Jumbo BIBLE Crossword Fun

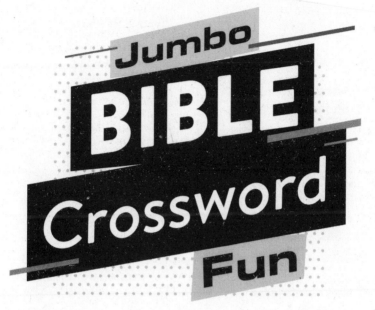

BARBOUR
PUBLISHING

ISBN 978-1-63609-464-9

Crosswords were created using licensed Crossword Weaver software (www.crosswordweaver.com).

Scripture quotations, unless otherwise noted, are taken from the King James Version of the Bible.

Scripture quotations marked AMP are taken from the Amplified® Bible, © 1954, 1958, 1962, 1964, 1965, 1987 by The Lockman Foundation. Used by permission.

Scripture quotations marked CEV are from the Contemporary English Version, Copyright © 1995 by American Bible Society. Used by permission.

Scripture quotations marked ESV are from The Holy Bible, English Standard Version®, copyright © 2001 by Crossway Bibles, a publishing ministry of Good News Publishers. The ESV® text has been reproduced in cooperation with and by permission of Good News Publishers.

Scripture quotations marked NASB are taken from the New American Standard Bible, © 1960, 1962, 1963, 1968, 1971, 1972, 1973, 1975, 1977, 1995, 2020 by The Lockman Foundation. Used by permission.

Scripture quotations marked NIV are taken from the HOLY BIBLE, NEW INTERNATIONAL VERSION®. NIV®. Copyright © 1973, 1978, 1984, 2011 by Biblica, Inc.™ Used by permission. All rights reserved worldwide.

Scripture quotations marked NKJV are taken from the New King James Version®. Copyright © 1982 by Thomas Nelson, Inc. Used by permission. All rights reserved.

Scripture quotations marked MSG are from *THE MESSAGE*. Copyright © by Eugene H. Peterson 1993, 1994, 1995, 1996, 2000, 2001, 2002. Used by permission of NavPress Publishing Group.

Scripture quotations marked NLT are taken from the *Holy Bible*. New Living Translation copyright© 1996, 2004, 2015 by Tyndale House Foundation. Used by permission of Tyndale House Publishers, Inc. Carol Stream, Illinois 60188. All rights reserved.

Published by Barbour Publishing, Inc., 1810 Barbour Drive, Uhrichsville, Ohio 44683, www.barbourbooks.com

Our mission is to inspire the world with the life-changing message of the Bible.

ecpa Member of the
Evangelical Christian
Publishers Association

Printed in the United States of America.

Spend your down time productively with a Bible crossword!

Enhance your Bible knowledge and your puzzle-solving skills with *Jumbo Bible Crossword Fun*. Here are more than 170 puzzles covering the fascinating people and places, times and teachings, objects and oddities of the Bible.

Bible crosswords are a great way to pass time while learning scripture. . .and this collection is sure to satisfy. With clues drawn from the breadth of scripture—from Genesis to Revelation—*Jumbo Bible Crossword Fun* is based on the King James Version of scripture. And, for added variety, there are some clues and answers drawn from other fields of study.

Perfect for puzzle lovers of all ages, *Jumbo Bible Crossword Fun* promises hours of wholesome fun!

NOTE: Crosswords are presented in two sections of eighty-six puzzles each, with answers immediately following each section. So look for the answers to the first section of puzzles in the *center* of this book—and the answers to the second section of puzzles in the *back* of the book.

Section 1

CRUCIAL QUESTION AND ANSWER

And ye shall know the truth, and the truth shall make you free.

JOHN 8:32

ACROSS

1 The mountain of God (Exodus 3:1)
6 Beginning of a **QUESTION** from Acts 16:30
10 "It is the gall of _____ within him" (Job 20:14)
14 "Christ, who is the _____ of God" (2 Corinthians 4:4)
15 "And all iniquity shall _____ her mouth" (Psalm 107:42)
16 **QUESTION**, cont.
17 "I understood their _____ destiny" (Psalm 73:17 NIV)
18 "And he said, I _____ thee, Peter" (Luke 22:34)
19 "That I may _____ piece of bread" (1 Samuel 2:36) (2 words)
20 Its capital is Roma
22 "For they shall _____ God" (Matthew 5:8)
23 Declare as a fact
24 Latin for "I"
26 Nocturnal resounders
28 Gad about
33 "Give us this _____ our daily bread" (Matthew 6:11)
34 Express feeling
35 Former Soviet republic (var.)
37 CCLI x II
40 Yorkshire river
41 "Came and _____ them into the pot" (2 Kings 4:39)
42 **QUESTION**, cont.
43 Esau's hair color (Genesis 25:25)
44 "For now thou numberest my ____" (Job 14:16)
45 "Cast me forth into the _____ shall the sea be calm" (Jonah 1:12) (2 words)
46 "When I _____ unto thee" (Psalm 56:9)
47 "And _____ heart" (Proverbs 7:10) (2 words)
49 Bantu language
53 "A third part shall be at the gate of _____" (2 Kings 11:6)
54 Guided trip
55 **QUESTION**, cont. (2 words)
57 Belonging to Judah's daughter-in-law and Absalom's sister (Genesis 38:11; 2 Samuel 13:4)
62 Ahab's father (1 Kings 16:28)
63 Royal address
65 Of ships
66 "Keep _____ the apple of the eye" (Psalm 17:8) (2 words)
67 **QUESTION**, cont. (2 words)
68 "So shalt thou _____ them out" (Deuteronomy 9:3)
69 "Spreadeth _____ for his feet" (Proverbs 29:5) (2 words)
70 Eyelid infection
71 End of **QUESTION**

DOWN

1 Stereo, once
2 "I command you; do not _____ a word" (Jeremiah 26:2 NIV)
3 "And there _____ young man" (Numbers 11:27) (2 words)
4 Arab headpiece
5 Beginning of part of the **ANSWER** from Acts 16:31
6 Concorde, for example
7 Residents of, suffix
8 Play parts
9 "Bear fruit and become a _____ vine" (Ezekiel 17:8 NIV)
10 "As the shadow of a great rock in _____ land" (Isaiah 32:2) (2 words)
11 "And she shall _____ her head" (Deuteronomy 21:12)
12 Latin father

by David K. Shortess

13 "Upon her head a crown of twelve
    _____" (Revelation 12:1)
21 Turkish honorific
25 **ANSWER**, cont. (2 words)
27 "I saw Absalom hanged in an
    ____" (2 Samuel 18:10)
28 Equipment
29 Parisian girlfriend
30 **ANSWER**, cont.
31 "And _____ it up"
    (Revelation 10:10)
32 Rain protectors
36 **ANSWER**, cont.
37 Composed of two similar parts
38 "Who _____ great a God as our
    God?" (Psalm 77:13) (2 words)
39 "For I neither received _____
    man" (Galatians 1:12) (2 words)
41 Beauticians
42 "Let _____ pray you"
    (Genesis 19:8) (2 words)
44 _____ Lanka
45 "But take a few _____ of hair"
    (Ezekiel 5:3 NIV)

46 The end of part of the **ANSWER**
48 "_____ of the tree" (Genesis
    2:17)
49 Leaf or stem pore
50 "Blessed art thou among _____"
    (Luke 1:28)
51 Having to do with optical
    sensations often preceding a
    seizure
52 Fool
56 "_____ the hearing of faith"
    (Galatians 3:2) (2 words)
58 Naomi's sad name (Ruth 1:20)
59 Tel _____
60 _____ review
61 Coaster
64 Wide shoe size

ACROSS

1 "Duke Magdiel, duke _____" (Genesis 36:43)
5 Simeon's second son (Genesis 46:10)
10 Hasty
14 Soldiers cast lots for Jesus' _____
15 A river of Damascus (2 Kings 5:12)
16 Jesus' cross saying (Matthew 27:46 NIV)
17 Zechariah's father (Ezra 5:1)
18 Consumed by flames
19 Clothed
20 "If thou _____" (Job 35:6)
22 Amoz's prophet son (2 Chronicles 32:20) (abbr.)
24 Gym class (abbr.)
25 Comfort
26 Great wickedness
27 Rimmon the Beerothite's son (2 Samuel 4:2)
30 "And _____ not his tongue" (James 1:26)
34 Eliud's father (Matthew 1:14)
35 Charge (noun)
36 "God created _____ heaven" (Genesis 1:1)
37 Shem's son (Genesis 10:22)
38 "Ivory and _____" (Ezekiel 27:15)
40 Show (var.)
41 Pastor's title (abbr.)
42 Small flying insect
43 Allotment
44 Asaph's son (1 Chronicles 25:2)
46 Crippled; disfigured
47 Shobal's son (Genesis 36:23)
48 "Take thy _____, and write fourscore" (Luke 16:7)
49 Opposite of *down*
51 Fight between countries
52 The eighth plague
55 Tibetan monk
57 "The hill of _____" (Joshua 24:30)
59 Delilah cut Samson's _____
61 "_____, Hizkijah, Azzur" (Nehemiah 10:17)
62 Sychem's father (Acts 7:16)
63 "Son of _____" (Nehemiah 11:12)
64 Repair
65 Shelomith's father (Leviticus 24:11)
66 Pay attention to

DOWN

1 Bela's son (1 Chronicles 7:7)
2 Staffs
3 Levite grandfather of Ethan (1 Chronicles 6:44)
4 "The plain of _____" (Judges 9:37)
5 Saul's body and his son's bodies were burnt in _____
6 Domestic violence
7 Market
8 Motel
9 Birth
10 Remember
11 "Destroy _____ kings and people" (Ezra 6:12)
12 Cleaning agent
13 Pelt (noun)
21 Caleb's son (1 Chronicles 4:15)
23 Riverbank (Exodus 2:5)
26 "Shuthelah: of _____" (Numbers 26:36)
27 One of Shaharaim's wives (1 Chronicles 8:8)
28 Land parcels
29 Ezra proclaimed a fast there (Ezra 8:21)
30 Soup
31 "And encamped in _____, in the edge of the wilderness" (Exodus 13:20)
32 "_____ I hated them" (Hosea 9:15)
33 Chopped
38 Made wider
39 "Remnant of _____" (Zephaniah 1:4)
40 Zophah's son (1 Chronicles 7:37)
42 A priestly city of Benjamin (2 Kings 23:8)
43 Zimri's father (Numbers 25:14)
45 Recompense

by N. Teri Grottke

46 Uzzi's father (1 Chronicles 9:8)
48 Balaam's father (2 Peter 2:15)
49 Sheresh's son (1 Chronicles 7:16)
50 Scalp (noun)
52 Baby sheep
53 Gentle
54 Dimensions
56 "Count all the _____ from thirty to fifty years of age" (Numbers 4:23 NIV)
58 A family of returned exiles (Ezra 2:57)
60 To free

3

ACROSS

1 Three hundred and sixty-five days
5 Work
9 Attached to the shoulder
12 Made a mistake
14 "Cast _____ the waters" (Exodus 15:25)
15 Not false
16 In labor (arch.)
18 "In_____ there was a voice" (Matthew 2:18)
19 Wicked
20 Isaac's mother (Genesis 17:19)
21 Nadab's son (1 Chronicles 2:30)
24 Pharaoh's daughter (1 Chronicles 4:18)
27 Construct
28 "And _____ them" (Mark 6:33)
29 Sick
30 "And _____ such as had separated themselves" (Ezra 6:21)
31 "_____ there yet the treasures" (Micah 6:10)
32 Consecrated by religious rite or word
35 "As thou _____" (Acts 7:28)
39 Zephaniah's son (Zechariah 6:14)
40 "No _____ is for him" (Amos 3:5)
41 Exclamation of affirmation
42 Adaiah's father (1 Chronicles 9:12)
44 Sleeping thought
46 Roused from sleep
47 Sewing tool
48 To tear repeatedly
49 Baby horse
50 Sheep product
51 "Worketh God _____ with man" (Job 33:29)
57 "Highways, _____! alas!" (Amos 5:16)
58 Jesus raised a young man from the dead here (Luke 7:11–15)
59 Hurl or cast
60 Follows the book of Ezra (abbr.)
61 "Day of _____ birth" (Ecclesiastes 7:1)
62 Dog parasite

DOWN

1 But nevertheless
2 To make a mistake
3 Jether's son (1 Chronicles 7:38)
4 Make known
5 Plow
6 Single
7 Possessive pronoun
8 Abraham's nephew (Genesis 12:5)
9 Resting place of Noah's ark
10 Pedaiah was from here (2 Kings 23:36)
11 "Even unto the tower of _____" (Nehemiah 3:1)
13 Jesse's son (Ruth 4:17)
15 Taught
17 "They departed from _____" (Numbers 33:45)
20 "_____ to take fire from the hearth" (Isaiah 30:14)
21 First month of the Hebrew year (Exodus 34:18)
22 Opposite of *push*
23 Heap
24 Eighth Hebrew month (1 Kings 6:38)
25 Location of Rome (abbr.)
26 "Compel thee to go a mile, go with him _____" (Matthew 5:41)
28 Elderly
30 A baptismal site of John the Baptist (John 3:23)
33 Bible money
34 Zebulun's son (Genesis 46:14)
35 "My eyes are _____ with grief" (Psalm 88:9 NIV)
36 Looked at
37 A ring engraved with some device
38 Gentle
40 Jacob's son (Genesis 35:26)
42 Huri's father (1 Chronicles 5:14)
43 Opposite of *she*
44 "Precious in the sight of the LORD is the _____ of his saints" (Psalm 116:15)
45 Respite
46 Entire
47 Prefix meaning *not*
48 Graceful water bird

by N. Teri Grottke

49 Swamps
51 The valley of craftsmen (Nehemiah 11:35)
52 Disperses air
53 Bind
54 The last book of the Old Testament (abbr.)
55 Adam's wife
56 _____ of Galilee

ACROSS

1 Steal
4 "The appointed barley and the
_____ in their place" (Isaiah
28:25)
7 Work farm ground
11 Abdiel's son (1 Chronicles 5:15)
12 Shammai's brother
(1 Chronicles 2:28)
13 "Intreat me not to _____ thee"
(Ruth 1:16)
14 What Lot did in the gate of
Sodom (Genesis 19:1)
15 Opposite of *begins*
16 "For what _____ he spake"
(John 13:28)
18 "Mushi; Mahli, and _____"
(1 Chronicles 23:23)
20 Received
21 Satisfy thirst
22 In a popular hymn, he saw a wheel
(Ezekiel 1:15) (abbr., var.)
24 Take to court
25 Opposite of *he*
26 Mar
30 Grasp onto
32 John the Baptist baptized here
(John 3:23)
33 Ram's son (1 Chronicles 2:27)
35 "Nevertheless _____ heart was
perfect" (1 Kings 15:14)
39 "Departed from the river of
_____ on the twelfth day" (Ezra
8:31)
40 Fish eggs
41 By yourself
42 The straight distance between two
points
43 A chair, stool, or bench
44 Igdaliah's son (Jeremiah 35:4)
45 Homes of wild animals
47 "By the _____ of men, and
cunning craftiness" (Ephesians
4:14)
49 Bela's son (1 Chronicles 7:7)
52 Put down
53 "Helez the Paltite, _____"
(2 Samuel 23:26)
54 Lumber

56 Eve was made from Adam's
_____
58 Stop
62 "Heaven _____ upon the great
sea" (Daniel 7:2)
63 "Of Harim, _____"
(Nehemiah 12:15)
65 "_____ that ye refuse not him"
(Hebrews 12:25)
66 "_____ nor sown, and shall
strike" (Deuteronomy 21:4)
67 "_____ the Ahohite"
(1 Chronicles 11:29)
68 Motel
69 "Set it between Mizpeh and
_____" (1 Samuel 7:12)
70 He came with Zerubbabel
(Ezra 2:2) (abbr.)
71 Increase

DOWN

1 "The day of Jerusalem; who said,
_____ it" (Psalm 137:7)
2 "Jemuel, and Jamin, and _____"
(Genesis 46:10)
3 "Suddenly that shall _____ thee"
(Habakkuk 2:7)
4 Cooking appliances
5 "Ahinadab the son of _____"
(1 Kings 4:14)
6 Opposite of *west*
7 Gedor's father (1 Chronicles 4:4)
8 Opposite of *early*
9 Bread bakes in these
10 Woman (arch.)
12 Precedes July (abbr., var.)
13 "Shall he drink any _____ of
grapes" (Numbers 6:3)
17 "Praise ye _____ Lord"
(Psalm 150:1)
19 Took away
23 Shimei's son (1 Chronicles 23:10)
24 Bed coverings
26 "Throw down the altar of _____"
(Judges 6:25)
27 Samson slew 1,000 Philistines here
(Judges 15:14)
28 Ahira's father (Numbers 1:15)
29 False teaching

by N. Teri Grottke

31 Elioenai's son (1 Chronicles 3:24)
34 Hawaiian tree for timber
36 Verbal music
37 Zibeon's daughter (Genesis 36:2)
38 Caused to go to a destination
41 "And Hushim, the sons of _____"
(1 Chronicles 7:12)
43 Trapped
46 Number of disciples left after
death of Judas
48 "The daughter of Jeremiah of
____" (Jeremiah 52:1)
49 Possessive pronoun
50 "According to all the _____ of it"
(Numbers 9:3)
51 Zophah's son (1 Chronicles 7:36)
55 Uninteresting person
56 Precipitation
57 Inactive
59 Largest continent
60 "Do good and _____" (Luke
6:35)

61 Take care of
64 Conquered by Joshua (Joshua 8:1)

THE BODY OF JESUS

Each of the theme answers is comprised of a portion of the verse given and contains a reference to a part of Jesus' body.

ACROSS

1 Rye fungus
6 City in northern Syria (var.)
10 Doorframe
14 Viola kin
15 Stadium division
16 "Why was it, _____, that you fled" (Psalm 114:5 NIV) (2 words)
17 "Around Jesus' _____ folded up by itself" (John 20:7 NIV) (4 words)
20 "The _____ number of them is to be" (Numbers 3:48)
21 "And of _____ speech" (Genesis 11:1)
22 Poisonous substance in snake venom (var.)
23 Facial flaw
25 Slangy negative
26 "That he should _____ them" (Matthew 19:13) (4 words)
31 "The storm and _____ from the heat" (Isaiah 25:4 NIV) (2 words)
32 "And for the _____ that is in the land" (Isaiah 7:18)
33 Expression of joy
36 "If a man _____ his male or female slave" (Exodus 21:20 NIV)
37 "And do not _____ among thorns" (Jeremiah 4:3 NIV)
38 "Wail, _____ tree" (Zechariah 11:2 NIV) (2 words)
40 "And they said unto her, Thou _____ mad" (Acts 12:15)
41 "Shall be at the gate of _____" (2 Kings 11:6)
42 Seasick symptom
43 "One of the soldiers pierced Jesus' _____" (John 19:34 NIV) (4 words)
47 Israeli Red Sea port
48 Little bit
49 Of the tip
52 Cleric's degree (abbr.)

53 Tiger's organization (abbr.)
56 "And when he saw him, _____" (Mark 5:22) (5 words)
60 Part of AARP (abbr.)
61 Bassoon relative
62 "Exalt thyself as the _____" (Obadiah 1:4)
63 "Every warrior's _____" (Isaiah 9:5 NIV)
64 "The waters _____ the stones" (Job 14:19)
65 Demi- ending

DOWN

1 "The woodwork will _____ it" (Habakkuk 2:11 NIV)
2 "With the measuring _____" (Ezekiel 42:18)
3 "Making him very _____" (Jeremiah 20:15)
4 "How _____ art thou?" (Genesis 47:8)
5 Youngster
6 "Gave _____ part of all" (Hebrews 7:2) (2 words)
7 "And _____ in all their coasts" (Psalm 105:31)
8 Lamprey
9 "But if any _____ not for his own" (1 Timothy 5:8)
10 "_____ the seven churches" (Revelation 1:4) (2 words)
11 "_____ have heard" (Psalm 48:8) (2 words)
12 "What _____ ye, that ye use this" (Ezekiel 18:2)
13 "Yea, children of _____ men" (Job 30:8)
18 "And I looked, and behold a pale _____" (Revelation 6:8)
19 "And rulers of _____" (Exodus 18:25)

by David K. Shortess

23 "_____ is man, that thou art mindful of him" (Psalm 8:4)
24 Succors
25 "Be in Christ, he is _____ creature" (2 Corinthians 5:17) (2 words)
26 Sunscreen ingredient (abbr.)
27 Computer operators
28 "_____ will pour out my spirit" (Joel 2:28) (2 words)
29 Terminate before completion
30 "Play skilfully with a loud _____" (Psalm 33:3)
34 "The _____ Pharisee, and the other a publican" (Luke 18:10) (2 words)
35 "_____, O Israel" (Deuteronomy 6:4)
37 "Many shall make _____ unto thee" (Job 11:19)
38 Drying kiln
39 Cocoon resident
41 "And _____ a camel" (Matthew 23:24)

42 Elimelech's wife (Ruth 1:2)
44 Morally upright
45 Airline to Haifa (2 words)
46 "Who brought thee _____" (Judges 18:3)
49 Ahaziah's father (1 Kings 22:40)
50 Cuban coin
51 "His mouth in the dust; _____ be there may be hope" (Lamentations 3:29) (2 words)
52 Greek colonnade
53 "Do they make _____ from it" (Ezekiel 15:3 NIV)
54 Hairstyling items
55 "To _____": exactly (2 words)
57 Presidential nickname, "Honest ____"
58 "And _____ it before them" (Genesis 18:8)
59 Government airline controller (abbr.)

ACROSS

1 What the devil is (John 8:44)
5 Remunerated
9 Open regions where animals graze
11 A chamberlain of Ahasuerus (Esther 1:10)
13 Meshelemiah's son (1 Chronicles 9:21) (abbr., var.)
14 A job
16 This city worshipped Diana (Acts 19:35) (abbr.)
17 Rahab hid them (Joshua 6:17 NIV)
18 Biblical father of twenty children
20 "Nathan the prophet, and Shimei, and _____" (1 Kings 1:8)
21 Keeper of the women (Esther 2:3 NIV)
23 Sugar plant
24 In place of
27 Meshach's Hebrew name (Daniel 1:7)
29 "A _____ in the flesh" (2 Corinthians 12:7)
30 "Her new _____, and her sabbaths" (Hosea 2:11)
31 "Wilt thou that _____ command" (Luke 9:54)
32 Titanium (sym.)
33 "Lord, _____ us to pray" (Luke 11:1)
36 Ahiam's father (1 Chronicles 11:35)
39 Harum's son (1 Chronicles 4:8)
41 "Aden of _____" (Mark 11:17)
43 Winged animal
44 Lower in place or position
46 Mighty tree
47 "No room for them in the _____" (Luke 2:7)
48 "Name of _____ before was Kirjathsepher" (Judges 1:11)
50 Bela's son (1 Chronicles 7:7)
51 Jesus' garden trial
55 Place of Daniel's lions
56 "Which _____ at a gnat" (Matthew 23:24)
57 "Ye have _____ treasure" (James 5:3)
59 Spiritual song
60 Went swiftly

DOWN

1 "O thou inhabitant of _____" (Micah 1:13)
2 Fort Wayne's state (abbr.)
3 Generations
4 "The star of your god _____" (Acts 7:43)
5 "_____ ye tribute also" (Romans 13:6)
6 "With great power and a stretched out _____" (2 Kings 17:36)
7 "Whose womb came the _____?" (Job 38:29)
8 "_____, and about to Zidon" (2 Samuel 24:6)
9 Turn away from sin
10 "He _____ an Egyptian" (Exodus 2:11)
11 Melchi's grandfather (Luke 3:28)
12 These would be thrown at adulterers in the OT
13 "Gedaliah, and _____" (1 Chronicles 25:3)
15 Lower appendage
19 God of Babylon (Isaiah 46:1)
22 "Baalah, and _____" (Joshua 15:29)
23 "She is the _____ one" (Song of Solomon 6:9)
25 "So great is his mercy _____ them that fear him" (Psalm 103:11)
26 "_____, and Accad, and Calneh" (Genesis 10:10)
28 Children of Solomon's servants (Nehemiah 7:57)
33 "My goodly pleasant _____" (Joel 3:5)
34 "Wages _____ wages" (Haggai 1:6)
35 "Be not servants unto the _____" (1 Samuel 4:9) (abbr.)
36 Places of idol worship
37 "And David _____ out of his presence twice" (1 Samuel 18:11)
38 "He _____ up altars for Baal" (2 Kings 21:3)
39 King Hezekiah's mother (2 Kings 18:1–2)

by N. Teri Grottke

40 "Ye that labour and are heavy
   _____" (Matthew 11:28)
41 Reumah's son (Genesis 22:24)
42 Epidermis
45 One goes here to become a
   minister (abbr.)
49 Harvest (verb)
52 "But _____ the spirits whether
   they are of God" (1 John 4:1)
53 Noah's son (Genesis 5:32)
54 Transgression
58 Gym class (abbr.)

ACROSS

1 Received
4 "I _____ above all things" (3 John 1:2)
8 Twenty-first letter of the Greek alphabet
11 "Hath said against Jerusalem, ____" (Ezekiel 26:2)
12 "And Jozabad, and _____" (2 Chronicles 31:13)
14 "And _____ with her suburbs" (Joshua 21:16)
15 "On the _____" from the law
16 "Should be holy and without _____" (Ephesians 1:4)
17 "And beginning to _____, he cried" (Matthew 14:30)
18 Home for Daniel's lions
20 "_____ the prophet" (Ezra 5:1)
23 Pagiel's father (Numbers 1:13)
26 Are (arch.)
27 Horse holdings
30 Goliath was one
32 Opposite of *him*
33 Conquered by Joshua (Joshua 8:20)
34 "_____ lieth at the door" (Genesis 4:7)
35 "To meet the Lord in the _____" (1 Thessalonians 4:17)
37 "O satisfy us _____" (Psalm 90:14)
39 The story of Creation is told here (abbr.)
40 Her household reported contentions in the Corinthian church (1 Corinthians 1:11)
42 "Deliver thyself as a _____" (Proverbs 6:5)
43 This book contains an ancient census (abbr.)
44 In the direction of; toward
45 He took 100 prophets and hid them in caves (1 Kings 18:4) (abbr., var.)
46 Two hydrogen molecules and an oxygen
48 Type of stinging insect
50 Make angry

51 "While he thought on _____ things" (Matthew 1:20)
53 Whole
55 Oath
58 Idols
61 "Brought him again from the well of _____" (2 Samuel 3:26)
64 Verbalize
66 "Lod, and _____, the valley of craftsmen" (Nehemiah 11:35)
67 "I am from _____" (John 8:23)
68 Before (poet.)
69 Panhandle
70 "Tappuah, and _____" (Joshua 15:34)
71 Her decree confirmed the matters of Purim (Esther 9:32) (abbr.)

DOWN

1 Girl (slang)
2 Simeon's son (Genesis 46:10)
3 "No man can _____ the tongue" (James 3:8)
4 Spider's art
5 Sick
6 Returning exiles (Ezra 2:44)
7 Mahol's son (1 Kings 4:31)
8 "The name of his city was _____" (1 Chronicles 1:50)
9 A liquid measure (Leviticus 23:13)
10 Writing fluid
13 Part of a journey
17 "He called the name of it _____" (Genesis 26:21)
19 A city of the priests (1 Samuel 22:19)
21 Increase
22 Jether's son (1 Chronicles 7:38)
24 "How much less in them that dwell in houses of _____" (Job 4:19)
25 "Nathan the prophet, and Shimei, and _____" (1 Kings 1:8)
27 Opposite of *he*
28 Rip
29 "The _____ cannot make him flee" (Job 41:28)
30 "The _____ shall take him" (Job 18:9)

by N. Teri Grottke

31 Shimon's son
(1 Chronicles 4:20)
34 Place of religious study (abbr.)
36 Soldiers cast lots for Jesus'
38 "_____ of the tree" (Revelation 22:2)
39 "Going up to _____"
(2 Kings 9:27)
40 Sounds made by doves
41 Consume food
43 "Our _____ kinsmen" (Ruth 2:20)
44 "_____ old lion" (Job 4:11)
47 "Hundred and _____ years old" (Joshua 24:29)
49 Last book of the Bible (abbr.)
51 "Of the _____ of Benjamin" (Philippians 3:5)
52 "The _____ after her kind" (Leviticus 11:19)
54 He prescribed figs for a boil (2 Kings 20:7) (abbr.)

56 "As he saith also in _____" (Romans 9:25)
57 "From whence come _____ and fightings" (James 4:1)
58 Battle where Goliath's brother was slain (2 Samuel 21:19)
59 Single
60 Canine
62 Area near Babylon (2 Kings 17:24)
63 The edge of a garment
65 In addition

8

ACROSS

1 "Name of his city was _____"
(1 Chronicles 1:50)
4 "And from Cuthah, and from
_____" (2 Kings 17:24)
7 Gad's son (Genesis 46:16)
10 "Ye shall _____ up early"
(Genesis 19:2)
12 "Also were accounted giants. . .
called _____" (Deuteronomy
2:11)
14 Seir's son (1 Chronicles 1:38)
15 Hand-driven boat propellers
16 American low-growing tree type
17 "The troops of _____ looked"
(Job 6:19)
18 "They _____ cockatrice' eggs"
(Isaiah 59:5)
20 "Adam, Sheth, _____"
(1 Chronicles 1:1)
22 Benjamin's son (Genesis 46:21)
23 "Having a _____, or scurvy"
(Leviticus 22:22)
24 Hectare (abbr.)
26 Consecrated by religious rite or
word
30 "They could not drink of the
waters of _____" (Exodus 15:23)
32 "I do not fight like a man beating
the _____" (1 Corinthians 9:26
NIV)
33 "_____ the Mahavite, and Jeribai"
(1 Chronicles 11:46)
36 Salathiel's father (Luke 3:27)
37 "_____ is finished" (John 19:30)
38 "The parts of _____ about
Cyrene" (Acts 2:10)
39 Denver's state (abbr.)
40 Deviation from straight line
42 "Rich man. . ._____
sumptuously" (Luke 16:19)
43 "Valley of _____ shadow"
(Psalm 23:4)
44 "Though I forbare, what am I
_____?" (Job 16:6)
46 Kept from detection
47 Ulla's son (1 Chronicles 7:39)
48 Aluminum (sym.)
49 "Bore his ear through with an
_____" (Exodus 21:6)
51 Eve was made from Adam's
_____
52 Found in a mollusk
55 "Inhabitants of _____ gather
themselves" (Isaiah 10:31)
57 Bethuel's brother (Genesis 22:22)
60 "_____ from anger" (Psalm 37:8)
62 "Went to the top of the rock
_____" (Judges 15:11)
64 Jerahmeel's son (1 Chronicles
2:25)
65 "Hast thou _____ of the tree?"
(Genesis 3:11)
66 "Land from _____ to the
wilderness" (Isaiah 16:1)
67 Tree juice
68 Ground moisture
69 Place (verb)

DOWN

1 Not an amateur
2 Zibeon's son (1 Chronicles 1:40)
3 Jacob's descendants
4 A family of returned exiles
(Ezra 2:57)
5 Grapes grow here
6 "_____ trespassed more and
more" (2 Chronicles 33:23)
7 Follows Lamentations (abbr., var.)
8 A male sheep
9 Savings account for the future
11 Hadassah's other name
12 Residents of Ephesus (abbr.)
13 White precipitation
14 Helah's son (1 Chronicles 4:7)
19 King Saul's father (Acts 13:21)
21 Punctuation mark (abbr.)
24 Shobal's son (1 Chronicles 2:52)
25 Abdiel's son (1 Chronicles 5:15)
26 Russian lake
27 "Swarest by thine own _____"
(Exodus 32:13)
28 Elam's son (Ezra 10:26)
29 Shelomith's father (Leviticus
24:11)
31 They wouldn't drink wine
(Jeremiah 35:6)

by N. Teri Grottke

34 Looked at
35 Boy
40 "Through the way of the wilderness of the Red _____" (Exodus 13:18)
41 "His destroying _____ in his hand" (Ezekiel 9:1)
43 There were twelve in Israel
45 _____ process
47 "_____ there yet the treasures" (Micah 6:10)
50 "_____ of blue, to fasten it on high" (Exodus 39:31)
53 "They were _____ before the king" (Esther 6:1)
54 "Even of _____ my people is risen up as an enemy" (Micah 2:8)
55 First book of the Bible (abbr.)
56 "There is neither _____ nor female" (Galatians 3:28)
57 Follows Daniel (abbr.)
58 Jether's son (1 Chronicles 7:38)

59 Josiah's father (Zechariah 6:10) (abbr., var.)
61 To stitch
63 Floor covering

ESTHER'S PEOPLE

The book of Esther has some interesting characters.
Can you find them in this story of intrigue and courage?

ACROSS

1 Edom (Genesis 36:19)
5 Robber to crowd: "Stick 'em up, all _____" (2 words, slang)
9 "Therefore will I change their glory into _____" (Hosea 4:7)
14 Coarse file
15 "Do nothing" in Java cybertalk
16 "Came upon me to _____ my flesh" (Psalm 27:2) (2 words)
17 Esther's king (Esther 1:1)
19 Allan _____ (Robin Hood's pal)
20 Artist's studio
22 Away from the wind
23 "_____ truth shall be established for ever" (Proverbs 12:19) (3 words)
26 Appraise
28 Esther's chamberlain (Esther 4:5)
29 "That in the _____ to come" (Ephesians 2:7)
30 "He planteth an _____" (Isaiah 44:14)
31 Moses' brother (Exodus 4:14)
34 "How _____ be quiet" (Jeremiah 47:7) (2 words)
38 "Whatever _____ it is" (Leviticus 11:32 NKJV)
40 Esther's nemesis (Esther 3:1)
42 "For the labourer is worthy of his _____" (Luke 10:7)
43 "_____ chose for himself the whole plain of Jordan" (Genesis 13:11 NIV) (2 words)
45 "If that is so, I'll eat _____" (2 words)
47 "And stand in the _____ before me" (Ezekiel 22:30)
48 "That shall he also _____" (Galatians 6:7)
50 An Old Testament queen (Esther 1:9)
52 Marks

55 Called forth
57 "Gather a certain _____ every day" (Exodus 16:4)
58 "Prophesy and say _____" (Ezekiel 38:14) (2 words)
60 Frozen (2 words)
62 Esther's king's chamberlain (Esther 2:14)
66 Philippine island
67 "Then Daniel _____ in" (Daniel 2:16)
68 "He _____ his clothes" (Genesis 37:29 NIV)
69 American author, Gertrude
70 Gaelic
71 "And I will give him the morning _____" (Revelation 2:28)

DOWN

1 "Roaring Twenties," for example
2 African desert (abbr.)
3 Jehoshaphat's dad (1 Kings 22:41)
4 College in New Jersey
5 "Three bullocks, and _____ of flour" (1 Samuel 1:24) (2 words)
6 "_____, thou shalt conceive" (Judges 13:5) (2 words)
7 "But I will return again unto _____ God will" (Acts 18:21) (2 words)
8 Cathedral's altar area
9 "And cast out the wheat into the _____" (Acts 27:38)
10 Esther's other name (Esther 2:7)
11 "We spend our years as _____ that is told" (Psalm 90:9) (2 words)
12 "And riders on _____" (Esther 8:10)
13 Swords
18 City on the Erie Canal
21 Word with doll or time
23 Siamese's, today (poss.)

by David K. Shortess

24 "Fear _____ do with punishment" (1 John 4:18 NIV) (2 words)
25 Singer Waters
27 Short time (abbr.)
29 One of Esau's in-laws (Genesis 36:2)
32 "Build a _____ up to it" (Ezekiel 4:2 NIV)
33 "Bless the Lord, _____ soul" (Psalm 103:1) (2 words)
35 "Nor the pillar of fire by _____" (Exodus 13:22)
36 In a severe pique
37 Another word that might describe the Laodiceans (Revelation 3:14–16)
39 Esther's guardian (Esther 2:5)
41 Emulate Magellan
44 Golf helper
46 Juan's snacks
49 Tempe school (abbr.)

51 "And fearful _____ and great signs" (Luke 21:11)
52 "For this people's heart is waxed _____" (Matthew 13:15)
53 "And _____ flood stage as before" (Joshua 4:18 NIV) (2 words)
54 "_____ to be born" (Ecclesiastes 3:2) (2 words)
55 "Libnah, and _____, and Ashan" (Joshua 15:42)
56 Things given temporarily
59 Letters on a weather vane
61 Directional suffix
63 "Which he had _____ in the land of Canaan" (Genesis 36:6)
64 One of the three sons of Jether (1 Chronicles 7:38)
65 One of the fenced (fortified) cities of Ziddim (Joshua 19:35)

ACROSS

1 "_____ *ne sais quoi*" (Fr., lit.) "I know not what"
3 "They will _____ me to pieces" (Psalm 7:2 NIV)
6 Became acquainted
9 Sprint
10 Middle Eastern country
12 Uzai's son (Nehemiah 3:25)
14 Strange
15 "Them unto _____, and slew" (Judges 20:45)
17 Enan's son (Numbers 1:15)
18 "Thou shalt _____ them diligently" (Deuteronomy 6:7)
20 Jephunneh and Pispah's brother (1 Chronicles 7:38)
21 Wild animals can sometimes be _____
22 "Have _____ I commanded thee?" (Joshua 1:9)
23 "Men of Cuth made _____" (2 Kings 17:30)
25 Time past: long _____
26 Home to Nelson Mandela (abbr.)
27 Belonging to Bathsheba's first husband (2 Samuel 11:3) (poss.)
31 "Babylon is taken, _____ is confounded" (Jeremiah 50:2)
32 "Agar is mount Sinai in _____" (Galatians 4:25)
35 Untruth
36 "_____ was an hair of their head singed" (Daniel 3:27)
37 "The breast may be _____" (Leviticus 7:30)
38 "How long. . ._____ they believe me?" (Numbers 14:11)
39 "Mother of all living" (Genesis 3:20)
40 "A _____ without blemish" (Leviticus 4:28)
41 Big hatchet
42 Walls of shrubs
44 Present tense, third person singular of *be*
45 Insane
46 _____ for the night
49 Adam was the first

50 Baanah's son (2 Samuel 23:29)
53 Minister (noun) (abbr.)
54 "_____ and Medad do prophesy in the camp" (Numbers 11:27)
57 "And Zechariah, and _____" (1 Chronicles 15:20)
58 "As thou _____ to do unto those that love my name" (Psalm 119:132)
60 "For ye tithe mint and _____" (Luke 11:42)
61 "And Noah found _____ in the eyes of the LORD" (Genesis 6:8)
62 Apples grow on this
63 "In the _____. . .the LORD met him" (Exodus 4:24)
64 "_____ there yet the treasures of wickedness" (Micah 6:10)
65 Unhappy
66 There

DOWN

1 The patron saint of impossible causes
2 Nearly extinct
3 Opposite of *wrong*
4 Bela's son (1 Chronicles 7:7)
5 Rebekah was from here (Genesis 25:20)
6 Merari's son (Exodus 6:19)
7 "In _____ were twelve fountains of water" (Numbers 33:9)
8 Type of weed
9 Decay
11 Mutiny of the _____ Lightship (1797)
12 "From thence unto _____" (Acts 21:1)
13 "And God was with the _____" (Genesis 21:20)
16 Disfigure
19 Not warm
24 "Woe unto you, ye blind _____" (Matthew 23:16)
25 "Send thine hand from _____" (Psalm 144:7)
26 "Thou _____ till that a stone was cut" (Daniel 2:34)

by N. Teri Grottke

28 "We departed in a ship of _____"
   (Acts 28:11)
29 Employed
30 "_____ that ye refuse"
   (Hebrews 12:25)
33 Area near Babylon (2 Kings 17:24)
34 "_____ were the more added to
   the Lord" (Acts 5:14)
36 Precedes Esther (abbr.)
40 Weak
41 Helem's son (1 Chronicles 7:35)
43 Country Athens is in
47 Caleb's son (1 Chronicles 4:15)
48 "Give thyself no _____"
   (Lamentations 2:18)
49 Gave out in measured portions
50 He prophesied to the Jews
   (Ezra 5:1) (abbr.)
51 This priest rebuilt the temple
   (Ezra 1:2)
52 "Who will make me a _____"
   (Job 24:25)

55 Sister of a parent
56 "I will make Jerusalem. . .a _____
   of dragons" (Jeremiah 7:11)
59 "Walking by the _____ of
   Galilee, saw two brethren"
   (Matthew 4:18)

ACROSS

1 Relatives
4 Popular hymn: "How Great Thou _____"
7 "Midian, _____, and Rekem" (Joshua 13:21)
10 Heap
11 Title of respect for men
13 To use up
15 Zibeon's daughter (Genesis 36:2)
16 "Abiezer the _____" (1 Chronicles 27:12)
18 "_____, and goeth out to Cabul" (Joshua 19:27)
20 "And the herdmen of _____" (Genesis 26:20)
21 Prefix meaning *non*
22 A measurement for oil (Leviticus 14:10)
24 Partook
25 "No _____ that is formed against thee shall prosper" (Isaiah 54:17)
28 "_____ flour shalt thou make them" (Exodus 29:2)
33 Father of the Canaanites (Genesis 9:18)
34 Nahor's son (Genesis 22:20–21)
36 To struggle
37 Lotan's son (Genesis 36:22)
38 Became acquainted
40 Team
41 King of Damascus (2 Corinthians 11:32)
44 Cousin, shortened (abbr.)
46 Zephaniah's son (Zechariah 6:14)
47 A city of Judah's inheritance (Joshua 15:36)
49 "Or _____ ought of thy neighbour's hand" (Leviticus 25:14)
51 Genus of macaws
52 To stir up; excite
53 Female sheep
56 "But ye have _____" (Amos 5:26)
59 "And these from the land of _____" (Isaiah 49:12)
63 "Sent thither twelve thousand men of the _____" (Judges 21:10)

66 Exhaust
67 Methusalah's father (Genesis 5:21)
68 "Cometh of the _____ of his patrimony" (Deuteronomy 18:8)
69 "From the sea to Hazar _____" (Ezekiel 47:17 NIV)
70 Bind
71 A liquid measure (Exodus 29:40)
72 Arphaxad's father (Luke 3:36)

DOWN

1 "Seven well favoured _____ and fatfleshed" (Genesis 41:2)
2 "_____ the Ahohite" (1 Chronicles 11:29)
3 Shemaiah was one (Jeremiah 29:31)
4 David's son (1 Kings 15:11)
5 Circle
6 Elm or oak
7 "Great is Diana of the _____" (Acts 19:28) (abbr.)
8 Blood vessel
9 "Go _____ the ark, you and your whole family" (Genesis 7:1 NIV)
10 "In a _____ it shall be made with oil" (Leviticus 6:21)
12 People searched Egypt for stubble rather than this (Exodus 5:12)
13 Lane
14 "Become a _____ of robbers" (Jeremiah 7:11)
17 Vows
19 Cut off
23 Lump; large amount
25 "They shall not take a wife that is a _____" (Leviticus 21:7)
26 "Which is neither _____ nor sown" (Deuteronomy 21:4)
27 Fourth book of the Old Testament (abbr.)
29 Rehum and Shimshai's companions (Ezra 4:9)
30 "Round _____ like the moon" (Isaiah 3:18)
31 Incident
32 "There arose up a _____ king over Egypt" (Exodus 1:8)

by N. Teri Grottke

35 Alphabetically, the next to the last book of the Bible (abbr., var.)
37 An evil-looking old woman
39 Jephthah fled to here (Judges 11:3)
42 "And went down unto _____" (Joshua 18:18)
43 "And all that dwell at Lydda and _____" (Acts 9:35)
45 A king of Midian (Numbers 31:8)
48 "Become like _____ that find no pasture" (Lamentations 1:6)
50 "_____ verily, their sound" (Romans 10:18)
53 Night before special day
54 Desire
55 Means "My God" (Mark 15:34)
57 The border from Remmonmethoar to here (Joshua 19:13)
58 Nagge's son (Luke 3:25)

60 "And Nahor lived _____ and twenty years" (Genesis 11:24)
61 He was a duke of Edom (Genesis 36:43)
62 The Wise _____ came to see Jesus
64 "Out of whose womb came the _____?" (Job 38:29)
65 "_____ cubits shall be the length of a board" (Exodus 26:16)

ACROSS

1 "_____ opened her mouth with wisdom" (Proverbs 31:26)
4 Pork
7 "This woman was taken in adultery, in the very _____" (John 8:4)
10 "And his _____ drew the third part" (Revelation 12:4)
11 He hid prophets in a cave (1 Kings 18:4) (abbr.)
12 One of Job's friends (Job 2:11)
15 "I beseech thee for my son _____, whom I have begotten in my bonds" (Philemon 1:10)
17 Kingdom
18 "She. . .eateth not the bread of _____" (Proverbs 31:27)
19 Skinned
20 Reverend Martin Luther King Jr.'s famous speech, "I have a _____"
22 Jacob's son (Genesis 35:26)
23 Teacher of Judaism
27 Nathan of Zobah's son (2 Samuel 23:36)
29 "Driven up and down in _____" (Acts 27:27)
30 Advertisements made for the benefit of the public (abbr.)
31 "Fourth part of a _____ of dove's dung" (2 Kings 6:25)
34 "Ye shall find a colt _____" (Mark 11:2)
35 Damp
37 Gaddi's father (Numbers 13:11)
38 "Kindness in the latter _____" (Ruth 3:10)
39 Unusually capable
40 "Why _____ ye God?" (Acts 15:10)
41 Cattle (arch.)
43 "_____ up seed to thy brother" (Genesis 38:8)
44 Religious college (abbr.)
45 One of the twelve spies (Numbers 13:14)
49 Hamath's idol (2 Kings 17:30)
52 "Inhabitant of _____: he shall come" (Micah 1:15)
57 "The treacherous _____" (Isaiah 21:2)
58 He was in the fiery furnace (Daniel 3:19)
59 Leave
60 Sem's father (Luke 3:36)
61 "Than the day of _____ birth" (Ecclesiastes 7:1)
62 He came with Zerubbabel (Ezra 2:2) (abbr.)
63 Bela's son (Numbers 26:40)
64 "Before Abraham _____, I am" (John 8:58)

DOWN

1 Beach surface
2 "_____ the Bethelite build Jericho" (1 Kings 16:34)
3 Otherwise
4 Measurement of barley (Hosea 3:2)
5 "I _____ not my power in the gospel" (1 Corinthians 9:18)
6 Ishmael's son (Genesis 25:13–14)
7 Plea
8 Very young person
9 Ripped (arch.) (2 Samuel 13:31)
10 "When _____ king of Hamath" (2 Samuel 8:9)
12 Alphabetically, the last book of the Bible (abbr., var.)
13 "I am Alpha and _____" (Revelation 1:8)
14 "The wine is _____" (Psalm 75:8)
16 Home to Ghandi
21 Single female's title
23 Premium per unit (noun)
24 "The children of _____, four hundred fifty and four" (Ezra 2:15)
25 "It _____ worms, and stank" (Exodus 16:20)
26 "Will do all that thou shalt _____ us" (2 Kings 10:5)
28 "We _____ our bread with the peril of our lives" (Lamentations 5:9)
30 Deep hole
31 "Said unto her, Talitha _____" (Mark 5:41)
32 Poisonous snakes

by N. Teri Grottke

33 "That shall _____ thee"
   (Habakkuk 2:7)
35 "A mighty _____ of wealth"
   (Ruth 2:1)
36 Opposite of *closed*
37 Black _____
40 Put forth effort
41 "And _____, and Achzib, and
   Mareshah" (Joshua 15:44)
42 He had 1,052 children
   (Nehemiah 7:40)
44 "Bodily _____ like a dove"
   (Luke 3:22)
46 Brand-name refrigerator (obs.)
47 "Brought them unto Halah, and
   _____, and Hara"
   (1 Chronicles 5:26)
48 Type of dog, as Chihauhau
49 Increase
50 Viewed

51 "Thou _____ cursed above all
   cattle" (Genesis 3:14)
53 Needed for white Christmas
54 "City of Sepharvaim, _____, and
   Ivah" (Isaiah 37:13)
55 Generations
56 Follows the book of Daniel (abbr.)

WINDOWS OF OPPORTUNITY

Take this opportunity to see what these windows reveal to you.

ACROSS

1 Victor's companion
4 Gun (the engine)
7 Volga feeder
10 "Much learning doth make thee _____" (Acts 26:24)
13 Swiss river (var.)
14 Of aircraft electrical systems
16 "But I am slow of speech, and _____ slow tongue" (Exodus 4:10) (2 words)
17 "And _____ them about thy neck" (Proverbs 6:21)
18 Where Jezebel was thrown from a **WINDOW** and died (2 Kings 9:30–33)
19 October follower (abbr.)
20 "Whether he be a sinner _____, I know not" (John 9:25) (2 words)
22 "God: _____ me according to thy mercy" (Psalm 109:26) (2 words)
23 Meaning three (comb. form)
24 Where a raven and a dove were released from a **WINDOW** (Genesis 8:6–8) (2 words)
27 Responded vocally to a tongue depressor
29 Baseball great Ott
30 Rockies and Cascades (abbr.)
32 "And _____ did that which was right in the eyes of the Lord" (1 Kings 15:11)
35 Click beetle
38 "Take thee a _____, and lay it before thee" (Ezekiel 4:1)
42 The direction Daniel's **WINDOWS** faced (Daniel 6:10) (2 words)
45 Part of CEO (abbr.)
46 "She gave me some fruit from the tree, and _____" (Genesis 3:12 NIV) (3 words)
47 "Your lightning _____ up the world" (Psalm 77:18 NIV)
48 _____-do-well (slang)
50 "Unto us a _____ is given" (Isaiah 9:6)
52 "And took a _____, and girded himself" (John 13:4)

55 Where Paul escaped through a **WINDOW** (2 Corinthians 11:32–33)
60 "For ye tithe mint and _____ and all" (Luke 11:42)
61 Muslim women's garments
64 "His children, their _____ is the sword" (Job 27:14 NIV)
65 Similar to O.C.S. (abbr.)
66 Where Rahab tied a thread in a **WINDOW** (Joshua 2:1–21)
69 "He maketh me to _____ down in green pastures" (Psalm 23:2)
70 "As though I shot _____ mark" (1 Samuel 20:20) (2 words)
71 "Therefore I said, Surely these _____" (Jeremiah 5:4) (2 words)
72 Shimei's father (1 Kings 4:18 NIV)
73 "They that _____ in tears shall reap in joy" (Psalm 126:5)
74 "And _____ him in the sand" (Exodus 2:12)
75 Oolong or mint
76 "In the Valley of _____ Hinnom" (2 Kings 23:10 NIV)

DOWN

1 Betray (2 words, slang)
2 Capital on the Nile
3 "Men condemned to die in the _____" (1 Corinthians 4:9 NIV)
4 British rule in India
5 Grandmother of Enos (Genesis 4:25–26)
6 Eyeshade (var.)
7 "To every _____ loaf of bread" (1 Chronicles 16:3) (2 words)
8 Capital of Ukraine
9 "Create in me _____ heart, O God" (Psalm 51:10) (2 words)
10 "Which is the _____ Adar" (Esther 8:12)
11 "As I wrote _____ in few words" (Ephesians 3:3)
12 Who Michal let down from a **WINDOW** (1 Samuel 19:12)
15 Russian city on the Ural River
21 Bit of electrical resistance
25 Soothsayer or clairvoyant

by David K. Shortess

26 "For as in Adam _____ "
   (1 Corinthians 15:22) (2 words)
28 Nick and Nora Charles'
   cinematic pup
30 "Are you not _____ men"
   (1 Corinthians 3:4 NIV)
31 Self-evident verity
32 "And _____ the sacrifices of the
   dead" (Psalm 106:28)
33 Red or white in baseball
34 "Stand in _____, and sin not"
   (Psalm 4:4)
36 "Go into the city, and a man
   carrying _____ of water will meet
   you" (Mark 14:13 NIV) (2 words)
37 Vietnamese holiday
39 "Wherefore dealt ye so _____
   with me" (Genesis 43:6)
40 Island garland
41 9-1-1 responder (abbr.)
43 Teen bane
44 Greek portico
49 He slew 450 prophets of Baal
   (1 Kings 18:40)
51 It may cause a check to bounce
   (abbr.)

52 Where Eutychus went to sleep and
   fell from a **WINDOW**
   (Acts 20:6–9)
53 "And led him _____ crucify him"
   (Mark 15:20) (2 words)
54 "And there _____ the giants, the
   sons of Anak" (Numbers 13:33)
   (2 words)
55 "The mountains will _____ new
   wine" (Joel 3:18 NIV)
56 It's a tie
57 One of the twelve spies (Numbers
   13:6)
58 Useful
59 "And thou shalt _____ enemy in
   my habitation" (1 Samuel 2:32)
   (2 words)
62 A son of Jeduthun
   (1 Chronicles 25:3)
63 "That they bring thee _____
   heifer" (Numbers 19:2) (2 words)
67 "Once cultivated by the _____"
   (Isaiah 7:25 NIV)
68 "Or athirst, _____ stranger"
   (Matthew 25:44) (2 words)

ACROSS

1 "Loose thy shoe from _____ thy foot" (Joshua 5:15)
4 Shoham's brother (1 Chronicles 24:27)
8 Sea rhythm
12 Weeps
14 Hananiah's father (Jeremiah 28:1)
15 Asa's father (1 Chronicles 3:10)
16 The figure formed by two intersecting lines
17 "Land of _____ brought water to him that was thirsty" (Isaiah 21:14)
18 "Pharaoh took off his _____" (Genesis 41:42)
19 Zelophehad's daughter (Numbers 26:33)
21 "Between Paran, and _____, and Laban" (Deuteronomy 1:1)
23 Came in
25 "Many of the _____ hearing believed and were baptized" (Acts 18:8) (abbr.)
26 Utilize
27 Othniel was this (Judges 3:9)
30 "And the angels of God _____ him" (Genesis 32:1)
33 Satan
34 "As vinegar upon _____" (Proverbs 25:20)
38 Jehiel's son (1 Chronicles 9:35–37)
40 They grind flour
42 Female sheep
43 Give up
45 Bible measurement for flour (Leviticus 14:10)
47 "A river went _____ of Eden" (Genesis 2:10)
48 "Man _____ his anger" (Proverbs 19:11)
51 "Get up, take your _____ and go home" (Matthew 9:6 NIV)
54 Gave food to
55 Tanhumeth's son (2 Kings 25:23)
59 Belonging to the adversary
61 "Wheat with a _____" (Proverbs 27:22)
62 "Which is above every _____" (Philippians 2:9)
63 Rip
67 "Encamped in _____, in the edge of the wilderness" (Exodus 13:20)
68 "And Ahijah, Hanan, _____" (Nehemiah 10:26)
69 "Began to _____ him vehemently" (Luke 11:53)
70 Product of weeping
71 "He had _____ hundred chariots of iron" (Judges 4:3)
72 "And to thy _____, which is Christ" (Galatians 3:16)
73 "How the gold is become _____!" (Lamentations 4:1)

DOWN

1 Solomon's temple was built on his threshing floor (1 Chronicles 21:15)
2 Altercation
3 Cut down
4 A small, furry animal that flies
5 Follows Lamentations (abbr., var.)
6 Follows Leviticus (abbr.)
7 Speaker
8 To bend out of shape, distort
9 Aaron's son (Exodus 6:23)
10 "No place of seed, or of figs, or of _____" (Numbers 20:5)
11 Fowl that should not be eaten (Leviticus 11:13)
12 Arrived
13 Charred
20 "Crowns shall be to _____, and to Tobijah" (Zechariah 6:14)
22 Jerahmeel's son (1 Chronicles 2:25)
24 Partitioned
25 Basements
28 More disgusting
29 "Wheat and the _____ were not smitten" (Exodus 9:32)
30 Species of hawthorn
31 Benjamin's son (Genesis 46:21)
32 Bind
35 "_____ wings of a great eagle" (Revelation 12:14)

by N. Teri Grottke

36 Peleg's son (Genesis 11:18)
37 Jewish heroine of the Old Testament (abbr.)
39 Elderly
41 Slumber
44 "Curse me Jacob, and come, _____ Israel" (Numbers 23:7)
46 City passageway
49 Felix's replacement (Acts 24:27)
50 "My foot hath _____ to deceit" (Job 31:5)
51 Melea's father (Luke 3:31)
52 Elioenai's son (1 Chronicles 3:24)
53 Eliphaz's son (Genesis 36:11)
56 Ribai's son (1 Chronicles 11:31)
57 "Day of the trumpet and _____ against the fenced cities" (Zephaniah 1:16)
58 Edges of garments
60 Part of the handwriting on the wall (Daniel 5:25)

64 "How long will it be _____ they believe me" (Numbers 14:11)
65 Get older
66 _____ Sea

15

ACROSS

1 "The devil threw him down, and
_____ him" (Luke 9:42)
5 Taxi
8 David lived here (2 Samuel 5:9)
12 Belly button
13 "Thy princes _____ rebellious,
and companions of thieves" (Isaiah
1:23)
14 Manna was measured this way
(Exodus 16:33)
15 Oily fruit
16 Untruth
17 She hid the Hebrew spies
(Joshua 6:17)
19 Rope web
20 Grapes grow here
22 "Children of _____" (Ezra 2:55)
23 "And Anab, and _____"
(Joshua 15:50)
25 We
26 Museum in New York City (abbr.)
27 Type of lodging
28 Construct
30 Letter addressed to early
Christians (abbr.)
33 Shammah's father (2 Samuel
23:11)
36 Type of golf clubs
40 Honed
43 "Garments, _____ stood before
the angel" (Zechariah 3:3)
44 "Hariph, Anathoth, _____"
(Nehemiah 10:19)
45 King of nations (Genesis 14:1)
46 Arad's brother (1 Chronicles 8:15)
48 "Against Jerusalem, _____, she is
broken" (Ezekiel 26:2)
49 Crucifixion instrument
51 Gad's son (Genesis 46:16)
54 Pork
57 Venice's country (abbr.)
58 Hannah's adversary (1 Samuel 1:2,
6)
63 Chooses
65 Picnic pests
66 Herdsman of Tekoa (Amos 1:1)
(abbr., var.)

67 Levi's grandson (1 Chronicles
6:47)
68 Not young
69 "Let us watch and be _____"
(1 Thessalonians 5:6)
71 Ostracize
72 Partook
73 Hodaiah's brother
(1 Chronicles 3:24)
74 Suspend
75 To free
76 Gripped

DOWN

1 Stories
2 Where Hadad reigned
(Genesis 36:35)
3 "Day of wrath and _____ of the
righteous judgment" (Romans 2:5)
(abbr.)
4 Number of disciples minus one
5 "Is not _____ as Carchemish?"
(Isaiah 10:9)
6 "Argob and _____" (2 Kings
15:25)
7 Buzzing insect
8 "Let thy _____ be uncovered"
(Habakkuk 2:16)
9 A grandson of Esau
(Genesis 36:15 NIV)
10 The commanding officer
(Ezra 4:9 NIV)
11 Commerce
12 Not any
18 Cave-dwelling mammal
21 Helem's son (1 Chronicles 7:35)
22 Issachar's son (Numbers 26:23)
24 U.S. calculator company (abbr.)
28 Darius was one (Daniel 11:1)
29 "Between their teeth, _____ it
was chewed" (Numbers 11:33)
30 Superlative (suffix)
31 _____ Beta Kappa
32 "He _____ horns" (Habakkuk
3:4)
34 Ebed's son (Judges 9:26)
35 "It came to pass at the _____ of
two full years (Genesis 41:1)

by N. Teri Grottke

37 A Hebrew prophet (abbr., var.)
38 Book of the Bible that tells the vision of an Elkoshite (abbr.)
39 "Of Keros, the children of _____" (Nehemiah 7:47)
41 "_____ greedily after the error of Balaam" (Jude 1:11)
42 Braiding
47 Lease
50 "That which groweth of _____ own accord" (Leviticus 25:5)
52 "Journeyed from _____, and pitched in Kehelathah" (Numbers 33:22)
53 "So shall my righteousness answer for me _____ time to come" (Genesis 30:33)
54 "Upon the _____ of the robe round about" (Exodus 28:34)
55 Encampment in the wilderness (Numbers 33:13)
56 King of Moab (2 Kings 3:4)

58 Raphu's son (Numbers 13:9)
59 Finished
60 Abigail's "churlish and evil" husband (1 Samuel 25:3)
61 Make a correction
62 Lotan's son (Genesis 36:22)
64 A city of Hadarezer (1 Chronicles 18:8)
68 Boat paddle
70 Single

16

ACROSS

1 Drinking vessel
4 Land measurement
8 Asher didn't drive out these inhabitants (Judges 1:31)
13 "Shall say in all the highways, ____!" (Amos 5:16)
15 "Suffer ye _____ far" (Luke 22:51)
16 Flatland
17 Neri's son (Luke 3:27)
19 Steed
20 "They take the _____ and harp, and rejoice" (Job 21:12)
21 Problems
23 Musical group
24 "They are _____ with the showers of the mountains" (Job 24:8)
25 "They dwelt in their _____ until the captivity" (1 Chronicles 5:22)
28 "Thou _____ the springing thereof" (Psalm 65:10)
33 Flavor
34 "Thy thoughts are very _____" (Psalm 92:5)
35 "God created _____ heaven" (Genesis 1:1)
36 "From _____ of the Sidonians as far as Aphek" (Joshua 13:4)
37 Most horrible
38 He provoked more anger than all the kings of Israel before him (1 Kings 16:30)
39 Peleg's son (Genesis 11:18)
40 "Swift as the _____ upon the mountain" (1 Chronicles 12:8)
41 A city in Judah (Joshua 15:26)
42 Direction of the sunrise
45 "And Avim, and _____" (Joshua 18:23)
46 "We _____ not what is become of him" (Acts 7:40)
47 Bambi is one
48 Shimrath's father (1 Chronicles 8:21)
51 Belonging to Old Testament heroine
55 Zadok's father (Nehemiah 3:4)
56 Eran's father (Numbers 26:36)
58 Frequently
59 "In his days did _____ the Bethelite" (1 Kings 16:34)
60 "People shall be as the burnings of _____" (Isaiah 33:12)
61 Troublesome plants
62 _____ of Man (place)
63 "Two cheeks, and the _____" (Deuteronomy 18:3)

DOWN

1 "_____ out this bondwoman and her son" (Genesis 21:10)
2 Daniel had a vision by this river (Daniel 8:2)
3 Part of the hand
4 Large Greek city
5 "Thou art with _____" (Genesis 16:11)
6 Regret, sorrow
7 Nagge's son (Luke 3:25)
8 Levite chief (1 Chronicles 24:15)
9 "Old cast _____ and old rotten rags" (Jeremiah 38:11)
10 A worldwide relief organization (abbr.)
11 Cat's sound of displeasure
12 In agreement or union
14 Day of rest
18 Swap
22 Used a broom
25 Look hard
26 Micah's son (1 Chronicles 8:35)
27 Belonging to Jacob's brother (Genesis 25:26)
28 Ephraim's son (1 Chronicles 7:20)
29 Greater than or _____ than
30 "Libnah, and _____, and Ashan" (Joshua 15:42)
31 Hothan the Aroerite's son (1 Chronicles 11:44)
32 Reumah's son (Genesis 22:24)
34 Entrance
37 "And their _____, for it was cruel" (Genesis 49:7)
38 Harum's son (1 Chronicles 4:8)
41 "Destroy all the children of _____" (Numbers 24:17)

by N. Teri Grottke

43 "Fine _____ linen of cunning
   work" (Exodus 26:31)
44 "And the Israelitish _____ son
   blasphemed the name of the Lord,
   and cursed" (Leviticus 24:11)
45 "Mortar among wheat with a
   _____" (Proverbs 27:22)
47 Eliasaph's father (Numbers 1:14)
48 Out of danger
49 Detest
50 Rephaiah's father
   (1 Chronicles 4:42)
52 There were twelve wells of water
   here (Exodus 15:27)
53 "In _____ was there a voice
   heard" (Matthew 2:18)
54 "Kindness which thou shalt
   _____ unto me" (Genesis 20:13)
55 Arrow ejector
57 "The priest shall have in _____
   hand the bitter water that causeth
   the curse" (Numbers 5:18)

TIT FOR TAT

But as for me, it is good to be near God.
I have made the sovereign LORD my refuge.
PSALM 73:28 NIV

ACROSS

1 Neighbor of 69 Across (abbr.)
5 "The _____ principles of the world" (Galatians 4:3 NIV)
10 Sergeant Snorkel's dog
14 "I that speak unto thee _____ " (John 4:26) (2 words)
15 "It is only _____ " (Leviticus 13:6 NIV) (2 words)
16 "They shall _____ themselves"
18 It is found between many stories
19 "And Moses diligently sought the _____ " (Leviticus 10:16)
20 Start of a **PROMISE** from James 4:8 NIV (4 words)
23 Exodus (the movie) hero
24 Means for saving money and data (abbr.)
25 "And it came to pass, when _____ was past" (1 Kings 18:29)
28 Cow catcher
30 "Now the coat was without _____ " (John 19:23)
32 "Sir, come down _____ my child die" (John 4:49)
33 "Der _____ " (Konrad Adenauer)
34 Perspicacious
36 "As a wild bull in a _____ " (Isaiah 51:20)
37 **PROMISE**, cont. (3 words)
40 Type of sleep (abbr.)
43 "Are not his days like those of _____ man?" (Job 7:1 NIV) (2 words)
44 Patron saint and once king of Norway
48 "But I _____ worm" (Psalm 22:6) (2 words)
49 "And they made upon the _____ of the robe" (Exodus 39:24)
50 "They look and _____ upon me" (Psalm 22:17)
51 "_____ not among yourselves" (John 6:43)

53 "And for the _____ that is in the land of Assyria" (Isaiah 7:18)
55 "And his body was _____ " (Daniel 4:33)
56 End of the **PROMISE** (4 words)
60 Follower of Joel
62 "And bring _____ reign of terror" (Amos 6:3 NIV) (2 words)
63 L.D.S. and J.W. (abbr.)
64 "And the _____ said unto them" (Judges 9:13)
65 Lugs
66 Glasgow bank
67 Allies' opponents
68 "He walketh upon a _____ " (Job 18:8)
69 Lat. and Est., once (abbr., poss.)

DOWN

1 Milan opera house (2 words)
2 "People of this world who are _____ " (1 Corinthians 5:10 NIV)
3 "To whom _____ of darkness is reserved" (2 Peter 2:17) (2 words)
4 "I and _____ dreamed each man" (Genesis 41:11) (2 words)
5 "The law is not _____ on faith" (Galatians 3:12 NIV)
6 "And thou _____ a whale in the seas" (Ezekiel 32:2) (2 words)
7 Industrial region in southwest Germany
8 "How _____ that I hear this of thee?" (Luke 16:2) (2 words)
9 Half a chromosome
10 "For in the image _____ made he man" (Genesis 9:6) (2 words)
11 "And it shall be _____ down" (Isaiah 5:5)
12 Crumpets' buddy
13 Giants' Mel

by David K. Shortess

21 Sergeant York, for example (abbr.)
22 Word preceding Psalm 119:17
26 "Three angels which _____. . .
   (cont. in 27 Down)
27 . . ._____ to sound"
   (Revelation 8:13)
29 "And made the _____ dry land"
   (Exodus 14:21)
30 Suffix for young and old alike
31 World chess champ Max,
   1935–1937
34 Enthusiasts
35 Leveler, at times
38 Follower of Micah
39 "One _____ for the Lord"
   (Leviticus 16:8)
40 "And a _____ on every altar"
   (Numbers 23:14)
41 It's grounded in Australia
42 Radio pioneer
45 Tertullus and Zenas
   (Acts 24:1 and Titus 3:13 NIV) (pl.)

46 Concerning the inner part of the
   iris
47 Prenatal babies (pl.)
50 "O God, _____ me up on high"
   (Psalm 69:29)
52 "And she called his name _____"
   (Exodus 2:10)
53 More austere
54 Expunge
57 Dodge model
58 "That they may _____ whole
   month" (Numbers 11:21)
   (2 words)
59 Eyes, poetically
60 "From Babylon, and from Cuthah,
   and from _____" (2 Kings 17:24)
61 "_____ her a double portion from
   her own cup" (Revelation 18:6 NIV)

18

ACROSS

1 Give for temporary use
5 "Tappuah, and _____"
(Joshua 15:34)
9 Baby horses
14 Mushi's son (1 Chronicles 23:23)
15 This was to be made all of blue
(Exodus 28:31)
16 New Delhi's country
17 Jehoiada was their leader
(1 Chronicles 12:27)
19 Hosea's wife (Hosea 1:3)
20 To propel a motor vehicle
21 Otherwise
23 Abijam's son (1 Kings 15:8)
24 Left-handed son of Gera
(Judges 3:15)
26 Esther replaced her (Esther 2:17)
29 Paul's hometown (Acts 21:39)
32 Amount owed
33 Alphabetically, the second book of
the Bible (abbr., var.)
34 "Ship boards of fir trees of _____"
(Ezekiel 27:5)
37 David fought the Syrians here
(2 Samuel 10:17)
41 David fled to here
(1 Samuel 19:18)
43 Ikkesh's son (2 Samuel 23:26)
44 The *last* of "the First and the Last"
(Revelation 22:13 NIV)
45 Selected ones
46 Simeon was called this
(Acts 13:1)
48 Number of commandments
49 Endurance test
51 They were "five and twenty cubits
long, and five cubits broad"
(Ezekiel 40:30)
53 Naarah's son (1 Chronicles 4:6)
56 Father of ninety-eight children
(Ezra 2:16)
57 Big hatchet
58 "Ho, _____ a one!" (Ruth 4:1)
61 "They shall lament for the _____"
(Isaiah 32:12)
65 Burdened
68 "Then _____ stood and cried
with a loud voice" (2 Kings 18:28)

70 Jeroham's father (1 Samuel 1:1)
71 "The city of Sepharvaim, of Hena,
and _____" (2 Kings 19:13)
72 Not feral
73 Blemish
74 "The writing that was written,
_____" (Daniel 5:25)
75 Naphtali tribe member
(Numbers 2:29)

DOWN

1 Guide
2 "Spread his tent beyond the tower
of _____" (Genesis 35:21)
3 Salathiel's father (Luke 3:27)
4 Herds
5 Gad's son (Genesis 46:16)
6 Marked down
7 Cain's victim
8 Chaos
9 Jesus cursed this tree (Mark 11:21)
10 "The children of Lod, Hadid, and
_____" (Ezra 2:33)
11 "Shall I make thee as _____?"
(Hosea 11:8)
12 "When thou _____ down, thou
shalt not be afraid"
(Proverbs 3:24)
13 Abram's wife
18 Brass serpent (2 Kings 18:4)
22 January 20 is Saint Agnes' _____
25 To put into practicality
27 "Their soul _____ all manner of
meat" (Psalm 107:18)
28 Part of a flower
29 "Straightway the spirit _____
him" (Mark 9:20)
30 Imna's brother (1 Chronicles 7:35)
31 Geographical center of New
Testament politics
32 Pull
35 "_____ ladies dancing" in the
holiday counting song
36 Bela's son (1 Chronicles 7:7)
38 Danish director Jørgen _____
39 Shammah's father (2 Samuel
23:11)
40 "For the tree of the field is _____
life" (Deuteronomy 20:19) (poss.)

by N. Teri Grottke

42 Unit of land
47 Consume food
50 Saul's father (Acts 13:21)
52 Make from nothing
53 Canterbury _____
54 "Let us _____ his name together" (Psalm 34:3)
55 Esther's husband was king here (Esther 1:2–4)
56 Abishur's son (1 Chronicles 2:29)
59 "Let thy Thummim and thy _____ be with thy holy one" (Deuteronomy 33:8)
60 Where Lot and his two daughters dwelled (Genesis 19:30)
62 Ezer's child (Genesis 36:27)
63 "The troops of _____ looked, the companies of Sheba waited" (Job 6:19)
64 "Set it between Mizpeh and _____" (1 Samuel 7:12)
66 Benjamin's son (Genesis 46:21)

67 Joshua's father (Exodus 33:11)
69 "_____ was a woman of a fair countenance" (2 Samuel 14:27)

ACROSS

1 It was not smitten (Exodus 9:32)
4 "In _____ was there a voice" (Matthew 2:18)
8 Get up
13 Weapons
15 Duke of Edom (Genesis 36:43)
16 Gomer's husband (Hosea 1:2–3)
17 "My _____ shall live because of thee" (Genesis 12:13)
18 Currently
19 Haggeri's son (1 Chronicles 11:38)
20 "Enlarge the place of thy tent" (Isaiah 54:2)
22 "There was _____ again with the Philistines" (1 Chronicles 20:5)
23 "Therefore _____ name is called Babel" (Genesis 11:9 NKJV)
24 "They will _____ thee alive" (Genesis 12:12)
25 Shamer's son (1 Chronicles 7:34)
28 "Hundred and _____ years old" (Joshua 24:29)
29 Kept from detection
30 "The sons of Mushi; Mahli, and _____, and Jeremoth, three" (1 Chronicles 23:23)
34 Hadad's city (1 Chronicles 1:50)
36 Goliath compared himself to this animal before David
39 Child's favorite seat
41 "Abraham set seven _____ lambs of the flock by themselves" (Genesis 21:28)
42 Fuss
43 Cain's mother
44 Hophni's father (1 Samuel 1:3)
45 First book of the Bible (abbr.)
46 The good Samaritan took the man here (Luke 10:33–34)
47 "First came out _____, all over like a hairy garment" (Genesis 25:25)
48 College entrance exam (abbr.)
49 Hadassah (abbr.)
50 Skin breakout
52 "_____, and the mighty men which belonged to David" (1 Kings 1:8)

54 Zephaniah's son (Zechariah 6:14)
56 "_____, Shophan, and Jaazer" (Numbers 32:35)
59 "According to his eating, an _____ for every man" (Exodus 16:16)
61 "Destroy _____ kings and people" (Ezra 6:12)
64 "The servant _____ to meet her" (Genesis 24:17)
65 Esteemed
68 "Sighed by _____ of the bondage" (Exodus 2:23)
70 Earlier than (arch.)
71 "Gilalai, _____, Nethaneel" (Nehemiah 12:36)
72 Subdued
73 Dishan's son (1 Chronicles 1:42)
74 Mix
75 Disgrace
76 Christ died for our _____
77 When fasting, one does not _____

DOWN

1 "_____ it, even to the foundation" (Psalm 137:7)
2 Heavy chains
3 Imitations
4 Pharaoh put this on Joseph's hand (Genesis 41:42)
5 City on the bank of the river Arnon (Deuteronomy 4:48)
6 "Two cheeks, and the _____" (Deuteronomy 18:3)
7 "Before Abraham was, I _____" (John 8:58)
8 Enan's son (Numbers 1:15)
9 Expression: "_____ him blind"
10 Zoheth's father (1 Chronicles 4:20)
11 Resting place
12 "Seven _____ of corn came up on one stalk" (Genesis 41:5)
14 _____ trade was an issue in the early 1800s
19 "He sent away the multitude, and took ship, and came into the coasts of _____" (Matthew 15:39)

by N. Teri Grottke

21 "All the evil. . .did God _____ upon their heads" (Judges 9:57)
22 "And _____ I was speaking, and praying" (Daniel 9:20)
26 The Buckeye State (abbr.)
27 "_____ is become great" (Genesis 24:35)
31 "Turned into the _____ plant" (Jeremiah 2:21)
32 "Thy _____ and thy she goats" (Genesis 31:38)
33 "Joseph is without doubt _____ in pieces" (Genesis 37:33)
34 Couple
35 Pahathmoab's son (Ezra 10:30)
37 "Ran by the way of the plain, and _____ Cushi" (2 Samuel 18:23)
38 "Time would fail me to tell of ____" (Hebrews 11:32)
40 One of Pharaoh's treasure cities (Exodus 1:11)
51 Short laugh

53 Birthplace of Christopher Columbus (abbr.)
55 Giants (Deuteronomy 2:10–11)
57 "_____ them down with ease over against Gibeah" (Judges 20:43)
58 Abram's brother (Genesis 11:26)
60 "Micah his son, _____ his son" (1 Chronicles 5:5)
61 "Used curious _____ brought their books" (Acts 19:19)
62 Rachel's sister (Genesis 29:16)
63 Dali _____
66 "Then the beasts go into _____" (Job 37:8)
67 Grime
69 Arphaxad's father (Luke 3:36)
70 Haggi's brother (Genesis 46:16)
73 "_____ Time Goes By"

ACROSS

1 He was not with Adonijah
(1 Kings 1:8)
4 Jehoshaphat's father (1 Kings
22:41)
7 "_____ obtained favour in his
sight" (Esther 5:2)
10 "Any of his _____" (Job 34:27)
11 Ground moisture
12 "Which was diverse from all the
_____" (Daniel 7:19)
15 The field of blood (Acts 1:19)
17 Azareel's father (Nehemiah 11:13)
18 Savior
19 Turn away from sin
20 Jehu's great-grandfather
(1 Chronicles 4:35)
22 Gave food
23 "And they _____ against me"
(Hosea 7:14)
27 "The magicians tried to produce
gnats by their secret _____"
(Exodus 8:18 NIV)
29 "As thou _____ to do"
(Psalm 119:132)
30 Peleg's son (Genesis 11:18)
31 They descended from Shem
through Eber (abbr.)
34 Pepper's tablemate
35 "Let him that _____"
(Ephesians 4:28)
37 "_____ in speech"
(2 Corinthians 11:6)
38 Uz's brother (Genesis 10:23)
39 Bela's son (Numbers 26:40)
40 "Whether he have _____ a son"
(Exodus 21:31)
41 "Harvest is _____" (Joel 3:13)
43 "Enter into my _____"
(Lamentations 3:13)
44 "A _____ of dove's dung"
(2 Kings 6:25)
45 "Seek peace, and _____ it"
(1 Peter 3:11)
49 "And _____, and Kedemoth"
(Joshua 13:18)
52 King of Shinar (Genesis 14:1)
57 A city in Naphtali
(Joshua 19:35–36)
58 Teresh's coconspirator (Esther 6:2)
59 Immer's son (Ezra 10:20)
60 Partook
61 Sheresh's son (1 Chronicles 7:16)
62 Good hand (abbr.)
63 Commanded
64 "Abram had been living in Canaan
_____ years" (Genesis 16:3 NIV)

DOWN

1 Endurance test
2 Looked at
3 Island
4 Belonging to the first man (poss.)
5 Joseph's son (Luke 3:26)
6 "Or ever I was _____"
(Song of Solomon 6:12)
7 Molds
8 "The son of _____" (1 Kings 4:10)
9 Descendant of Shuthelah
(Numbers 26:36 NASB)
10 Conflict as Korean, Vietnam, and
Civil
12 Boat paddle
13 "Sold for his _____" (Exodus
22:3)
14 "Turn aside, _____ down here"
(Ruth 4:1)
16 "When Sarai _____ hardly with
her" (Genesis 16:6)
21 Eliasaph's father (Numbers 3:24)
23 "Branch and _____, in one day"
(Isaiah 9:14)
24 Jacob's brother (Genesis 25:27)
25 "A _____ and a pomegranate"
(Exodus 39:26)
26 New York time in the winter
(abbr.)
28 Expression: "_____ the day"
30 Staff
31 Jaroah's son (1 Chronicles 5:14)
32 First garden
33 "_____ of spices"
(Song of Solomon 6:2)
35 Tree juice
36 Mighty oak
37 _____ v. Wade
40 "And God made two _____
lights" (Genesis 1:16)

by N. Teri Grottke

41 Cush's son (Genesis 10:7)
42 Judge after Jephthah
(Judges 12:7–8)
44 "That _____ to the sound of the
viol" (Amos 6:5)
46 Abigail's churlish husband
(1 Samuel 25:3)
47 "_____ a scorner"
(Proverbs 19:25)
48 "They _____ him till he was
ashamed" (2 Kings 2:17)
49 "By his name _____"
(Psalm 68:4)
50 This Hebrew month is the twelfth
month of the year (Esther 9:1)
51 Abdiel's son (1 Chronicles 5:15)
53 Ham's son (Genesis 10:6)
54 "Lest he _____ thee"
(Luke 12:58)
55 Ahira's father (Numbers 1:15)
56 Comes between Jeremiah and
Ezekiel (abbr.)

BIG BIBLICAL WORDS

So likewise ye, except ye utter by the tongue words easy to be understood, how shall it be known what is spoken?

1 CORINTHIANS 14:9

ACROSS

1 "No one _____ a patch of unshrunk" (Mark 2:21 NIV)
5 Sailors of yesteryear
9 "He maketh them also to _____ like a calf" (Psalm 29:6)
13 "In Pontus, and _____" (Acts 2:9)
14 "Answered and said, Master, _____ I?" (Matthew 26:25) (2 words)
15 "And he said _____ him" (2 Kings 4:13)
16 A big biblical word meaning "lewdness" (Jude 1:4)
19 A word of mild reproof
20 "Was I ever _____ to do so unto thee?" (Numbers 22:30)
21 "Even upon _____ by the wall" (1 Samuel 20:25) (2 words)
22 Have a bug
23 "And one _____ lamb of the first year" (Leviticus 14:10)
24 A big biblical word meaning "deceit" (Romans 12:9)
31 "The _____ of tabrets ceaseth" (Isaiah 24:8)
32 "And _____ they tell him of her" (Mark 1:30)
33 Sign at a full house (abbr.)
34 Take _____ view, be skeptical (2 words)
35 "Depart, and _____ peace" (Acts 16:36) (2 words)
36 "Jehu destroyed _____ out of Israel" (2 Kings 10:28)
37 Genetic carrier (abbr.)
38 "They _____ my garments among them" (Psalm 22:18)
39 Lariat
40 A big biblical word meaning "lust" (Romans 7:8)

43 "Where _____ you?" (Genesis 3:9 NIV)
44 "Out of whose womb came the _____?" (Job 38:29)
45 "Shew I unto you _____ excellent way" (1 Corinthians 12:31) (2 words)
48 Ninth Greek letter
50 "Blessed are _____ poor" (Matthew 5:3)
53 A big biblical word meaning "thing written over" (Mark 15:26)
56 "Casting _____ into the sea" (Matthew 4:18) (2 words)
57 "Then Jacob _____ up" (Genesis 31:17)
58 Consequently
59 "And the crisping _____" (Isaiah 3:22)
60 Signs (as a pact)
61 "How much _____ man" (Job 25:6)

DOWN

1 "Ye are the _____ of the earth" (Matthew 5:13)
2 Isaac's firstborn (Genesis 27:32)
3 "For he _____ not what to say" (Mark 9:6)
4 Animal pouch
5 Italian fountain city
6 "So, as much _____ me is" (Romans 1:15) (2 words)
7 "Not accused of _____ or unruly" (Titus 1:6)
8 Catholic school in Miami, Florida (abbr.)
9 "Return it to him by _____" (Exodus 22:26 NIV)
10 "At the name of Jesus every _____ should bow" (Philippians 2:10)

by David K. Shortess

11 "_____ ghost" (Matthew 14:26 NIV) (2 words)
12 "Or unto the door _____"
   (Exodus 21:6)
17 "Beloved, _____ above all things"
   (3 John 1:2) (2 words)
18 "And I _____ angel" (Revelation
   20:1) (2 words)
22 Independent standards
   organization (abbr.)
23 "The daughter of _____ the
   Hittite" (Genesis 36:2)
24 "Who _____ sin" (1 Peter 2:22)
   (2 words)
25 _____ Jaya, Indonesia
26 New Zealand tribe
27 "The rear guard for all the _____"
   (Numbers 10:25 NIV)
28 Sarah's firstborn (Genesis 21:3)
29 Speechify
30 New Orleans' nickname
31 Artist Chagall

35 "They ____ at me" (Psalm 35:21
   NIV)
36 Climbing vine
38 "Were _____ than snow"
   (Lamentations 4:7)
39 Tire type
41 Insertion marks
42 "And repaired the _____"
   (Judges 21:23)
45 Posthaste (abbr.)
46 Actor Paul, who played Pasteur
47 "Lord, Lord, _____ to us"
   (Matthew 25:11)
48 Computer symbol
49 City on the Ural
50 "Bind the _____ of thine head"
   (Ezekiel 24:17)
51 Swine
52 Seth's son (Genesis 4:26)
54 _____ Lanka
55 "In _____ Assar" (Isaiah 37:12 NIV)

ACROSS

1 Tasks
5 "Twenty thousand _____ of gold" (Nehemiah 7:72)
10 Skeletal component
14 "_____, lama sabachthani" (Mark 15:34)
15 Rulers' nationality at Jesus' time
16 Manna was measured this way (Exodus 16:33)
17 Circle
18 A river of Damascus (2 Kings 5:12)
19 Anak's father (Joshua 15:13)
20 "High places also of _____" (Hosea 10:8)
21 Forty years
23 "The son of _____" (1 Kings 4:10)
25 "And Hushim, the sons of _____" (1 Chronicles 7:12)
26 Homes of wild animals
29 "The treacherous _____" (Isaiah 21:2)
34 Area near Babylon (2 Kings 17:24)
37 "Compassed me about like _____" (Psalm 118:12)
39 "Land from _____ to" (Isaiah 16:1)
40 Elkanah's hometown (1 Samuel 1:1)
45 "Shall say in all the highways, _____!" (Amos 5:16)
46 Precipitation
47 Follows Song of Solomon (abbr.)
48 "Entering in of _____ unto the river" (Amos 6:14)
51 Caleb's son (1 Chronicles 4:15)
53 "That which _____ been is named already" (Ecclesiastes 6:10)
56 "It was the _____ month and the king was sitting in the winter apartment" (Jeremiah 36:22)
60 "_____ the soul" (Proverbs 25:13)
66 "The plain of _____" (Daniel 3:1)
67 Chelub's son (1 Chronicles 27:26)
68 "_____ the Carmelite" (1 Chronicles 11:37)
69 Enoch's son (Genesis 4:18)
70 "_____, and Dumah, and Eshean" (Joshua 15:52)
71 Michaiah's father (2 Chronicles 13:2)
72 Poisonous snakes
73 Weeks are made of these
74 "Daughter of Pharaoh, which _____ took" (1 Chronicles 4:18)
75 The phrase "empty _____" is used when the children have left home

DOWN

1 Joktan's son (Genesis 10:26)
2 Oily fruit
3 "Rottenness entered into my _____" (Habakkuk 3:16)
4 "Darius _____ the writing" (Daniel 6:9)
5 A bore
6 This was made of blue (Exodus 28:31)
7 "Look from the top of _____" (Song of Solomon 4:8)
8 "Shall be your _____" (Ezekiel 45:12)
9 Trapped
10 "There was none other _____ there" (John 6:22)
11 Ahab's father (1 Kings 16:28)
12 "The men of the other _____" (Nehemiah 7:33)
13 "_____, the family of" (Numbers 26:36)
22 "Your remembrances _____ like unto ashes" (Job 13:12)
24 "Go, sell the oil, and pay thy _____" (2 Kings 4:7)
27 He came with Zerubbabel (Ezra 2:2) (abbr.)
28 Body of water
30 "Child shall play on the hole of the _____" (Isaiah 11:8)
31 Philistines "spread themselves" here (Judges 15:9)
32 Belonging to Hophni's father (1 Samuel 4:11) (poss.)
33 Deity of Hinduism, like Vishnu
34 Ulla's son (1 Chronicles 7:39)

by N. Teri Grottke

35 "And in the _____"
(Deuteronomy 1:7)

36 "_____, and Shema"
(Joshua 15:26)

38 A knight

41 He destroyed his mother's idol
(1 Kings 15:13)

42 He shall not live by bread alone

43 Jachan's brother (1 Chronicles
5:13)

44 Judah's son (Genesis 46:12)

49 "God created _____ heaven"
(Genesis 1:1)

50 "The children of _____"
(Ezra 2:19)

52 A son of Abraham by Keturah
(Genesis 25:1–2)

54 "For _____ I hated them"
(Hosea 9:15)

55 The seventeenth order of the
priesthood (1 Chronicles 24:15)

57 A caretaker

58 "They shall be snares and _____
unto you" (Joshua 23:13)

59 "Little which thou _____ before I
came" (Genesis 30:30)

60 "They were _____ before the
king" (Esther 6:1)

61 He brought the law of Moses
before the congregation
(Nehemiah 8:2)

62 Wear out

63 Eve was made from one of these

64 _____ of the Knowledge of Good
and Evil

65 "And _____ him in thine hand"
(Genesis 21:18)

ACROSS

1 Scalp
5 "An _____ for every man" (Exodus 16:16)
9 Minor prophet's book after Nahum (abbr.)
12 Shechem's father (Genesis 33:19)
13 Binea's father (1 Chronicles 8:37)
14 Naomi wanted to be called this (Ruth 1:20)
15 These cities are forsaken (Isaiah 17:2)
16 Begat the Eranites (Numbers 26:36)
17 One of the chief of the priests (Nehemiah 12:7)
18 Rahab received these (Joshua 6:17)
20 "Shall in no _____ enter" (Matthew 5:20)
21 "Son of _____" (1 Chronicles 6:34)
22 "Thine enemies have _____ their mouth" (Lamentations 2:16)
24 "Hallohesh, _____, Shobek" (Nehemiah 10:24)
28 "Alammelech, and _____" (Joshua 19:26)
29 Manasseh's son (2 Kings 21:18)
30 Caanan's son (Genesis 10:15)
33 The sons of Reuben, the Gadites, and the tribe of Manasseh made war with them (1 Chronicles 5:18–19)
37 Anger
39 "Against Jerusalem, _____, she is broken" (Ezekiel 26:2)
40 Type of drum
41 "Come to the desert of _____" (Exodus 19:2)
42 "_____ shall offer gifts" (Psalm 72:10)
44 Grandfather of Methusael (Genesis 4:18)
45 "Thou puttest they _____ in a rock" (Numbers 24:21)
47 "Thou shalt die the _____ of the uncircumcised" (Ezekiel 28:10)
49 Unmarried
52 Jesus' first miracle was here (John 2:11)

54 Helem's son (1 Chronicles 7:35)
55 Works of the flesh (Galatians 5:20)
61 "Let them eat _____!" says Marie Antoinette
62 Market
63 Naarai's father (1 Chronicles 11:37)
64 Grown older
65 "Or _____," expressing a threat
66 "_____ up a child in the way he should go" (Proverbs 22:6)
67 The _____ Sea was parted
68 "The fallow _____, and the wild goat" (Deuteronomy 14:5)
69 "Worship at his holy _____" (Psalm 99:9)

DOWN

1 Peel
2 Naum's son (Luke 3:25)
3 The giant had six of these (2 Samuel 21:20)
4 "Refuseth reproof _____" (Proverbs 10:17)
5 The End
6 "Beside the plains of _____" (Deuteronomy 11:30)
7 Seir's son (1 Chronicles 1:38)
8 "Who gave himself a _____ for all" (1 Timothy 2:6)
9 Mordecai's enemy (Esther 3:5)
10 Jesus did this at the resurrection
11 Cooked in an oven
12 This meat can be eaten at Christmas
14 "I departed from _____" (Philippians 4:15)
19 He was a preacher of righteousness (2 Peter 2:5)
23 Pots and _____
24 "Goeth upon his _____" (Leviticus 11:27)
25 Zaccur's father (Nehemiah 3:2)
26 Mortgage
27 "They are again _____ therein" (2 Peter 2:20)
28 He gathered the prophets on Mount Carmel (1 Kings 18:20)
31 Middle _____

by N. Teri Grottke

32 "Note _____ place where he is lying" (Ruth 3:4 NIV)
34 Move quickly
35 Had 775 "children" (Ezra 2:5)
36 "_____ of spices" (Song of Solomon 6:2)
38 "In his days did _____ the Bethelite" (1 Kings 16:34)
43 Pahathmoab's son (Ezra 10:30)
46 "Of these who _____ to be somewhat" (Galatians 2:6)
48 "Let not him that _____ despise" (Romans 14:3)
49 Ahiam's father (1 Chronicles 11:35)
50 Idol
51 Not clothed
52 "Law are under the _____" (Galatians 3:10)
53 "Nor _____ the thing that is gone" (Psalm 89:34)

56 _____ and female they were brought into the ark
57 "The fourth to _____" (1 Chronicles 25:11)
58 Brother to Sheba (Genesis 10:26–29)
59 "Sisera lay dead, and the _____ was in his temples" (Judges 4:22)
60 Transgression

24

ACROSS

1 Esau's son (Genesis 36:5)
6 Type of snake
9 _____ of the earth
13 "A tower of _____" (Song of Solomon 7:4)
14 "Mingled people, and _____" (Ezekiel 30:5)
16 Eshcol's brother (Genesis 14:13)
17 "All the fowls of heaven made their _____ in his boughs" (Ezekiel 31:6)
18 "Habor, and _____, and to the river Gozan" (1 Chronicles 5:26)
19 "Harvest is _____: come, get you down" (Joel 3:13)
20 Before (poet.)
21 "Thou shalt make _____ of shittim wood" (Exodus 25:13)
23 "As he saith also in _____" (Romans 9:25)
24 "Of the oaks of Bashan have they made thine _____" (Ezekiel 27:6)
25 Entrepreneurs
27 Hanun's father (Nehemiah 3:30)
31 "City of Sepharvaim, _____, and Ivah" (Isaiah 37:13)
33 "Engannim, Tappuah, and _____" (Joshua 15:34)
34 Belonging to a king of Judah (1 Kings 16:8) (poss.)
36 "Hariph, Anathoth, _____" (Nehemiah 10:19)
41 Clothing
43 "So she wrote _____ in Ahab's name" (1 Kings 21:8)
45 Eastern border of Persian rule
46 Largest continent
48 "He was the son-in-law of Shechaniah the son of _____" (Nehemiah 6:18)
49 Classify
51 "Land of _____ reigned in his stead" (Genesis 36:34)
53 "Talent for a _____" (Exodus 38:27)
57 One-tenth of an ephah (Exodus 16:36)
59 Strong metal
60 Immer's son (Ezra 10:20)
62 "The same _____ great city" (Genesis 10:12) (2 words)
65 "And the burning _____, that shall consume the eyes" (Leviticus 26:16)
66 "And the children of _____ which were in Thelasar?" (2 Kings 19:12)
67 "And a net spread upon _____" (Hosea 5:1)
69 Rabbit
70 "Who said, _____ it" (Psalm 137:7)
71 Phares's son (Matthew 1:3)
72 Picnic pests
73 Arithmetic (abbr., var.)
74 God made coats of these

DOWN

1 Cattle
2 "Let them have dominion _____ the fish of the sea" (Genesis 1:26)
3 Thorny flower
4 Hymn: "How Great Thou _____"
5 "Wool, and _____, and sprinkled" (Hebrews 9:19)
6 "The sons of Carmi; _____, the troubler of Israel" (1 Chronicles 2:7)
7 This man was a scribe (1 Chronicles 18:16)
8 Untainted
9 "At Lydda and _____ saw him" (Acts 9:35)
10 "Mint and _____ and cummin" (Matthew 23:23)
11 One afflicted with a skin disease
12 "_____ whose fruit withereth" (Jude 1:12)
15 "Blood that is in the _____" (Exodus 12:22)
22 Ephraim's son (Numbers 26:35)
26 Desire
27 Jeduthun's son (1 Chronicles 25:3)
28 "And Ahijah, Hanan, _____" (Nehemiah 10:26)

by N. Teri Grottke

29 "Have _____ a wound under thee" (Obadiah 1:7)

30 "Say ye unto your brethren, _____" (Hosea 2:1)

32 Father of Naum (Luke 3:25)

35 Night sky illuminator

37 "The rock _____, and said to Samson" (Judges 15:11)

38 King of Sodom (Genesis 14:2)

39 Dishan's child (Genesis 36:28)

40 Rephaiah's father (1 Chronicles 4:42)

42 Comfort

44 "In one house shall it be _____" (Exodus 12:46)

47 "And _____ them that are sent unto thee" (Luke 13:34)

50 "Name of the _____ Ruth" (Ruth 1:4)

52 Descendants of Eri (Numbers 26:16)

53 "Children of _____ (Ezra 2:44)

54 "Rejoice at the sound of the _____" (Job 21:12)

55 "The _____ which is without the temple" (Revelation 11:2)

56 "_____ smite together, and much pain" (Nahum 2:10)

58 "Shall be your _____" (Ezekiel 45:12)

61 "Death reigned from _____ to Moses" (Romans 5:14)

62 A son of Merari (1 Chronicles 24:27)

63 In a short time

64 "Underneath are the everlasting _____" (Deuteronomy 33:27)

68 Question

25

SPRING!

For as the earth bringeth forth her bud. . .so the Lord GOD will cause righteousness and praise to spring forth before all the nations.

ISAIAH 61:11

ACROSS

1 "Am I a _____ hand" (Jeremiah 23:23) (2 words)
6 "They shoot out the _____ " (Psalm 22:7)
9 "And set a _____ upon him" (Revelation 20:3)
13 " _____ the plague was stayed" (Psalm 106:30) (2 words)
14 "And Abia begat _____ " (Matthew 1:7)
15 "Naomi _____ son" (Ruth 4:17 NIV) (2 words)
16 Start of a seasonal scripture **VERSE**, from Song of Solomon 2:11 NIV (4 words)
19 "And poured _____ upon the top of it" (Genesis 28:18)
20 "And given _____ nation bringing" (Matthew 21:43) (2 words)
21 Branch of women GIs in WWII (abbr.)
24 "And she is a _____ of nations" (Isaiah 23:3)
27 "And walk after _____ gods" (Jeremiah 13:10)
31 "It goes through _____ places" (Matthew 12:43 NIV)
33 "It is a _____ offering" (Leviticus 2:6)
35 "Ye prisoners of _____ " (Zechariah 9:12)
36 "So went _____ forth from" (Job 2:7)
38 "He _____ on the ground" (John 9:6)
40 " _____ them out of the hand of the wicked" (Psalm 82:4)
41 **VERSE**, cont. (3 words)
44 "And it _____ ten horns" (Daniel 7:7)
45 " _____ me when I call" (Psalm 4:1)
46 "Great things _____ he" (Job 37:5)
48 "And Hushim, the sons of _____ "

DOWN

(1 Chronicles 7:12)
50 "Ivory, and _____, and peacocks" (1 Kings 10:22)
52 Capital of Manche (partial abbr.)
53 Mandibular grinder
55 "Whereas _____ saith" (Malachi 1:4)
57 "A time to _____ " (Ecclesiastes 3:7)
58 Thirteenth letter of the Hebrew alphabet
60 " _____ unto the wicked" (Isaiah 3:11)
62 End of **VERSE** (4 words)
70 "In the _____, and all deep places" (Psalm 135:6)
71 "Arise and come to my _____ " (Psalm 35:2 NIV)
72 White heron
73 "Of them that _____ me" (Deuteronomy 5:9)
74 "In the land of _____ " (Genesis 4:16)
75 "They have harps and _____ " (Isaiah 5:12 NIV)

DOWN

1 Neon, for example
2 "This is _____ thing" (Job 9:22)
3 Number 34, he succeeded H.S.T. (initials)
4 "I speak _____ wise men" (1 Corinthians 10:15) (2 words)
5 "And Laban said _____ " (Genesis 29:14) (2 words)
6 "But by the _____ of faith" (Romans 3:27)
7 "That it _____ myself" (Luke 24:39) (2 words)
8 "That _____ after the dust" (Amos 2:7)
9 "Return into his _____ " (Ezekiel 21:30)
10 "And cut off his _____ " (Mark 14:47)
11 "As many _____ love" (Revelation 3:19) (2 words)

by David K. Shortess

12 _____ Cruces, NM
17 "The children of _____"
(Nehemiah 7:12)
18 "It was _____ painful for me"
(Psalm 73:16)
21 "And there _____ light"
(Genesis 1:3)
22 Buffalo-hunting plains Indians
23 "While I was in the _____ of
Susa" (Nehemiah 1:1 NIV)
25 Mold again
26 Gradually lessened
28 "And I will send _____ before
thee" (Exodus 23:28)
29 "Ye are our _____"
(2 Corinthians 3:2)
30 "With that same _____ pottage"
(Genesis 25:30)
32 _____ Kapital (Karl Marx work)
34 "Of stone, and _____ for mortar"
(Genesis 11:3 NIV)
37 To the _____ degree (uttermost)
39 Skosh
42 Earl Grey, for one
43 Midwest bone association (abbr.)
44 Second of Noah's three sons

(Genesis 6:10)
47 "_____ many loaves have ye?"
(Matthew 15:34)
49 Highly branched
51 "Ye have _____ much" (Haggai 1:6)
54 Ministerial title, for example (abbr.)
56 "You were the _____ of perfection"
(Ezekiel 28:12 NIV)
59 "In Cilicia, a citizen of no _____
city" (Acts 21:39)
61 Like a familiar breakfast item
62 "He planteth an _____"
(Isaiah 44:14)
63 New Deal organization (abbr.)
64 "Take, _____: this is my body"
(1 Corinthians 11:24)
65 River, for Juan
66 "Shall _____ unto these things"
(Revelation 22:18)
67 Canadian-born star of the Boston
Bruins, Bobby
68 Born
69 Aliens, briefly

26

ACROSS

1 "The wicked _____ their bow" (Psalm 11:2)
5 Chopped
10 An online marketplace
14 "Spread his tent beyond the tower of _____" (Genesis 35:21)
15 Woman's fruity name
16 Smelling orifice
17 A fit of shivering
18 "Pestilence, and _____ them" (Numbers 14:12)
20 Pekah's father (2 Kings 15:25)
22 Asher's firstborn (1 Chronicles 7:30)
23 Lot's son and grandson (Genesis 19:37)
24 Solomon made one in Eziongeber (1 Kings 9:26)
26 "And _____ learning to his lips" (Proverbs 16:23)
29 Jesus' grandfather (Luke 3:23)
30 "It will no longer yield _____ crops" (Genesis 4:12)
33 "_____ about the paps with a golden girdle" (Revelation 1:13)
34 "And _____ great bulwarks against it" (Ecclesiastes 9:14)
35 "_____ Star Spangled Banner"
36 Aaron's son (Exodus 6:23)
38 "Blessed _____ those servants" (Luke 12:37)
39 One of Zerah's sons (1 Chronicles 2:6)
41 Connected to the foot
42 Abigail's churlish husband (1 Samuel 25:3)
44 Unusual
45 "But her _____ is bitter as wormwood" (Proverbs 5:4)
46 "_____ lived after he begat" (Genesis 11:11)
47 King Josiah's servant (2 Chronicles 34:1, 20)
49 "Been done to Mordecai for ___" (Esther 6:3)
50 "His _____ also shall not wither" (Psalm 1:3)
51 Heber's son (1 Chronicles 4:18)

54 "Some of the _____ of purpose" (Ruth 2:16)
58 "Uncleanness, _____ affection, evil" (Colossians 3:5)
61 He was an Ahohite (1 Chronicles 11:29)
62 "It _____ to pass" (Genesis 4:8)
63 "Children" of Asher (1 Chronicles 7:39)
64 Abel's murderer
65 "Unto me every _____ shall bow" (Isaiah 45:23)
66 Presses
67 Baby goats

DOWN

1 "Every man should _____ rule" (Esther 1:22)
2 Cutting side of blade
3 Amos's father (Luke 3:25)
4 "Thirsty man _____, and, behold, he drinketh" (Isaiah 29:8)
5 Naham's sister (1 Chronicles 4:19)
6 One of David's brothers (1 Samuel 17:28)
7 "I _____ above all things" (3 John 1:2)
8 A king of Midian (Numbers 31:8)
9 "Has this house. . .become a _____ of robbers to you?" (Jeremiah 7:11 NIV)
10 Foe
11 "Moses, when he was _____" (Hebrews 11:23)
12 "He was accompanied by. . . Trophimus from the province of _____" (Acts 20:4 NIV)
13 Affirmative, with a lisp
19 Zibeon was one (Genesis 36:2)
21 Abraham's nephew (Genesis 12:5)
24 "_____, and goeth out to Cabul" (Joshua 19:27)
25 "Destroy _____ kings and people" (Ezra 6:12)
26 A gem on the third row of the ephod (Exodus 28:19)
27 Moab went here to weep (Isaiah 15:2)

by N. Teri Grottke

28 "New wine is _____ up" (Joel 1:10)
29 King of Tyre (2 Chronicles 2:11)
30 Ribai's son (1 Chronicles 11:31)
31 Isaac's grandfather (Luke 3:34)
32 "The name of the other _____" (1 Samuel 14:4)
34 "As newborn _____" (1 Peter 2:2)
37 "Withhold thy foot from being _____" (Jeremiah 2:25)
40 Trade, especially in illegal items (var.)
43 Abdiel's son (1 Chronicles 5:15)
47 "Found a certain man named _____" (Acts 9:33)
48 Sorrowful
49 Number of gifts brought to the baby Jesus
50 Dead language
51 "Behold, thy father is _____" (Genesis 48:1)
52 Judah's son (Genesis 46:12)

53 "O _____, All Ye Faithful"
54 Bethuel's brother (Genesis 22:22)
55 Daniel had a vision by this river (Daniel 8:2)
56 Placed
57 "The goat will carry on itself all their _____" (Leviticus 16:22 NIV)
59 Bela's son (1 Chronicles 7:7)
60 Abner's father (1 Samuel 14:51)

ACROSS

1 "If thy father at all _____ me" (1 Samuel 20:6)
5 Cut back
9 "Even unto _____" (Genesis 10:19)
14 Jesus' last earthly words (Mark 15:34, 37)
15 "Rabbith, and Kishion, and _____" (Joshua 19:20)
16 Beriah's son (1 Chronicles 8:16)
17 "Seven _____ came up in one stalk" (Genesis 41:22)
18 To tear down (arch.)
19 "Call me no more _____" (Hosea 2:16)
20 "_____ after his kind" (Leviticus 11:14)
21 "Ye were as sheep going _____" (1 Peter 2:25)
23 Type of Asian and Pacific tree and shrub
24 "Make the _____ of the ephod all of blue" (Exodus 28:31)
26 Caught in Abraham's bush (Genesis 22:13)
28 "As a _____ which melteth" (Psalm 58:8)
30 Issachar's son (Numbers 26:23)
32 "With the _____, whereof thou canst not be healed" (Deuteronomy 28:27)
36 Dined
37 Belonging to Jacob's first wife (poss.)
39 Story
40 "Aaron _____ it up before the Testimony" (Exodus 16:34)
42 "Light a candle, and _____ the house" (Luke 15:8)
44 Salah's son (Genesis 10:24)
45 "_____, Hizkijah, Azzur" (Nehemiah 10:17)
46 Hillel's son (Judges 12:13)
48 Boy
49 "Land from _____ to the wilderness" (Isaiah 16:1)
50 "But the _____ of their God" (Ezra 5:5)
51 "Were among thy honourable _____" (Psalm 45:9)
53 "Stand in the _____ before me" (Ezekiel 22:30)
55 Shoham's brother (1 Chronicles 24:27)
56 "_____, and sin no more" (John 8:11)
58 Ezekiel's vision was by this river (Ezekiel 1:1)
61 "According to this _____, peace be on them" (Galatians 6:16)
65 Mattathias's son (Luke 3:26)
67 Bread comes in this shape
68 "I am _____ of speech" (Exodus 4:10)
69 "Driven up and down in _____" (Acts 27:27)
70 Zimri's father (Numbers 25:14)
71 "Among these nations shalt thou find no _____" (Deuteronomy 28:65)
72 "_____ again from the dead" (Acts 17:3)
73 David hid by this stone (1 Samuel 20:19)
74 "Behold, thou has mocked me, and told me _____" (Judges 6:10)

DOWN

1 They shall inherit the earth
2 An Ahohite (1 Chronicles 11:29)
3 Kind, class
4 Jael killed him (Judges 4:22)
5 Jesus told stories in this form
6 To humble
7 "Give thyself no _____" (Lamentations 2:18)
8 Jeshua's son (Nehemiah 3:19)
9 "The parts of _____ about Cyrene" (Acts 2:10)
10 Solomon's great-grandson (Matthew 1:7)
11 "When he had thus spoken, he _____ on the ground and made clay" (John 9:6)
12 "Their border was Helkath, and _____" (Joshua 19:25)
13 Abdiel's son (1 Chronicles 5:15)
22 Jether's son (1 Chronicles 7:38)
25 Petroleum product
27 "Paid the very last _____" (Luke 12:59)

by N. Teri Grottke

28 Vermont is one, as is Nebraska
29 "Toward the north side of Beth-emek, and _____" (Joshua 19:27)
30 A servant of the church at Cenchrea (Romans 16:1)
31 "Have _____ the office of a deacon" (1 Timothy 3:13)
33 "Crumbs which fall from their masters' _____" (Matthew 15:27)
34 "Those that were _____ escaped" (2 Peter 2:18)
35 "Shall be no _____ in the stalls" (Habakkuk 3:17)
36 "_____ for the day!" (Joel 1:15)
38 "Abram drove them _____" (Genesis 15:11)
41 Expression: "Knock-down-_____-out," as in a fight
43 The voice of the Lord is this (Psalm 29:4)
47 Jehoshua's father (1 Chronicles 7:27)

50 A letter to early Christians (abbr.)
52 Tidbit
54 Disobedient at Ai (Joshua 7:1–3)
55 "_____ of Judah" (2 Samuel 6:2)
56 Menahem's father (2 Kings 15:17)
57 Rowers
59 "Give me children, or _____ I die" (Genesis 30:1)
60 Ruth's second husband (Ruth 4:13)
62 "Between the banks of _____" (Daniel 8:16)
63 Misplace
64 "Thy _____ and thy she goats" (Genesis 31:28)
65 "Neither shalt thou _____ the corners of thy beard" (Leviticus 19:27)
66 "_____ them about thy neck" (Proverbs 6:21)

## 28

ACROSS

1 Little girl (Mark 5:41)
5 "I _____ you with blasting" (Haggai 2:17)
10 Jeduthun's son (1 Chronicles 25:3)
14 Larger than monkeys
15 A duke of Edom (Genesis 36:41)
16 Hananiah's father (Jeremiah 28:1)
17 "_____, the eighth person, a preacher of righteousness" (2 Peter 2:5)
18 Son of Shemaiah (1 Chronicles 3:22)
19 Another name for *Zoar* (Genesis 14:2)
20 Nicolas was a proselyte here (Acts 6:5)
22 Touched
24 "She _____ my feet with her tears" (Luke 7:44 NIV)
25 He was not with Adonijah (1 Kings 1:8)
26 Gihon was this river coming out of Eden (Genesis 2:13)
30 "Drowsiness shall clothe a man with _____" (Proverbs 23:21)
32 Caleb's son (1 Chronicles 4:15)
35 Micaiah's father (2 Chronicles 18:7)
36 "Ourselves also were _____ foolish" (Titus 3:3)
38 He was a chief of the priests in the days of Jeshua (Nehemiah 12:7)
39 "At Ezem, and at _____" (1 Chronicles 4:29)
40 "_____ it, even to the foundation" (Psalm 137:7)
41 "Will command his children and his _____" (Genesis 18:19)
43 "_____ 5 and Up"
44 Bela's son (Numbers 26:40)
45 "So is my beloved among the _____" (Song of Solomon 2:3)
46 "Kingdoms of the world in a _____ of time" (Luke 4:5)
48 "The name of his city was _____" (Genesis 36:39)

49 "I _____ do everything through him who gives me strength" (Philippians 4:13 NIV)
50 "_____ the LORD did there confound the language of all the earth" (Genesis 11:9)
54 "Among _____ eaters of flesh" (Proverbs 23:20)
59 Sadoc's father (Matthew 1:14)
60 "Made of the _____ trees terraces" (2 Chronicles 9:11)
62 Steward of the house in Tirzah (1 Kings 16:9)
63 To throw out
64 "The _____ of a whip" (Nahum 3:2)
65 Close tight
66 _____ and crafts
67 Ate in style
68 "Being _____ together in love" (Colossians 2:2)

DOWN

1 Jesus' first miracle was here
2 "Consume it _____ your lusts" (James 4:3)
3 Flesh food
4 Rephaiah's father (1 Chronicles 4:42)
5 "Drink of _____ wine" (Song of Solomon 8:2)
6 Power and strength
7 Single
8 Son of _____ (1 Chronicles 6:34)
9 Made bigger
10 Micha's father (Nehemiah 11:17)
11 "Wait by the stone _____" (1 Samuel 20:19)
12 "Walk according to this _____" (Galatians 6:16)
13 Enoch's son (Genesis 4:18)
21 Have possession
23 Residence for birds
26 Returning exiles (Ezra 2:44)
27 Sychem's father (Acts 7:16)
28 Jesus was received into this (Acts 1:9)
29 Strong trees

by N. Teri Grottke

30 "Made in the house of the _____" (Ezra 6:1)
31 "Alammelech, and _____, and Misheal" (Joshua 19:26)
32 Idol
33 "_____ between Ninevah and Calah" (Genesis 10:12)
34 "Thou _____ to do unto those that love thy name" (Psalm 119:132)
36 As _____ as possible
37 Duke of Edom (1 Chronicles 1:54)
39 "A _____ years as one day" (2 Peter 3:8)
42 Jacob's brother (Genesis 25:27)
46 They were made whole (Matthew 15:31)
47 "Let us meet together. . .in the plain of _____" (Nehemiah 6:2)
48 Separates

49 "Bring me a new _____, and put salt therein" (2 Kings 2:20)
50 "Valley of _____ make it a well" (Psalm 84:6)
51 Seir's son (1 Chronicles 1:38)
52 "Counteth the _____" (Luke 14:28)
53 "_____, lama sabachthani" (Mark 15:34)
55 Job
56 Jerahmeel's son (1 Chronicles 2:25)
57 Palal's father (Nehemiah 3:25)
58 Lot's wife became a pillar of this (Genesis 19:26)
61 "The _____ shall take him by the heel" (Job 18:9)

## 29

PAY ATTENTION!

"You have seen many things, but you pay no attention;
your ears are open, but you do not listen."

ISAIAH 42:20 NIV

ACROSS

1 "For I have born him _____ in his old age" (Genesis 21:7) (2 words)
5 "And hide it there in _____ of the rock" (Jeremiah 13:4) (2 words)
10 "Go forth, and _____" (1 Kings 22:22) (2 words)
14 "He _____ a man before them" (Psalm 105:17)
15 Filled or covered with wax (arch.)
16 "And _____ for a burnt offering" (Leviticus 9:2) (2 words)
17 **QUOTE** found in several verses in Revelation 2 and 3 (5 words)
20 Previously, Tokyo
21 "Then Samuel took a _____ of oil" (1 Samuel 10:1)
22 Halos
23 Promote
24 "His life is bound up in the _____ life" (Genesis 44:30) (poss.)
26 **QUOTE**, cont. (4 words)
32 "_____ shaken with the wind" (Luke 7:24) (2 words)
33 "Are ye angry _____" (John 7:23) (2 words)
34 _____ de mer
36 "_____; God hath numbered thy kingdom" (Daniel 5:26)
37 Theater boxes
39 "At the _____ of the droves before me" (Genesis 33:14 NIV)
40 "In the very _____" (John 8:4)
41 Swiss river
42 Mouthlike openings in bodily organs
43 **QUOTE**, cont. (3 words)
47 "I shall die in my _____" (Job 29:18)
48 "Concerning this _____" (Acts 28:22)

49 "Go, _____ lookout and have him report what he sees" (Isaiah 21:6 NIV) (2 words)
52 Sicilian volcano
53 Greek letter
56 End of **QUOTE** (3 words)
60 Swindle
61 "And bread to the _____" (Isaiah 55:10)
62 An unclean animal (Leviticus 11:6)
63 "And _____ for the service of man" (Psalm 104:14)
64 "Tables of _____, written with" (Exodus 31:18)
65 Once (arch.)

DOWN

1 "Out of joint, _____ wrestled with him" (Genesis 32:25) (2 words)
2 "The _____ is the word of God" (Luke 8:11)
3 "And pass _____ Azmon" (Numbers 34:4) (2 words)
4 Ultimate, as degree
5 Town in old Greece where Mark Antony was defeated
6 "Because _____ no son" (Numbers 27:4) (2 words)
7 Of the mouth
8 "Rise, _____ us be going" (Matthew 26:46)
9 Icelandic letter
10 Sweet breakfast pastry
11 City in Utah, north of Provo
12 Swedish automobile
13 Evil king of Israel (1 Kings 16:25)
18 "_____ it, pass not by it" (Proverbs 4:15)
19 "_____ beseech you, brethren" (1 Thessalonians 5:12) (2 words)
23 "I would lead _____" (Song of Solomon 8:2)

by N. Teri Grottke

24 "The Jews of _____ sought" (John 11:8)
25 "And underneath are the everlasting _____" (Deuteronomy 33:27)
26 "Eli, Eli, _____ sabachthani" (Matthew 27:46)
27 "_____ siege works" (Ezekiel 4:2 NIV)
28 "Abraham gave the _____ of the spoils" (Hebrews 7:4)
29 "I was very _____ to write to you" (Jude 1:3 NIV)
30 Noted violin maker of yore
31 Unspoken
35 Laban's oldest daughter (Genesis 29:16)
37 "I will pay it back into their _____" (Isaiah 65:6 NIV)
38 "_____ will kill us and our people" (1 Samuel 5:11 NIV) (2 words)
39 High school junior test hurdle (abbr.)

41 "Even upon _____ by the wall" (1 Samuel 20:25) (2 words)
42 Hammerstein
44 Bury a body
45 "Where _____ the blessedness" (Galatians 4:15) (2 words)
46 Professorial job security
49 "To _____ in time past" (Exodus 21:36)
50 "_____ have I spoken" (Job 40:5)
51 "When they saw the _____" (Matthew 2:10)
52 Prefix for *outer* (var.)
53 Scorch
54 "Restore all that was _____" (2 Kings 8:6)
55 "Yet have _____ my king" (Psalm 2:6) (2 words)
57 "_____ alive" (Acts 20:10 NIV) (contr.)
58 "And he did _____" (Genesis 3:6)
59 Fidel's cohort Guevara

## 30

ACROSS

1 Uncooked
4 Poisonous snakes
8 King of Hebron (Joshua 10:3)
13 There were twelve wells of water here (Exodus 15:27)
15 "Bindeth me about as the collar of my _____" (Job 30:18)
16 Absalom's captain (2 Samuel 17:25)
17 "Thy sister in law is _____ back unto her people" (Ruth 1:15)
18 Center
19 A rebuilder of the wall (Nehemiah 3:25)
20 "In the two _____ of the mercy seat" (Exodus 25:18)
21 Venture
23 "Sent _____ unto them" (Genesis 43:34)
25 "_____ thee out of my mouth" (Revelation 3:16)
26 In a different way
28 An old disciple of Cyprus (Acts 21:16)
33 Zerah's son (1 Chronicles 6:41)
36 Assist
39 Translation: "God hath numbered thy kingdom, and finished it" (Daniel 5:25)
40 "Thou hast drunken the _____ of the cup of trembling" (Isaiah 51:17)
41 "The porters; Shallum, and Telem, and _____" (Ezra 10:24)
42 "For her _____ is far above rubies" (Proverbs 31:10)
43 Entrance
44 Returned exiles (Ezra 2:15)
45 "Which is neither _____ nor sown" (Deuteronomy 21:4)
46 Abraham bought the cave of Machpelah from him (Genesis 49:30)
48 "O daughter of _____" (Lamentations 4:21)
50 Type of organ
53 A captain of the ward, the son of Shelemiah (Jeremiah 37:13)
57 "Blood of the sin offering of _____" (Exodus 30:10)
62 Arabian city (Job 6:19)
63 "Border went up to the stone of _____" (Joshua 15:6)
64 Jabal's mother (Genesis 4:20)
65 Fathered the Eranites (Numbers 26:36)
66 "Holy and without _____ before him in love" (Ephesians 1:4)
67 "Wickedness is _____ up before me" (Jonah 1:2)
68 "Multiply my days as the _____" (Job 29:18)
69 Increased
70 "I must care for the _____ and cows" (Genesis 33:13 NIV)
71 "He _____ not so much grieved me as he has grieved all of you" (2 Corinthians 2:5 NIV)

DOWN

1 Jahdai's son (1 Chronicles 2:47)
2 By yourself
3 "Without water, carried about of _____" (Jude 1:12)
4 "_____ by faith into this grace" (Romans 5:2)
5 "Not selfwilled, not _____ angry" (Titus 1:7)
6 "The outmost _____ of heaven" (Deuteronomy 30:4)
7 "The herd ran violently down a _____ place into the lake" (Luke 8:33)
8 "Began to tell them what things should _____ unto him" (Mark 10:32)
9 Eliphaz's son (Genesis 36:11)
10 "Helkath, and _____, and Beten" (Joshua 19:25)
11 His heart was perfect (1 Kings 15:14) (poss.)
12 "That same day he removed all the _____ goats that were streaked or spotted" (Genesis 30:35 NIV)
14 "Behold, I will send my _____" (Malachi 3:1)
22 Rear end of an animal

by N. Teri Grottke

24 Belonging to Hophni's father (1 Samuel 1:3) (poss.)
27 He brought a message from God to the king (Judges 3:19–20)
29 A family of Kohath (Numbers 3:27)
30 Esau lived here (Genesis 36:8)
31 The earth was destroyed by a flood this many times
32 Lack
33 Brim
34 Snare
35 Caanan's son (Genesis 10:15)
37 Gad's son (Genesis 46:16)
38 "Bind this _____ of scarlet thread in the window" (Joshua 2:18)
42 Balak brought Balaam to the top of this mountain (Numbers 23:28)
44 "Anab, and Eshtemoh, and _____" (Joshua 15:50)
47 "All thine enemies have _____ their mouth" (Lamentations 2:16)

49 Eating vessels
51 Jesus is the prince of this (Isaiah 9:6)
52 "He shall surely _____ her to be his wife" (Exodus 22:16)
54 Almodad's brother (Genesis 10:26)
55 "Look from the top of _____" (Song of Solomon 4:8)
56 "Submit thyself under her _____" (Genesis 16:9)
57 Father (Galatians 4:6)
58 Spoke
59 Simeon's son (Genesis 46:10)
60 "Which is above every _____" (Philippians 2:9)
61 "But the tongue can no man _____" (James 3:8)

## 31

ACROSS

1 "That drink wine in _____"
(Amos 6:6)
6 "Of Harim, _____; of Meraioth"
(Nehemiah 12:15)
10 Hastens
14 Hezron's wife (1 Chronicles 2:24)
15 "Should thy _____ make men
hold their peace?" (Job 11:3)
16 Precipice
17 "_____ not the proud" (Psalm
40:4)
19 "_____ the door after her"
(2 Samuel 13:17)
20 "But the _____ of their God"
(Ezra 5:5)
21 Wine is made with this
22 Benjamin's son (Genesis 46:21)
23 The devil knows his time is this
24 Abraham's father (Genesis 11:26)
25 An altar (Joshua 22:34)
27 Hymn: "_____ Great Thou Art"
28 "_____ thou well to be angry?"
(Jonah 4:4)
29 A _____ of contention
31 These were in the tops of the cur-
tains of the tabernacle (Exodus
26:5)
33 Precedes Nehemiah (abbr., var.)
36 A king of Midian (Numbers 31:8)
37 A seraphim used this tool to take a
live coal off the altar (Isaiah 6:6)
38 "_____, and the mighty men
which belonged to David" (1
Kings 1:8)
39 "Secretly as a lion in his _____"
(Psalm 10:9)
40 "Came the next day over against
_____" (Acts 20:15)
41 Previously owned
42 Belonging to Jacob's brother
(Genesis 25:25) (poss.)
44 "God saw that it _____ good"
(Genesis 1:21)
46 Beatles song: "Let It _____"
47 Bread bakes in these
48 Color of purity
50 "Let us swallow them up _____"
(Proverbs 1:12)

51 Trunk
52 "Arise, lift up the _____"
(Genesis 21:18)
55 "Suddenly that shall _____ thee"
(Habakkuk 2:7)
56 "He has condemned the great
_____ who corrupted the earth
by her adulteries" (Revelation 19:2
NIV)
58 "_____ the death of the cross"
(Philippians 2:8)
59 Get higher
60 It was between Ninevah and Calah
(Genesis 10:12)
61 _____ than or greater than
62 Naomi's "son" (Ruth 4:17)
63 "At the _____ of the city"
(Proverbs 8:3)

DOWN

1 Uncovered
2 "_____ my voice" (Genesis 27:8)
3 These kind of men came from
the East to find the king of the
Jews
4 Child's favorite seat
5 Shobal's son (Genesis 36:23)
6 Change
7 "Where thou _____, will I die"
(Ruth 1:17)
8 Peter fished with these
9 A tree (Isaiah 44:14)
10 Belonging to Jael's husband
(Judges 4:17) (poss.)
11 "Neither be ye _____, as were
some of them" (1 Corinthians
10:7)
12 One of David's wives (2 Samuel
3:5)
13 Younger son of Adam
18 Before the cock would do this,
Peter denied the Lord
(Matthew 26:34)
22 "They compassed me about like
_____" (Psalm 118:12)
23 "_____ was buried beneath
Bethel under an oak" (Genesis
35:8)
24 Spinning toys

by N. Teri Grottke

25 Gaal's father (Judges 9:26)
26 Bird from the ark sent out twice (Genesis 8:8)
28 Canines not of teeth
30 "For as Jonas was a sign unto the _____" (Luke 11:30)
31 Timothy's grandmother (2 Timothy 1:5)
32 The sons of Elpaal built this place (1 Chronicles 8:12 NIV)
34 A prince of the Midianites (Judges 7:25)
35 Travel other than on foot
37 In this manner
40 Sugar plant
41 "Neither shall ye _____ enchantment" (Leviticus 19:26)
43 The numbers of the clean animals on the ark (Genesis 7:2)
44 "For he _____ not what to say" (Mark 9:6)
45 Fancy dressings

47 "They also brought spices and _____ oil for the light" (Exodus 35:28 NIV)
48 "_____ name was Mordecai" (Esther 2:5)
49 "The son of _____, in Aruboth" (1 Kings 4:10)
50 Cain's victim
51 "Where no oxen are, the _____ is clean" (Proverbs 14:4)
52 "Ye shall not fulfil the _____ of the flesh" (Galatians 5:16)
53 They were children of porters (Ezra 2:42)
54 Will not take responsibility
56 Jack Nicklaus, golf _____ (abbr.)
57 In the song, _____ lords are a-leaping

## 32

ACROSS

1 "Even thou _____ as one of them" (Obadiah 1:11)
5 In the edge of the wilderness (Exodus 13:20)
10 "I will give it thee, unto the _____ of my kingdom" (Mark 6:23)
14 Abinadab's son (2 Samuel 6:3)
15 Zorobabel's son (Luke 3:27)
16 Helem's son (1 Chronicles 7:35)
17 Golf can be played in _____ holes or eighteen
18 Rulers' nationality at Jesus' time
19 "Claudius had commanded all Jews to depart from _____" (Acts 18:2)
20 "And if he _____ against thee seven times" (Luke 17:4)
22 "Upon this I _____" (Jeremiah 31:26)
24 Sharp-toothed tool
25 Lyrics: "_____ is the loneliest number"
26 A prophet and son of Amoz (2 Kings 20:1) (abbr.)
27 Cows chew this
28 Hiddekel goes toward the east of this place (Genesis 2:14)
32 Ishmael's mother (Genesis 16:15)
35 _____ blue; genuine
36 Ahab's father (1 Kings 16:28)
38 Ahira's father (Numbers 1:15)
39 This place is on the left hand of Damascus (Genesis 14:15)
40 "I will requite thee in this _____" (2 Kings 9:26)
41 Winged mammals
42 King Hoshea's father (2 Kings 15:30)
43 Belonging to Jacob's first wife (Genesis 30:9) (poss.)
44 A wife of Abraham (Genesis 25:1)
46 Past tense of *is*
47 To free
48 One of Jacob's sons (Genesis 30:6)
49 Hold or obtain
52 "Thou shalt not _____ adultery" (Matthew 5:27)
56 Historic building
58 Easternmost continent
59 Separate
61 "Jesus cried with a loud voice, saying, _____" (Mark 15:34)
62 Not as much
63 "Bear children, _____ the house" (1 Timothy 5:14)
64 "My father did _____ you with a heavy yoke" (1 Kings 12:11)
65 John Wesley's denomination (abbr.)
66 He remained in the camp (Numbers 11:26)
67 "Who knows but that you have come. . .for such a time as _____?" (Esther 4:14 NIV)

DOWN

1 "He that ministered to my _____" (Philippians 2:25)
2 Enan's son (Numbers 1:15)
3 "Eat not of the _____ which shrank" (Genesis 32:32)
4 The giant had six of these (2 Samuel 21:20)
5 "I have an _____ to thee, O captain" (2 Kings 9:5)
6 Particular ones
7 "They made upon the _____ of the robe pomegranates" (Exodus 39:24)
8 Solomon's great-grandson (Matthew 1:7)
9 Joseph's firstborn (Genesis 41:51)
10 "Habor, and _____, and to the river Gozan" (1 Chronicles 5:26)
11 "Sallu, _____, Hilkiah" (Nehemiah 12:7)
12 "Jonathan. . .had a son that was _____ of his feet" (2 Samuel 4:4)
13 "He _____ from the presence of the LORD" (Jonah 1:10)
21 "Thou shalt _____ it upon the ground as water" (Deuteronomy 15:23)
23 "I am the _____, the truth, and the life" (John 14:6)
26 Asher's son (1 Chronicles 7:30)

by N. Teri Grottke

27 "Thou _____ understand a dream to interpret it" (Genesis 41:15)
28 Another name for *Hebron* (Genesis 35:27)
29 Thick cords
30 Micaiah's father (2 Chronicles 18:7)
31 Had 775 "children" (Ezra 2:5)
32 Egyptians were told not to eat bread with them (abbr.) (Genesis 43:32)
33 Talmai's father (Joshua 15:14)
34 "Lot sat in the ____ of Sodom" (Genesis 19:1)
35 "And at Ezem, and at _____" (1 Chronicles 4:29)
37 "Each dream had a meaning of _____ own" (Genesis 40:5 NIV)
39 "Neither as being lords over God's _____" (1 Peter 5:3)
43 Real estate
45 Bezaleel's father (Exodus 31:2)

46 Sought by law enforcement
48 "Heman, and Chalcol, and _____" (1 Kings 4:31)
49 The king of Assyria took Israel here in their captivity (2 Kings 17:6)
50 Progeny of Gad (Genesis 46:16)
51 "Dark waters, and thick clouds of the _____" (2 Samuel 22:12)
52 Peaceful
53 "As he saith also in _____" (Romans 9:25)
54 How the earth was watered before the flood (Genesis 2:6)
55 Crush
56 "Thy bread have _____ a wound under thee" (Obadiah 1:7)
57 Thaw
60 King of Assyria (2 Kings 15:19)

## 33

NEAR THE CROSS

*For the preaching of the cross is to them that perish foolishness;
but unto us which are saved it is the power of God.*

1 Corinthians 1:18

ACROSS

1 "They made _____ in Horeb"
   (Psalm 106:19) (2 words)
6 Jekyll's alter ego
10 "It shall be _____ instant
   suddenly" (Isaiah 29:5) (2 words)
14 "And fine linen, and _____, and
   agate" (Ezekiel 27:16)
15 U.S. scientific organization (abbr.)
16 "Behold a _____ in the wall"
   (Ezekiel 8:7)
17 "And whosoever doth _____
   CROSS" (Luke 14:27) (3 words)
19 Greek colonnade
20 Urban trains, sometimes
21 Perfume solvent
22 FDR follower (initials)
23 Former British prime minister,
   David _____ George
25 Enos's father (Genesis 5:6)
26 "That which groweth of _____
   own accord" (Leviticus 25:5)
29 "Arise, go thy _____" (Luke
   17:19)
30 The sound of TV
32 "And he that taketh _____
   CROSS" (Matthew 10:38)
   (2 words)
34 "For he is the Lord's _____"
   (1 Samuel 24:10)
37 "To temper with the fine _____"
   (Ezekiel 46:14)
38 "But they _____ not hear"
   (Zechariah 1:4)
39 First prime minister of free India
40 It just shows how far you've gone
42 "Carrying his own **CROSS**,
   _____ out to the place" (John
   19:17 NIV) (2 words)
43 Egyptian corn
44 Prefix for day or night (Nehemiah
   8:3 and Mark 13:35)
45 Spanish king (Sp.)

46 Spheres
48 "Libnah, and _____" (Joshua
   15:42)
50 Suburb of Ogden
51 Gomer's husband (Hosea 1:3)
53 "And he did _____" (Genesis 3:6)
56 Camp beds
58 "And they forced him _____
   CROSS" (Matthew 27:32 NIV)
   (3 words)
60 "For _____ thinketh in his heart,
   so is he" (Proverbs 23:7) (2 words)
61 "And Coz begat _____"
   (1 Chronicles 4:8)
62 They're found at 44 Down
63 "When Jacob was cooking some
   _____" (Genesis 25:29 NIV)
64 "Feet _____ to the lame"
   (Job 29:15) (2 words)
65 Bridges

DOWN

1 Teen bane
2 "In the ____ of the day" (Genesis
   3:8)
3 Carney and Linkletter (pl.)
4 Retriever (abbr.)
5 "After a _____" (1 Samuel 24:14)
6 "And, _____ passing it" (Acts
   27:8)
7 Cowboy cry
8 "And take up his **CROSS** _____
   follow me" (Luke 9:23) (2 words)
9 Ogee shape
10 Interjections of satisfaction
11 "He gave orders to **CROSS**
   _____ side of the lake" (Matthew
   8:18 NIV) (3 words)
12 "Gone astray like _____ sheep"
   (Psalm 119:176) (2 words)
13 Under, to Keats

by David K. Shortess

18 "But we are _____ an unclean thing" (Isaiah 64:6) (2 words)
24 Couple
25 "And thy neck is an iron _____" (Isaiah 48:4)
26 News, in short
27 "As it was _____ unto them" (Luke 2:20)
28 "Now there _____ **CROSS** of Jesus his mother" (John 19:25) (3 words)
29 Electrician
31 "So when they had _____" (John 21:15)
33 Organic soil component
34 "That no _____ can come between them" (Job 41:16)
35 Sea eagle
36 "For this is the whole _____ of man" (Ecclesiastes 12:13)
38 "Even _____ **CROSS**" (Philippians 2:8 NIV) (3 words)
41 Cornwall name prefix
42 Employer
44 Iron-rich range
46 Killer whales
47 "Screech owl will _____ on her columns" (Zephaniah 2:14 NIV)
49 _____-pocus
52 "And strengtheneth her _____" (Proverbs 31:17)
53 Sicilian volcano
54 "As _____ doth gather her brood under her wings" (Luke 13:34) (2 words)
55 D'Urberville girl
57 "And a time to _____" (Ecclesiastes 3:7)
58 Word preceding Psalm 119:169 (NIV)
59 Puppy's cry

34

ACROSS

1 "He was at the _____ of death" (John 4:47)
6 Mix
10 Marching or concert group
14 "The colour of _____, out of the midst of the fire" (Ezekiel 1:4)
15 "Why beholdest thou the _____ that is in thy brother's eye?" (Matthew 7:3)
16 "_____ was a cunning hunter" (Genesis 25:27)
17 "_____ me through visions" (Job 7:14)
19 Docile
20 Gad's son (Genesis 46:16)
21 Horses are steered with these
22 Levite chief (1 Chronicles 24:15)
24 Absalom rode on this (2 Samuel 13:29)
25 Identifier of marriage status
26 "Who remembered us in our low _____" (Psalm 136:23)
29 Shobal's child (Genesis 36:23)
33 "The land is. . . _____ enough for them (Genesis 34:21)
34 Hymn verse: "I _____ to the garden alone"
35 God (Mark 15:34)
36 The Ahohite (1 Chronicles 11:29)
37 "It was told Laban on the _____ day that Jacob was fled" (Genesis 31:22)
38 "Shall come down like rain upon the _____ grass" (Psalm 72:6)
39 Baby goats
40 On the third day, Jesus did this
41 "Saul _____ with Samuel that day" (1 Samuel 9:24 NIV)
42 Purple gem
44 "Andrew, Simon _____ brother" (John 6:8)
45 "Put ye in the sickle, for the harvest is _____" (Joel 3:13)
46 "In the hills, and in the _____" (Deuteronomy 1:7)
47 Jahdai's son (1 Chronicles 2:47)
50 Greek form of *Sinai* (Acts 7:30)
51 "_____, she is broken that was the gates of the people" (Ezekiel 26:2)
54 "He placed on the _____ side of the Garden of Eden cherubim" (Genesis 3:24 NIV)
55 "I have _____ the death of all" (1 Samuel 22:22)
58 "To guard the way to the _____ of life" (Genesis 3:24 NIV)
59 Human being
60 Cognitive
61 "Restore all that was _____" (2 Kings 8:6)
62 "That thine _____ may be in secret" (Matthew 6:4)
63 Asher's grandson (Genesis 46:17)

DOWN

1 Meat or fish pie
2 Manna measurement (Exodus 16:36)
3 Merari's son (1 Chronicles 24:27)
4 Abner's father (2 Samuel 3:25)
5 "_____ or duty will be paid" (Ezra 4:13 NIV)
6 "_____ a scorner, and the simple will beware" (Proverbs 19:25)
7 Most have five digits here
8 "Set the door of the ark in _____ side" (Genesis 6:16 NKJV)
9 Kept
10 "And the cart came into the field of Joshua, a _____" (1 Samuel 6:14)
11 Belonging to the king of Judah (1 Kings 15:17) (poss.)
12 Personal title
13 "Render therefore to all their _____" (Romans 13:7)
18 Sharpening tool
23 A biblical poem (abbr.)
24 They "sent the serjeants" (Acts 16:35)
25 Abram lived in this plain (Genesis 13:18)
26 David's Harodite guard (2 Samuel 23:25)

by N. Teri Grottke

27 John was baptizing near here (John 3:23)
28 Commerce
29 Damp
30 Isolated
31 "Thy neck is like the _____ of David" (Song of Solomon 4:4)
32 "He will make my feet like _____ feet" (Habakkuk 3:19)
34 "Then Lot _____ him all the plain of Jordan" (Genesis 13:11)
37 "Salute Tryphena and _____, who labour in the Lord" (Romans 16:12)
41 Mehetabeel's son (Nehemiah 6:10)
43 "The socket of Jacob's _____ was out of joint as He wrestled with him" (Genesis 32:25 NKJV)
44 "Make his _____ to receive his ashes" (Exodus 27:3)
46 The prayers of the saints are in these (Revelation 5:8)

47 Cain and Abel's brother (Genesis 4:25)
48 Aesop's fables included the _____ and the tortoise
49 Greek form of *Asher* (Revelation 7:6)
50 "The _____ of it may be consumed" (Ezekiel 24:11)
51 Canaanite city (Joshua 11:21)
52 In this place
53 Arad's brother (1 Chronicles 8:15)
56 Follows Philippians (abbr.)
57 Indebted

35

ACROSS

1 "Girt about the _____ with a golden girdle" (Revelation 1:13)
5 A tenth
10 Follows Romans (abbr.)
13 King Hoshea's father (2 Kings 15:30)
14 The judge of Israel who put out a fleece (Judges 6:39)
15 Distressed cry (var.) (2 words)
16 "The flowers _____ on the earth" (Song of Solomon 2:12)
18 According to Scarlett O'Hara's father, this is the only thing worth fighting or dying for
19 A battering weapon
20 Mouse food
21 "Are delivered _____ the midwives come in unto them" (Exodus 1:19)
22 "And in process of _____ it came to pass" (Genesis 4:3)
23 "But we have this treasure in _____ vessels" (2 Corinthians 4:7)
25 Cyrenius was governor here (Luke 2:2)
27 Ahiam's father (1 Chronicles 11:35)
29 Solomon's temple was built on his threshing floor (1 Chronicles 21:21)
32 Would-be lawyers' test
35 Jeroboam's father (1 Kings 11:26)
37 "Golden _____ of Ophir" (Isaiah 13:12)
38 Twelfth Hebrew month (Esther 3:7)
40 "_____, I am warm, I have seen the fire" (Isaiah 44:16)
41 Prophet
42 Er's wife (Genesis 38:6)
44 "He shall gather the _____ with his arm" (Isaiah 40:11)
47 He was with Nathan and Shimei (1 Kings 1:8)
48 "Bodily _____ like a dove upon him" (Luke 3:22)
49 Beef, pork, mutton, for example (pl.)
51 Aaron had blood applied to this part of his hand (Exodus 29:20)

54 Joseph's brothers called him this (Genesis 37:19)
58 Elihu's father (1 Samuel 1:1)
60 Hophni's father (1 Samuel 1:3)
62 "I...will _____ them as silver" (Zechariah 13:9)
63 A king of Midian (Numbers 31:8)
64 Belonging to the temple priest (1 Samuel 1:9) (poss.)
65 Chooses a candidate
66 "The angels of God _____ him" (Genesis 32:1)
67 Gedor's father (1 Chronicles 4:4)
69 You, like Thou (arch.)
70 "These _____ to find grace in the sight of my lord" (Genesis 33:8)
71 Lod's child (Ezra 2:33)
72 "The linen _____ at a price" (1 Kings 10:28)

DOWN

1 War and _____ by Tolstoy
2 First letter of the Greek alphabet
3 "I would not write with _____ and ink" (2 John 1:12)
4 Bed coverings
5 Asian tree or shrub
6 Inactive
7 "Mine eye poureth out _____ unto God" (Job 16:20)
8 Bee product
9 "The _____ of all flesh is come before me" (Genesis 6:13)
10 Manna tasted like this seed (Numbers 11:7)
11 Shammai's father (1 Chronicles 2:28)
12 Capital of Italy
14 Country of Athens
17 "Tochen, and _____, five cities" (1 Chronicles 4:32)
22 "Their round _____ like the moon" (Isaiah 3:18)
24 A Carmelite (1 Samuel 30:5)
26 "Hewed stone, and a _____ of cedar beams" (1 Kings 6:36)
28 Jorkoam's father (1 Chronicles 2:44)
30 Shammah's father (2 Samuel 23:11)
31 Salathiel's father (Luke 3:27)

by N. Teri Grottke

32 Swings in baseball
33 Jabal's mother (Genesis 4:20)
34 "Over the vineyards was Shimei the _____" (1 Chronicles 27:27)
36 "For every kind of beast. . .is _____" (James 3:7)
39 Palti's father (Numbers 13:9)
43 Lived two and thirty years (Genesis 11:20)
45 The daring use this at Niagara Falls
46 "The bow of _____ shall strike him through" (Job 20:24)
50 "Peace and _____; then sudden destruction cometh" (1 Thessalonians 5:3)
52 Menan's son (Luke 3:31)
53 "A gift doth _____ the eyes of the wise" (Deuteronomy 16:19)
55 Mephibosheth's son (2 Samuel 9:12)
56 Come in
57 "And _____ between" (Genesis 10:12)

58 Arabian city (Job 6:19)
59 Prepositions meaning *above*
61 Asher's son (Genesis 46:17)
64 Biblical letter to early Christians (abbr.)
68 "Children of Gad called the altar _____" (Joshua 22:34)

ACROSS

1 Hasty
5 "In _____ was there a voice" (Matthew 2:18)
9 A son of Hothan the Aroerite (1 Chronicles 11:44)
14 _____ or false
15 Eliphaz's son (1 Chronicles 1:36)
16 Zerah's son (1 Chronicles 2:6)
17 "Halah, and Habor, and _____" (1 Chronicles 5:26)
18 This woman's name means *bitter* (Ruth 1:20)
19 The disciples did this to Jesus in the storm (Luke 8:24)
20 A prince of the king of Babylon (Jeremiah 39:3)
23 Fully cooked (slang)
24 East of Eden (Genesis 4:16)
25 "Neither shall ye _____ enchantment" (Leviticus 19:26)
28 One of five royal Philistine cities (1 Samuel 6:17)
31 Institution for religious preparation (abbr.)
34 "Set down at the _____ hand of the throne of God" (Hebrews 12:2)
36 "_____ greedily after the error" (Jude 1:11)
37 "Hills, and in the _____, and in the south" (Deuteronomy 1:7)
38 Micaiah's father (1 Kings 22:9)
39 The fifth angel was given this (Revelation 9:1)
40 Paul and Silas were sent by night here (Acts 17:10)
41 "Of _____, the family" (Numbers 26:17)
42 Voice amplification device (abbr.)
43 "_____ no more than that which is appointed you" (Luke 3:13)
44 "I acknowledge my _____ unto thee" (Psalm 32:5)
45 Maybe
48 "_____ clusters produced ripe grapes" (Genesis 40:10 NASB)
49 "Some shall _____ before his chariots" (1 Samuel 8:11)
50 He was a Bethelite (1 Kings 16:34)

52 "Whose is this image and _____?" (Matthew 22:20)
59 "Why say the scribes that _____ must first come?" (Mark 9:11)
60 Green citrus
61 "Ye shall keep it a feast by an ordinance for _____" (Exodus 12:14)
63 Spear
64 "Passed along to Hezron, and went up to _____" (Joshua 15:3)
65 "_____ shall offer gifts" (Psalm 72:10)
66 Jonah was inside a great _____ belly (Jonah 1:17) (poss.)
67 "From the lions' _____, from the mountains of the leopards" (Song of Solomon 4:8)
68 "I _____ not" (Luke 17:9)

DOWN

1 A female ancestor of Jesus (abbr., var.)
2 Dishan's child (Genesis 36:28)
3 Certain
4 Listened
5 They controlled Israel during the time of Christ
6 "When he let down his hand, _____ prevailed" (Exodus 17:11)
7 "Paul stood in the midst of _____' hill" (Acts 17:22)
8 He had 652 "sons" (Nehemiah 7:10 NKJV)
9 "I am the rose of _____" (Song of Solomon 2:1)
10 Chopped
11 Isaiah's father (2 Kings 19:2)
12 Construct
13 Eshcol's brother (Genesis 14:13)
21 "Shall compass about to _____" (Jeremiah 31:39)
22 Writer unknown (abbr.)
25 Greek form of *Uriah* (Matthew 1:6)
26 Hosah's chief son (1 Chronicles 26:10)
27 King of Moab (Judges 3:12)
29 "_____, and Accad, and Calneh" (Genesis 10:10)

by N. Teri Grottke

30 Put down
31 Pharaoh and his house suffered great plagues because of her (Genesis 12:17)
32 Special group
33 "Commanding to abstain from _____" (1 Timothy 4:3)
35 "The servants of David _____ smitten of Benjamin" (2 Samuel 2:31)
37 "Thou shalt neither _____ a stranger, nor oppress him" (Exodus 22:21)
39 The people of Syria shall go into captivity here (2 Kings 16:9)
40 "The sin which doth so easily _____ us" (Hebrews 12:1)
42 Belonging to more than one man (poss.)
45 "Neither gold, nor silver, nor brass in your _____" (Matthew 10:9)
46 He was a porter (1 Chronicles 9:17)

47 "Voice of harpers, and musicians, and of _____" (Revelation 18:22)
49 Stretch out one's arm
51 "When thou _____ down, and when thou risest up" (Deuteronomy 6:7)
52 "Swarest by thine own _____" (Exodus 32:13)
53 Daniel had a vision by this river (Daniel 8:2)
54 Brooches
55 Clothed
56 Travel other than on foot
57 "He was head _____ a people" (Numbers 25:15)
58 "The men of the other _____" (Nehemiah 7:33)
62 Fresh

BIBLICAL A.K.A.S

And thou shalt be called by a new name,
which the mouth of the LORD shall name.
ISAIAH 62:2

ACROSS

1 **NAOMI** (Ruth 1:20)
5 _____ California
9 Gator kin (abbr.)
13 Last writes (abbr.)
14 Esrom's son (Matthew 1:3)
15 Nadab's father (Exodus 6:23)
17 Friskies' competitor
18 Of sound mind
19 Swelling, the result of the accumulation of excess fluids
20 **SATAN** (Matthew 12:24–27)
22 **PETER** (Matthew 4:18)
23 _____ Alamos, NM
24 **SARAH** (Genesis 17:15)
26 Room for family fun (abbr.)
29 Giants' Hall of Famer Mel
31 Patriotic organization (abbr.)
32 Opposite of NNW
35 Greek god of love
37 "But flesh with the life thereof, which is the blood thereof, shall ye not _____" (Genesis 9:4)
39 In the South, it's a goober
41 **JOSEPH** (Genesis 41:45)
44 **JACOB** (Genesis 32:28)
45 And so on (abbr.)
46 Jazz man Brubeck
47 It may be split in your soup
48 "I pray you give _____ him to wife" (Genesis 34:8)
50 "And the sun and the _____ were darkened" (Revelation 9:2)
52 Article, in Bonn (Ger. punc.)
53 One of the seven princes of Persia and Media (Esther 1:14)
55 "And again he sent forth the dove _____ of the ark" (Genesis 8:10)
57 **ABRAHAM** (Genesis 17:5)
60 **GIDEON** (Judges 7:1)
65 _____-comedy
66 Gabor and Peron (pl.)

67 Exxon competitor
68 West Side Story heroine
69 "And a light shone in the _____" (Acts 12:7 NIV)
70 Small stream
71 "We dreamed _____ man according to the interpretation" (Genesis 41:11)
72 Domino with three spots
73 **PAUL** (Acts 13:9)

DOWN

1 "_____ is my washpot" (Psalm 60:8)
2 "All that are _____ to go forth to war in Israel" (Numbers 1:3)
3 "Even like the figs that are first _____" (Jeremiah 24:2)
4 Reef structure
5 Diamond thief? (2 words)
6 "No _____ will pitch his tent there" (Isaiah 13:20 NIV)
7 Two-faced Roman god
8 Shapeless protozoans (var.)
9 Cornelius's hometown (Acts 10:1)
10 Spokes (pl.)
11 Utah city by Provo
12 Singer Perry
16 One of the Bobbsey twins
21 Petting, for one
25 Greedily
26 Close again, as a jacket
27 Expunge
28 Dried coconut meat
30 Tit for _____
32 Golf great Sam
33 Urbane
34 "Libnah, and _____, and Ashan" (Joshua 15:42)
36 Music group, _____ Na Na
38 "_____ words of the Preacher, the son" (Ecclesiastes 1:1)

by David K. Shortess

40 "_____ there were born unto him" (Job 1:2)
42 "After him repaired _____ the son of Azbuk" (Nehemiah 3:16)
43 School organization (abbr.)
49 "I will also _____ thee" (Hosea 4:6)
51 "Grain, _____ them in their hands and eat the kernels" (Luke 6:1 NIV)
53 "Amazed them for a long time with his _____" (Acts 8:11 NIV)
54 "And _____ the wicked from among the just" (Matthew 13:49)
56 Lifts at the slopes (hyphenated)
57 Withdrawal spot (abbr.)
58 Scottish hillside
59 _____ *avis* (Lat.)
61 Abnormal breathing sound
62 Beverly Sills' specialty
63 Human rights organization (abbr.)
64 Be relaxed

ACROSS

1. "Ten women shall bake your bread in one _____" (Leviticus 26:26)
5. "And the archers _____ at king Josiah" (2 Chronicles 35:23)
9. The king of Assyria took Israel here in their captivity (2 Kings 17:6)
14. "Let him offer a _____ without blemish" (Leviticus 1:3)
15. Type of weed
16. "Ye pay tithe of mint and _____" (Matthew 23:23)
17. Charity
18. "A river watering the garden flowed from _____" (Genesis 2:10)
19. Creator
20. "There is no _____ to the Lord" (1 Samuel 14:6)
22. "They gathered twice as much— two _____ for each person" (Exodus 16:22 NIV)
23. Independent Order of the _____ Fellows
24. "Shallum, and Telem, and _____" (Ezra 10:24)
25. "Now I know of a _____" (Acts 12:11)
29. "Our God _____ delivered Samson, our enemy, into our hands" (Judges 16:23 NIV)
31. "In the evening it is _____ down and withers" (Psalm 90:6 NASB)
35. "Every day they _____ my words" (Psalm 56:5)
36. "Bound in their coats, their _____, and their hats" (Daniel 3:21)
38. Falsehood
39. A gem on the third row of the ephod (Exodus 28:19)
40. Type of snake
41. Get up
43. He was not with Adonijah (1 Kings 1:8)
44. "Axeltrees and their _____, and their felloes" (1 Kings 7:33)
46. "My bowels were _____ for him" (Song of Solomon 5:4)
47. There was a tower here (Genesis 35:21)
49. Large lake
50. Cutters
51. Prophetic book of canonical Jewish and Hebrew scripture (abbr., var.)
53. Gideon's fleece was first _____ then dry
54. Bend (noun)
57. Hezron's son (1 Chronicles 2:9)
63. "The children of _____, the children of Darkon" (Nehemiah 7:58)
64. Nehemiah's wall was finished in this month (Nehemiah 6:15)
65. Jether's father (1 Chronicles 4:17)
66. Fossilized tree sap
67. "Seven times more than it was _____ to be heated" (Daniel 3:19)
68. "When king _____ the Canaanite" (Numbers 21:1)
69. Listened
70. "Her gates are desolate: her priests _____" (Lamentations 1:4)
71. The straight distance between two points

DOWN

1. Teman's brother (Genesis 36:11)
2. Valley
3. Type of trees
4. "Thou makest thy _____ in the cedars" (Jeremiah 22:23)
5. Aaron and Hur held up Moses' hands to keep them this way (Exodus 17:12)
6. Ono's brother (Ezra 2:33)
7. Jerahmeel's son (1 Chronicles 2:25)
8. Cloth shelter
9. Shechem's father (Genesis 33:19)
10. Mizraim's son (Genesis 10:13)
11. Fond of
12. Greek form of *Asher* (Revelation 7:6)
13. "Five damsels of _____ that went after her" (1 Samuel 25:42)
21. "And he, as a _____ thing, consumeth" (Job 13:28)
24. "_____ not vain repetitions" (Matthew 6:7)

by N. Teri Grottke

25 Take an oath (arch.)
26 "Pressed him daily with her words, and _____ him" (Judges 16:16)
27 "Micah his son, _____" (1 Chronicles 5:5)
28 New England time zone (abbr.)
29 Gomer's husband (Hosea 1:3)
30 "It is the gall of _____ within him" (Job 20:14)
32 Noah's dove brought back an _____ leaf (Genesis 8:11)
33 "The foolishness of God is _____ than men" (1 Corinthians 1:25)
34 "He must _____ go through Samaria" (John 4:4)
36 Has ownership
37 "Let every one that _____ the name" (2 Timothy 2:19)
42 A quarrel
45 "_____ did that which was right" (1 Kings 15:11)
48 "Put a _____ to bind it" (Ezekiel 30:21)

50 "That thou mayest prosper and be in _____" (3 John 1:2)
52 "Mar the corners of thy _____" (Leviticus 19:27)
53 "Cup of trembling, and _____ them out" (Isaiah 51:17)
54 Zibeon's son (Genesis 36:24)
55 "Given him a _____ which is above every name" (Philippians 2:9)
56 "The children of Ramah and _____" (Ezra 2:26)
57 Descendants of Abraham
58 Jesus' final cry (Mark 15:34)
59 Repast
60 Chelub's son (1 Chronicles 27:26)
61 "Shuthelah: of _____" (Numbers 26:36)
62 "_____ your beasts, and go" (Genesis 45:17)

ACROSS

1 Feel deeply about
5 Clergyman (abbr., var.)
8 Fire product
13 Naum's son (Luke 3:25)
14 Unhappy destiny
16 "Let him that _____ steal no more" (Ephesians 4:28)
17 "Neither by the blood of _____ and calves" (Hebrews 9:12)
19 A work of _____
20 Moses' brother (Exodus 4:14)
21 Jether's father (1 Chronicles 4:17) (abbr., var.)
22 Deep hole
24 "He saith among the trumpets _____" (Job 39:25)
26 "A fool uttereth all his _____" (Proverbs 29:11)
27 Marshes
28 Quick swim
30 Dishon's child (Genesis 36:26)
33 "Said unto her, Talitha _____" (Mark 5:41)
35 Mattathias's father (Luke 3:25) (abbr., var.)
38 "But a _____ of hospitality" (Titus 1:8)
39 Melchi's grandfather (Luke 3:28)
40 Book about burnt offerings (abbr.)
41 "As he saith also in _____" (Romans 9:25)
42 "Fifteen shekels, shall be your ____" (Ezekiel 45:12)
43 "Walk according to this _____" (Galatians 6:16)
44 "As a lion in his ____" (Psalm 10:9)
45 Alleviated
46 "_____ again from the dead" (Acts 17:3)
47 Rachel _____ on the images (Genesis 31:34)
48 "Will a lion roar in the forest, when he hath no _____?" (Amos 3:4)
49 Simon's new name (John 1:42)
50 "Against Jerusalem, _____, she is broken" (Ezekiel 26:2)
51 "Let fall also _____ of the handfuls" (Ruth 2:16)
52 Samuel killed this Amelekite king (1 Samuel 15:33)
55 "_____, every one that thirsteth" (Isaiah 55:1)
57 Samuel's priest (1 Samuel 1:3)
58 Dull
61 He took Kenath (Numbers 32:42)
63 Hymn lyric: "But now I'm _____"
65 Barter
67 Eastern border of Persian rule
68 Final
70 "Thy shoes shall be _____ and brass" (Deuteronomy 33:25)
71 "If by any _____ I may provoke" (Romans 11:14)
72 Was not with Adonijah (1 Kings 1:8)
73 "Valley of Shaveh, which is the king's _____" (Genesis 14:17)

DOWN

1 Prison
2 Isaiah's father (2 Kings 19:2)
3 "The LORD also shall _____ out of Zion" (Joel 3:16)
4 Time zone in Pennsylvania (abbr.)
5 An altar (Joshua 22:34)
6 "The LORD God make _____ of skins, and clothed them" (Genesis 3:21)
7 "Many of the _____ hearing believed" (Acts 18:8) (abbr.)
8 Quiet _____ mouse (2 words)
9 Mail requires this
10 Lotan's son (Genesis 36:22)
11 Esau's father-in-law (Genesis 26:34)
12 "I will even _____ a curse upon you" (Malachi 2:2)
15 Arithmetic (abbr., var.)
18 "Saul leaned upon his _____" (2 Samuel 1:6)
23 The Samaritan went to this lodging (Luke 10:33–34)
25 "How shall I make thee as _____?" (Hosea 11:8)
27 Having liberty

by N. Teri Grottke

29 "They departed from _____" (Numbers 33:45)
30 "The seed is rotten under their _____" (Joel 1:17)
31 Faithful to Gomer (Hosea 1:2–3)
32 Incident
33 An unclean animal (Deuteronomy 14:7)
34 "_____ the office of a deacon" (1 Timothy 3:13)
35 Encampment in the wilderness (Numbers 33:13)
36 Menan's son (Luke 3:31)
37 "The Tower of the _____" (Nehemiah 3:11 NIV)
39 "Shall in no _____ enter into the kingdom of heaven" (Matthew 5:20)
42 The waters were bitter here (Exodus 15:23)
43 Fruit ready to pick
45 Follows Galatians (abbr.)
46 Pay

49 Officer's title (abbr.)
50 "His spirit came ____" (Judges 15:19)
51 Hearing is one
52 "Anab, and Eshtemoh, and _____" (Joshua 15:50)
53 "Thy sister in law is _____ back" (Ruth 1:15)
54 Adoniram's father (1 Kings 4:6)
56 Night flier
58 Zerah's son (1 Chronicles 2:6)
59 Image
60 Belshazzar saw this on the wall (Daniel 5:5, 25)
62 "'Naboth _____ been stoned and is dead'" (1 Kings 21:14 NIV)
64 Boat paddle
66 To make free of
69 Metallic element used in alloys (sym.)

ACROSS

1 A city of Lycaonia (Acts 14:6)
6 Cleaning agent
10 "Ephod with a _____ of blue" (Exodus 39:21)
14 Elijah in the New Testament (Mark 6:15)
15 Rephaiah's father (1 Chronicles 4:42)
16 The *Titanic* was a ship made of _____
17 "There made him a _____" (Jonah 4:5)
18 "Shall be eaten: as a _____ tree" (Isaiah 6:13)
19 "So David dwelt in the _____" (2 Samuel 5:9)
20 "_____ all the increase of thy seed" (Deuteronomy 14:22)
21 To make as new
22 "Beyond the tower of _____" (Genesis 35:21)
23 Simon Peter cut off one (John 18:10)
25 "Go not forth _____ to strive" (Proverbs 25:8)
27 "Neither yet the _____ of Sarah's womb" (Romans 4:19)
32 "Nathan the prophet, and Shimei, and _____" (1 Kings 1:8)
33 "_____ opened the book in sight of all the people" (Nehemiah 8:5) (abbr., var.)
34 "They shall _____ like torches" (Nahum 2:4)
36 Absalom's captain (2 Samuel 17:25)
40 Shechaniah's father (Nehemiah 6:18)
42 A porter (Ezra 10:24)
44 Salah's son (Genesis 10:24)
45 A city of the tribe of the children of Benjamin (Joshua 18:25)
47 "A daily _____ for every day" (2 Kings 25:30)
48 "Seven days it shall be with his _____" (Exodus 22:30)
49 A power color

51 "Do it _____, as to the Lord" (Colossians 3:23)
54 "I was an _____, and a gatherer of sycomore fruit" (Amos 7:14)
58 "_____ the knot"
59 Baking place
60 Almonds, cashews, etc.
63 Intelligent
67 Dimensions
68 "Before the cock _____, thou shalt deny me thrice" (Matthew 26:34)
69 "The name of the other _____" (1 Samuel 14:4)
70 Belonging to Phinehas's father (1 Samuel 1:3) (poss.)
71 Amos's grandfather (Luke 3:25)
72 Elioenai's son (1 Chronicles 3:24)
73 Belonging to a king of Judah (1 Kings 15:17) (poss.)
74 Jesus' coat didn't have one (John 19:23)
75 "Maketh the _____ to calve" (Psalm 29:9)

DOWN

1 "I forgave thee all that _____" (Matthew 18:32)
2 "Cried with a loud voice, saying, _____" (Mark 15:34)
3 "The same excess of _____, speaking evil of you" (1 Peter 4:4)
4 "My sword shall be _____ in heaven" (Isaiah 34:5)
5 A city of Judah (Joshua 15:52)
6 "_____ thou hast not hated blood" (Ezekiel 35:6)
7 Lyric: "_____ say can you _____" (2 words)
8 Ahitub's son (1 Samuel 14:3)
9 "Will I make a _____ in the temple of my God" (Revelation 3:12)
10 "All their _____ subject to bondage" (Hebrews 2:15)
11 Progeny of Gad (Genesis 46:16)
12 "No mention shall be made of ____" (Job 28:18)

by N. Teri Grottke

13 "At the _____ of the city" (Proverbs 8:3)
24 "Give thyself no _____" (Lamentations 2:18)
26 Dead _____ Scrolls
27 Darling
28 He brought the law before the congregation (Nehemiah 8:2)
29 Shem's son (Genesis 10:22)
30 Indian unit of weight
31 A pause or musical note used in the psalms
35 Measure
37 Levite grandfather of Ethan (1 Chronicles 6:44)
38 To close tightly
39 Land branch of service
41 "Endure _____, as a good soldier" (2 Timothy 2:3)
43 Non-earthy food group
46 This edge can be let out for more room

50 "Sang one to another in _____" (1 Samuel 29:5)
52 "They journeyed from _____" (Numbers 33:22)
53 Naarah's son (1 Chronicles 4:6)
54 Gomer's prophet (Hosea 1:2–3)
55 "For innumerable _____ have compassed me" (Psalm 40:12)
56 Asher's son (1 Chronicles 7:39-40)
57 Sister of mercy
61 Puah's son (Judges 10:1)
62 "He cut down a stick, and cast it in thither; and the iron did _____" (2 Kings 6:6)
64 "And Ahijah, Hanan, _____" (Nehemiah 10:26)
65 Tear apart
66 "What. . .hath been done to Mordecai for _____?" (Esther 6:3)

41

SOWING THE WORD

Hearken; behold, there went out a sower to sow:
and it came to pass, as he sowed. . .
MARK 4:3–4

ACROSS

1 "Who _____ thou?"
  (Genesis 27:32)
4 "_____ a watch, O LORD"
  (Psalm 141:3)
7 "How right they are to _____
  you!" (Song of Solomon 1:4 NIV)
12 Constrictors
14 Japheth's father (Genesis 5:32)
15 "No mention shall be made of
  _____" (Job 28:18)
16 Ambience
17 "There is none _____"
  (Deuteronomy 4:39)
18 Short news pieces
19 "Some fell _____" (Mark 4:4)
  (4 words)
22 One who stores fodder on a farm
23 Lots of ounces (abbr.)
24 Its agents work underground
  (abbr.)
27 Repeat in music
28 Used in posting a letter to oneself
29 "And it became _____ in his
  hand" (Exodus 4:4) (2 words)
30 Naval initials
33 "And some fell on _____"
  (Mark 4:5) (2 words)
36 Indian princess or rajah's wife
38 "Have gone into exile, captive
  before the _____" (Lamentations
  1:5 NIV)
39 It may be a golden one
40 "And some fell _____" (Mark
  4:7) (2 words)
43 "Doth not the _____ try words?"
  (Job 12:11)
44 "And cried with a _____ voice"
  (Mark 5:7)
45 "To _____, Jerusalem"
  (Jeremiah 25:18)

46 "Which strain _____ gnat"
  (Matthew 23:24) (2 words)
48 "And it _____ upon each of
  them" (Acts 2:3)
49 Brother's sibling (abbr.)
50 "Even on the _____ laid a very
  heavy yoke" (Isaiah 47:6 NIV)
  (2 words)
54 "And other fell _____" (Mark
  4:8) (3 words)
56 "Let me _____" (Deuteronomy
  9:14)
59 "But thou art _____" (Daniel
  4:18)
60 Son of Boaz (Ruth 4:21)
61 Sweet, musically (Ital.)
62 Homophone for land amphibian
63 "And mules, a _____ year by
  year" (2 Chronicles 9:24)
64 More strange
65 "And the moon shall not give
  _____ light" (Ezekiel 32:7)
66 "Let them not feed, _____ drink
  water" (Jonah 3:7)

DOWN

1 "For he is _____" (Hebrews
  5:13) (2 words)
2 City in southwest Quebec
3 Small pies
4 Free energy?
5 "For my yoke is _____"
  (Matthew 11:30)
6 "Then shall _____ return"
  (Joshua 20:6) (2 words)
7 Sulfuric and nitric
8 "And they shall _____"
  (Jeremiah 50:36)
9 "And my people the _____"
  (Jeremiah 6:27 NIV)
10 "And a _____ on every altar"
  (Numbers 23:30)

by David K. Shortess

11 Golfer Ernie
13 Indian honorific
14 Latest
20 Pillar in Wales
21 "_____ you, don't torture me!" (Luke 8:28 NIV) (2 words)
24 Indecorous
25 Western Turkey, at one time
26 "By the way, an _____ in the path" (Genesis 49:17)
28 Snob
29 Popular ISP (abbr.)
30 They separate Asia from Europe
31 Apia location
32 "As a jewel of gold in a swine's _____" (Proverbs 11:22)
34 "Abraham, and _____ unto Isaac" (1 Chronicles 16:16) (3 words)
35 List of names
37 "Nor _____ of life" (Hebrews 7:3)
41 "Away like a _____ on the surface of the waters" (Hosea 10:7 NIV)

42 Griped and whined
47 "I had digged in the wall, behold _____" (Ezekiel 8:8) (2 words)
49 "At whom do you _____ and stick out your tongue?" (Isaiah 57:4 NIV)
50 Psychiatrist who rejected Freud
51 Coffee type
52 "Every _____ his brother" (Jeremiah 34:17) (2 words)
53 Milk faucet
54 "Saying, Come up this _____" (Judges 16:18)
55 Bassoon relative
56 "Why make ye this _____, and weep?" (Mark 5:39)
57 "The children of _____" (Nehemiah 7:37)
58 "I am an _____ man" (Luke 1:18)

## 42

ACROSS

1 Furious driver (2 Kings 9:20)
5 Cognitive
10 _____ and lass
13 "_____ for the day!" (Joel 1:15)
14 "_____ away the gods your forefathers worshiped" (Joshua 24:14 NIV)
15 Some women are afraid of these
16 Expression: "On Cloud _____"
17 "He reasoned of righteousness, _____" (Acts 24:25)
19 Joshua's father (Exodus 33:11)
20 "Then my anger will _____ and my wrath. . .will subside" (Ezekiel 5:13 NIV)
21 Zabad's son (1 Chronicles 7:21)
22 "As an _____ harder than flint" (Ezekiel 3:9)
24 Make recompense
25 Boy Scouts are well versed in pitching one of these
26 "Maintain good works for necessary _____" (Titus 3:14)
27 Jediael's brother (1 Chronicles 11:45)
29 Enoch's son (Genesis 4:18)
30 Issachar's son (Numbers 26:23)
33 "Bear ye one _____ burdens" (Galatians 6:2) (poss.)
37 Emmor's son (Acts 7:16)
39 A fussy, middle-aged woman
40 Asa's father (Matthew 1:7)
41 "Their border was Helkath, and _____" (Joshua 19:25)
42 "There is but a _____ between me and death" (1 Samuel 20:3)
43 Expression: "The eleventh _____"
45 "Waters were _____ from off the earth" (Genesis 8:11)
48 Garbage
51 Ishmael's son (Genesis 25:15–16)
52 "Look from the top of _____" (Song of Solomon 4:8)
54 Mediterranean _____
55 Exile
57 "In the covert of the reed, and _____" (Job 40:21)
58 _____ Wildlife Observatory in Alaska
59 "Let us make man in our _____" (Genesis 1:26)
60 Respite
61 Follows Micah (abbr.)
62 Supped
63 "_____, I will call them my people" (Romans 9:25)

DOWN

1 Melchi's father (Luke 3:24)
2 Achim's son (Matthew 1:14)
3 "On the north side to _____" (Joshua 19:14)
4 Take advantage of
5 "Let thine ears be _____" (2 Chronicles 6:40)
6 Small bread grain
7 "The _____ of his hands were made strong" (Genesis 49:24)
8 "And sin as it were with a cart _____" (Isaiah 5:18)
9 This animal was used in the rich man/poor man parable to King David (2 Samuel 12:2–4)
10 Flax cloth
11 "_____, and Calneh, in the land of Shinar" (Genesis 10:10)
12 Works
15 "Count all the firstborn Israelite _____" (Numbers 3:40 NIV)
18 Cure
20 Expression: "A _____ of worms"
23 Chicken, ham, turkey, etc.
24 "Nevertheless _____ heart was perfect" (1 Kings 15:14) (poss.)
26 Abram's birthplace (Genesis 11:31)
27 "Upon the heavens by his name _____" (Psalm 68:4)
28 Expression: "Two heads are better than _____"
29 The prophet (2 Kings 19:2) (abbr.)
30 Paul was of this sect (Acts 23:6)
31 Bani's son (Ezra 10:34)
32 A family of returned exiles (Ezra 2:57)

by N. Teri Grottke

34 "Backbiters, _____ of God"
   (Romans 1:30)
35 Gaal's father (Judges 9:26)
36 This cord is used with a balloon or
   parachute
38 "The mingled people, and _____"
   (Ezekiel 30:5)
42 Blemish
43 Sought after
44 Called by Ahab (1 Kings 18:3)
   (abbr., var.)
45 Abishur's son (1 Chronicles 2:29)
46 Zadok's father (Nehemiah 3:4)
47 Jehosaphat's chief captain of Judah
   (2 Chronicles 17:14)
48 Realm
49 Keen perception; sixth _____
50 Expression: "_____ makes waste"
52 "Say ye unto your brethren,
   _____" (Hosea 2:1)
53 "What _____ ye to weep"
   (Acts 21:13)

56 Kept from detection
57 Satan went to and _____ in the
   earth (Job 2:2)

## 43

ACROSS

1 A long, slender column in the ground to carry a load
5 Venomous Egyptian snake (pl.)
9 "And Bethzur, and _____, and Adullam" (2 Chronicles 11:7)
14 The month when the Hebrews left Egypt (Exodus 34:18)
15 "Land from _____ to the wilderness" (Isaiah 16:1)
16 "Children of Sisera, the children of _____" (Nehemiah 7:55)
17 Late 1800s English actor-manager known for Dickens
18 Wily plot
19 Absalom's captain (2 Samuel 19:13)
20 "Is persecuted, and none _____" (Isaiah 14:6)
22 "And _____ sumptuously every day" (Luke 16:19)
23 Chemical imbalance disorder based on season
24 Often (arch.)
25 "Sweetness of a man's friend by _____ counsel" (Proverbs 27:9)
29 "Bore his _____ through with a thorn" (Job 41:2)
31 Neither _____ nor there
35 Measurement a little over a bushel
36 "The difficult _____ they brought to Moses" (Exodus 18:26 NIV)
38 To rent or lease (verb)
39 The sun does this
40 "The porters; Shallum, and Telem, and _____" (Ezra 10:24)
41 Bela's son (1 Chronicles 8:3–4)
43 "The barley was in the _____" (Exodus 9:31)
44 Binea's son (1 Chronicles 8:37)
46 Dead language
47 "Gone down in the sun _____ of Ahaz" (Isaiah 38:8)
49 Hezekiah's servants came to him (2 Kings 19:5) (abbr.)
50 David's spy among Absalom's counselors (2 Samuel 16:16)
51 Have possession
53 Joseph was thrown into this (Genesis 37)

54 "Hushai was in Asher and in _____" (1 Kings 4:16)
57 "Save that one _____ his disciples were entered" (John 6:22)
63 Agar is this mount in Arabia (Galatians 4:25)
64 Employ
65 Formerly a prophet, now also a fortune-teller
66 "_____ measure that is abominable" (Micah 6:10)
67 Farm children gather these
68 Saul's grandson was this (2 Samuel 4:4)
69 Sound judgment is common _____
70 This, _____, these, those
71 "Shuthelah: of _____" (Numbers 26:36)

DOWN

1 Way
2 Merari's son
3 "Though ye have _____ among the pots" (Psalm 68:13)
4 Gaal's father (Judges 9:28)
5 "Ye were as sheep going _____" (1 Peter 2:25)
6 Zebulun's son (Genesis 46:14)
7 "I will requite thee in this _____" (2 Kings 9:26)
8 A giant (2 Samuel 21:18)
9 "Thy rod and thy _____ they comfort me" (Psalm 23:4)
10 Toi was king of this country (2 Samuel 8:9)
11 Baseball player Vizquel
12 "Will you argue the _____ for God?" (Job 13:8 NIV)
13 Simeon's son (Genesis 46:10)
21 Ahasuerus's new wife (Esther 2:16–17)
24 Indebted
25 "The son of _____" (1 Kings 4:10)
26 This man was a Netophathite (Jeremiah 40:8)
27 Enan's son (Numbers 1:15)
28 "_____ greedily after the error" (Jude 1:11)

by N. Teri Grottke

29 Attai's father (1 Chronicles 2:35)
30 Largest continent
32 "He built _____, and restored it to Judah" (2 Chronicles 26:2)
33 "Micah his son, _____ his son" (1 Chronicles 5:5)
34 Zerah's son (1 Chronicles 6:41)
36 Drinking vessels
37 Military greeting
42 "These he _____ kept in darkness" (Jude 1:6 NIV)
45 "Riblah, on the east side of _____" (Numbers 34:11)
48 "_____ sister was Timna" (Genesis 36:22) (poss.)
50 "Thou givest thy gifts to all thy lovers, and _____ them" (Ezekiel 16:33)
52 A polar bear's color
53 "They came to _____ in Pamphylia" (Acts 13:13)

54 "Sitting on an _____ colt" (John 12:15) (poss.)
55 One of the plagues on Egypt (Exodus 8:16)
56 Judah's son (Genesis 46:12)
57 "Do not _____ the edge" (Ecclesiastes 10:10)
58 "Wisdom is too _____ for a fool" (Proverbs 24:7)
59 _____ of Wight in the Channel
60 "Moses drew _____" (Exodus 20:21)
61 Arabian city (Job 6:19)
62 Jerahmeel's son (1 Chronicles 2:25)

ACROSS

1 Before (arch.)
4 Unit of electricity
7 Tiny insect that carries 20 times its weight
10 "Dove found no _____ for the sole of her foot" (Genesis 8:9)
12 Jesus' forlorn cry (Mark 15:34)
13 "Children of Sisera, the children of _____" (Nehemiah 7:55)
15 "Booz begat Obed of _____" (Matthew 1:5)
16 "He had greaves of brass upon his _____" (1 Samuel 17:6)
17 Over and _____ the call of duty
18 Zepho's brother (Genesis 36:11)
19 Valley
20 "_____ are fallen unto me in pleasant places" (Psalm 16:6)
21 Score or grade
22 "Spread his tent beyond the tower of _____" (Genesis 35:21)
23 Winged symbol of the United States
24 "Which come to you in _____ clothing" (Matthew 7:15) (sing. poss.)
26 Spiritual song
28 Cain and Abel's younger brother (Genesis 5:3)
30 Jerahmeel's wife (1 Chronicles 2:26)
35 "And Bethzur, and _____, and Adullam" (2 Chronicles 11:7)
38 Esau's father-in-law (Genesis 26:34)
41 One now deceased
42 Higher-pitched male voice
43 "Moses took the _____ of God in his hand" (Exodus 4:20)
44 Bathsheba's father (2 Samuel 11:3)
45 Greek form of *Hagar* (Galatians 4:24)
46 Furthest part
47 "Burst thy _____ in sunder" (Nahum 1:13)
48 "Suddenly shall he be broken without _____" (Proverbs 6:15)

50 "Ran again unto the well to _____ water" (Genesis 24:20)
52 A lease is often for this length of time
55 Voting _____ some governments
59 "Seek peace, and _____ it" (1 Peter 3:11)
63 "And he _____ upon a cherub" (Psalm 18:10)
65 A defensive football play
66 This plant was shade for Jonah (Jonah 4:6)
67 Naomi's "son" (Ruth 4:17)
68 "Her merchandise and her _____ shall be holiness" (Isaiah 23:18)
69 First book of the Bible (abbr.)
70 "When they couch in their _____" (Job 38:40)
71 Sleeping place

DOWN

1 Mistakes
2 Tebah's mother (Genesis 22:24)
3 "Who remembered us in our low _____" (Psalm 136:23)
4 Hymn: "_____ my blindness by the hand" (2 words)
5 Zelophehad's daughter (Numbers 26:33)
6 "Destruction and _____ are in their ways" (Romans 3:16)
7 In the midst of
8 Type of orange
9 "_____ are the generations of the heavens" (Genesis 2:4)
11 "Egyptians mourned for him _____ and ten days" (Genesis 50:3)
12 Firstborn
13 Ability
14 Roboam's son (Matthew 1:7)
25 Balak brought Balaam to the top of this mountain (Numbers 23:28)
27 In the movie *Mulan*, she emulates a _____
29 "There shall be no _____ in the stalls" (Habakkuk 3:17)
31 "That thing which he _____" (Romans 14:22)

by N. Teri Grottke

32 Precipitation
33 "Canaanites, saw the mourning in the floor of _____" (Genesis 50:11)
34 _____ and haws
35 Jewish symbol of David
36 The king's chamberlain (Esther 2:3)
37 Shobal's child (Genesis 36:23)
39 "Moses kept a _____ of every time they moved" (Numbers 33:2 THE MESSAGE)
40 Azariah's father (2 Chronicles 15:1)
44 There was a curse here (Deuteronomy 11:29)
46 "But the _____ of their God was upon the elders" (Ezra 5:5)
49 Colored
51 Measures of length (Ezekiel 42:16) (pl.)

53 "Of _____, the family" (Numbers 26:17)
54 It was purple (John 19:5)
56 "Where no oxen are, the _____ is clean" (Proverbs 14:4)
57 Homophone for rip
58 Went swiftly
59 Ovum
60 Greek form of Noah (Matthew 24:38)
61 Biggest star in our solar system
62 "Brought thee out of _____ of the Chaldees" (Genesis 15:7)
64 Subdivision of a Cub Scout pack

BIBLICAL TREES

*"You will go out in joy and be led forth in peace. . .
and all the trees of the field will clap their hands."*

Isaiah 55:12 NIV

ACROSS

1 "_____, Ham, and Japheth"
   (Genesis 6:10)
5 *Les Misérables* author Victor
9 "As a piece of string _____"
   (Judges 16:9 NIV)
14 **TREE** found in Isaiah 60:13
15 "Houses to live _____ had vine-
    yards" (Jeremiah 35:9 NIV) (2 words)
16 Rationale
17 Wield a blue pencil
18 "Thee down that the rain _____
    thee not" (1 Kings 18:44)
19 **TREE** found in Psalm 52:8
20 **TREES** found in Isaiah 2:13
    (3 words)
23 "Your lightning _____ up the
    world" (Psalm 77:18 NIV)
24 "And brought the _____ upon
    them" (Joshua 24:7)
25 Telephone company (abbr.)
26 "Because thou saidst, _____"
    (Ezekiel 25:3)
29 "The spiritual man is _____"
    (Hosea 9:7)
31 "That thou _____ virtuous
    woman" (Ruth 3:11) (2 words)
34 "A dead _____ flea" (1 Samuel
    24:14 NIV) (2 words)
36 Game official, for short
38 **TREE** found in Genesis 30:37
42 A place Texans will never forget
44 **TREE** found in Hosea 14:8
46 "One _____ was rained upon"
    (Amos 4:7)
47 **TREE** found in Isaiah 55:13
49 "For they shall see _____"
    (Matthew 5:8)
51 "Perfume, made of pure _____"
    (Mark 14:3 NIV)
52 "Here am I; _____ me"
    (Isaiah 6:8)
54 "They are _____ with the
    showers" (Job 24:8)

56 "_____ blaspheming!" (Mark 2:7
    NIV) (contr.)
57 Madrid Mrs. (abbr.)
60 Prosecuting attorneys (abbr.)
62 Government Native American
    agency (abbr.)
64 **TREES** found in Isaiah 6:13 NIV
    (3 words)
71 **TREE** found in Song of
    Solomon 2:3
72 The Jairite and the Tekoite (2
    Samuel 20:26 and 23:26) (pl.)
73 Italian noble family
74 Western grass
75 Irish Free State
76 **TREE** found in Jeremiah 10:5
77 Lot's wicked city
    (Genesis 13:12–13)
78 "Bless the _____" (Genesis 48:16)
79 "Who plan to _____ my feet"
    (Psalm 140:4 NIV)

DOWN

1 On _____ (without assurance of
   profit) (abbr.)
2 "_____ thy face from my sins"
   (Psalm 51:9)
3 Oklahoma city
4 "Looked like glowing _____"
   (Ezekiel 1:4 NIV)
5 "For we have seen _____ in the
   east" (Matthew 2:2) (2 words)
6 "And said _____ them"
   (Luke 9:48)
7 Bloopers
8 "When a prayer _____ is made"
   (1 Kings 8:38 NIV) (2 words)
9 Vulgarian
10 Vincent Lopez's theme song
11 "And _____ will soon disappear"
    (Hebrews 8:13 NIV)
12 Turning point

by David K. Shortess

13 "A crowd was running to the
   _____" (Mark 9:25 NIV)
21 "Was like the _____ of a cup"
   (1 Kings 7:26 NIV)
22 Wyatt of O.K. Corral fame
26 "And _____ gave names to all"
   (Genesis 2:20)
27 "The _____ One in Israel"
   (Ezekiel 39:7)
28 Mount Sinai in Galatians 4:25
30 Meaning (abbr.)
32 "The _____ of the hill"
   (Exodus 17:10)
33 "Or will men take _____ of it?"
   (Ezekiel 15:3) (2 words)
35 Quantities (abbr.)
37 **TREE** found in Micah 4:4
39 Dinah's mother (Genesis 34:1)
40 "Were an half _____ of land"
   (1 Samuel 14:14)
41 Carmine and ruby
43 Corrida cry
45 "Fifteen in a _____"
   (1 Kings 7:3)

48 "To this _____ labor" (2 words)
   (Colossians 1:29 NIV)
50 Runs down
53 "Behold, thou art wiser than
   _____" (Ezekiel 28:3)
55 "Take away all thy ____" (Isaiah
   1:25)
57 Bambi's father, et al.
58 Printing proof (abbr.)
59 "And the king of _____"
   (2 Kings 19:13)
61 One of a series of parallel lines
63 Highly skilled
65 Sailors' patron saint
66 "A spear like a weaver's _____"
   (1 Chronicles 11:23)
67 "Speak _____ things"
   (Psalm 94:4)
68 Eskers
69 Gudrun's second husband
70 1996 V.P. candidate

ACROSS

1 "Thou shalt not _____ the harlot" (Hosea 3:3)
5 Eliezer's son (Luke 3:29)
9 "Shall be astonished, and _____ his head" (Jeremiah 18:16)
12 Lubricated
14 Naum's son (Luke 3:25)
15 "_____ shall offer gifts" (Psalm 72:10)
16 "I _____ you with blasting and with mildew" (Haggai 2:17)
17 Retained
18 Tarry
19 Type of foil
20 Greek form of *Asher* (Revelation 7:6)
22 Jerahmeel's wife (1 Chronicles 2:26)
24 High-flying aircraft with little radar return
26 Zerah's son (1 Chronicles 6:41)
27 Sacred songs or poems (abbr.)
28 Guilty or not guilty
29 A knight
32 "Of the tribe of _____ were sealed twelve thousand" (Revelation 7:5)
35 "Have ye made a _____ to day?" (1 Samuel 27:10)
37 Particular ones
39 Jeshua's son (Nehemiah 3:19)
40 Made a mistake
42 Micaiah's father (2 Chronicles 18:7)
43 Garbage
45 Cut back
46 Lack
47 "Turn aside, _____ down here" (Ruth 4:1)
48 Breadth
50 Insane
52 A prophet's father (1 Kings 22:8)
54 "He shewed himself alive after his _____" (Acts 1:3)
58 Keep
60 Flow amply
61 "Woman were given _____ wings of a great eagle" (Revelation 12:14)
62 Nehemiah's wall was finished in this month (Nehemiah 6:15)
63 Crucifixion instrument
65 Old-time anesthetic
67 "_____ that man, and have no company with him" (2 Thessalonians 3:14)
68 Hymn: "Rock of _____"
69 Cook
70 "_____ them about thy neck" (Proverbs 6:21)
71 To pierce with horns
72 "He that winketh _____ the eye" (Proverbs 10:10)

DOWN

1 "Waiting at the _____ of my doors" (Proverbs 8:34)
2 Boundary
3 "It is not good that the man should be _____" (Genesis 2:18)
4 "The iniquity of the Amorites is not _____ full" (Genesis 15:16)
5 Agur's father (Proverbs 30:1)
6 Biblical measurement (Exodus 16:18)
7 The giving of this revealed Jesus' betrayer (John 13:26)
8 "_____ of a man of high degree" (1 Chronicles 17:17)
9 "_____ nights are appointed to me" (Job 7:3)
10 Asa's father (1 Chronicles 3:10)
11 Goliath was from here (1 Samuel 17:4)
13 Bible measurement for flour (Leviticus 14:10)
15 Graceful water bird
21 Look hard
23 Specific one
25 "She shall be put _____ seven days" (Leviticus 15:19)
26 Older person
28 Ishmael and Hagar lived in this wilderness (Genesis 21:21)
30 Island
31 "They were _____ before the king" (Esther 6:1)
32 Descendants of Jacob

by N. Teri Grottke

33 Palal's father (Nehemiah 3:25)
34 Totally without resources
36 Ruth's sister-in-law (Ruth 1:14–15)
38 "He will make my feet like _____ feet" (Habakkuk 3:19) (pl. poss.)
41 He forsook Paul (2 Timothy 4:10)
44 Nagge's son (Luke 3:25)
49 "Minnith, and _____, and honey" (Ezekiel 27:17)
51 One of Jacob's sons (Genesis 35:26)
53 "Every _____ by their polls" (Numbers 1:2)
54 Heartbeat
55 Ribai's son (1 Chronicles 11:31)
56 "Pay me that thou _____" (Matthew 18:28)
57 _____ Dakota
58 Lease
59 This was interpreted as God (Mark 15:34)
60 A type of eagle (Leviticus 11:18)

64 Time past
66 "As a thread of _____ is broken" (Judges 16:9)

ACROSS

1 A king of Judah (Hosea 1:1)
5 Get up
10 To throw out
14 Fossil matter
15 The king at the time of Jesus' birth
16 Detest
17 "Plentifully rewardeth the proud _____" (Psalm 31:23)
18 Type of refrigerator (obs.)
19 Of the family of the Eranites (Numbers 26:36)
20 "From the going up to _____, from the rock, and upward" (Judges 1:36)
22 "People _____ unto him again" (Mark 10:1)
24 "Where _____ thou gleaned to day?" (Ruth 2:19)
25 "Even with two _____ measured he to put to death" (2 Samuel 8:2)
26 Korah's son (Exodus 6:24)
29 "_____ thou know that the most High ruleth in the kingdom" (Daniel 4:32)
32 Heber's father (Luke 3:35)
33 "_____ whose fruit withereth" (Jude 1:12)
34 "Destroy _____ kings and people" (Ezra 6:12)
37 Zibeon's daughter (Genesis 36:2)
38 Shemidah's son (1 Chronicles 7:19)
39 Paul preached in _____ Minor
40 "So many as the stars of the _____ in multitude" (Hebrews 11:12)
41 Asher's son (1 Chronicles 7:30)
42 Expression: "_____ as a doornail"
43 "Beholding his natural face in a _____" (James 1:23)
44 Regretful
45 One of Shaharaim's wives (1 Chronicles 8:8)
48 A city of Hadarezer (1 Chronicles 18:8)
50 "The Lord saith it; _____ I have not spoken" (Ezekiel 13:7)
52 One nation's citizens present on the day of Pentecost (Acts 2:9)
56 Expression: "Less is _____"
57 Eliadah's son (1 Kings 11:23)
59 Cattle
60 Talmai's father (Numbers 13:22)
61 "Nor _____ my love, until he please" (Song of Solomon 8:4)
62 Dishan's son (Genesis 36:28)
63 Garment edges
64 "_____; Thy kingdom is divided" (Daniel 5:28)
65 Repair

DOWN

1 Adoniram's father (1 Kings 4:6)
2 Used to catch fish
3 "_____ with her suburbs" (1 Chronicles 6:70)
4 Uzzi's son (1 Chronicles 6:6)
5 "So she wrote letters in _____ name" (1 Kings 21:8) (poss.)
6 "The Son of Man has authority on earth to forgive sins and _____ the penalty" (Matthew 9:6 AMP)
7 Duke of Edom (1 Chronicles 1:54)
8 "Came to Joel the _____ of Pethuel" (Joel 1:1)
9 Biblical tower (Genesis 35:21)
10 "And Eltolad, and _____, and Hormah" (Joshua 15:30)
11 Moses' brother (Exodus 4:14)
12 Look fixedly
13 "I saw the _____ of Cushan" (Habakkuk 3:7)
21 Barrier
23 Belonging to Hophni's father (1 Samuel 1:3) (poss.)
26 Belonging to a king of Judah (1 Kings 15:17) (poss.)
27 The Egyptians in the Red Sea _____ (Exodus 15:10)
28 To amuse immensely
29 Greek form of *Uriah* (Matthew 1:6)
30 The border went to here from Remmonmethoar (Joshua 19:13)
31 "Hundred and _____ years old" (Joshua 24:29)
33 In this manner

by N. Teri Grottke

34 Greek form of *Asher* (Revelation 7:6)
35 A person who makes untrue statements
36 "The elder unto the elect _____ and her children" (2 John 1:1)
38 "_____ his son reigned in his stead" (1 Kings 15:8)
39 Eliphelet's father (Ezra 8:13)
41 An Ahohite (1 Chronicles 11:29)
43 "I am debtor both to the _____" (Romans 1:14)
44 Total
45 "Is called _____ unto this day" (Ezekiel 20:29)
46 "Who can forgive sins, but God _____?" (Luke 5:21)
47 Sarai's husband (Genesis 11:29)
48 "Liberty for a _____ of maliciousness" (1 Peter 2:16)
49 "His ambassadors came to _____" (Isaiah 30:4)

51 Set to capture animals
52 A son of Seir (1 Chronicles 1:38)
53 Exhaust
54 Ahira's father (Numbers 1:15)
55 "I will even _____ a curse upon you" (Malachi 2:2)
58 "_____, ye shall not kill it and her young both in one day" (Leviticus 22:28)

ACROSS

1 "An _____ for every man" (Exodus 16:16)
5 Rachel wept for her children where? (Matthew 2:18)
9 "I saw as the colour of _____" (Ezekiel 1:27)
14 Zerah's son (1 Chronicles 2:6)
15 "From following the _____ great with young" (Psalm 78:71)
16 Zadok's father (Nehemiah 3:4)
17 Dental method (sing.)
18 The crown of the head
19 An altar was built on his threshing floor (1 Chronicles 21:18)
20 Response
22 "Her princes within her are _____ lions" (Zephaniah 3:3)
24 "Gathered together unto _____ place" (Genesis 1:9)
25 A plaintive sound from one's young
26 "God _____ be tempted with evil" (James 1:13)
30 Winged animal
32 Expression: "On the _____"
35 Jerusalem (Isaiah 29:1)
36 Another name for *Zoar* (Genesis 14:2)
37 Look at
38 Disordered, untidy
39 "Dost thou know the _____ of the clouds?" (Job 37:16)
41 "Cast him into the _____ of ground" (2 Kings 9:26)
42 Nagge's son (Luke 3:25)
43 Er's son (1 Chronicles 4:21)
44 This causes estrangement from God
45 "Swift as the _____ upon the mountains" (1 Chronicles 12:8)
46 Jeroboam, son of Nebat, was from here (1 Kings 11:26)
47 "Zechariah, _____, and Jaaziel" (1 Chronicles 15:18)
48 _____ of Galilee
49 Keturah's son (1 Chronicles 1:32)

52 "What man is like Job, who drinketh up _____ like water?" (Job 34:7)
57 Zabad's son (1 Chronicles 7:21)
58 "The devil threw him down, and _____ him" (Luke 9:42)
59 "Besought him to _____ with him" (Luke 11:37)
61 "Not many mighty, not many _____, are called" (1 Corinthians 1:26)
62 Picnic pests
63 Judah's son (Genesis 46:12)
64 Come in
65 Many instances in little time
66 "Which are ashamed of thy _____ way" (Ezekiel 16:27)

DOWN

1 Strange
2 Naomi's new name
3 "Son of Shuthelah" (Numbers 26:36)
4 "All our righteousnesses are as filthy _____" (Isaiah 64:6)
5 "_____ in dust and ashes" (Job 42:6)
6 Cognitive
7 *When Harry _____ Sally*
8 Greek form of *Asher* (Revelation 7:6)
9 On a ship
10 "Let them _____ to whom they think best" (Numbers 36:6)
11 A mighty man of David (2 Samuel 23:36)
12 Ahira's father (Numbers 2:29)
13 Resounded
21 Sheep product
23 Pagiel's father (Numbers 2:27)
26 "Stink of your _____ to come up unto your nostrils" (Amos 4:10)
27 Gad's son (Genesis 46:16)
28 The first Hebrew month (Esther 3:7)
29 "I shall die in my _____" (Job 29:18)
30 "And they made _____ of pure gold" (Exodus 39:25)

by David K. Shortess

31 "_____ the Ahohite"
(1 Chronicles 11:29)
32 Spear
33 "The children of _____, a
thousand two hundred twenty and
two" (Ezra 2:12)
34 "Their dwelling was from _____"
(Genesis 10:30)
36 "Who in presence am _____
among you" (2 Corinthians 10:1)
37 A type of eagle
(Deuteronomy 14:17)
39 "Shebam, and Nebo, and _____"
(Numbers 32:3)
40 "Those that were _____ escaped"
(2 Peter 2:18)
45 "I will _____ vengeance to
mine enemies"
(Deuteronomy 32:41)
46 Haman's wife (Esther 5:10)
47 "With him from _____ of Judah"
(2 Samuel 6:2)

48 "Clothed with all _____ of
armour" (Ezekiel 38:4)
49 Part of the handwriting on the
wall (Daniel 5:25)
50 Esau's father-in-law (Genesis
26:34)
51 Formerly, one could end up in
prison for this
52 "Your images, the _____ of your
god" (Amos 5:26)
53 Jesus' first miracle was here at a
wedding (John 2:11)
54 "Offered sacrifice unto the _____,
and rejoiced in the works"
(Acts 7:41)
55 Number of tribes of Israel in
Numbers 34:13
56 Chew a bone
60 "The _____ of that mirth is
heaviness" (Proverbs 14:13)

49

QUESTION AND ANSWER

*Then he. . .fell down before Paul and Silas, and brought
them out, and said, Sirs, what must I do to be saved?*

ACTS 16:29–30

ACROSS

1 "The enemy has _____
everything in the sanctuary"
(Psalm 74:3)
8 September follower (abbr.)
11 Federal lending agency (abbr.)
14 Learned (adj.)
15 "And the _____ shouted, Day
after day, my lord" (Isaiah 21:8
NIV)
17 "The full fruitage of the _____ of
his sin" (Isaiah 27:9 NIV)
18 Encroach on
19 Beginning of **ANSWER** to theme
question (Acts 16:31) (3 words)
21 "He may give her divorce _____"
(Deuteronomy 24:1 THE MESSAGE)
24 Animal doctors (shortened)
25 Tropical cuckoos
26 "Neither shall they learn _____
any more" (Micah 4:3)
27 "And he _____ son, whose name
was Saul" (1 Samuel 9:2) (2 words)
31 Soap ingredient, at one time
32 "_____ with thy servant
according unto thy mercy" (Psalm
119:124)
34 "Yet it _____ its provisions in
summer" (Proverbs 6:8 NIV)
36 **ANSWER**, cont. (3 words)
39 "_____ them sharply"
(Deuteronomy 27:8 THE MESSAGE)
40 "Their inheritance, _____ said
unto them" (Joshua 13:33) (2
words)
41 "_____, I have no man" (John
5:7)
42 "For this _____ of the queen shall
come abroad" (Esther 1:17)
43 Country address, rural _____
(abbr.)

44 "The _____ and warrior, the
judge and prophet" (Isaiah 3:2 NIV)
45 Reed instrument
47 British pastries
49 **ANSWER**, cont. (3 words)
54 Oppressed farm laborer
55 How something egglike is shaped
59 Nonresident hospital physician
(var.)
60 End of **ANSWER**
61 Sault _____ Marie (abbr.)
62 River in Scotland
63 Fish hawks

DOWN

1 City Paul came to (Acts 16:1)
(shortened)
2 "Her prophets _____ light"
(Zephaniah 3:4)
3 Fall flower
4 Unfired bricks
5 "For God loveth a cheerful
_____" (2 Corinthians 9:7)
6 List enders (abbr.)
7 It's full of bologna
8 _____ Twist
9 "A grand _____ of fireworks"
(2 Samuel 22:13 THE MESSAGE)
10 Maps showing relative elevation,
for short
11 Type of type
12 _____ Downs, radio and TV
personality
13 "That just suits me to _____"
(2 words)
16 "The man is near of _____ unto
us" (Ruth 2:20)
20 Appraises
21 Luminousless
22 "If _____ of the common people
sin" (Leviticus 4:27) (2 words)

by David K. Shortess

23 "And _____ them through with his arrows" (Numbers 24:8)
26 "_____ the Lord displeased against the rivers?" (Habakkuk 3:8)
27 "And came unto mount _____" (Numbers 20:22)
28 "That wicked men have _____ among you" (Deuteronomy 13:13 NIV)
29 "For he gave them their own _____" (Psalm 78:29)
30 Houston ball club
32 They handle CDs (abbr.)
33 Wide shoe size
34 Elementary or middle (abbr.)
35 "Make strong _____ brickkiln" (Nahum 3:14)
37 "Those of his that _____ remain in the day of distress" (Obadiah 1:14)
38 Georgia is this direction from Nebraska (abbr.)
43 Shaping tool in the woodshop

44 Built-up roof component (2 words)
45 Scarlett _____
46 Pretty, in Glasgow (Scot.)
47 "But I call to God, and the Lord _____ me" (Psalm 55:16 NIV)
48 "And _____ hands with pagans" (Isaiah 2:6 NIV)
49 Some things King Solomon got from the Tharshish ships (1 Kings 10:22)
50 "And the _____ unto him was Carshena, Shethar, Admatha" (Esther 1:14)
51 "Son of man, record this _____" (Ezekiel 24:2 NIV)
52 Mao _____-tung
53 Vagrant
56 Mother of all humans
57 Meadow (var.)
58 Gain units on the gridiron (abbr.)

50

ACROSS

1 "Compassed me about like _____" (Psalm 118:12)
5 Despise
10 Smelling spot
14 Mattathias's great-grandfather (Luke 3:25))
15 Ahilud's son (1 Kings 4:12)
16 Great wickedness
17 "Ye shall see the abomination of _____" (Mark 13:14)
19 Shoham's brother (1 Chronicles 24:27)
20 Nobah took this province (Numbers 32:42)
21 "Machnadebai, Shashai, _____" (Ezra 10:40)
23 Quilting get-together
24 Keats, Yeats, Frost, and Whitman, for example
25 Chislon's son (Numbers 34:21)
29 Without speech
30 Bear's hand
33 A baptismal site of John the Baptist (John 3:23)
34 To make a hole
35 Anak's father (Joshua 15:13)
36 This computer function keeps your work available
37 "Jacob _____ in the land of Egypt" (Genesis 47:28)
38 Not appetizing to vegans
39 Always
40 Brother to Mamre the Amorite (Genesis 14:13)
41 "Day and night shall not _____" (Genesis 8:22)
42 "As a lion in his _____" (Psalm 10:9)
43 Larger than monkeys
44 "They shall _____ from sea to sea" (Amos 8:12)
45 Jehaleleel's son (1 Chronicles 4:16)
47 Writing tool
48 Crippled
50 Tikvath's father (2 Chronicles 34:22)
54 Manasseh's son (2 Kings 21:18)
55 "These things worketh God _____ with man" (Job 33:29)
59 Brother to Amal (1 Chronicles 7:35)
60 "Stock of Israel, of the _____ of Benjamin" (Philippians 3:5)
61 Little color
62 "That dippeth with me in the _____" (Mark 14:20)
63 "Faith is the substance of things _____ for" (Hebrews 11:1)
64 There were seventy palm trees here (Exodus 15:27)

DOWN

1 Sleigh, four-poster, king
2 Well of strife (Genesis 26:20)
3 "I am the LORD, and there is none _____" (Isaiah 45:5)
4 "There shall come out of _____ the Deliverer" (Romans 11:26)
5 "Waters were _____ from off the earth" (Genesis 8:11)
6 "He shall _____ his flesh in water" (Numbers 19:7)
7 "Between Bethel and _____" (Genesis 13:3)
8 Distressed cry (var.)
9 "_____ him from the hand of him that was stronger than he" (Jeremiah 31:11)
10 Jeroboam's father (1 Kings 11:26)
11 "Of them was the whole earth _____" (Genesis 9:19)
12 Greek form of *Sinai* (Acts 7:30)
13 Jesus cried this on the cross (Mark 15:34)
18 Rachel and Leah's father (Genesis 29:16)
22 Comes before James (abbr.)
24 "Thou art of _____ eyes than to behold evil" (Habakkuk 1:13)
25 "For I mean not that other men be _____, and ye burdened" (2 Corinthians 8:13)
26 "Intreat me not to _____ thee" (Ruth 1:16)
27 "They have sought out many _____" (Ecclesiastes 7:29)

by N. Teri Grottke

28 "Rewardeth the proud _____"
   (Psalm 31:23)
29 "Cab of _____ dung"
   (2 Kings 6:25) (sing. poss.)
31 To lower in rank or esteem
32 "See, here is _____; what doth
   hinder me to be baptized?"
   (Acts 8:36)
34 Moza's son (1 Chronicles 8:37)
35 So be it
37 Deborah's husband (Judges 4:4)
41 "Thou _____ understand a
   dream" (Genesis 41:15)
43 "All _____ come to pass unto
   you" (Joshua 23:14)
44 "Now when she had _____
   Loruhamah" (Hosea 1:8)
46 Asher's firstborn (1 Chronicles
   7:30)
47 A servant of the church at
   Cenchrea (Romans 16:1)

48 "A little _____; and she waited on
   Naaman's wife" (2 Kings 5:2)
49 "Say ye unto your brethren,
   _____" (Hosea 2:1)
51 "Harvest is _____: come, get you
   down" (Joel 3:13)
52 Helem's son (1 Chronicles 7:35)
53 Jesus' grandfather (Luke 3:23)
56 To and _____
57 "_____ of the right ear of Aaron"
   (Exodus 29:20)
58 School of religious teaching (abbr.)

ACROSS

1 Hodesh's son (1 Chronicles 8:9–10)
5 "Tochen, and _____, five cities" (1 Chronicles 4:32)
10 Shobal's son (Genesis 36:23)
14 A child of Gad (Numbers 26:15–16)
15 Not *these*
16 Tibetan monk
17 "From the villages of _____" (Nehemiah 12:28)
19 Enoch's son (Genesis 4:18)
20 "For one _____ of meat sold his birthright" (Hebrews 12:16)
21 Watchmen
23 "Go to the _____, thou sluggard" (Proverbs 6:6)
24 This woman worshiped at Cenchrea (Romans 16:1)
25 "There shall be no herd in the _____" (Habakkuk 3:17)
29 "His _____ drew the third part of the stars of heaven" (Revelation 12:4)
30 Abner's father (1 Samuel 26:5)
33 Lotan's child (Genesis 36:22)
34 "The _____ ears devoured the seven good ears" (Genesis 41:24)
35 Zibeon's daughter (Genesis 36:2)
36 He was with Zanoah and Engannim (Joshua 15:34)
37 "And the _____ pleased the king" (Esther 2:4)
38 Expression: "In the _____ and now"
39 Underground rodent
40 Corn grows on these
41 Deliberate pauses in music
42 "We _____ the clay, and thou our potter" (Isaiah 64:8)
43 Sailors' cry: "_____, ho!"
44 "Children of Mehida, the children of _____" (Ezra 2:52)
45 "Ye shall find _____, and it shall be opened unto you" (Luke 11:9)
47 Fluid from a plant
48 "The arrow that _____ by day" (Psalm 91:5)
50 "Diverse from all the _____" (Daniel 7:19)
54 Fee scale
55 "He evil _____ the barren" (Job 24:21)
59 Azariah's father (2 Chronicles 15:1)
60 "Plucked up by the _____" (Jude 1:12)
61 Solomon's grandson (Matthew 1:7)
62 Military meal
63 "What thou _____, write in a book" (Revelation 1:11)
64 "Paul stood in the midst of _____' hill" (Acts 17:22) (pl. poss.)

DOWN

1 Swallowed by a whale (abbr.)
2 "And at Bilhah, and at _____, and at Tolad" (1 Chronicles 4:29)
3 "I have stretched out my hands _____ thee" (Psalm 88:9)
4 "Hebron, and _____; nine cities" (Joshua 15:54)
5 Large Greek city
6 "Thou _____ love thy neighbour as thyself" (James 2:8)
7 "Can one go upon _____ coals. . . ?" (Proverbs 6:28)
8 A tree
9 Horse noises
10 Dathan and Abiram were his sons (Deuteronomy 11:6)
11 "A fruitful land into _____" (Psalm 107:34)
12 "Alammelech, and _____, and Misheal" (Joshua 19:26)
13 Boys
18 Biblical song
22 Married a foreign wife in exile (Ezra 10:34, 44)
24 "Having loosed the _____ of death" (Acts 2:24)
25 Raham's father (1 Chronicles 2:44)
26 Higher-pitched male voice
27 God told Saul to destroy these people (1 Samuel 15:6)

by N. Teri Grottke

28 "Blind man, or a _____, or he that hath a flat nose" (Leviticus 21:18)
29 "Joseph saw Ephraim's children of the _____ generation" (Genesis 50:23)
31 One of the two things God created in the beginning
32 Zorobabel's son (Luke 3:27)
34 Express gratitude
35 "Sons of _____" (1 Chronicles 7:12)
37 "Desiring to be _____ of the law" (1 Timothy 1:7)
41 Binea's son (1 Chronicles 8:37)
43 Abram's nephew (Genesis 11:27)
44 "Thou _____ the deeds of the Nicolaitanes" (Revelation 2:6)
46 "And he must _____ go through Samaria" (John 4:4)
47 "There came divers _____ of flies" (Psalm 105:31)

48 "He had rested _____ all his work" (Genesis 2:3)
49 "My father did _____ you with a heavy yoke" (1 Kings 12:11)
51 "Went to the top of the rock _____" (Judges 15:11)
52 Midian prince (Joshua 13:21)
53 Mix
56 Greek form of *Noah* (Matthew 24:38)
57 Digit connected to the foot
58 "Jacob _____ taken everything our father owned" (Genesis 31:1 NIV)

ACROSS

1 "And the sons of Jonathan; Peleth, and _____" (1 Chronicles 2:33)
5 "Praise the Lord from the earth, ye dragons, and all _____" (Psalm 148:7)
10 Pull, as a boat
13 "Having a _____, or scurvy" (Leviticus 22:22)
14 Shaphat's father (1 Chronicles 27:29)
15 Belonging to the priest who sat by a post (1 Samuel 1:9) (poss.)
17 Zerah's son (1 Chronicles 2:6)
18 Metal pegs
19 Not previously recorded
20 Weightlifters pump this
21 "Make for it a _____ of network of brass" (Exodus 27:4)
22 "High places also of _____" (Hosea 10:8)
23 "They shall _____ every strong hold" (Habakkuk 1:10)
25 Respectful address for a man
26 First place
27 Bezaleel's father (Exodus 31:2)
29 King Hezekiah's mother (2 Kings 18:1–2)
31 "Began to _____ him vehemently" (Luke 11:53)
34 Also
37 Father (Galatians 4:6)
40 He was born red and hairy (Genesis 25:25)
41 They put _____ the strange gods" (Judges 10:16)
43 "_____, against my sanctuary, when it was profaned" (Ezekiel 25:3)
45 Inheritor
46 Entrances to cities
48 Date tree
49 "_____ iron point weighed six hundred shekels" (1 Samuel 17:7 NIV)
50 "What _____ the Lord require of thee?" (Micah 6:8)
51 Daniel had a vision by this river (Daniel 8:2)
52 "City of Sepharvaim, _____, and Ivah" (Isaiah 37:13)

54 Time zone in Boston (abbr.)
56 "Brought the heads of _____ and Zeeb to Gideon" (Judges 7:25)
57 "But the _____ of their God was upon the elders" (Ezra 5:5)
59 Follows Nahum (abbr.)
61 "Some would even _____ to die" (Romans 5:7)
64 Fire residue
67 "_____, and Kirjathsannah, which is Debir" (Joshua 15:49)
72 Enoch's son (Genesis 4:18)
73 "You will never _____ to serve as woodcutters" (Joshua 9:23 NIV)
75 Lessen
76 "Having _____ persons in admiration" (Jude 1:16) (pl. poss.)
77 Ishmael's son (Genesis 25:13–15)
78 "Now the serpent was more subtil _____ any beast" (Genesis 3:1)

DOWN

2 Wary or watchful (arch.)
3 Bechorath's son (1 Samuel 9:1)
4 Elioenai's son (1 Chronicles 3:24)
5 "Thou fool, shall be in _____ of hell fire" (Matthew 5:22)
6 Where Israel spread his tent (Genesis 35:21)
7 Elijah in the New Testament (Matthew 11:14)
8 Raphu's son (Numbers 13:9)
9 Jael killed him (Judges 4:18–21)
10 "Came to them of the captivity at _____" (Ezekiel 3:15)
11 Canaan was "a land of _____ oil and honey" (Deuteronomy 8:8 NKJV)
12 Lamech had two _____, Adah and Zillah (Genesis 4:19)
16 Caused to go to a destination
17 "God _____ tempt Abraham" (Genesis 22:1)
24 Expected
28 Boot-shaped country (abbr.)
30 Color of a horse
31 "The tongue of the wise _____ knowledge aright" (Proverbs 15:2)
32 Elevate
33 "Going up to _____" (2 Kings 9:27)

by N. Teri Grottke

35 "Shalt perform unto the Lord thine _____" (Matthew 5:33)
36 "_____ no man any thing" (Romans 13:8)
38 "Were with him from _____ of Judah" (2 Samuel 6:2)
39 Asher didn't drive out the inhabitants of this town (Judges 1:31)
40 Benjamin's son (Genesis 46:21)
42 Common conjunction
44 Means "friend" (Fr.)
46 "_____ and take the little book which is open" (Revelation 10:8)
47 "I _____ no pleasant bread" (Daniel 10:3)
48 "Had cast _____, that is, the lot" (Esther 9:24)
50 "God called the light _____" (Genesis 1:5)
53 "Thou wouldest _____ be gone" (Genesis 31:30)
55 Ordinal suffix

56 Ahab called him (1 Kings 18:3) (abbr., var.)
58 Individually
60 Arad's brother (1 Chronicles 8:15)
61 Chinese food variety, a little at a time: _____ sum
62 "The small and great _____ there" (Job 3:19)
63 The prodigal's father _____ to meet him (Luke 15:20)
65 "Dominion over the fish of the _____" (Genesis 1:26)
66 "He _____ horns coming out" (Habakkuk 3:4)
68 Rope web
69 This Elkoshite had a vision (Nahum 1:1) (abbr.)
70 He destroyed his mother's idol (1 Kings 15:13)
71 Zephaniah's son (Zechariah 6:14)
75 Johannesburg is its capital (abbr.)

BIBLICAL MOUNTS

And seeing the multitudes, he went up into a mountain: and when he was set, his disciples came unto him.

MATTHEW 5:1

ACROSS

1 Where the Greeks got their groceries
6 Wrath
9 "Said, Then bring _____ " (2 Kings 4:41)
13 Evened up (var.)
14 "Our rafters of _____ " (Song of Solomon 1:17)
15 Spanish pot
16 **BIBLICAL MOUNT** (Genesis 31:21)
17 "As _____ these four" (Daniel 1:17)
18 Mr. Olds's cars of old
19 Confederate soldier, for short
20 "Out of the miry _____ " (Psalm 40:2)
22 **BIBLICAL MOUNT** (Zechariah 14:4)
24 "There was _____ wall parallel to" (Ezekiel 42:7 NIV) (2 words)
26 Malayan sailboat
27 Raiment for Rani
28 *Phi* follower
30 "Stretch forth _____ hand" (Mark 3:5)
34 "_____ been wronged!" (Job 19:7 NIV) (contr.)
36 Giants' Mel
38 "And they did so at the going up to _____ " (2 Kings 9:27)
39 "Which is the salt _____ " (Genesis 14:3)
42 **BIBLICAL MOUNT** (Joshua 17:15)
45 "Rows, six _____ row" (Leviticus 24:6) (2 words)
46 "The _____ is better" (Luke 5:39)
47 "Once cultivated by the _____ " (Isaiah 7:25 NIV)
48 Hole in one
50 "If she lose one _____ " (Luke 15:8)

53 Batter's stat (abbr.)
55 **BIBLICAL MOUNT** (Deuteronomy 32:49)
58 "And she took _____ " (2 Samuel 13:9) (2 words)
60 Regional tongue
63 **BIBLICAL MOUNT** (Genesis 8:4)
66 Part of FCC (abbr.)
67 Pipe joint
68 Residence hall, in short
69 "But I tell you _____ truth" (Luke 4:25) (2 words)
71 **BIBLICAL MOUNT** (Psalm 68:15 NIV)
73 "That they should believe_____ " (2 Thessalonians 2:11) (2 words)
74 Siesta
75 The East
76 "Will _____ their land" (2 Chronicles 7:14)
77 "Sir, come down _____ my child die" (John 4:49)
78 Juggler's tools

DOWN

1 "Our houses to _____ " (Lamentations 5:2)
2 **BIBLICAL MOUNT** (1 Samuel 31:1)
3 "The voice of _____ crying in the wilderness" (Matthew 3:3)
4 Tending to respond to a stimulus
5 Discombobulate
6 Doubtful (slang)
7 Spanish river
8 "The last _____ shall be worse than the first" (Matthew 27:64)
9 **BIBLICAL MOUNT** (2 Chronicles 3:1)
10 Altitude (abbr.)
11 Plant that produces a medicinal spice (see Song of Solomon 4:14)
12 Girl, on Skye

by N. Teri Grottke

13 Taj Mahal city
21 _____ de Triomphe
23 "And the _____ fell upon Jonah" (Jonah 1:7)
25 Bezaleel's father (Exodus 31:2)
26 Pocket bread
29 **BIBLICAL MOUNT** (Exodus 33:6)
31 "_____ a fishing" (John 21:3) (2 words)
32 Joshua's father (Exodus 33:11)
33 Historical period
35 Galatians follower (abbr.)
37 Pedro's aunt (Sp.)
39 "And after the _____" (John 13:27)
40 "Jesus cried with a loud voice, saying, _____" (Matthew 27:46)
41 Lemon or orange suffix
43 "For I will make thine _____ iron" (Micah 4:13)
44 Kennedy's defense secretary
49 Lamprey, for one
51 **BIBLICAL MOUNT** (1 Kings 18:19)

52 Government ecological group (abbr.)
54 "O Judah, what shall _____ unto thee?" (Hosea 6:4) (2 words)
56 **BIBLICAL MOUNT** (Joshua 16:1)
57 "When there were no _____, I was given birth" (Proverbs 8:24 NIV)
59 "Whom he slew _____ time" (2 Samuel 23:8) (2 words)
61 Mr. Hope's reply to, "Who are you?" (2 words)
62 "Enlarge the place of thy _____" (Isaiah 54:2)
63 One of Esau's three Canaanite wives (Genesis 36:2)
64 Play part
65 Diva's forte
66 Superhero's garb
70 "In that day shall the decree be _____ removed" (Micah 7:11)
72 Wycliffe organization (abbr.)

ACROSS

1 "Behold, they come up by the cliff of _____" (2 Chronicles 20:16)
4 Lard
7 Absalom's captain (2 Samuel 17:25)
12 Takes advantage of
14 Cain's victim
16 "When I came from _____, Rachel died by me" (Genesis 48:7)
17 "I will requite thee in this _____" (2 Kings 9:26)
18 An angel in the flame of the burning bush appeared here (Acts 7:30)
19 A Harodite guard of David's (2 Samuel 23:25)
20 Joseph's father (Luke 3:23)
21 "The children of Shephatiah, the children of _____" (Nehemiah 7:59)
23 Between Ezra and Esther (abbr.)
24 "Shimei, and _____, and the mighty men which belonged to David" (1 Kings 1:8)
26 "The sorrows of _____ compassed me about" (2 Samuel 22:6)
27 "The name of the town _____ been Beersheba" (Genesis 26:33 NIV)
30 "A _____ of cedar beams" (1 Kings 6:36)
32 What Dan was called before they captured it (Joshua 19:47)
37 "And they tarried until _____, and they did eat both of them" (Judges 19:8)
41 "Let him that _____ steal no more" (Ephesians 4:28)
42 "The gold of that land is _____" (Genesis 2:12 NIV)
43 Solemn
45 "Nevertheless _____ heart was perfect" (1 Kings 15:14) (poss.)
46 "The _____ cannot make him flee" (Job 41:28)
48 "The husbandman that _____ must be first partaker of the fruits" (2 Timothy 2:6)
50 "Ain, _____, and Ether, and Ashan; four cities and their villages" (Joshua 19:7)

52 "All that handle the _____. . . shall come down from their ships" (Ezekiel 27:29)
53 "Hath said against Jerusalem, ____" (Ezekiel 26:2)
54 Not easily found
57 "Abner. . .smote him under the fifth _____" (2 Samuel 2:23)
59 Received
62 Ziza's father (1 Chronicles 4:37)
64 "Deliver thy servant into the hand of _____" (1 Kings 18:9)
68 Hezron's wife (1 Chronicles 2:24)
70 A city of Hadarezer (1 Chronicles 18:8)
71 Sugar plant
72 Raphu's son (Numbers 13:9)
73 Suspend
74 "Tie the _____ to the cart" (1 Samuel 6:7)
75 "She made him _____ upon her knees" (Judges 16:19)
76 "All _____ utensils he made of bronze" (Exodus 38:3 NKJV)
77 Stood for election

DOWN

1 Tohu's father (1 Samuel 1:1)
2 "Be still, ye inhabitants of the _____" (Isaiah 23:2)
3 "Yea, what _____, yea, what revenge!" (2 Corinthians 7:11)
4 "All their goings out were both according to their ____" (Ezekiel 42:11)
5 Asa's father (Matthew 1:7)
6 "Abraham gave the _____ of the spoils" (Hebrews 7:4)
7 "Salute _____ approved in Christ" (Romans 16:10)
8 Follows Zechariah (abbr.)
9 There were 454 children of _____ (Ezra 2:15)
10 "Oh save me for thy mercies' _____" (Psalm 6:4)
11 Zibeon's son (Genesis 36:24)
13 Cause a ruckus or _____
15 "The Jews of _____ sought to stone thee" (John 11:8)
22 "Wherefore dealt ye so _____ with me. . . ?" (Genesis 43:6)

by N. Teri Grottke

25 "Do they not _____ that devise evil?" (Proverbs 14:22)
27 Ishmael's mother (Genesis 16:15)
28 "Which withereth _____ it groweth up" (Psalm 129:6)
29 "His way in the whirlwind and in the _____" (Nahum 1:3)
31 "I will put a fleece of _____ in the floor" (Judges 6:37)
33 "The day _____ arise in your hearts" (2 Peter 1:19)
34 Gomer's husband (Hosea 1:3)
35 "Way of the plain from _____" (Deuteronomy 2:8)
36 "Their dwelling was from _____" (Genesis 10:30)
38 "O daughter of _____, that dwellest in the land of Uz" (Lamentations 4:21)
39 Governor of Ahab's house (1 Kings 18:3) (abbr., var.)
40 "Men of the other _____" (Nehemiah 7:33)

44 "My _____ are poured out like the waters" (Job 3:24)
47 The act of adoration
49 "Shallum, and Telem, and _____" (Ezra 10:24)
51 Negative expression (slang)
55 Wealthy
56 This man was a Netophathite (Jeremiah 40:8)
58 Lot's wife looked this direction (Genesis 19:26)
59 Breaches
60 Joktan's son (Genesis 10:28–29)
61 "Thou also, son of man, take thee a _____" (Ezekiel 4:1)
63 "Wilt thou _____ the prey for the lion?" (Job 38:39)
65 Delilah cut Samson's
66 Temple prophetess in Jesus' time (Luke 2:36)
67 "Ye have _____ rebellious against the Lord" (Deuteronomy 31:27)
69 "They. . ._____ the sacrifices of the dead" (Psalm 106:28)

ACROSS

1 "Thy neck is like the _____ of David" (Song of Solomon 4:4)
6 Turn quickly
10 "All the hills shall ____" (Amos 9:13)
14 City in Naphtali (Joshua 19:32–33)
15 "He made the stars _____" (Genesis 1:16)
16 King Hoshea's father (2 Kings 15:30)
17 "Daughter of Pharaoh, which _____ took" (1 Chronicles 4:18)
18 "My skin is broken, and become _____" (Job 7:5)
20 Mushi's son (1 Chronicles 23:23)
21 Ground moisture
22 Shemidah's son (1 Chronicles 7:19)
23 The first father
25 Arabian city (see Job 6:19)
27 "Lift up thy voice, O daughter of _____" (Isaiah 10:30)
30 Shoham's brother (1 Chronicles 24:27)
31 Course of study or a meeting (abbr.)
34 "And he _____ with him the space of a month" (Genesis 29:14)
35 "The son of _____, in Makaz" (1 Kings 4:9)
36 "Between Bethel and _____" (Genesis 13:3)
37 Head covers
38 "For every high priest _____ from among men" (Hebrews 5:1)
39 To fasten by girth (arch.)
40 Quiet _____ mouse (2 words)
41 "No mention shall be made of _____" (Job 28:18)
42 Measurement of barley (Hosea 3:2)
43 Mighty _____ served David
44 Distance from one end of an object to the other (abbr.)
45 "Take this, and _____ it among yourselves" (Luke 22:17)
46 Throw gently
47 "That we _____ not those things" (2 John 1:8)
48 Aaron's son (Exodus 6:23)

51 This is by Ibleam (2 Kings 9:27)
52 "In _____ was there a voice" (Matthew 2:18)
56 "Took counsel with the _____ against him" (Mark 3:6)
59 "Fathers, provoke not your children to _____" (Colossians 3:21)
60 "_____ for the day" (Joel 1:15)
61 "The young man _____ kept the watch" (2 Samuel 13:34)
62 To tally
63 "Her mother in law _____ her" (Ruth 3:6)
64 "Put them under _____, and under harrows of iron" (2 Samuel 12:31)
65 "_____ whose fruit withereth" (Jude 1:12)

DOWN

1 Not wild
2 Azariah's father (2 Chronicles 15:1)
3 "They were _____ of it, and fled" (Acts 14:6)
4 Green gems
5 To free
6 Peace (Hebrews 7:2)
7 Till
8 Follows Song of Solomon (abbr.)
9 Mary was told by the angel to be _____ afraid (Luke 1:30)
10 "Dwelling was from _____" (Genesis 10:30)
11 "_____, lama sabachthani" (Mark 15:34)
12 Tibetan monk
13 "See _____ that ye walk circumspectly" (Ephesians 5:15)
19 Shechem's father (Genesis 33:19)
21 "His _____; on the eighth day" (Exodus 22:30)
24 Elijah did not _____ but was taken up in a whirlwind (2 Kings 2:11)
25 "Thou art weighed in the balances, and art found wanting" (Daniel 5:27)
26 Ahira's father (Numbers 7:78)

by N. Teri Grottke

27 Reumah's child (Genesis 22:24)
28 To humble
29 Seir's son (Genesis 36:20)
30 "_____ for every man, that is, half a shekel, after the shekel of the sanctuary" (Exodus 38:26)
31 Gershon's son (Exodus 6:17)
32 "Which is neither _____ nor sown" (Deuteronomy 21:4)
33 "Let them set a fair _____ upon his head" (Zechariah 3:5)
35 "Quench all the fiery _____ of the wicked" (Ephesians 6:16)
38 Clothing
39 "Zerubbabel the son of Shealtiel, _____ of Judah" (Haggai 1:1)
41 Jesus was received into this (Acts 1:9)
42 Opposite of *hers*
45 "Borders of _____ on the west" (Joshua 11:2)
46 "There were giants in the earth in _____ days" (Genesis 6:4)
47 Selfish desires

48 He did evil in the Lord's view above all who had come before (1 Kings 16:30)
49 Another name for Zoar (Genesis 14:2)
50 Enoch's son (Genesis 4:18)
51 Chew a bone
53 "Burning _____, that shall consume the eyes" (Leviticus 26:16)
54 Part of the handwriting on the wall (Daniel 5:25)
55 "Used curious _____ brought their books together" (Acts 19:19)
57 "A ram was caught in a thicket by _____ horns" (Genesis 22:13 NKJV)
58 "Against Jerusalem, _____" (Ezekiel 26:2)
59 Take action

ACROSS

1 "And if thy _____ offend thee, cut it off" (Mark 9:45)
5 "Sharper than any twoedged _____" (Hebrews 4:12)
10 "And they filled them up to the _____" (John 2:7)
14 "Unto your brethren, _____; and to your sisters" (Hosea 2:1)
15 "_____, and Hara, and to the river Gozan" (1 Chronicles 5:26)
16 Relieve
17 "_____; God hath numbered thy kingdom, and finished it" (Daniel 5:26)
18 "I have bought all that was _____" (Ruth 4:9) (poss.)
20 A son of Gad (Genesis 46:16)
21 Topple
22 "And he said, Hagar, _____ maid, whence camest thou" (Genesis 16:8) (poss.)
23 "Your own _____ have said, For we are also his offspring" (Acts 17:28)
25 Largest continent
26 A porter with Obededom (1 Chronicles 16:38)
27 Ishi's son (1 Chronicles 2:31)
30 "Cast ye the unprofitable servant into _____ darkness" (Matthew 25:30)
31 "For what _____ the scripture" (Romans 4:3)
32 Fits in a horse's mouth
34 Not enslaved
35 He was from Mount Ephraim (Judges 17:1)
36 Smelling function
37 Cooling device
38 Ashur's wife, the father of Tekoa (1 Chronicles 4:5)
39 Eliphaz's son (Genesis 36:11)
40 Aaron's son (Exodus 6:23)
42 "Until they had destroyed _____ king of Canaan" (Judges 4:24)
43 Naum's son (Luke 3:25)
44 "Dwelt at Lydda and _____" (Acts 9:35)
45 "I have not hastened from being a _____ to follow thee" (Jeremiah 17:16)
48 Opposite of *despair*
49 Cured hunger
52 "According to his inheritance which he _____" (Numbers 35:8)
54 Naomi's son (Ruth 4:17)
55 Destitute
56 Sheshan's child (1 Chronicles 2:31)
57 Banner
58 Opposite of *begins*
59 A seller of purple (Acts 16:14)
60 "Herod was highly displeased with them of _____ and Sidon" (Acts 12:20)

DOWN

1 Renown
2 One-tenth of an ephah (Exodus 16:36)
3 Almighty
4 Bind
5 "Put up thy sword into the _____" (John 18:11)
6 "By faith the _____ of Jericho fell down" (Hebrews 11:30)
7 Ishmaelite camel driver (1 Chronicles 27:30)
8 Male gypsy
9 "When he _____ the lamps, he shall burn incense upon it" (Exodus 30:7)
10 "_____ his son" (1 Chronicles 5:6)
11 "Whosoever shall say to his brother, _____, shall be in danger of the council" (Matthew 5:22)
12 Rephaiah's father (1 Chronicles 4:42)
13 Hall of military meals
19 Phalti's father (1 Samuel 25:44)
21 "God hath not given us the spirit of _____" (2 Timothy 1:7)
24 Lyric: "_____ say can you _____"
25 Ahitub's son (1 Samuel 14:3)
26 "_____ of the brooks of Gaash" (1 Chronicles 11:32)

by N. Teri Grottke

27 Ahiam's father (1 Chronicles 11:35)
28 "He did very _____ in following idols" (1 Kings 21:26)
29 The first Hebrew month (Esther 3:7)
30 Cut the power
31 Paul's missionary partner (Acts 15:40)
33 "Hundred and _____ years old" (Joshua 24:29)
35 "Thine alms are come up for a _____ before God" (Acts 10:4)
36 "The men of the other _____" (Nehemiah 7:33)
38 Shechem's father (Genesis 33:19)
39 "The king arose, and _____ his garments" (2 Samuel 13:31)
41 "Backbiters, _____ of God" (Romans 1:30)
42 King of Lachish (Joshua 10:3)

44 "The children of _____" (Nehemiah 7:57)
45 "Without life giving sound, whether _____ or harp" (1 Corinthians 14:7)
46 "_____ they tell him of her" (Mark 1:30)
47 "And your feet _____ with the preparation of the gospel of peace" (Ephesians 6:15)
48 Gripped
50 To well up emotionally
51 Precipice
53 "So shall _____ seed be" (Romans 4:18)
54 "How _____ is the candle of the wicked put out" (Job 21:17)

TO SEE OR NOT TO SEE. . .

*Now faith is the substance of things hoped for,
the evidence of things not seen.*

HEBREWS 11:1

ACROSS

1 "The heart of _____ was perfect all his days" (2 Chronicles 15:17)
4 Tibetan priests
9 Overindulgence
14 "Whither the men went I _____ not" (Joshua 2:5)
15 "The LORD smelled the pleasing _____" (Genesis 8:21 NIV)
16 One way to fish
17 Beginning of **QUOTE** from 2 Corinthians 4:18 NIV (5 words)
20 Disinter
21 "Yea, there is no God; I know not _____" (Isaiah 44:8)
22 "But ye are forgers of _____" (Job 13:4)
23 Director Preminger
25 "Or if the _____ flesh turn again" (Leviticus 13:16)
28 "For the soil nor for the _____ pile" (Luke 14:35 NIV)
31 "In _____ was there a voice heard" (Matthew 2:18)
32 **QUOTE**, cont.
36 "Simon, son of _____" (John 21:15)
37 "And _____ out of the flock" (Ezekiel 45:15) (2 words)
38 Leaf pores
40 Crusoe's domain
41 **QUOTE**, cont. (3 words)
43 Bass brass
44 "Now learn this _____ from the fig tree" (Matthew 24:32 NIV)
45 "And made the _____ dry land" (Exodus 14:21)
46 "And they _____ a calf in those days" (Acts 7:41)
47 West African nation
51 "Behold, I make all things _____" (Revelation 21:5)
52 Uses a towel again

55 End of **QUOTE** (3 words)
60 "And the screech owl will _____ on her columns" (Zephaniah 2:14 NIV)
61 "His _____ shall fall backward" (Genesis 49:17)
62 "How long will it be _____ thou be quiet" (Jeremiah 47:6)
63 "_____ busybody in other men's" (1 Peter 4:15) (3 words)
64 "When God _____ to judgment" (Psalm 76:9)
65 "_____ God said" (Genesis 1:3)

DOWN

1 "How _____ that day will be" (Jeremiah 30:7 NIV)
2 "_____ will return to fight against" (Daniel 10:20 NIV) (2 words)
3 "Cursed is every one that hangeth on _____" (Galatians 3:13) (2 words)
4 Cowardly Lion Bert
5 "Smells _____": is suspicious (2 words)
6 "The _____ shall eat them up" (Isaiah 50:9)
7 "Here _____; send me" (Isaiah 6:8) (2 words)
8 Carrier to Oslo
9 Dictation taker, in short
10 "We took for a _____ to ourselves" (Deuteronomy 3:7)
11 Former White House nickname
12 Means "My God" (Matthew 27:46)
13 Pro golfer Ernie
18 "And the Word ____ God" (John 1:1)
19 Satisfy fully
23 "Even _____ own God" (Psalm 67:6)

by David K. Shortess

24 Secret meetings between lovers
25 "And _____ flood stage as before" (Joshua 4:18 NIV) (2 words)
26 Stradivari's teacher
27 "I _____ a beast" (Psalm 73:22) (2 words)
28 Castle protection
29 "And to whom hath the _____ of the Lord" (John 12:38)
30 Snatched
31 Salad tomato
32 "Love does no harm _____ neighbor" (Romans 13:10 NIV) (2 words)
33 "Let him seek peace, and _____ it" (1 Peter 3:11)
34 Word with peach or toast
35 "Hear now my argument; listen to the _____ of my lips" (Job 13:6 NIV)
36 A son of Zebedee (Matthew 4:21)
39 Number of Lot's daughters (Genesis 19:15)
42 "That _____ their tongues, and

say" (Jeremiah 23:31)
44 Yard
46 "Let a bear robbed of her whelps _____ man" (Proverbs 17:12) (2 words)
47 Defunct Soviet space station
48 Temporary asphyxia
49 "_____ to do well" (Isaiah 1:17)
50 "Whoever _____ astray by them" (Proverbs 20:1 NIV) (2 words)
51 Famous monster loch
52 Perform again
53 Seine summers (Fr.)
54 "All things _____ made by him" (John 1:3)
55 Comb. form for *tail*
56 "_____ thy fathers' fathers have seen" (Exodus 10:6)
57 "_____ fire was kindled against Jacob" (Psalm 78:21) (2 words)
58 A son of Ikkesh (1 Chronicles 27:9)
59 "And I said unto him, _____, thou knowest" (Revelation 7:14)

ACROSS

1 Jump
5 An Ahohite (1 Chronicles 11:29)
9 Short subject study (abbr.)
12 Jehiel's son (1 Chronicles 9:35–37)
13 "As he that lieth upon the top of a
   _____" (Proverbs 23:34)
14 To glisten
16 "Cast it into the great _____ of
   the wrath of God"
   (Revelation 14:19)
18 Troublesome plants
19 "And his _____ drew the third
   part" (Revelation 12:4)
20 "_____ of the tree were for the
   healing of the nations"
   (Revelation 22:2)
21 "My people hath been _____
   sheep" (Jeremiah 50:6)
23 "One that _____ God with all his
   house" (Acts 10:2)
24 Like jelly
25 "They are white already to
   _____" (John 4:35)
29 The _____ and only
30 Set of steps
31 Belonging to cotton gin inventor
   (poss.)
35 Salathiel's father (Luke 3:27)
37 Disfigure
38 Uncontrolled anger
39 "Sitting on an _____ colt"
   (John 12:15) (poss.)
40 "Hallohesh, _____, Shobek"
   (Nehemiah 10:24)
43 Zephaniah's son (Zechariah 6:14)
44 "Seven thin ears and _____with
   the east wind" (Genesis 41:6)
45 Rabid
46 Shobal's son (1 Chronicles 2:52)
49 Body armor
51 Family of exiles
   (Nehemiah 7:6, 48)
52 Rachel's sister (Genesis 29:16)
54 Get up
55 Asa's maternal grandfather
   (1 Kings 15:10)
60 A palace was located in this
   province (Ezra 6:2)
61 Abysmal
62 "The _____ lying in a manger"
   (Luke 2:16)
63 Book of songs (abbr., var.)
64 Will not take responsibility
65 Breadth

DOWN

1 "Sin is the transgression of the
   _____" (1 John 3:4)
2 Benjamin's son (Genesis 46:21)
3 Riblah was on its east side
   (Numbers 34:11)
4 Angelou, Plath, and Sandburg,
   for example
5 Zaccur's father (Nehemiah 3:2)
6 Eliasaph's father (Numbers 3:24)
7 Donkey
8 "The earth opened _____ mouth
   and swallowed them"
   (Numbers 26:10 NIV)
9 Strainer
10 "The boundary _____ at the sea"
   (Joshua 15:11 NIV)
11 Military meal
14 "His _____ was as it were great
   drops of blood" (Luke 22:44)
15 "_____, O Israel: the LORD our
   God is one LORD"
   (Deuteronomy 6:4)
17 Trails
20 Opposite of *more*
21 "Streets and _____ of the city"
   (Luke 14:21)
22 Manna was measured this way
   (Exodus 16:32)
23 Unclean animal to eat
   (Leviticus 11:30)
24 Simon Peter's father (John 1:42)
26 "For the goodman is not _____
   home" (Proverbs 7:19)
27 Parosh's son (Ezra 10:25)
28 Prayers of the saints are in these
   (Revelation 5:8)
31 Judah's firstborn (Genesis 38:6)
32 Goliath's brother
   (1 Chronicles 20:5)
33 Hattush's brother
   (1 Chronicles 3:22)

by N. Teri Grottke

34 "I will even _____ a curse upon you" (Malachi 2:2)
36 "Mine hour _____ not yet come" (John 2:4)
40 Answer to a charge
41 "_____ which soweth bountifully shall reap also bountifully" (2 Corinthians 9:6)
42 "Shall I make thee as _____" (Hosea 11:8)
44 "Rottenness entered into my _____" (Habakkuk 3:16)
46 "Amorites would dwell in mount _____" (Judges 1:35)
47 "Henoch, and _____, and Eldaah" (1 Chronicles 1:33)
48 "Who said, _____ it" (Psalm 137:7)
50 Belonging to the one in whose name letters were written (1 Kings 21:8) (poss.)

51 "Thy word is a _____ unto my feet" (Psalm 119:105)
52 "Though ye have _____ among the pots" (Psalm 68:13)
53 "Sent me from Kadeshbarnea to _____ out the land" (Joshua 14:7)
55 Increase
56 Buzzing stinger
57 Child's favorite seat
58 Follows the book of Amos (abbr.)
59 "_____ began to multiply" (Genesis 6:1)

ACROSS

1 "If any of you lack _____, let him ask of God" (James 1:5)
7 Benjamin's son (Genesis 46:21)
11 "Two cheeks, and the _____" (Deuteronomy 18:3)
14 Clothing
15 Rehoboam's son (1 Chronicles 3:10)
16 "Helez the Paltite, _____" (2 Samuel 23:26)
17 Lyric: "My Country 'Tis of _____"
18 Sorrow
20 "In the borders of _____ on the west" (Joshua 11:2)
21 Small wagon
22 "_____ shall see God" (Matthew 5:8)
23 Watched secretly
25 Liquid measure (Leviticus 23:13)
26 "In vain shalt thou _____ many medicines" (Jeremiah 46:11)
27 "Of the oaks of Bashan have they made thine _____" (Ezekiel 27:6)
28 "And Simon Peter stood and _____ himself" (John 18:25)
31 Gained the victory in a contest
32 "Thou art John the Baptist: some, Elias; and others, _____" (Matthew 16:14)
35 Seir's nationality (Genesis 36:20)
38 Splits wood (var.)
39 King Hezekiah's mother (2 Kings 18:1–2)
40 "We trust in the Lord _____ God" (2 Kings 18:22)
41 "Dip the _____ of his finger in water" (Luke 16:24)
42 "And Mordecai walked every day before the court of the _____ house" (Esther 2:11) (pl. poss.)
44 "The wicked flee when no man _____" (Proverbs 28:1)
46 Jether's son (1 Chronicles 7:38)
47 "Doeth not any of those _____, but even hath eaten" (Ezekiel 18:11)
48 Micaiah's father (2 Chronicles 18:7)
50 To make a mistake

51 "Fourth part of a _____ of dove's dung" (2 Kings 6:25)
54 A very holy person
56 "I will _____ thee out of my mouth" (Revelation 3:16)
58 "Syrians of Bethrehob, and the Syrians of _____" (2 Samuel 10:6)
59 Test for prostate cancer (abbr.)
60 "Leeks, and the _____, and the garlick" (Numbers 11:5)
62 Duke of Edom (Genesis 36:43)
63 Tree
64 "Let us kill him, and the inheritance shall be _____" (Mark 12:7)
65 Nethinim children (Nehemiah 7:46, 48)
67 "The LORD _____ seen my misery" (Genesis 29:32 NIV)
68 "Every _____ should bow" (Philippians 2:10)
69 "Shimron, and _____, and Bethlehem: twelve cities" (Joshua 19:15)

DOWN

1 "For they _____ for your souls" (Hebrews 13:17)
2 Ribai's son (1 Chronicles 11:31)
3 "They cast four anchors out of the _____, and wished for the day" (Acts 27:29)
4 "There was a continual _____ given him of the king of Babylon" (Jeremiah 52:34)
5 Surgical suite (abbr.)
6 "All the inhabitants of Canaan shall _____ away" (Exodus 15:15)
7 "And the children of Israel removed from _____" (Numbers 33:5)
8 "But they have not all _____ the gospel" (Romans 10:16)
9 This was the cause for OT sacrifice
10 Head covers
11 Moses' father-in-law was one (Numbers 10:29)
12 These cities are forsaken (Isaiah 17:2)

by N. Teri Grottke

13 "Appointed the _____ of the priests and the Levites" (Nehemiah 13:30)
19 Lahad's brother (1 Chronicles 4:2)
24 Destitute
28 "Wilt thou that _____ command" (Luke 9:54)
29 "Look from the top of _____" (Song of Solomon 4:8)
30 Eve's beginning
31 "Is _____ than an infidel" (1 Timothy 5:8)
32 "Bore his _____ through with a thorn" (Job 41:2)
33 Contains the story of the flight from Egypt (abbr., var.)
34 "Head of Samaria is _____ son" (Isaiah 7:9) (poss.)
35 Jaroah's son (1 Chronicles 5:14)
36 Small, plump, long-tailed bird
37 Follows Galatians (abbr.)
40 "So they ran both together: and the other disciple did _____ Peter" (John 20:4)

43 "Shuthelah: of _____" (Numbers 26:36)
44 "According to the eternal _____" (Ephesians 3:11)
45 "Woe unto _____!" (1 Samuel 4:8)
47 "As newborn babes, _____ the sincere milk of the word" (1 Peter 2:2)
48 Beriah's son (1 Chronicles 8:16)
49 Ishmael's son (Genesis 25:13–14)
51 This was sold in the fairs (Ezekiel 27:16)
52 River of Damascus (2 Kings 5:12)
53 "Called _____ unto this day" (Ezekiel 20:29)
55 "_____ upon him the form of a servant" (Philippians 2:7)
57 Naum's father (Luke 3:25)
58 A servant of Saul (2 Samuel 9:2)
61 Joshua's father (Numbers 11:28)
66 The altar in Joshua 22:34

## 60

ACROSS

1 The skin of an animal
5 "_____, and Ivah" (Isaiah 37:13)
9 Eliphaz's son (Genesis 36:11)
14 The "sin of Israel" (Hosea 10:8)
15 Azariah's father (2 Chronicles 15:1)
16 Enan's son (Numbers 1:15)
17 Real property
18 "Wherefore _____ up the loins of your mind" (1 Peter 1:13)
19 _____ "without blemish" were given in OT sacrifice (Leviticus 14:10)
20 "Love thy neighbour as _____" (James 2:8)
22 "And at Enrimmon, and at _____, and at Jarmuth" (Nehemiah 11:29)
23 Put down
24 "Land from _____ to the wilderness" (Isaiah 16:1)
25 "The children of _____, an hundred and twelve" (Nehemiah 7:24)
29 "_____ altar of Baal was cast down" (Judges 6:28)
30 Type of Mass
34 River of Damascus (2 Kings 5:12)
35 "I commend unto you _____ our sister" (Romans 16:1)
37 Along with
38 Bread from heaven
39 Jether's son (1 Chronicles 7:38)
40 "Purge the _____ and purify it" (Ezekiel 43:26)
42 Question
43 "This shall be the law of the _____ in the day of his cleansing" (Leviticus 14:2)
45 "They shall lament for the _____" (Isaiah 32:12)
46 Those with young away have an empty _____
48 Hymn lyric: "While the _____ is still on the roses"
49 "Woe to them that _____ iniquity" (Micah 2:1)
50 Eshcol's brother (Genesis 14:13)
52 Aaron died on this mountain (Numbers 33:38)
53 "For thy name's sake, O LORD, _____ mine iniquity; for it is great" (Psalm 25:11)
56 Bleak
61 City in Naphtali (Joshua 19:33)
62 Coz's son (1 Chronicles 4:8)
64 "For in the month _____ thou camest out from Egypt" (Exodus 34:18)
65 "Next day we arrived at _____" (Acts 20:15)
66 "Wilt thou _____ the prey for the lion" (Job 38:39)
67 Darius was one (Daniel 11:1)
68 Allotment
69 Lifts up to 20 times its weight
70 Mushi's son (1 Chronicles 23:23)

DOWN

1 Command to stop
2 "City of Sepharvaim, of Hena, and _____" (2 Kings 19:13)
3 Refute
4 "All the _____ of the world shall remember" (Psalm 22:27)
5 Zelophehad's daughter (Numbers 26:33)
6 "All things are lawful for me, but all things _____ not" (1 Corinthians 10:23)
7 Abner's father (1 Chronicles 26:28)
8 Increase
9 Jeduthun's son (1 Chronicles 9:16)
10 Benjamin's third son (1 Chronicles 8:1)
11 "And in process of _____ it came to pass" (Genesis 4:3)
12 Anak's father (Joshua 15:13)
13 1970s military hospital show
21 Hushim's son (1 Chronicles 8:11)
22 A prince of the Midianites (Judges 7:25)
24 "And Laban went to _____ his sheep" (Genesis 31:19)
25 Mordecai's enemy (Esther 3:6)
26 To humble
27 Membership
28 The good Samaritan went to this lodging (Luke 10:33–34 NIV)

by N. Teri Grottke

29 "She _____ in two mites, which make a farthing" (Mark 12:42)
31 Ribai's son (2 Samuel 23:29)
32 "Neither by the blood of _____ and calves" (Hebrews 9:12)
33 Steed
35 "I would not write with _____ and ink" (2 John 1:12)
36 Those who consume
41 Eating restrictions are found in this book (abbr.)
44 "A river went out of _____ to water the garden" (Genesis 2:10)
47 Solomon built this city in the wilderness (2 Chronicles 8:4)
49 "I have heard of thee, that thou canst make interpretations, and dissolve _____" (Daniel 5:16)
51 "The _____ of a whip" (Nahum 3:2)
52 "David himself and his men were wont to _____" (1 Samuel 30:31)

53 "Heavens shall _____ away with a great noise" (2 Peter 3:10)
54 Jabal's mother (Genesis 4:20)
55 "In _____ was there a voice" (Matthew 2:18)
57 "The tongue can no man _____" (James 3:8)
58 Gaal's father (Judges 9:26)
59 Travel other than on foot
60 Salah's son (Genesis 10:24)
62 "Against Jerusalem, _____, she is broken" (Ezekiel 26:2)
63 Joshua's father (Exodus 33:11)

SCRIPTURAL ILLUMINATION

But if a man walk in the night,
he stumbleth, because there is no light in him.

JOHN 11:10

ACROSS

1 "And did _____ upon him" (Mark 15:19)
5 "That ye _____ me hither" (Genesis 45:5)
9 "They look and _____ upon me" (Psalm 22:17)
14 Healing plant
15 "Lest he _____ my soul like a lion" (Psalm 7:2)
16 "And the _____ of this world" (Mark 4:19)
17 Start of **VERSE** from Psalm 119:105 NIV (5 words)
20 "I will attack them and _____ them open" (Hosea 13:8 NIV)
21 "In the ____ of Siddim" (Genesis 14:8)
22 "And the _____ after her kind" (Leviticus 11:19)
25 "The _____ is wasted, the land mourneth" (Joel 1:10)
27 Father of Cush (1 Chronicles 1:8)
30 "And it shall stand for _____" (Daniel 2:44)
31 Unit of petrol
32 "He who _____ wise son delights in him" (Proverbs 23:24 NIV) (2 words)
33 "In him _____ life" (John 1:4)
34 Cultivator
35 "If I make my _____ hell" (Psalm 139:8) (2 words)
36 **VERSE**, cont. (4 words)
40 "And Jacob shall break his _____" (Hosea 10:11)
42 "Or the price of _____" (Deuteronomy 23:18) (2 words)
43 "And he said, _____" (Judges 13:11) (2 words)
46 "Shave her head, and _____ her nails" (Deuteronomy 21:12)
47 Emblem of honor
49 Folk singer Seeger

50 "_____ hospitality one to" (1 Peter 4:9)
51 "They, _____ also, die" (Numbers 18:3) (2 words)
52 "And he was _____ that saying" (Mark 10:22) (2 words)
53 "Was the son of _____" (Luke 3:35)
54 After-hours money source (abbr.)
55 End of **VERSE** (5 words)
63 Central African language group
64 "That they should believe _____" (2 Thessalonians 2:11) (2 words)
65 "The ants _____ people not" (Proverbs 30:25) (2 words)
66 Convulsion
67 Alabama neighbor (abbr.)
68 "If my _____ hath turned" (Job 31:7)

DOWN

1 "What shall we _____ then" (Romans 6:1)
2 Organization of 48 Down (abbr.)
3 Chit letters (abbr.)
4 "Be not a _____ unto me" (Jeremiah 17:17)
5 "And _____ all wells of water" (2 Kings 3:19)
6 Above, to Keats
7 "Lay not thine hand upon the _____" (Genesis 22:12)
8 "The crying of the _____" (Job 39:7)
9 Burn with hot water
10 "As a _____ that is told" (Psalm 90:9)
11 Jether's son (1 Chronicles 7:38)
12 Type of sleep (abbr.)
13 Sixth sense (abbr.)
18 "That I may _____ Christ" (Philippians 3:8)
19 "Of the _____ of his patrimony" (Deuteronomy 18:8)

by David K. Shortess

22 "_____ ye down trees" (Jeremiah 6:6)
23 Braun or Perón
24 "And ____ all things" (Matthew 17:11)
25 Feudal land fee
26 "He hath bent his bow, and made _____" (Psalm 7:12) (2 words)
27 "All we _____ this day" (2 Samuel 19:6) (2 words)
28 "As truly _____ live" (Numbers 14:28) (2 words)
29 "What is _____, that thou" (Psalm 8:4)
31 Actress Myrna
32 Zephaniah's son (Zechariah 6:14)
34 USS in Britain
35 "Judas had the _____" (John 13:29)
37 Pindar product
38 "Smite them with the _____ of the sword" (Jeremiah 21:7)
39 "And upon the great _____ of his right foot" (Leviticus 14:14)
40 Computer "brain" (abbr.)
41 _____ Vegas, Nevada

44 "Strain _____ gnat" (Matthew 23:24) (2 words)
45 "And God _____ Balaam" (Numbers 23:4)
47 "And _____ the door after her" (2 Samuel 13:17)
48 Yasir of the Middle East
49 Grassy South American plains
51 Micah follower
52 Filthy place
53 NCOs over corporals (abbr.)
54 "And all the people shall answer and say, _____" (Deuteronomy 27:15)
55 Kin to Fahrenheit or Celsius (abbr.)
56 "The lot is cast into the _____" (Proverbs 16:33)
57 "_____ way not cast up" (Jeremiah 18:15) (2 words)
58 Cheer in the ring
59 _____ Tin Tin
60 "Behold, thou _____ with child" (Genesis 16:11)
61 Golf item
62 "And her _____ was to" (Ruth 2:3)

ACROSS

1 A cooking direction
5 Peace (Hebrews 7:2)
10 "The poison of _____ is under their lips" (Romans 3:13 NASB)
14 To reduce or diminish
15 Commerce
16 "Lamb to the ruler of the land from _____" (Isaiah 16:1)
17 Sheresh's son (1 Chronicles 7:16)
18 City of Benjamin (Joshua 18:21, 25)
19 "Wizards that _____, and that mutter" (Isaiah 8:19)
20 Cosam's father (Luke 3:28)
22 "And to your sisters, _____" (Hosea 2:1)
24 Oath
25 Tangled mess
26 Cut off
30 "Is not this written in the book of _____" (Joshua 10:13)
33 "Of _____, the family" (Numbers 26:17)
34 "And upon _____, and upon Nebo" (Jeremiah 48:22)
36 Coz's son (1 Chronicles 4:8)
38 Bela's son (1 Chronicles 7:7)
39 Joshua's father (Numbers 14:6)
40 "Keros, the children of _____" (Nehemiah 7:47)
41 Make secure
43 "Eldad and _____ do prophesy in the camp" (Numbers 11:27)
45 Sister of a parent
46 "And the earth was _____" (Revelation 14:16)
48 "Even so we also should walk in _____ of life" (Romans 6:4)
50 Owed
51 Place
52 "And the fenced cities are Ziddim, Zer, and _____" (Joshua 19:35)
56 "Had severed himself from the _____" (Judges 4:11)
60 Palal's father (Nehemiah 3:25)
61 "Out of the _____ came something to eat" (Judges 14:14 NASB)

63 "Make thee bald, and _____ thee for thy delicate children" (Micah 1:16)
64 Entrance
65 "Many bodies of the saints which _____ arose" (Matthew 27:52)
66 Likewise
67 David hid by this stone (1 Samuel 20:18–19)
68 "I saw the _____ of Cushan in affliction" (Habakkuk 3:7)
69 Killed

DOWN

1 "_____ thee out of my mouth" (Revelation 3:16)
2 Having great height
3 A duke of Edom (Genesis 36:43)
4 Taken away
5 "Others cut down branches off the trees, and _____ them in the way" (Mark 11:8)
6 Shem's son (Genesis 10:22)
7 Book describing the fall of Jerusalem (abbr.)
8 Biblical tower (Genesis 35:21)
9 A chamberlain of King Ahasuerus (Esther 1:10)
10 A son of Haman (Esther 9:7, 10)
11 "They shall _____ like torches" (Nahum 2:4)
12 Comes before the verdict
13 A giant (2 Samuel 21:18)
21 "Borders of _____ on the west" (Joshua 11:2)
23 "'God _____ come into the camp!'" (1 Samuel 4:7 NKJV)
26 "God hath given thee all them that _____ with thee" (Acts 27:24)
27 "Smote him there for his _____" (2 Samuel 6:7)
28 "With the _____ of the archangel" (1 Thessalonians 4:16)
29 Feasted fancily
30 Eliakim's son (Luke 3:30)
31 "Let him seek peace, and _____ it" (1 Peter 3:11)

by N. Teri Grottke

32 "I will raise up his _____,
   and I will build it as in the days
   of old" (Amos 9:11)
35 "The pomegranates _____ forth"
   (Song of Solomon 7:12)
37 Winged mammals
42 A Levite on the stairs
   (Nehemiah 9:4)
43 "Look even out the best and
   _____ of your master's sons"
   (2 Kings 10:3)
44 Places of very little rain
45 "_____ was my faithful martyr"
   (Revelation 2:13)
47 Issachar's son (Numbers 26:23)
49 "Having a _____, or scurvy, or
   scabbed" (Leviticus 22:22)
52 Very large
53 Bela's father (1 Chronicles 5:8)
54 Spouse
55 "Lest he _____ thee to the judge"
   (Luke 12:58)

56 Retained
57 "It shall not be lawful to impose
   _____" (Ezra 7:24)
58 Otherwise
59 A lumbering pace
62 The greater number of tribes split
   after Solomon's reign

ACROSS

1 Zophah's son (1 Chronicles 7:36)
6 Pashur's father (Jeremiah 20:1)
11 "_____ is God, save the Lord?" (2 Samuel 22:32)
14 Elevate
15 "Land whereon thou _____, to thee will I give it" (Genesis 28:13)
16 "Her _____ was to light" (Ruth 2:3)
17 "These were they which went up from Telmelah, Telharsa, Cherub, _____" (Ezra 2:59)
18 Shamgar's father (Judges 3:31)
19 Follows Lamentations (abbr., var.)
20 Jehu's great-grandfather (1 Chronicles 4:35)
22 "The _____ did swim" (2 Kings 6:6)
23 Out of the sun
26 "He lodgeth with one Simon a _____" (Acts 10:6)
29 Ashur's son (1 Chronicles 4:5–6)
30 Belonging to Judas Iscariot's father (John 13:26) (poss.)
31 Titled
32 Eliphaz's son (Genesis 36:11)
33 Brand of insect repellent
36 Thummim's partner (Exodus 28:30)
37 "And we went over the brook _____" (Deuteronomy 2:13)
39 Jesus' grandfather (Luke 3:23)
40 God of Babylon (Isaiah 46:1)
41 Olive and corn
42 "Filled his holes with prey, and his dens with _____" (Nahum 2:12)
43 A son of Keturah (1 Chronicles 1:32)
45 Another name for Mizpah (Genesis 31:48–49)
46 "And Cabbon, and _____, and Kithlish" (Joshua 15:40)
47 Manna was measured this way (Exodus 16:22)
48 "Lot sat in the _____ of Sodom" (Genesis 19:1)
49 "The workman melteth a graven _____" (Isaiah 40:19)

52 Bela's son (1 Chronicles 7:7)
53 "_____. . .incited David to take a census of Israel" (1 Chronicles 21:1 NIV)
55 "And God _____ unto Noah" (Genesis 8:15)
60 Time past
61 "Pay me that thou _____" (Matthew 18:28)
62 "Ran greedily after the _____ of Balaam for reward" (Jude 1:11)
63 She lays eggs
64 "Foxes have holes and birds of the air have _____" (Matthew 8:20 NKJV)
65 Children of Solomon's servants (Nehemiah 7:57)

DOWN

1 "Helez the Paltite, _____" (2 Samuel 23:26)
2 Angry
3 To free of a pest
4 He took all the silver and gold left in the houses of the Lord (1 Kings 15:18)
5 Bavai's father (Nehemiah 3:18)
6 An Ahohite (1 Chronicles 11:29)
7 Belonging to me
8 "At _____ come thou hither, and eat of the bread" (Ruth 2:14)
9 Time zone for Ohio (abbr.)
10 Naomi's daughter-in-law (abbr., var.)
11 "_____ the body is, thither will the eagles be gathered together" (Luke 17:37)
12 Sisera was captain of this host (Judges 4:2)
13 Students attending a school other than assigned is _____ enrollment
21 School for ministers (abbr., var.)
22 "It came to pass by the way in the _____" (Exodus 4:24)
23 Allotment
24 "In his _____ his judgment was taken away" (Acts 8:33)

by N. Teri Grottke

25 "Baalah, and Iim, and _____" (Joshua 15:29)
27 "Alammelech, and _____, and Misheal" (Joshua 19:26)
28 "_____ was an hair of their head singed" (Daniel 3:27)
29 Coz's son (1 Chronicles 4:8)
30 Site of molybdenum plant in Russia near Mongolia
34 What a bird does
35 Opposite of *lose*
37 A servant of Saul (2 Samuel 9:2)
38 Nation that signed the letter to Artaxerxes (Ezra 4:9)
39 Hearty
41 A unit of electricity
42 "And the children of Israel removed from _____, and pitched in Succoth" (Numbers 33:5)
44 "_____ went after the messengers of David" (1 Samuel 25:42)

45 "_____, and Magog, to gather them together to battle" (Revelation 20:8)
46 General clothing size
48 "Before _____ by the way of the wilderness" (2 Samuel 2:24)
50 "As he that lieth upon the top of a _____" (Proverbs 23:34)
51 Homophone for parents' sisters
53 "Came to Joel the _____ of Pethuel" (Joel 1:1)
54 Reverent fear
56 Positive side of a thing (abbr.)
57 "Thou _____ cursed above all" (Genesis 3:14)
58 Hawaii airport code
59 Gad's son (Genesis 46:16)

ACROSS

1 Unpaid broadcast announcement of (abbr.)
4 Wound covering
8 Fire by-products
13 "I will _____ all that afflict thee" (Zephaniah 3:19)
15 Jehiel's son (1 Chronicles 9:35, 37)
16 Keep out of the sun
17 "This woman for the _____ which is lent" (1 Samuel 2:20)
18 Give for temporary use
19 "The city was _____ and great" (Nehemiah 7:4)
20 "From _____ come wars and fightings among you?" (James 4:1)
22 "Choked it, and it _____ no fruit" (Mark 4:7)
24 Strong wood
25 Place
26 Johanan and Jonathan's father (Jeremiah 40:8)
30 Assist
32 Before James (abbr.)
35 "Adam, Sheth, _____" (1 Chronicles 1:1)
36 Cattle (arch.)
37 "Land from _____ to" (Isaiah 16:1)
38 Identifications
39 Personal retirement fund (abbr.)
40 "Until they had destroyed _____ king of Canaan" (Judges 4:24)
41 Talmai's father (Numbers 13:22)
42 Cherubims were stationed at the east of this place (Genesis 3:24)
43 "_____, whom the men of Gath that were born in that land slew" (1 Chronicles 7:21)
44 "Maalehacrabbim, and passed along to _____" (Joshua 15:3)
45 "The heavens shall _____ away with a great noise" (2 Peter 3:10)
46 "I will send _____ of flies upon thee" (Exodus 8:21)
47 Comes between Daniel and Joel (abbr.)

48 "_____ saith in her heart, I sit a queen" (Revelation 18:7)
49 "Children, obey your _____ in all things" (Colossians 3:20)
53 Spoke
57 Change
58 Shem's son (Genesis 10:22)
60 False image
62 Spear
63 Salathiel's father (Luke 3:27)
64 Speed
65 "An _____ must be blameless" (Titus 1:6 NIV)
66 Type of eagle (Leviticus 11:18)
67 Color of love

DOWN

1 King of Assyria (2 Kings 15:19)
2 High mountains have this at the top
3 Jabal's mother (Genesis 4:20)
4 "All Bashan unto _____" (Joshua 13:11)
5 "Whosoever shall smite thee on thy right _____, turn to him the other also" (Matthew 5:39)
6 "To Riblah, on the east side of _____" (Numbers 34:11)
7 "He disputed about the _____ of Moses" (Jude 1:9)
8 Slumbering
9 "Good and evil, thou _____ not eat of it" (Genesis 2:17)
10 As Christians, we should not have this kind of heart
11 Guardrails protect this
12 Germ
14 Single
21 Belonging to Shem's father (Genesis 7:13) (poss.)
23 Body of land surrounded by water
26 Othniel's father (Judges 1:13)
27 Elioenai's son (1 Chronicles 3:24)
28 Rulers' nationality at Jesus' time
29 Well of strife (Genesis 26:20)
30 Employs
31 Ahira's father (Numbers 1:15)

by N. Teri Grottke

32 A grandson of Asher (Genesis 46:17)
33 Bathsheba's father (2 Samuel 11:3)
34 "By joints and _____ having nourishment ministered" (Colossians 2:19)
36 Children (slang)
37 Heber's father (Luke 3:35)
40 Gem
42 The sun rises this way
45 Meditate
46 Michah's son (1 Chronicles 24:24)
47 "Come they not _____, even of your lusts" (James 4:1)
48 Unwavering look
49 Little color
50 Helem's son (1 Chronicles 7:35)
51 Tear apart as a sign of anger, grief, or despair
52 "They _____ his praise" (Psalm 106:12)

54 "People of Syria shall go into captivity unto _____" (Amos 1:5)
55 Biblical tower (Genesis 35:21)
56 Feel affection for
59 "Shimei, and _____, and the mighty men which belonged to David" (1 Kings 1:8)
61 Commanded

## 65

JOSHUA'S PROCLAMATION

Serve the LORD with gladness:
come before his presence with singing.
PSALM 100:2

ACROSS

1 Communication code for the letter *P*
5 Home of the Incas
9 "_____ for the widow" (Isaiah 1:17)
14 Stork relative
15 "And Geshem the _____ heard about it" (Nehemiah 2:19 NIV)
16 Leap forward suddenly
17 "I _____; it is sealed" (Isaiah 29:11 NIV)
18 Capital of 5 Across
19 "Ye are not under the law, but _____ grace" (Romans 6:14)
20 Beginning of **QUOTE** from Joshua 24:15 (5 words)
23 Biah preceder (see second in Nehemiah 10:12)
24 Talk idly
25 "Out of the _____" (Ezekiel 45:14)
28 Sailing skill
32 "And the night be _____" (Job 7:4)
33 Table scrap
34 "The LORD _____ to me" (Ruth 1:17) (2 words)
35 "And after that also King of _____" (Hebrews 7:2)
36 **QUOTE**, cont. (3 words)
40 "Judah is a lion's _____" (Genesis 49:9)
42 Large, open wagon
43 "_____ their words like deadly arrows" (Psalm 64:3 NIV)
46 "Is any thing too _____ for the LORD" (Genesis 18:14)
47 Reclusive actress of the silents (2 words)
50 GI's duds (abbr.)
51 Language of Laos

52 Maliciously false public statement
53 End of **QUOTE** (3 words)
57 "Tell me, art thou a _____" (Acts 22:27)
60 "Or _____ I will come unto thee quickly" (Revelation 2:5)
61 We, at the start, makes it a hot dog
62 "_____ all that we ask or think" (Ephesians 3:20)
63 "Let the sea _____" (Psalm 96:11)
64 "Neither _____ you up a standing image" (Leviticus 26:1)
65 Its capital is Lhasa
66 "_____, what must I do to be saved?" (Acts 16:30)
67 Common IDs (abbr.)

DOWN

1 Spanish artist
2 Embarrasser
3 Undeveloped plumage (2 words)
4 "As _____ against the wall" (Isaiah 25:4) (2 words)
5 "The _____ tree also" (Joel 1:12)
6 Pennsylvania port
7 "In _____ was there a voice heard" (Matthew 2:18)
8 African lady with stretched lips
9 "Look, I am setting a _____ line among my people Israel" (Amos 7:8 NIV)
10 Crazy (var.)
11 "And keepeth my works unto the _____" (Revelation 2:26)
12 "A child when she was past _____" (Hebrews 11:11)
13 _____ *Rosenkavalier*
21 Research, with *on* (2 words)
22 Skip, as a stone
25 Clavicles

by N. Teri Grottke

26 "As of many; but as of _____" (Galatians 3:16)
27 Dream indicator (abbr.)
29 Negative votes
30 157.5° from North (abbr.)
31 "And _____ came through the nations" (Deuteronomy 29:16) (2 words)
32 Four quarts (abbr.)
35 "If therefore thine eye be _____" (Matthew 6:22)
37 "Became mighty men which were of _____, men of renown" (Genesis 6:4)
38 "And Moses said, _____ that to day" (Exodus 16:25)
39 Purple Heart recipient, for example (abbr.)
40 "And _____ will go for us" (Isaiah 6:8)
41 "Yea, he _____ power over the angel" (Hosea 12:4)

44 Of Portugal and Spain's peninsula
45 Shapers
47 Needlefish
48 "Like a tree planted by the _____ of water" (Psalm 1:3)
49 Sick people
51 Dogma presented as truth
53 "Lord, _____ me" (Matthew 14:30)
54 A word spoken from the cross (Mark 15:34)
55 Russian emperor
56 "As though they were not _____" (Job 39:16)
57 "The weasel, the _____, any kind" (Leviticus 11:29 NIV)
58 Kimono holder
59 "The _____ will stone them" (Ezekiel 23:47 NIV)

## 66

ACROSS

1 Refuse
6 Primary color
10 "Mahli, and _____, and Jeremoth, three" (1 Chronicles 23:23)
14 Elkanah's grandfather (1 Samuel 1:1)
15 "Punish the men that are settled on their _____" (Zephaniah 1:12)
16 "They shall enter in at the windows _____ a thief" (Joel 2:9)
17 "When he came to the den, he cried with a _____ voice unto Daniel" (Daniel 6:20)
19 Merari's son (1 Chronicles 24:27)
20 Man's neck accessory
21 "I will send a fire on the wall of _____" (Amos 1:7)
22 "Asa destroyed her idol, and burnt it by the brook _____" (1 Kings 15:13)
24 "And the fame _____ went abroad into all that land" (Matthew 9:26)
26 "Hope of their _____ was gone" (Acts 16:19)
27 "The like _____ whereunto even baptism doth also now save us" (1 Peter 3:21)
30 Put forth effort
32 "Spread his tent beyond the tower of _____" (Genesis 35:21)
33 "King of the city of Sepharvaim, _____, and Ivah" (Isaiah 37:13)
34 Impede
37 "But with the well _____ is wisdom" (Proverbs 13:10)
41 Make bigger
43 Small deer
44 "The fourth to _____" (1 Chronicles 25:11)
46 "Though ye have _____ among the pots" (Psalm 68:13)
47 "That were _____ escaped from them" (2 Peter 2:18)
48 "The building fitly _____ together groweth unto an holy temple in the Lord" (Ephesians 2:21)

50 Paul and Silas were sent by night here (Acts 17:10)
53 "And _____ I was speaking, and praying" (Daniel 9:20)
55 "Thou _____ affliction upon our loins" (Psalm 66:11)
57 "Judah went to the top of the rock _____" (Judges 15:11)
58 Jehoshuah's father (1 Chronicles 7:27)
61 Anak's father (Joshua 15:13)
62 "Being absent now I write to them which _____ have sinned" (2 Corinthians 13:2)
65 The North one guided slaves to freedom
66 "And _____, and Parah, and Ophrah" (Joshua 18:23)
67 "There came a _____ out of the heat, and fastened on his hand" (Acts 28:3)
68 "Send me good speed _____ day" (Genesis 24:12)
69 Peter fished with these
70 Zerah's son (1 Chronicles 6:41)

DOWN

1 "She _____ in her body that she was healed of that plague" (Mark 5:29)
2 The Ahohite (1 Chronicles 11:29)
3 One of the cures for scurvy
4 Amaziah. . . . went to _____ valley of salt" (2 Chronicles 25:11)
5 Effect without food
6 Streak or outburst
7 "And _____, and Shilhim, and Ain" (Joshua 15:32)
8 Maadai's brother (Ezra 10:34)
9 "He called the name of the well _____" (Genesis 26:20)
10 Chislon's son (Numbers 34:21)
11 Shelomith's father (Leviticus 24:11)
12 "I will turn mine hand against _____" (Amos 1:8)
13 "His quiver to enter into my _____" (Lamentations 3:13)
18 Type of vetch
23 Shemaiah's son (1 Chronicles 3:22)

by N. Teri Grottke

24 Jaroah's son (1 Chronicles 5:14)
25 Relieved from or lacking
27 "God hath not given us the spirit of _____" (2 Timothy 1:7)
28 Zechariah's father (Ezra 5:1)
29 "Abraham _____ the tenth of the spoils" (Hebrews 7:4)
31 Type of motel
34 "And they filled them up to the _____" (John 2:7)
35 Shammah's father (2 Samuel 23:11)
36 Tear apart in anger or grief
38 "Notwithstanding it pleased _____ to abide there still" (Acts 15:34)
39 Follows Lamentations (abbr, var.)
40 "Ran again unto the well to _____ water" (Genesis 24:20)
42 "_____ for the day" (Joel 1:15)
45 "He that overcometh shall _____ all things" (Revelation 21:7)
47 "His countenance is as Lebanon, excellent as the _____" (Song of Solomon 5:15)
48 "He that hath a _____ nose, or any thing superfluous" (Leviticus 21:18)
49 "All faith, so that I could _____ mountains" (1 Corinthians 13:2)
50 "By the _____ of God they perish" (Job 4:9)
51 "Elements shall melt with fervent heat, the _____ also" (2 Peter 3:10)
52 Ithai's father (1 Chronicles 11:31)
54 Things
56 "Now the serpent was more subtil _____ any beast" (Genesis 3:1)
58 "_____ shall have distresses daily" (Ezekiel 30:16)
59 Jerahmeel's son (1 Chronicles 2:25)
60 Salathiel's father (Luke 3:27)
63 Adam's wife
64 "No man, having put his hand to the plow, and looking back, is _____ for the kingdom" (Luke 9:62)

## 67

ACROSS

1 Meat from pigs
4 Panhandle
7 Where the mercy seat is (Exodus 25:21)
10 Boaz's son (Ruth 4:21)
12 Zibeon's son (Genesis 36:24)
14 "_____that ye refuse not him that speaketh" (Hebrews 12:25)
15 Daniel had a vision by this river (Daniel 8:2)
16 The Ural Mountains is one of its boundaries
17 Suspend
19 "Not _____ evil for evil" (1 Peter 3:9)
21 Abraham's heir (Genesis 21:3)
23 "Bound two talents of silver in two _____" (2 Kings 5:23)
24 "This is the sixth _____ with her, who was called barren" (Luke 1:36)
25 Chief among the captains of David's mighty men (2 Samuel 23:8)
29 An ancestor of Jesus (Luke 3:31)
32 "I will speak: I will _____ of thee" (Job 42:4)
34 Not me
35 Land measurement
39 "I made haste, and _____ not to keep thy commandments" (Psalm 119:60)
41 Saul's son (1 Chronicles 8:33)
43 Duke of Edom (Genesis 36:43)
44 "Bore his ear through with an ____" (Exodus 21:6)
46 Kelaiah (Ezra 10:23)
47 Jairus's daughter was not dead but _____ (Luke 8:51–52 NIV)
50 "The name of the other _____" (1 Samuel 14:4)
51 "Behold, every one that _____ proverbs shall use this proverb against thee" (Ezekiel 16:44)
54 Biblical *you*
56 Palti's father (Numbers 13:9)
57 "Every man in his place by their _____" (Numbers 2:17)

62 Skinny
63 "Restore all that was _____" (2 Kings 8:6)
64 Rabbit
65 Samson did this with the honey in the lion (Judges 14:8–9)
66 He was a hunter and man of the field (Genesis 25:27)
67 Manasseh's son (2 Chronicles 33:20)
68 At the bottom of a garment
69 "_____ Star-Spangled Banner"
70 Capable

DOWN

1 "Could you not keep watch for one _____?" (Mark 14:37 NIV)
2 Having sufficient power to accomplish something
3 "What _____ ye to weep" (Acts 21:13)
4 Shaharaim's wife (1 Chronicles 8:8)
5 "Lifted up as an _____ upon his land" (Zechariah 9:16)
6 "Your adversaries shall not be able to _____ nor resist" (Luke 21:15)
7 An idol of Hamath (2 Kings 17:30)
8 "Bodies a living sacrifice, holy, acceptable unto God, which is your _____ service" (Romans 12:1)
9 "Adam, Sheth, Enosh, _____, Mahalaleel, Jered" (1 Chronicles 1:1–2)
11 "God _____ tempt Abraham" (Genesis 22:1)
13 Crone
18 "We _____ our bread" (Lamentations 5:9)
20 "Ivory and _____" (Ezekiel 27:15)
22 Part of a book (abbr.)
25 Melchi's father (Luke 3:28)
26 "The fallow _____, and the wild goat" (Deuteronomy 14:5)
27 Micaiah's father (2 Chronicles 18:7)
28 Zophar was one (Job 2:11)

by N. Teri Grottke

30 Ballerina's tool
31 "Full ears of corn in the _____ thereof" (2 Kings 4:42)
33 "Lookest thou upon them that ____ treacherously" (Habakkuk 1:13)
36 Abel's murderer
37 Fee scale
38 King Hoshea's father (2 Kings 15:30)
40 Once a thing is lent, it is _____
42 "The son of _____, in Aruboth" (1 Kings 4:10)
45 "Lord, now _____ thou thy servant depart in peace" (Luke 2:29)
48 "_____: and Saul gathered all Israel" (1 Samuel 28:4)
49 He was with Avim and Ophrah (Joshua 18:23)
51 Abram's birthplace (Nehemiah 9:7)

52 What Lot did in the gate of Sodom (Genesis 19:1)
53 Biblical measurement (Exodus 16:36)
55 "Let him seek peace, and _____ it" (1 Peter 3:11)
57 "_____ hath given up the ghost" (Jeremiah 15:9)
58 "_____, she is broken that was the gates of the people" (Ezekiel 26:2)
59 "In _____ was there a voice heard" (Matthew 2:18)
60 "Mountains shall _____ down new wine" (Joel 3:18)
61 Dispatched

68

ACROSS

1 Horse color
4 Aharhel's father (1 Chronicles 4:8)
9 Make a mistake
12 Get older
13 Elioenai's son (1 Chronicles 3:24)
14 An appeal
15 Boring
17 Farm buildings
18 A mortgage must
19 "And he erected there an altar, and called it _____" (Genesis 33:20)
22 An elevated Britisher
23 "Thou take the anointing _____, and pour it upon his head" (Exodus 29:7)
24 An animal unclean for eating (Leviticus 11:29)
27 "There was a cake _____ on the coals" (1 Kings 19:6)
30 With power to accomplish something
31 "Elimelech _____ husband died" (Ruth 1:3) (poss.)
33 Follows Nehemiah (abbr.)
36 What the devil is
37 Greek form of *Uriah* (Matthew 1:6)
38 King Hoshea's father (2 Kings 15:30)
39 Hophni's father (1 Samuel 1:3)
40 "There shall be no herd in the ____" (Habakkuk 3:17)
41 Only
42 Jonah prayed from the _____ belly (Jonah 2:1) (poss.)
43 Black and _____
44 Used to control a horse
45 You're completely wrong if you're all _____
46 "At _____, and Hazarsusim, and at Bethbirei, and at Shaaraim" (1 Chronicles 4:31)
53 Corridor
54 "An _____ of a sweet smell" (Philippians 4:18)
55 Eighth person (2 Peter 2:5)
57 "You _____ have I known of all the families" (Amos 3:2)
58 Type of drum
59 Comes before Daniel (abbr., var.)
60 "So many as the stars of the _____ in multitude" (Hebrews 11:12)
61 Weeds
62 "Thou art with child, and shalt bear a _____" (Genesis 16:11)

DOWN

1 Translated, it is also *mal* (Fr.)
2 "_____, that shall consume the eyes" (Leviticus 26:16)
3 Shout
4 The half tribe of Manasseh was brought here (1 Chronicles 5:26)
5 Zibeon's son (Genesis 36:2)
6 Not easily found
7 "Bakbukiah and _____, their brethren" (Nehemiah 12:9)
8 Unmarried woman
9 Overseer under Cononiah and Shimei (2 Chronicles 31:13)
10 "They _____ to and fro" (Psalm 107:27)
11 "Fire _____ along upon the ground" (Exodus 9:23)
14 "They found a _____ in the land of Shinar" (Genesis 11:2)
16 "_____ light to rule the night" (Genesis 1:16)
20 Deliberate misleading
21 Two or more deer
24 "Take a census. . .every _____ individually" (Numbers 1:2 NKJV)
25 Ishmaelite camel driver (1 Chronicles 27:30)
26 Biblical river (Daniel 8:16)
27 Job had these from the sole of his foot to the top of his head (Job 2:7)
28 Helem's son (1 Chronicles 7:35)
29 "_____ the Son, lest he be angry" (Psalm 2:12)
31 Walnuts and pecans, for example
32 Haniel and Rezia's brother (1 Chronicles 7:39)
33 Jesus cried this at the ninth hour (Mark 15:34)

by N. Teri Grottke

34 "Neither shalt thou suffer the
   _____ of the covenant"
   (Leviticus 2:13)
35 Biblical *you*
38 Paseah's father (1 Chronicles 4:12)
40 "_____ thou hast not hated
   blood" (Ezekiel 35:6)
42 "In whom all the building _____
   framed together groweth"
   (Ephesians 2:21)
43 Classic children's literature:
   Charlotte's _____
44 "Jonah was in the _____ of the
   fish three days" (Jonah 1:17)
45 Goods for sale
46 Side of the river
47 "Priest of the _____ high God"
   (Hebrews 7:1)
48 "Of Harim, _____; of Meraioth"
   (Nehemiah 12:15)
49 The Lord shall do this out of Zion
   (Joel 3:16)

50 Make well
51 The giant had six of these
   (2 Samuel 21:20)
52 Bethuel's brother (Genesis 22:22)
53 Comes before Joel (abbr.)
56 Zephaniah's son (Zechariah 6:14)

ALPHA-NUMERIC MIXUP

*For where two or three are gathered together
in my name, there am I in the midst of them.*

MATTHEW 18:20

ACROSS

1 Jehoshaphat's dad (1 Kings 15:24)
4 "Neither do they _____"
(Matthew 6:28)
8 Between-meal treats
14 One Bobbsey twin
15 Ambience
16 Beach shelter
17 "He will silence her noisy _____"
(Jeremiah 51:55 NIV)
18 "How we may _____ one
another" (Hebrews 10:24 NIV)
19 Thomas Alva _____
20 Jonah's stay in the fish (Jonah
1:17) (3 words, 2 numerals)
23 "Mine _____ is consumed with
grief" (Psalm 31:9)
24 "_____ the ramparts we watched"
25 Dewy
28 "____, give me this water"
(John 4:15)
30 "As _____ in heaven"
(Matthew 6:10) (2 words)
34 "There _____ lad here" (John 6:9)
(2 words)
35 Thursday was named after him
37 "And _____ and mourning shall
flee away" (Isaiah 51:11)
39 "The Father, the Word, and the
Holy Ghost: _____" (1 John 5:7)
(4 words, 1 numeral)
42 "Howbeit there is a kinsman
_____ than I" (Ruth 3:12)
43 "And _____ it in a book"
(Isaiah 30:8)
44 Contend
45 "Then came I with an _____"
(Acts 23:27)
46 Number of virgins who went to
meet the bridegroom
(Matthew 25:1)
47 "A shadow from the _____"
(Isaiah 25:4)
48 "Let us make _____ name"
(Genesis 11:4) (2 words)

50 "As for all the hills once cultivated
by the _____" (Isaiah 7:25 NIV)
52 In which the leaven was hidden
(Matthew 13:33)
(3 words, 1 numeral)
61 Band leader Glenn
62 "The same shall be _____ of all"
(Mark 9:35)
63 Attorneys' organization (abbr.)
64 Regal fur
65 Away from the wind and weather
66 "So a _____ tongue brings angry
looks" (Proverbs 25:23 NIV)
67 Wise old man of Greek mythology
68 "Saying, What _____ these
stones" (Joshua 4:21)
69 "_____, of the Gentiles also"
(Romans 3:29)

DOWN

1 "He had also seven sons _____
daughters" (Job 42:13) (1 word,
1 numeral)
2 "And God _____, Let there be
light" (Genesis 1:3)
3 "And there was one _____, a
prophetess" (Luke 2:36)
4 Impudent
5 Between caterpillars and butterflies
6 "_____ in the path of your com-
mands" (Psalm 119:32 NIV)
(2 words)
7 "Then Mary took about a pint of
pure _____" (John 12:3 NIV)
8 "A crowd was running to the
_____" (Mark 9:25 NIV)
9 Opposite the zenith
10 "He rolled _____ stone in front
of the entrance" (Matthew 27:60
NIV) (2 words)
11 Country singer Johnny
12 Nautical mile per hour
13 *Lacking* or *without* (Fr.)
21 Quick affirmative
22 "That when Jehudi had read _____
four leaves" (Jeremiah 36:23)
(1 word, 1 numeral)

by N. Teri Grottke

25 Ephesian goddess (Acts 19:34)
26 Lou Grant: Ed _____
27 Polite address
28 Call for help
29 "Good night" girl
30 Anger
31 Word with treasure
32 Greek region where Ephesus was located
33 "Eat the fat, and drink the _____" (Nehemiah 8:10)
35 "_____ LORD is my shepherd" (Psalm 23:1)
36 "And all _____ paths are peace" (Proverbs 3:17)
37 "And _____ upon the bed" (Genesis 48:2)
38 "For _____ in the blackest darkness" (Job 28:3 NIV)
40 "But _____ the spirits whether" (1 John 4:1)
41 "And _____ that side" (Ezekiel 40:10) (1 word, 1 numeral)
46 "And _____ for mortar" (Genesis 11:3 NIV)

47 "And touched the _____ of his garment" (Matthew 9:20)
48 "_____ HOOKS!" (crate marking; 2 words)
49 More certain
50 Son of Beeri (Hosea 1:1)
51 "For as _____ as ye eat this bread" (1 Corinthians 11:26)
52 "Behold, _____ seek thee" (Acts 10:19) (1 word, 1 numeral)
53 "I sink in deep _____" (Psalm 69:2)
54 "Under oaks and poplars and _____" (Hosea 4:13)
55 Stepped down, as from a carriage
56 Shem's son (Genesis 10:22)
57 "Then let him count the years of the _____ thereof" (Leviticus 25:27)
58 "For my yoke is _____, and my burden is light" (Matthew 11:30)
59 "They say unto him, We are _____" (Matthew 20:22)
60 "The good shepherd _____ down his life for the sheep" (John 10:11 NIV)

ACROSS

1 Diana was one of these (Acts 19:28) (abbr.)
4 "To the _____ ye shall give the less inheritance" (Numbers 33:54)
9 Philadelphia's time (abbr.)
12 He brought the law before the congregation on the first day of the seventh month (Nehemiah 8:2)
13 Ribai's son (1 Chronicles 11:31)
14 Saul and his men camped by this valley (1 Samuel 17:2)
15 Zophar was one (Job 2:11)
17 Shade of green
18 Deserts are this
19 "There is but a _____ between me and death" (1 Samuel 20:3)
20 Biblical river (Isaiah 23:3)
21 Type of eagle (Deuteronomy 14:17)
22 "Practise it, _____ it is in the power of their hand" (Micah 2:1)
24 "Benjamin shall possess _____" (Obadiah 1:19)
27 "Ira an Ithrite, _____ an Ithrite, Uriah the Hittite: thirty and seven in all" (2 Samuel 23:38–39)
28 "In the month _____ thou camest out from Egypt" (Exodus 34:18)
29 Massacred
30 "Against Jerusalem, ___" (Ezekiel 26:2)
33 "Wide is the gate, and _____ is the way, that leadeth to destruction" (Matthew 7:13)
35 Peter cut off one (John 18:10)
36 Toned down or softened
38 Riblah was on its east side (Numbers 34:11)
39 Zorobabel's son (Luke 3:27)
41 Puah's son (Judges 10:1)
42 "I bestow all my _____ to feed the poor" (1 Corinthians 13:3)
43 "From the top of _____ and Hermon" (Song of Solomon 4:8)
45 "_____ went always into the first tabernacle" (Hebrews 9:6)
48 "Round about the throne, were _____ beasts full of eyes" (Revelation 4:6)
49 This young animal can represent peace or purity (p1.)

50 "Their _____ shall be broken" (Psalm 37:15)
51 Solomon's great-grandson (1 Chronicles 3:10)
54 Temple prophetess in Jesus' time (Luke 2:36)
55 God told Saul to destroy these people (1 Samuel 15:18)
58 Nathan of Zobah's son (2 Samuel 23:36)
59 "For I bear in my body the _____ of the Lord Jesus" (Galatians 6:17)
60 "All these men of war, that could keep _____, came with a perfect heart" (1 Chronicles 12:38)
61 He came with Zerubbabel (Ezra 2:2) (abbr.)
62 "I do not say to thee how thou _____ unto me" (Philemon 1:19)
63 Increase

DOWN

1 Brother of Dishon and Dishan (1 Chronicles 1:38)
2 "_____ for the peace" (Psalm 122:6)
3 Father of Canaan (Genesis 9:22)
4 "Vessels of wrath _____ to destruction" (Romans 9:22)
5 "Libnah, and _____, and Ashan" (Joshua 15:42)
6 Beat
7 Should do three
8 "But the wheat and the _____ were not smitten" (Exodus 9:32)
9 Elkanah's grandfather (1 Samuel 1:1)
10 "Next day we arrived at _____" (Acts 20:15)
11 "For _____ I hated them" (Hosea 9:15)
12 "More kindness in the latter _____" (Ruth 3:10)
14 David's brother (1 Samuel 17:28)
16 This includes both Cyprus and Japan
20 Light smell
21 Priestly city of Benjamin (1 Kings 15:22)
22 Shaharaim's wife (1 Chronicles 8:8)
23 Gad's son (Genesis 46:16)

by N. Teri Grottke

24 "Ramah and _____, six hundred twenty and one" (Ezra 2:26)
25 Merari's son (1 Chronicles 24:27)
26 Samson killed this animal (Judges 14:5–6 NIV)
27 "Beholding his natural face in a _____" (James 1:23)
29 "When he sowed, some _____ fell by the way side" (Matthew 13:4)
30 Manasseh's son (2 Chronicles 33:20)
31 Jesus' grandfather (Luke 3:23)
32 Twelfth Hebrew month (Esther 3:7)
34 "Take away the _____ from the silver" (Proverbs 25:4)
37 "_____, Hizkijah, Azzur" (Nehemiah 10:17)
40 Not cold or lukewarm
42 "The ancients of _____ and the wise men thereof" (Ezekiel 27:9)

43 "That which thou _____ is not quickened, except it die" (1 Corinthians 15:36)
44 "Full ears of corn in the _____ thereof" (2 Kings 4:42)
45 Flat land
46 To rove or roam
47 Asher's son (1 Chronicles 7:30)
48 "Bringing sick _____, and them which were vexed with unclean spirits" (Acts 5:16)
50 Uncovered
51 Joseph mourned for Jacob at his threshing floor (Genesis 50:10)
52 "I will even _____ a curse upon you" (Malachi 2:2)
53 Question
55 Mattathias's father (Luke 3:25) (abbr., var.)
56 "Shoulder, and the two cheeks, and the _____" (Deuteronomy 18:3)
57 "Helez the Paltite, _____ the son of Ikkesh" (2 Samuel 23:26)

ACROSS

1 Travel by car
5 "Mar the corners of thy _____" (Leviticus 19:27)
10 "Stand in the _____ before me" (Ezekiel 22:30)
13 Isaiah's father (2 Kings 19:2)
14 "Seek peace, and _____ it" (1 Peter 3:11)
15 Anak's father (Joshua 15:13)
16 "The poor useth _____; but the rich answereth roughly" (Proverbs 18:23)
18 "She took a _____, and covered herself" (Genesis 24:65)
19 Comes before Habakkuk (abbr.)
20 "Plain of _____, in the province of Babylon" (Daniel 3:1)
21 "Mount of _____, which is before Jerusalem" (Zechariah 14:4)
23 "Jealous for his land, and _____ his people" (Joel 2:18)
24 "Aquila, born in Pontus, _____ come from Italy" (Acts 18:2)
25 "A wise man will _____ it" (Proverbs 16:14)
28 Stretch out
30 Oneness
31 "O my strength, _____ thee to help me" (Psalm 22:19)
32 "And _____ greedily after the error" (Jude 1:11)
35 Tiny insect, sometimes winged
36 Deceitful cunning
37 Application
38 Livestock feed
39 "Together against her the kingdoms of Ararat, _____" (Jeremiah 51:27)
40 Lower
42 Proverbs 8:12 speaks of this type of inventions
43 Sheba's father (2 Samuel 20:1)
44 Agreement
47 "The dung _____, and viewed the walls of Jerusalem" (Nehemiah 2:13)
48 Laish's son (1 Samuel 25:44)

49 "I will not _____ out his name out of the book of life" (Revelation 3:5)
50 Abdiel's son (1 Chronicles 5:15)
53 Throw forcefully
54 A family of the scribes that dwelt at Jabez (1 Chronicles 2:55)
57 Seth's son (Genesis 4:26)
58 "Babel, and _____, and Accad" (Genesis 10:10)
59 Zimri's father (Numbers 25:14)
60 Relatives
61 "Jonah was gone down into the _____ of the ship" (Jonah 1:5)
62 Melchi's father (Luke 3:28)

DOWN

1 Missing in a drought
2 Helem's son (1 Chronicles 7:35)
3 "What _____ the LORD require of thee" (Micah 6:8)
4 Before Nehemiah (abbr., var.)
5 "And from the daughter of Zion all her _____ is departed" (Lamentations 1:6)
6 "She crieth. . .at the _____ of the city" (Proverbs 8:3)
7 Eastern continent
8 *Street* (Fr.)
9 "The _____ hath many more children than she which hath an husband" (Galatians 4:27)
10 Place of the dead
11 Kish's father (1 Samuel 14:51)
12 "Whether is it easier to say to the sick of the _____" (Mark 2:9)
15 "The name of his city was _____" (1 Chronicles 1:46)
17 "All things are lawful for me, but all things _____ not" (1 Corinthians 10:23)
22 "Tied unto it a _____ of blue" (Exodus 39:31)
23 1904 card game of commodities
25 One of the Hebrew midwives (Exodus 1:15)
26 Phanuel's daughter (Luke 2:36)
27 Large town

by N. Teri Grottke

28 "Continual dropping in a very _____ day and a contentious woman are alike" (Proverbs 27:15)
29 Nagge's son (Luke 3:25)
31 "Wilt thou _____ the prey for the lion" (Job 38:39)
32 "Tail, branch and _____, in one day" (Isaiah 9:14)
33 "The tribe of _____ were sealed" (Revelation 7:6)
34 Salathiel's father (Luke 3:27)
36 "All the _____, six hundred men which came after him" (2 Samuel 15:18)
39 "For ye tithe _____ and rue and all manner of herbs" (Luke 11:42)
40 "I travail in _____ again until Christ be formed in you" (Galatians 4:19)
41 Role-play
42 "These are _____ without water" (2 Peter 2:17)

43 "Made _____ for his cattle" (Genesis 33:17)
44 Ahab defeated Benhadad there (1 Kings 20:30)
45 Gad's son (Genesis 46:16)
46 "All that dwelt at Lydda and _____ saw him" (Acts 9:35)
47 "In every _____ your faith to God-ward is spread abroad" (1 Thessalonians 1:8)
49 Impregnated
50 This threshingfloor was beyond Jordan (Genesis 50:10)
51 Gripped
52 Asher's son (Genesis 46:17)
55 Bela's son (1 Chronicles 7:7)
56 Amoz's son (2 Kings 19:2) (abbr.)

ACROSS

1 Cut
4 "I will put my _____ into their mind" (Hebrews 8:10)
8 Let us meet together. . .in the plain of _____" (Nehemiah 6:2)
11 The Gadite (2 Samuel 23:36)
12 Kohath's son (Exodus 6:18)
14 David's grandfather (Ruth 4:17)
15 Baking place
16 Ruth's mother-in-law (Ruth 2:20)
17 "Past the first and the second _____, they came unto the iron gate" (Acts 12:10)
18 "_____ verily, their sound" (Romans 10:18)
19 "Name thereof _____: which is the name thereof unto this day" (Judges 1:26)
20 "Fruit of righteousness is _____ in peace" (James 3:18)
22 "According to all the _____ of it" (Numbers 9:3)
24 "Name of the _____ Ruth" (Ruth 1:4)
26 "Wherein was the golden _____ that had manna" (Hebrews 9:4)
27 "Joshua. . .died, being an hundred and _____ years old" (Joshua 24:29)
29 Things
32 Samson slew 1,000 Philistines here (Judges 15:14–15)
34 Attached to the thigh
35 Caleb's daughter (Joshua 15:16)
36 Fuss
37 Ishmael's son (1 Chronicles 1:31)
39 Tacked to a shirt
40 "Hagar, _____ maid, whence camest thou" (Genesis 16:8) (poss.)
42 Noah's boat
43 "Thou, being a _____ olive tree, wert grafted in among them" (Romans 11:17)
44 "I _____ that through your prayers I shall be given unto you" (Philemon 1:22)
45 "Of Keros, the children of _____" (Nehemiah 7:47)

46 "No man. . .looking back, is _____ for the kingdom of God" (Luke 9:62)
47 Wheat by-product
49 "I desired _____, and with him I sent a brother" (2 Corinthians 12:18)
51 A prince of Midian (Joshua 13:21)
52 Two of Paul's epistles were sent to these people (abbr.)
53 Hymn: "_____ Old Rugged Cross"
55 Tibetan monk
58 "Let not thy _____ make me afraid" (Job 13:21)
60 Zibeon's son (1 Chronicles 1:40)
61 Not at home
62 "Look from the top of _____" (Song of Solomon 4:8)
63 Gaddiel's father (Numbers 13:10)
64 "Wait secretly as a lion in his _____" (Psalm 10:9)
65 Dog's command
66 No matter which

DOWN

1 Priests had to wash here (Exodus 30:18–19)
2 "The Lord give mercy unto the house of _____" (2 Timothy 1:16)
3 Bowling target
4 "Eubulus greeteth thee, and Pudens, and _____" (2 Timothy 4:21)
5 Bela's father (1 Chronicles 5:8)
6 "O foolish Galatians, _____ hath bewitched you" (Galatians 3:1)
7 Nazarite judge (Judges 13:7, 24)
8 Governor of Ahab's house who greatly feared the Lord (1 Kings 18:3) (abbr.)
9 Saul's uncle (1 Samuel 14:50)
10 Strange
11 Opposite of *girl*
13 "Same excess of _____, speaking evil of you" (1 Peter 4:4)
14 "Bind the man that _____ this girdle" (Acts 21:11)
19 Allow

by N. Teri Grottke

21 "Great grasshoppers, _____ camp in the hedges" (Nahum 3:17)
23 Hamath king (2 Samuel 8:9)
25 "Until the times of _____ of all things" (Acts 3:21)
27 Gratuity
28 This man was a Netophathite (Jeremiah 40:8)
30 Chain armor
31 "Shall his blood be _____: for in the image of God made he man" (Genesis 9:6)
32 Final
33 Biblical tower (Genesis 35:21)
34 "No falcon's eye _____ seen it" (Job 28:7 NIV)
35 "Now I _____ one petition of thee" (1 Kings 2:16)
37 Mineral potash (Proverbs 25:20)
38 Retirement plan (abbr.)
41 "For ye were as sheep going _____" (1 Peter 2:25)

43 "To _____, that God was in Christ, reconciling the world unto himself" (2 Corinthians 5:19)
45 "I will send _____ of flies upon thee" (Exodus 8:21)
46 Type of tree
48 Adoniram's father (1 Kings 4:6)
49 "_____ if ye will hear his voice" (Hebrews 3:7) (2 words)
50 "He lieth under the _____ trees" (Job 40:21)
52 "Into _____ of Galilee, where he made the water wine" (John 4:46)
54 Benjamin's son (Genesis 46:21)
55 Young fellow
56 Reverent fear
57 "He saw a wayfaring _____ in the street" (Judges 19:17)
59 Consume food
60 He did what was good and right according to God (2 Chronicles 14:2)

FINDING SALVATION

Sirs, what must I do to be saved? And they said,
Believe on the Lord Jesus Christ, and thou shalt be saved.
ACTS 16:30–31

ACROSS

1 Grain for grinding
6 "And they set the ark of God upon a new _____" (2 Samuel 6:3)
10 "I speak _____ wise men" (1 Corinthians 10:15) (2 words)
14 "Being the _____ hour" (Acts 3:1)
15 Bread spread
16 "More than one _____" (Mark 8:14)
17 He usually has a number of lines
18 Indonesian island southwest of Sumatra
19 "There is a great _____ fixed" (Luke 16:26)
20 Start of **QUOTE** from Acts 2:21 (2 words)
23 "And he said, _____" (2 Samuel 14:12) (2 words)
24 "Because I am not the _____" (1 Corinthians 12:16)
25 "And out of the _____ of the bear" (1 Samuel 17:37)
28 "The people of Eden who were in _____ Assar" (Isaiah 37:12 NIV)
29 Opposite of NNW (abbr.)
30 "Below Beth _____" (1 Samuel 7:11 NIV)
33 "There was _____ of glass" (Revelation 4:6) (2 words)
35 Cry of pain
37 "And became _____ unto it" (Ruth 4:16)
39 **QUOTE**, cont. (5 words)
42 Prank
43 Very wide shoe size
44 Window part
45 Part of CBS (abbr.)
46 Book by Frank McCourt
48 Singer Boone
50 "They _____ my path" (Job 30:13)
51 Compressible matter

52 *Vain* (Ger.)
54 **QUOTE**, cont. (4 words)
60 "With a rod of _____" (Revelation 2:27)
61 "And the _____ was not consumed" (Exodus 3:2)
62 End of **QUOTE**
63 Part in a play
64 "Where is _____ thy brother?" (Genesis 4:9)
65 Ham it up
66 "And he _____ no trouble to it" (Proverbs 10:22 NIV)
67 "You _____ on your sword, you do" (Ezekiel 33:26 NIV)
68 "And he sent forth a _____" (Genesis 8:7)

DOWN

1 "They _____ not the bones till the morrow" (Zephaniah 3:3)
2 "Labour not to be _____" (Proverbs 23:4)
3 "And cast _____ his garden; and it grew" (Luke 13:19)
4 Glacial direction
5 "Their _____ is an open sepulchre" (Romans 3:13)
6 Folds back on itself
7 "I have been an _____ in a strange land" (Exodus 18:3)
8 "Neither _____ you up a standing image" (Leviticus 26:1)
9 "The Daughter of Jerusalem _____ her head as you flee" (Isaiah 37:22 NIV)
10 Pond plants
11 "He restoreth my _____" (Psalm 23:3)
12 "A people great and _____" (Deuteronomy 9:2)

by David K. Shortess

13 "She lighted _____ the camel" (Genesis 24:64)
21 "Do you fix your _____ such a one" (Job 14:3 NIV) (2 words)
22 It may laugh a lot
25 South American rodents
26 "Five times so much _____ of theirs" (Genesis 43:34) (2 words)
27 "Wounds and _____ and open sores" (Isaiah 1:6 NIV)
29 With embarrassment
30 "Flowing with honey and _____" (Job 20:17 NIV)
31 "And engrave on it _____ seal" (Exodus 28:36 NIV) (3 words)
32 "I _____ to those whose sin" (1 John 5:16 NIV)
34 Formerly Clay
36 Ernesto Guevara
38 Diamond expert, in short
40 Of eight
41 Under (poet.)

47 Weather map line
49 Ad come-on
51 Hereditary units
52 Ford's big bomb
53 Andes carrier
54 "And _____ them down in my wrath" (Isaiah 63:3 NIV)
55 "And ye shall _____ your peace" (Exodus 14:14)
56 Cartoonist Goldberg
57 City in the Ukraine
58 _____ noire (a thing to be avoided)
59 "And a river went out of _____ to water" (Genesis 2:10)
60 One of David's mighty men (2 Samuel 23:26)

74

ACROSS

1 Small morsel
4 Follows Micah (abbr.)
7 "When they came to _____, they could not drink of the waters" (Exodus 15:23)
12 Salathiel's father (Luke 3:27)
13 Jether's son (1 Chronicles 7:38)
14 The ending
15 "With a rod of _____" (Revelation 2:27)
16 "Bows and the arrows, and the _____, and the spears" (Ezekiel 39:9)
19 First book of the Bible (abbr.)
20 Harum's son (1 Chronicles 4:8)
21 "The sons of _____ the Gizonite" (1 Chronicles 11:34)
24 Greek form of *Noah* (Matthew 24:38)
25 The ripened fruit of a rose, rose _____ can be used in teas, jellies, and skin care (sing.)
28 An altar (Joshua 22:34)
29 "Dip the _____ of his finger in water" (Luke 16:24)
30 Expression: "Quiet _____ mouse" (2 words)
31 "Chalcol, and _____, the sons of Mahol" (1 Kings 4:31)
33 Festus (Acts 24:27)
37 Elizur's father (Numbers 1:5)
39 "He that overcometh shall _____ all things" (Revelation 21:7)
40 "Many taken with _____, and that were lame" (Acts 8:7)
41 "Oppress the poor, which crush the _____" (Amos 4:1)
42 "_____, the son of Ikkesh the Tekoite" (2 Samuel 23:26)
43 Ugly old woman
45 Chile's continent (abbr.)
46 Negative voice vote
47 "Pharaoh told them _____ dream" (Genesis 41:8)
48 "Joash, and _____, who had the dominion in Moab" (1 Chronicles 4:22)
52 Javan's son (Genesis 10:4)

55 "Had been at the beginning, between Bethel and ____" (Genesis 13:3)
56 Elkanah was one (1 Samuel 1:1)
59 Title of respected men
60 Sharar's son (2 Samuel 23:33)
61 Disfigure
62 "Many of them also which used curious _____" (Acts 19:19)
63 Amalek's mother (Genesis 36:12)
64 Supplement
65 Past tense of *is*

DOWN

1 Paul and Silas were sent by night here (Acts 17:10)
2 Type of golf clubs
3 Dorothy's woodsman
4 Hodiah's brother (1 Chronicles 4:19)
5 Rizia's brother (1 Chronicles 7:39 NASB)
6 Immer's son (Ezra 10:20)
7 "Beholdest thou the _____ that is in thy brother's eye" (Matthew 7:3)
8 Imna's brother (1 Chronicles 7:35)
9 Last book of the Bible (abbr.)
10 A historical period of time
11 "He _____ heard your grumbling" (Exodus 16:7 NIV)
12 "Draw _____ to God, and he will draw" (James 4:8)
17 "His lips like lilies, _____ sweet smelling myrrh" (Song of Solomon 5:13)
18 "_____ was a woman of good understanding" (1 Samuel 25:3)
22 "Railed on him, wagging their _____" (Mark 15:29)
23 "Og the king of Bashan, which dwelt at Astaroth in _____" (Deuteronomy 1:4)
25 Hirsute
26 Asher's son (Genesis 46:17)
27 "For ask now of the days that are _____" (Deuteronomy 4:32)
29 Jonah tried to run here (Jonah 4:2)
31 "Thou shalt not _____ to offer the first of thy ripe fruits" (Exodus 22:29)

by N. Teri Grottke

32 Fee for group membership (sing.)
34 "He began to be a mighty _____ in the earth" (Genesis 10:8)
35 Zorobabel's son (Luke 3:27)
36 David's house was made of this (2 Samuel 5:11)
37 Turn quickly
38 "Brought them unto Halah, and Habor, and _____" (1 Chronicles 5:26)
44 An idol of Hamath (2 Kings 17:30)
47 Strike
48 "Bursting of it a _____ to take fire" (Isaiah 30:14)
49 Enan's son (Numbers 10:27)
50 "Into the lower _____ of the earth" (Ephesians 4:9)
51 Cat's sound of displeasure
52 "These are the sons of Shuthelah: of _____" (Numbers 26:36)
53 Dali _____

54 "The Canaanites saw the mourning in the floor of _____" (Genesis 50:11)
56 "Thou shalt _____ the spoil of thine enemies" (Deuteronomy 20:14)
57 _____ Beta Kappa
58 "I will cause _____ to draw near" (Jeremiah 30:21)
59 Sharp-toothed tool

## 75

ACROSS

1 Covering or wrap
4 Sarai's handmaid (Genesis 16:1)
9 Iraqi city near the Euphrates
12 Ahira's father (Numbers 1:15)
14 Banish
15 "As he saith also in _____, I will call them my people" (Romans 9:25)
17 Not narrow
18 Joel's son (1 Chronicles 5:4–5)
19 "A little leaven leaveneth the whole _____" (Galatians 5:9)
20 Greek form of *Isaiah* (Matthew 3:3)
22 Pedaiah's son (1 Chronicles 3:19–20)
24 "_____ them again unto repentance" (Hebrews 6:6)
25 Aaron died in this mountain (Numbers 33:39)
26 Smallest amount
30 Keliah the Garmite's father (1 Chronicles 4:19)
34 Samson used an ass' _____ to kill a thousand men (Judges 15:16)
37 Son of Hothan the Aroerite (1 Chronicles 11:44)
39 Press clothes
41 Ishmaelite camel driver (1 Chronicles 27:30)
43 Baanah's son (2 Samuel 23:29)
44 "_____ that man, and have no company with him" (2 Thessalonians 3:14)
45 City in Germany
46 Live there
47 "My speech shall distil as the _____" (Deuteronomy 32:2)
48 Eliphaz's son (Genesis 36:11)
50 "Herd ran violently down a _____ place into the lake" (Luke 8:33)
53 "The _____ number of them is to be redeemed" (Numbers 3:48)
55 Part of the Canaanite border (Genesis 10:19)
59 Jeroham's son (1 Chronicles 8:27)
64 "Shall mourn, and the top of Carmel shall _____" (Amos 1:2)
65 He fought against Israel when he heard they came by way of spies (Numbers 21:1)
66 "That we might be fellowhelpers to the _____" (3 John 1:8)
68 "Turned about with a very small _____" (James 3:4)
69 Deck officer
70 City of the kingdom Og in Bashan (Deuteronomy 3:10)
71 Computer command
72 "Brethren of the second degree, Zechariah, _____" (1 Chronicles 15:18)
73 "Salute every _____ in Christ Jesus" (Philippians 4:21)
74 "The shield of his mighty men is made _____" (Nahum 2:3)

DOWN

1 Woodsman
2 "Pay tithe of mint and _____" (Matthew 23:23)
3 "When I came from _____, Rachel died by me" (Genesis 48:7)
4 "Restore all that was _____" (2 Kings 8:6)
5 Big hatchet
6 "Hill of Ammah, that lieth before _____ by the way" (2 Samuel 2:24)
7 Duke of Edom (1 Chronicles 1:51)
8 "Living sacrifice, holy, acceptable unto God, which is your _____ service" (Romans 12:1)
9 Opposite of *release*
10 Asher's son (Genesis 46:17)
11 The companies of Sheba waited for the troops from this place (Job 6:19)
13 "_____, and goeth out to Cabul on the left" (Joshua 19:27)
16 Biblical letter (abbr.)
21 "But my heart standeth in _____ of thy word" (Psalm 119:161)
23 Jether's son (1 Chronicles 7:38)
27 "_____, heard that the walls of Jerusalem were made up" (Nehemiah 4:7)

by N. Teri Grottke

28 "Thy kindness which thou shalt _____ unto me" (Genesis 20:13)
29 Lies
31 Liquid measure (Leviticus 23:13)
32 "Of _____, the family" (Numbers 26:17)
33 "Pull out the _____ that is in thy brother's eye" (Luke 6:42)
34 Slight nudge
35 "Rabbith, and Kishion, and _____" (Joshua 19:20)
36 Metal filament
38 "All the hills shall ____" (Amos 9:13)
40 Contemporary
42 "The lot is cast into the _____" (Proverbs 16:33)
49 Comes before Joel (abbr.)
51 He thought Hannah was drunk (1 Samuel 1:13)
52 Trails
54 Mahol's son (1 Kings 4:31)

56 "Laban went to _____ his sheep" (Genesis 31:19)
57 "Head slippeth from the _____, and lighteth upon his neighbour" (Deuteronomy 19:5)
58 "When a strong man _____ keepeth his palace" (Luke 11:21)
59 Press into a tight space
60 "_____, and Dumah, and Eshean" (Joshua 15:52)
61 Evaluate on a scale
62 First garden
63 Jaroah's son (1 Chronicles 5:14)
64 "I suppose I was not a _____ behind the very chiefest apostles" (2 Corinthians 11:5)
67 Abram lived this many years in the land of Canaan (Genesis 16:3)

## 76

ACROSS

1 Enoch's son (Genesis 4:18)
5 "Lookest thou upon them that
   _____ treacherously"
   (Habakkuk 1:13)
9 "Her ways are _____, that thou
   canst not know them"
   (Proverbs 5:6)
14 "Make for it a _____ of network
   of brass" (Exodus 27:4)
15 "They. . .hoised up the _____ to
   the wind" (Acts 27:40)
16 "The furnace one seven times
   more than it was wont to be
   _____ " (Daniel 3:19)
17 Acronym for NASA's counterpart
   across the Atlantic
18 Staying away from
20 Like ENTER, it's one of the most
   used keys on a keyboard (abbr.)
21 Cooking vessel
22 "How long will it be _____ ye
   make an end of words" (Job 18:2)
23 Hadad's city (1 Chronicles 1:50)
26 Benjamin's son (Genesis 46:21)
27 Twelfth Hebrew month
   (Esther 3:7)
28 Gad's son (Genesis 46:16)
29 Steal
31 "When David was come to
   _____ " (2 Samuel 17:27)
33 Was indebted to
35 "_____, Remmon, and Ether,
   and Ashan; four cities and their
   villages" (Joshua 19:7)
36 One of the plagues on Egypt
   (Exodus 8:17)
37 "They sat down in ranks, by
   _____, and by fifties" (Mark 6:40)
39 Between Ezra and Esther (abbr.)
40 "_____ hospitality one to another
   without grudging" (1 Peter 4:9)
41 Belonging to the cotton gin
   inventor
42 Only
44 Fenced city (Joshua 19:35)
45 "A brother offended is harder to
   be _____ than a strong city"
   (Proverbs 18:19)

46 *Love* (Sp.)
47 Rebuilder of Jerusalem (abbr.)
50 Kept
52 Eggs
53 Disappear
56 "For he hath _____ the low estate
   of his handmaiden" (Luke 1:48)
58 "How much _____ thou unto my
   lord" (Luke 16:5)
59 "_____ brought him flocks"
   (2 Chronicles 17:11)
60 "Murmured, and _____ destroyed
   of the destroyer"
   (1 Corinthians 10:10)
61 Time used in the winter

DOWN

1 Pashur's father (Jeremiah 20:1)
2 Cook
3 Birdlike
4 "Secretly as a lion in his _____ "
   (Psalm 10:9)
5 A kind of racing
6 "_____ thy bread with joy"
   (Ecclesiastes 9:7)
7 "Mephibosheth _____ at David's
   table like one of the king's sons"
   (2 Samuel 9:11 NIV)
8 Commanded
10 King David's music leader
   (Nehemiah 12:46)
11 Henadad's son (Nehemiah 3:18)
12 "He. . .slew a _____ in the pit in
   a snowy day" (1 Chronicles 11:22)
13 Hophni's father (1 Samuel 1:3)
14 "To the _____ assembly and
   church of the firstborn"
   (Hebrews 12:23)
16 "Certain Adullamite, whose name
   was _____ " (Genesis 38:1)
19 Raamah's son (Genesis 10:7)
23 Jesus is the prince of this
24 "Palace of the king's house, with
   Argob and _____ "
   (2 Kings 15:25)
25 After they left _____, they
   camped in Dibongad
   (Numbers 33:45)
26 Gaal's father (Judges 9:26)

by N. Teri Grottke

27 Wrong
29 Wake up
30 "Believed the master and the
_____ of the ship" (Acts 27:11)
32 _____ tribes and a half-tribe
(Numbers 34:13)
34 "Thou _____ near in the day
that I called upon thee"
(Lamentations 3:57)
35 Son of Shiza the Reubenite
(1 Chronicles 11:42)
37 Nahor's firstborn
(Genesis 22:20–21)
38 "He built _____, and restored it
to Judah" (2 Chronicles 26:2)
42 "I am Alpha and _____"
(Revelation 1:8)
43 "Jetur, and Nephish, and _____"
(1 Chronicles 5:19)
46 Eshcol's brother (Genesis 14:13)
47 Pertaining to a swelling
48 Smooths away rough spots

49 "It was little which thou _____
before I came" (Genesis 30:30)
50 Get up
51 He was the Jairite and a chief ruler
(2 Samuel 20:26)
53 Made before God
54 "Stand in _____, and sin not"
(Psalm 4:4)
55 Abner's father (1 Samuel 14:50)
57 To free of a pest

## 77

BIBLICAL TOGETHERNESS

Let us not give up meeting together. . .
but let us encourage one another.
HEBREWS 10:25 NIV

ACROSS

1 Inhabitant (abbr.)
4 Grinder
9 Melchizedek's kingdom (Genesis 14:18)
14 "I _____ stranger" (Genesis 23:4) (2 words)
15 "And he came _____, and drew near" (2 Samuel 18:25)
16 Overly corpulent
17 "And no _____ can shut it" (Revelation 3:8)
18 Estate owner in Scotland
19 "So hath he _____ with us" (Zechariah 1:6)
20 Start of **QUOTE** taken from Ecclesiastes 4:12 (3 words)
23 Cowboys' town
24 Edible tuber
25 "And a just _____, shall ye have" (Leviticus 19:36)
28 Upon
29 "Come forth a rod out of the _____ of Jesse" (Isaiah 11:1)
31 "And _____ in all their coasts" (Psalm 105:31)
32 "As a wild bull in a _____" (Isaiah 51:20)
33 German industrial and mining region
35 Chemical "twin"
37 **QUOTE**, cont. (3 words)
39 Beach shelter
42 "Ye have eaten the fruit of _____" (Hosea 10:13)
43 "The _____ of the LORD is perfect" (Psalm 19:7)
46 "For as in _____ all die" (1 Corinthians 15:22)
47 "For every head shall be _____" (Jeremiah 48:37)
49 Jacques's dad

DOWN

50 "The _____ of the scribes is in vain" (Jeremiah 8:8)
51 -*Chief* or -*take* preceder
52 "You believe _____" (John 16:31 NIV) (2 words)
54 End of **QUOTE** (2 words)
58 "Blessed are they that _____" (Matthew 5:4)
60 "And read: _____ of these shall fail" (Isaiah 34:16) (2 words)
61 *Hum* or *germ* follower
62 "The last" (Revelation 1:11)
63 Legendary monsters
64 Range fuel
65 Computer data storage units
66 Stadium ranks
67 Pro golfer Ernie

1 Muslim annual period of fasting
2 Issue forth
3 Kind of baseball
4 Island where Paul was shipwrecked (Acts 28:1 NIV)
5 Moonfish
6 "What a ruin she has become, a _____ for wild beasts" (Zephaniah 2:15 NIV)
7 "Within as it were an half _____ of land" (1 Samuel 14:14)
8 Overnight plane flight, informally
9 "And pitched his tent toward _____" (Genesis 13:12)
10 First homicide victim (Genesis 4:8)
11 "Take him, and _____ away safely" (Mark 14:44) (2 words)
12 Language class for immigrants to the United States (abbr.)
13 "Mercy and truth are _____ together" (Psalm 85:10)
21 High mountain

by David K. Shortess

22 "And lay no _____ upon you" (Ezekiel 36:29)
26 "Out of whose womb came the _____" (Job 38:29)
27 Saul's uncle (1 Samuel 14:50)
29 "And he was _____ at that saying" (Mark 10:22)
30 Vibrato
31 Tent pitcher in 9 Down
33 "And what, the _____ of my vows" (Proverbs 31:2)
34 Spoken in Jordan
36 "Help!" on the air
37 Valve-lifting wheel in a car
38 Comic Caesar
39 Bottle or lens adjunct
40 Lemon or lime follower
41 "Came into the _____ house" (Daniel 5:10)
43 Slow fluid loss
44 "The LORD has opened his _____" (Jeremiah 50:25 NIV)

45 Moisture
48 "Yet ye have not, because ye _____" (James 4:2) (2 words)
49 Arafat's political party (abbr.)
51 "And gave them ten _____" (Luke 19:13 NIV)
52 Saul's army captain (1 Samuel 14:50)
53 Long lock
55 "Began to _____ him vehemently" (Luke 11:53)
56 It makes sense if you add "cal"
57 Time long past
58 "They will bring a _____ against you" (Ezekiel 16:40 NIV)
59 "Remember me, _____ God" (Nehemiah 13:14) (2 words)

## 78

ACROSS

1 "Turn aside, _____ down here" (Ruth 4:1)
4 "Egypt will _____ like a fleeing serpent" (Jeremiah 46:22 NIV)
8 "Proving _____ is acceptable unto the Lord" (Ephesians 5:10)
12 "Peninnah had children, but Hannah had _____" (1 Samuel 1:2 NIV)
13 "Tochen, and _____, five cities" (1 Chronicles 4:32)
15 Opposite of *despair*
16 His servants plotted against and killed him in his own house (2 Kings 21:23)
17 "Shalt call me no more _____" (Hosea 2:16)
18 Jerahmeel's son (1 Chronicles 2:25)
19 "_____ of cattle are perplexed" (Joel 1:18)
21 "Areopagite, and a woman named _____" (Acts 17:34)
23 "He sighed _____ in his spirit" (Mark 8:12)
26 "But the wheat and the _____ were not smitten" (Exodus 9:32)
27 Goodness
28 "Were all baptized of him in the river of _____" (Mark 1:5)
31 "Fools mock at making amends for _____" (Proverbs 14:9 NIV)
32 "I will come upon him while he is weary and weak _____" (2 Samuel 17:2)
34 Carry out directions
36 "Tappuah, and _____" (Joshua 15:34)
38 This was the sign with Gideon's fleece (Judges 6:37–40)
39 "For in him we live, and _____, and have our being" (Acts 17:28)
40 Measure
41 "And Jacob called the name of the place _____" (Genesis 32:30)
44 Became acquainted
45 Spy from the tribe of Asher (Numbers 13:13)
47 Michah's son (1 Chronicles 24:24)

49 Hearing tool
50 Benhanan's father (1 Chronicles 4:20)
51 "Eli sat upon a seat by the _____ watching" (1 Samuel 4:13)
54 "Every _____, which my heavenly Father hath not planted, shall be rooted up" (Matthew 15:13)
57 Tibetan monk
58 Jehaleleel's son (1 Chronicles 4:16)
61 Shelah's son (1 Chronicles 1:18)
62 Always
63 Long for
64 Potter's material
65 Take care of
66 "The Lord saved Israel _____ day" (Exodus 14:30)
67 "Is not _____ younger sister fairer than she?" (Judges 15:2)

DOWN

1 "Let fall also _____ of the handfuls" (Ruth 2:16)
2 "Uncleanness, _____ affection, evil" (Colossians 3:5)
3 Easy to chew
4 Follows Nahum (abbr.)
5 After Song of Solomon (abbr.)
6 "He lieth under the _____ trees" (Job 40:21)
7 Heber's father (Luke 3:35)
8 "O Ephraim, thou committest _____" (Hosea 5:3)
9 Lotan's son (Genesis 36:22)
10 Primates
11 Joshua's age at his death, "an hundred and _____ years old" (Joshua 24:29)
12 Follows Micah (abbr.)
14 Cush's son (Genesis 10:8)
20 Cain and Abel's brother (Genesis 4:25)
22 "Meet the Lord in the _____" (1 Thessalonians 4:17)
24 Issachar's son (Numbers 26:23)
25 "The borrower is servant to the _____" (Proverbs 22:7)
27 Pumpkins grow on these

by N. Teri Grottke

28 "Not giving heed to _____ fables" (Titus 1:14)
29 "But the fearful, and unbelieving, and the _____" (Revelation 21:8)
30 "For if ye do these things, ye shall _____ fall" (2 Peter 1:10)
31 Place of theological study (abbr.)
33 Where the lion waits (Psalm 10:9)
35 Even though
37 "Unrighteousness in judgment, in _____, in weight, or in measure" (Leviticus 19:35)
41 "Younger as sisters, with all _____" (1 Timothy 5:2)
42 Benjamin's son (Genesis 46:21)
43 "Thy word is a _____ unto my feet" (Psalm 119:105)
46 "The king of Israel _____ come out to seek a flea" (1 Samuel 26:30 NKJV)

48 The abomination of the children of Ammon (1 Kings 11:7)
50 Asher's daughter (Genesis 46:17)
51 Sea rhythm
52 So be it
53 "There was a continual _____ given him of the king of Babylon" (Jeremiah 52:34)
55 "Moses drew _____ unto the thick darkness" (Exodus 20:21)
56 Test
57 Allow
59 "_____ the son of Ikkesh the Tekoite" (2 Samuel 23:26)
60 The star of Pixar's *A Bug's Life*

79

ACROSS

1 Not an amateur (abbr.)
4 Barbecue pork specialty
8 Separate
13 Warmth
15 "As he saith also in _____, I will call them my people" (Romans 9:25)
16 Pedaiah was from here (2 Kings 23:36)
17 "Cast _____ the waters, the waters were made sweet" (Exodus 15:25)
18 One of journalism's five Ws
19 Jesus did this at the resurrection
20 "Watching _____ with all perseverance" (Ephesians 6:18)
23 Follows Lamentations (abbr., var.)
24 One of the porters (Ezra 10:24)
25 Keep out
27 "Tarry at Jericho until your _____ be grown" (2 Samuel 10:5)
31 "See _____ that ye walk circumspectly" (Ephesians 5:15)
33 Irritated or chafed
36 "The heathen _____, the kingdoms were moved" (Psalm 46:6)
37 "_____ the flock of God which is among you" (1 Peter 5:2)
38 Gaddiel's father (Numbers 13:10)
39 "Gold, or pearls, or costly _____" (1 Timothy 2:9)
40 Between Amos and Jonah (abbr.)
41 "He oft refreshed me, and was not ashamed of my _____" (2 Timothy 1:16)
42 Part of stairs
43 "Uttereth his mischievous desire: so they _____ it up" (Micah 7:3)
44 "The son of _____, in Aruboth" (1 Kings 4:10)
45 "_____ thought he was the gardener" (John 20:15 NASB)
46 Way
47 "Deal _____ for my sake with the young man" (2 Samuel 18:5)
48 "_____ ways are moveable" (Proverbs 5:6)
49 Before
50 Satan went to and _____ in the earth (Job 2:2)
52 "When sailing was now _____" (Acts 27:9)
58 Gad's son (Genesis 46:16)
60 Homophone for letter delivery
61 "Suburbs, and _____ with her suburbs" (1 Chronicles 6:73)
63 "Let us watch and be _____" (1 Thessalonians 5:6)
64 Undisciplined manner
65 "At the name of Jesus every _____ should bow" (Philippians 2:10)
66 Absalom's captain (2 Samuel 17:25)
67 "Great swelling words, having _____ persons in admiration" (Jude 1:16) (poss.)
68 "There was no room for them in the _____" (Luke 2:7)

DOWN

1 Twenty-first letter of the Greek alphabet
2 "Joseph is without doubt _____ in pieces" (Genesis 37:33)
3 Strong promise
4 "Thy _____ have brought thee into great waters" (Ezekiel 27:26)
5 Saul's son (1 Samuel 14:49)
6 "Ye have _____ rebellious against the LORD" (Deuteronomy 31:27)
7 "Whoever shall receive me receiveth him that _____ me" (Luke 9:48)
8 Jephunneh's brother (1 Chronicles 7:38)
9 "Thou art of _____ eyes than to behold evil" (Habakkuk 1:13)
10 Isaiah's father (2 Kings 19:2)
11 "In the day of Jerusalem; who said, _____ it" (Psalm 137:7)
12 "For I was _____ king's cupbearer" (Nehemiah 1:11)
14 "You won't so much as stub your _____ on a stone" (Matthew 4:6 MSG)
21 "They were more _____ in body than rubies" (Lamentations 4:7)
22 Jesse's father (Ruth 4:17)
26 "Forasmuch as _____ excellent spirit" (Daniel 5:12)
27 "Instructer of every artificer in _____ and iron" (Genesis 4:22)

by N. Teri Grottke

28 "Elements shall melt with fervent heat, the _____ also" (2 Peter 3:10)
29 "_____ with thine adversary quickly" (Matthew 5:25)
30 Harvest
31 Reumah's son (Genesis 22:24)
32 "For in so doing thou shalt _____ coals of fire on his head" (Romans 12:20)
33 "Thou shalt _____ and eat it in the place which the LORD thy God shall choose" (Deuteronomy 16:7)
34 Maasiai's father (1 Chronicles 9:12)
35 "I would hasten my escape from the _____ storm and tempest" (Psalm 55:8)
37 Pioneer refuge
38 "Set it between Mizpeh and _____" (1 Samuel 7:12)
41 "Then were they all of good _____" (Acts 27:36)
43 "Past the first and the second _____, they came unto the iron gate" (Acts 12:10)

46 Gym class (abbr.)
47 "I am debtor both to the _____, and to the Barbarians" (Romans 1:14)
48 "Foxes have _____, and birds of the air have nests" (Luke 9:58)
49 A king of Moab (Judges 3:12)
50 "He had rested _____ all his work" (Genesis 2:3)
51 A prince of Midian (Joshua 13:21)
53 "_____, and Shema, and Moladah" (Joshua 15:26)
54 Appellation
55 Strong wood
56 "Bakbukiah and _____, their brethren" (Nehemiah 12:9)
57 Viewed
58 He was at war with Baasha, king of Israel (1 Kings 15:16)
59 Ikkesh's son (2 Samuel 23:26)
62 "Bring out the _____ who have come to you" (Joshua 2:3 NKJV)

ACROSS

1 Phares's brother (Matthew 1:3)
5 Zerah's son (1 Chronicles 2:6)
9 "For they _____ for your souls"
(Hebrews 13:17)
14 Belonging to Hophni's father
(1 Samuel 4:4)
15 Gaal's father (Judges 9:28)
16 This man was a Netophathite
(Jeremiah 40:8)
17 Get higher
18 Group of people, like gypsies
19 Things
20 "He hath reserved in _____
chains" (Jude 1:6)
23 "_____ verily, their sound went
into all the earth" (Romans 10:18)
24 "I will make Jerusalem heaps, and
a _____ of dragons"
(Jeremiah 9:11)
25 "We remember the fish we _____
in Egypt at no cost"
(Numbers 11:5 NIV)
26 Benjamin's son (Genesis 46:21)
28 "_____ of your faith in Christ"
(Colossians 2:5)
34 Strive to attain
37 The only New Testament history
book
38 King James affirmation
39 "_____ not unto thine own
understanding" (Proverbs 3:5)
40 "The changeable _____ of
apparel, and the mantles"
(Isaiah 3:22)
42 "I am this day _____, though
anointed king" (2 Samuel 3:39)
43 Last book of the Old Testament
(abbr.)
44 "Do not _____ the edge"
(Ecclesiastes 10:10)
45 This makes waste
46 Family of one of Ephraim's sons
(Numbers 26:35)
50 "He told _____ all his heart"
(Judges 16:17)
51 Stomach
52 Solomon's great-grandson
(1 Chronicles 3:10)
55 Take advantage of

58 "At _____ also the day shall be
darkened" (Ezekiel 30:18)
62 Manoah was from here
(Judges 13:2)
64 Sadoc's father (Matthew 1:14)
65 "What do thy eyes _____ at"
(Job 15:12)
66 "He was not _____ that his face
was radiant" (Exodus 34:29 NIV)
67 "Who said, _____ it"
(Psalm 137:7)
68 To lessen
69 Nearer the center
70 "Listen to the _____ of my lips"
(Job 13:6 NIV)
71 Lose fur

DOWN

1 "And we went over the brook
_____" (Deuteronomy 2:13)
2 "He. . .gave many convincing
proofs that he was _____"
(Acts 1:3 NIV)
3 "_____ again from the dead"
(Acts 17:3)
4 Greek form of *Asher*
(Revelation 7:6)
5 "Behold, ye fast for strife and
_____" (Isaiah 58:4)
6 "I know both how to be _____"
(Philippians 4:12)
7 "He will _____ the vineyard to
other tenants" (Matthew 21:41 NIV)
8 Melchi's father (Luke 3:28)
9 "Divers _____ are an
abomination unto the LORD"
(Proverbs 20:23)
10 Capable
11 "_____ shall see God"
(Matthew 5:8)
12 "The LORD _____ down to see
the city" (Genesis 11:5 NIV)
13 "The merchants among the
nations _____ at you"
(Ezekiel 27:36 NIV)
21 Now deceased
22 "I have robbed their _____ of
riches" (Isaiah 10:14 NLT)
27 Hoosier state (abbr.)
28 Our solar system's star

by N. Teri Grottke

29 "The just shall live by his _____"
   (Habakkuk 2:4)
30 Pretend
31 "Noah found grace in the _____
   of the Lord" (Genesis 6:8)
32 "I will commune with thee from
   above the mercy _____"
   (Exodus 25:22)
33 "Oh save me for thy mercies'
   _____" (Psalm 6:4)
34 Type of trees
35 The border went to here from
   Remmonmethoar (Joshua 19:13)
36 Zimri's father (Numbers 25:14)
40 Allotment
41 Bani's son (Ezra 10:34)
42 "God saw that it _____ good"
   (Genesis 1:21)
44 "Examine yourselves, _____ ye be
   in the faith" (2 Corinthians 13:5)
45 To fell by an ax, past tense
47 Fifth day of the week (abbr.)

48 "It shall not be lawful to _____
   toll, tribute, or custom, upon them"
   (Ezra 7:24)
49 Micah's son (1 Chronicles 9:41)
52 Ahitub's son (1 Samuel 14:3)
53 Hearing, sight, and smell are each
   this (sing.)
54 Questioned
55 Palal's father (Nehemiah 3:25)
56 "Fruit of righteousness is _____
   in peace" (James 3:18)
57 Shuthelah's son (Numbers 26:36)
59 "Joy of the _____ ceaseth"
   (Isaiah 24:8)
60 "Mountains shall reach unto
   _____" (Zechariah 14:5)
61 "_____ great with young"
   (Psalm 78:71)
63 "_____ there yet the treasures"
   (Micah 6:10)

## 81

BIBLICAL PLANTS

And God said, Behold, I have given you every herb bearing seed,
which is upon the face of all the earth, and every tree.

GENESIS 1:29

ACROSS

1 "James the son of Zebedee, and
_____ his brother"
(Matthew 10:2)
5 "And Geshem the _____ heard
about it" (Nehemiah 2:19 NIV)
9 "Whether it be good or _____
thou valuest it" (Leviticus 27:12)
(2 words)
14 Ann Arbor campus, initially
15 Italian money
16 "And set it upon _____"
(Numbers 21:8) (2 words)
17 Delhi garb
18 "The glory _____ the only
begotten of the Father" (John
1:14) (2 words)
19 *Eta* follower
20 Biblical plant found in Song of
Solomon 2:1 (4 words)
23 Mead's island of study
24 Flood and rip
25 Englishmen
28 "_____ them with cords of
human kindness" (Hosea 11:4 NIV)
(2 words)
32 Biblical plants, with 44 Across,
found in Matthew 6:28
(2 words)
35 "It was a _____, and a stone lay
upon it" (John 11:38)
36 Poem of praise
37 "The sun shall not smite thee by
_____" (Psalm 121:6)
38 Sign of a play's success (abbr.)
41 "Ye shall not surely _____"
(Genesis 3:4)
42 "Neither _____ you up a standing
image" (Leviticus 26:1)
44 See 32 Across (2 words)
46 "Some would even _____ to die"
(Romans 5:7)

47 Sky-colored jammies (2 words)
49 Parody
51 Use the soapbox
55 Biblical plants found in Isaiah 2:13
(3 words)
60 "Shall compel thee to go _____"
(Matthew 5:41) (2 words)
61 "O thou _____, go" (Amos 7:12)
62 Oklahoma city
63 Horse fathers
64 Sicilian volcano
65 Humdinger
66 Lock
67 Concordes, for example
68 Pirate in *Peter Pan*

DOWN

1 Tilting matches (var.)
2 Early Nebraska resident
3 "Singers, and a _____ as well"
(Ecclesiastes 2:8 NIV)
4 Capital of Kenya
5 "_____ for the day" (Joel 1:15 NIV)
6 "And ye shall _____ up early"
(Genesis 19:2)
7 "There shall be _____ Jesse"
(Romans 15:12) (3 words)
8 Island in northern Canada
9 "And _____ himself in water"
(Leviticus 15:5)
10 Incomprehensible, as a result of
brain damage
11 "But a _____ of the work"
(James 1:25)
12 A kind of sax
13 Irish playwright O'Casey
21 Rowed
22 1960s radical political group (abbr.)
26 "For what _____ man profited"
(Matthew 16:26) (2 words)
27 Plaything

by David K. Shortess

29 "This do ye; _____ your beasts, and go" (Genesis 45:17)
30 "But deliver us from _____" (Matthew 6:13)
31 "What _____ is this" (Genesis 44:15)
32 "Where, _____?" (Luke 17:37)
33 "The _____ seemed good to me" (Deuteronomy 1:23 NIV)
34 One of Shakespeare's kings
38 "And _____ said unto them" (Ruth 1:20)
39 Company agent, in short
40 "Ye have heard of the patience _____" (James 5:11) (2 words)
43 Used cars
44 Little Miss Muffet's seats
45 "Of the children of _____ half" (Numbers 31:47) (poss.)
47 Derek and Jangles (pl.)
48 Sets free
50 "For the _____ is full" (Joel 3:13)

52 Per _____ (once a year)
53 Sheer linen fabric
54 Provide with a gift or quality
55 "First _____ out the beam out of thine own eye" (Matthew 7:5)
56 Arabian chieftain
57 "A _____ vision has been shown to me" (Isaiah 21:2 NIV)
58 "I have _____ him to the LORD" (1 Samuel 1:28)
59 Significant historic periods

## 82

ACROSS

1 Negative response (slang)
4 Solomon's great-grandson (Matthew 1:7)
7 Before Daniel (abbr., var.)
10 "_____ nor sown, and shall strike off the heifer's neck" (Deuteronomy 21:4)
12 Belonging to Hophni's father (1 Samuel 1:3) (poss.)
13 Mary was told by the angel to regard fear this way
14 A servant of the church at Cenchrea (Romans 16:1)
15 Tubs
16 "Children of Ramah and _____" (Ezra 2:26)
17 Uz's brother (Genesis 10:23)
18 "_____ tables of the heart" (2 Corinthians 3:3)
20 "_____, and Shema, and Moladah" (Joshua 15:26)
21 Abraham's son by Keturah (Genesis 25:4)
23 National association of U.S. sign language interpreters (abbr.)
25 _____ Dominion University in Norfolk
26 "Doors of the gates, and for the _____" (1 Chronicles 22:3)
31 It took Jonah this many days to get to Nineveh (Jonah 3:3)
34 Rulers' nationality at Jesus' time
35 Gad's son (Genesis 46:16)
36 Delilah cut Samson's
37 The first Hebrew month (Esther 3:7)
38 "God hath not given us the spirit of _____" (2 Timothy 1:7)
39 "Fasten the ephod on him by _____ . . .waistband" (Exodus 29:5 NIV)
40 "There shall come forth a vessel for the _____" (Proverbs 25:4)
41 "Afflictions of Christ in my flesh for his _____ sake" (Colossians 1:24) (poss.)
42 "By his _____ a light doth shine" (Job 41:18)

44 "Keep thee _____ from a false matter" (Exodus 23:7)
45 "How long will it be _____ they believe me. . . ?" (Numbers 14:11)
46 "Vessels of wrath _____ to destruction" (Romans 9:22)
49 A symbol of peace is a lion laying with this animal
52 "_____ he were a Son, yet learned he obedience" (Hebrews 5:8)
55 Plural form of *is*
57 Of the Caucasus Mountains and Sri Lanka
58 "His soul shall dwell at _____" (Psalm 25:13)
59 "I have not _____ the rams of your flock" (Genesis 31:38 NKJV)
61 Adam was the first
62 David hid by this stone (1 Samuel 20:19)
63 "Let not thy _____ make me afraid" (Job 13:21)
64 Atlanta's time zone (abbr.)
65 Greek form of *Noah* (Matthew 24:38)
66 "With him is an _____ of flesh" (2 Chronicles 32:8)

DOWN

1 "The book of the vision of _____ the Elkoshite" (Nahum 1:1)
2 Gad's son (Genesis 46:16)
3 Before James (abbr.)
4 "_____ for the day" (Joel 1:15)
5 "_____ thou hast not hated blood" (Ezekiel 35:6)
6 "Behold, the _____ was a cedar" (Ezekiel 31:3)
7 "Tappuah, and _____" (Joshua 15:34)
8 "Syrians of Bethrehob, and the Syrians of _____" (2 Samuel 10:6)
9 "To the top of the rock _____" (Judges 15:11)
10 "Great is Diana of the _____" (Acts 19:28) (abbr.)
11 "_____ not yourselves with the idols of Egypt" (Ezekiel 20:7)
12 "_____ the death of the cross" (Philippians 2:8)

by N. Teri Grottke

16 Menahem's father (2 Kings 15:14)
19 "God heard the voice of the
____" (Genesis 21:17)
22 "Rewardeth the proud ____"
(Psalm 31:23)
24 Biblical lodging
26 One of Jesus' brothers
(Matthew 13:55)
27 Eliphaz's son (Genesis 36:11)
28 Lack
29 "Bring down my ____ hairs
with sorrow" (Genesis 42:38)
30 Title for knights
31 Through thick and ____: every
obstacle
32 Detest
33 Increase in height
34 Circle
37 "There lacked of David's servants
____ men and Asahel"
(2 Samuel 2:30)
38 Place of refuge
40 Type of tree

41 "My sword shall be ____ in
heaven" (Isaiah 34:5)
43 "____ shall offer gifts"
(Psalm 72:10)
44 Jesus cursed this tree (Matthew
21:19)
46 "Thou shalt be for ____ to the
fire" (Ezekiel 21:32)
47 Samson's riddle: "Out of the
____ came forth meat"
(Judges 14:14)
48 Sleeping thought
49 Crippled
50 "Nevertheless ____ heart was
perfect" (1 Kings 15:14) (poss.)
51 "Tithe ____ and rue and all
manner of herbs" (Luke 11:42)
53 Bethuel's brother (Genesis 22:22)
54 "As he saith also in ____"
(Romans 9:25)
56 "Latter ____ than at the
beginning" (Ruth 3:10)
60 Jether's son (1 Chronicles 7:38)

## 83

ACROSS

1 Many times (arch.)
4 "_____ name is called Babel" (Genesis 11:9 NKJV)
7 Became acquainted
10 John was baptizing near here (John 3:23)
12 "I _____ not" (Luke 17:9)
14 Heber's father (Luke 3:35)
15 Gad's son (Genesis 46:16)
16 "Their border was Helkath, and _____" (Joshua 19:25)
17 "Than the day of _____ birth" (Ecclesiastes 7:1) (poss.)
18 "Harps also and _____ for singers" (1 Kings 10:12)
20 "Millstone were hanged about his _____" (Matthew 18:6)
21 Ahira's father (Numbers 7:83)
22 This many souls were saved in the ark (1 Peter 3:20)
24 "Thou _____ till that a stone was cut" (Daniel 2:34)
28 "He that hath _____ to hear, let him hear" (Matthew 11:15)
30 Shobal's son (1 Chronicles 1:40)
31 Opposite of *begins*
33 "Thou hast put gladness in my _____" (Psalm 4:7)
38 "They had no _____ so much as to eat" (Mark 6:31)
40 Rezon's father (1 Kings 11:23)
42 "Will I not break, nor _____ the thing" (Psalm 89:34)
43 Not easily found
45 Identical
46 Increase
48 "Ye were as sheep going _____" (1 Peter 2:25)
50 "Crowns shall be to _____" (Zechariah 6:14)
53 David hid from Saul here (1 Samuel 24:3)
55 Priests burned incense from here to Beersheba (2 Kings 23:8)
56 Amasa's father was one of these (1 Chronicles 2:17)
62 Manasseh's son (2 Chronicles 33:20)
63 "All the Chaldeans, Pekod, and _____, and Koa" (Ezekiel 23:23)
64 "Rinnah, Benhanan, and _____" (1 Chronicles 4:20)
65 Musical group
66 Title of respect for men
67 Listened
68 No matter which
69 Asaph wrote numbers 73–83 of these (abbr.)
70 Iniquity

DOWN

1 "Wherein shall go no galley with _____" (Isaiah 33:21)
2 Animal parasite
3 Plow
4 Amasa's father (2 Samuel 17:25)
5 Taught
6 Shoe bottom
7 "Shall be your _____" (Ezekiel 45:12)
8 Special group by vote
9 Job
10 Gullible person
11 Two of these make a farthing (Mark 12:42)
13 "Foolishness of God is _____ than men" (1 Corinthians 1:25)
14 Verbal music
19 Come in
23 Rephaiah's father (1 Chronicles 4:42)
24 "Land from _____ to the wilderness" (Isaiah 16:1)
25 "_____ was a keeper of sheep" (Genesis 4:2)
26 Stay in place
27 "_____ by the life of Pharaoh surely ye are spies" (Genesis 42:16)
29 Greek form of *Asher* (Revelation 7:6)
32 Salathiel's father (Luke 3:27)
34 Wise men's direction (Matthew 2:1)
35 Twelfth Hebrew month (Esther 3:13)
36 "In _____ was there a voice" (Matthew 2:18)

by N. Teri Grottke

37 "Blessed are the pure in heart: for
_____ shall see God"
(Matthew 5:8)
39 "Pharisees began to _____ him
vehemently" (Luke 11:53)
41 "Intreat me not to _____ thee"
(Ruth 1:16)
44 "They cast four _____ out of the
stern" (Acts 27:29)
47 Wrong
49 "When he _____ that the lad is
not with us" (Genesis 44:31)
50 "_____, and Chalcol, and Darda"
(1 Kings 4:31)
51 "Brought thee for a present horns
of ivory and _____" (Ezekiel
27:15)
52 Real estate
54 Joab took him by the beard to kiss
him (2 Samuel 20:9)
55 A garrison of Philistines was here
(1 Samuel 13:3)

57 Deep water vehicle
58 Untruths
59 "_____ the Ahohite"
(1 Chronicles 11:29)
60 Ripped
61 Finish

84

ACROSS

1 "_____ of dove's dung for five pieces of silver" (2 Kings 6:25)
4 "Therefore God give thee of the _____ of heaven" (Genesis 27:28)
7 After Philippians (abbr.)
10 "The child was _____ from that very hour" (Matthew 17:18)
12 He was an Ahohite (1 Chronicles 11:29)
14 Elihu's father (1 Samuel 1:1)
15 A photograph
16 Address to group of men
17 A Canaanite king (Numbers 21:1)
18 "These from the land of _____" (Isaiah 49:12)
19 "Having _____ persons in admiration" (Jude 1:16) (poss.)
20 "My _____ shall comfort me" (Job 7:13)
21 The Lord smote him (1 Samuel 25:38)
23 A porter (Ezra 10:24)
25 "The _____ of Sodom were wicked and sinners before the LORD" (Genesis 13:13)
28 Negative voice vote
29 "Thou _____ thereof thou shalt surely die" (Genesis 2:17)
33 "_____ there yet the treasures" (Micah 6:10)
34 Expiring
37 Large sea mammal
38 "Kings of Sheba and _____ shall offer gifts" (Psalm 72:10)
40 Abner's father (1 Samuel 14:51)
41 Shammah's father (2 Samuel 23:11)
42 Head's skin
44 Spirit
47 To rent or lease
48 "The son of _____, was the ruler of the house of God" (Nehemiah 11:11)
50 "Meet the Lord in the _____" (1 Thessalonians 4:17)
51 Book of letters by Paul (abbr.)
52 Peter cut off one (John 18:10)
53 "As a _____ which melteth" (Psalm 58:8)

55 Ancient measure of capacity (Ezekiel 45:14)
57 Rephaiah's father (1 Chronicles 4:42)
59 Zadok's father (Nehemiah 3:4)
63 Feel deeply
64 Esau's father-in-law (Genesis 26:34)
65 Saul's witch was from here (1 Samuel 28:7)
66 "_____ the office of a deacon" (1 Timothy 3:13)
67 Resounded
68 Light smell
69 Lion's home
70 "_____ verily, their sound" (Romans 10:18)
71 "Come down _____ my child die" (John 4:49)

DOWN

1 "Talitha _____" (Mark 5:41)
2 Dishan's son (Genesis 36:28)
3 Start
4 "So shall Moab be a derision and a _____ to all" (Jeremiah 48:39)
5 An overseer (2 Chronicles 31:13)
6 To tell about danger
7 Center
8 "Jemuel, and Jamin, and _____" (Genesis 46:10)
9 Shem's child (Genesis 10:22)
10 King Saul's father (Acts 13:21)
11 "I will speak: I will _____ of thee" (Job 42:4)
13 "An _____ of blood twelve years" (Mark 5:25)
14 "Turning him to the body said, _____, arise" (Acts 9:40)
22 Type of window
24 Most fruits and vegetables are fine this way
25 Ishmael's son (Genesis 25:14)
26 "_____, and Accad, and Calneh" (Genesis 10:10)
27 "Hariph, Anathoth, _____" (Nehemiah 10:19)

by N. Teri Grottke

30 Winged symbol of the United States
31 Rejuvenation process
32 Grinders
35 He came with Jeshua and Seraiah (Ezra 2:2) (abbr.)
36 "With _____ which cannot be uttered" (Romans 8:26)
39 Changed
43 Issachar's son (Numbers 26:23)
45 "Keros, the children of _____" (Nehemiah 7:47)
46 There were twelve in Israel
49 "The best of them is as a _____" (Micah 7:4)
53 "Suddenly there _____ from heaven a great light" (Acts 22:6)
54 Spear
55 "Shall in no _____ enter into the kingdom of heaven" (Matthew 5:20)

56 Jerahmeel's son (1 Chronicles 2:25)
58 Kill
60 Arad's brother (1 Chronicles 8:15)
61 Not any
62 Form of expression
63 Cows chew this

EASTER DISCOVERIES

*In the end of the sabbath. . .came Mary Magdalene
and the other Mary to see the sepulchre.*

MATTHEW 28:1

ACROSS

1 "The LORD hath _____ king over you" (1 Samuel 12:13) (2 words)
5 Play boisterously
9 "From the _____ of evil and cruel men" (Psalm 71:4 NIV)
14 Unit of matter
15 Charles Lamb's pen name
16 Sudsy brothers
17 "And joined the _____ of Egypt" (Joshua 15:4 NIV)
18 "And because I _____ you the truth" (John 8:45)
19 Ancient Greek marketplace
20 Discovered on the first **EASTER** morn (Mark 16:4) (3 words)
23 "And _____ of them be gone astray" (Matthew 18:12)
24 Hair salon item
25 Radon or xenon
28 Female cat coat, sometimes
32 "Straightway ye shall find an _____ tied" (Matthew 21:2)
35 Discovered on the first **EASTER** morn (Luke 24:3) (2 words)
37 Tête topper
39 "And their round _____ like the moon" (Isaiah 3:18)
40 -*Rain* or -*race* preceder
41 "I am _____ for evermore, Amen" (Revelation 1:18)
42 "An _____ of wrath to bring" (Romans 13:4 NIV)
43 Discovered on the first **EASTER** morn (Matthew 28:6) (3 words)
45 "And upon the great _____" (Exodus 29:20)
46 Corporate union
47 Naval officer (abbr.)
48 Resort
50 Ruby or Sandra

52 Discovered on the first **EASTER** morn (John 20:12) (3 words)
61 Automaton
62 Stepped down
63 "But deliver us from _____" (Matthew 6:13)
64 "_____ all that we ask or think" (Ephesians 3:20)
65 Philosopher Descartes
66 Highway hauler
67 "I will ransom them from the _____ of the grave" (Hosea 13:14)
68 "Mighty in _____ and word" (Luke 24:19)
69 "Let it become a _____" (Psalm 69:22)

DOWN

1 "And put them under _____" (2 Samuel 12:31)
2 *State* (Fr.)
3 "Yea, and what have ye _____ with me" (Joel 3:4) (2 words)
4 Kind of acid
5 "They _____ before his thrashing" (Job 41:25 NIV)
6 Margarine
7 "Two women shall be grinding at the _____" (Matthew 24:41)
8 Coffin cover
9 Forest opening
10 Royal
11 "Four men which have _____ on them" (Acts 21:23) (2 words)
12 Blood fluids
13 "Watch and ____" (Matthew 26:41)
21 Capsulate, biologically
22 Self, to Caesar
25 "Could not _____ the truth because of the uproar" (Acts 21:34 NIV) (2 words)

by David K. Shortess

26 *Pal* (Sp.)
27 Overindulgence
29 "For, _____ winter is past"
(Song of Solomon 2:11) (2 words)
30 Middle Eastern chief (var.)
31 "Good buddy's" radio (2 words)
32 "_____, my love, my fair one,
and come away"
(Song of Solomon 2:13)
33 How many sons had Sceva?
(Acts 19:14)
34 British guns
36 How many sons had Haman?
(Esther 9:10)
37 What Sarai was (Genesis 11:30)
38 "And brought the child to _____"
(1 Samuel 1:25)
44 Tranquilized
46 Apple type, in short
48 Heater
49 "When _____ was come down
out of the ship" (Matthew 14:29)

51 Opposite of *ingest*
52 "That he can _____ himself in it"
(Isaiah 28:20)
53 King of the road
54 "For this cause _____ my knees"
(Ephesians 3:14) (2 words)
55 Hog fat
56 Away from the wind
57 "These men shall _____ with me"
(Genesis 43:16)
58 "Neither will he keep his anger for
_____" (Psalm 103:9)
59 Ohio city or bean
60 "That my feet did not _____"
(Psalm 18:36)

ACROSS

1 "Tyrus hath said against Jerusalem, _____" (Ezekiel 26:2)
4 She hid the Hebrew spies (Joshua 2:1)
9 Hotham's sister (1 Chronicles 7:32)
13 Not wild
15 "Jonathan _____ from the table in fierce anger" (1 Samuel 20:34)
16 Opposite of *release*
17 "Departed in a ship of _____" (Acts 28:11)
19 Shuthelah's son (Numbers 26:36)
20 "Simeon and Levi, _____ brethren" (Genesis 34:25) (poss.)
21 Nisroch's sons escaped to here (Isaiah 37:38)
23 Daniel was almost lunch for these
26 Took in food
27 Mother's sister
30 Follows Zechariah (abbr.)
31 "Who hath gathered the wind in his _____" (Proverbs 30:4)
33 Caleb's son (1 Chronicles 4:15)
34 Judean ruler at the time of Jesus' birth
36 Fifth day (abbr.)
38 Riblah was on its east side (Numbers 34:11)
39 "Hewers of wood and _____ of water for the congregation" (Joshua 9:27)
41 "_____ that ye refuse not him that speaketh" (Hebrews 12:25)
42 Syllable of derision or doubt
43 "Daughters were among thy honourable _____" (Psalm 45:9)
44 "Hear, O ye kings, give _____" (Judges 5:3)
45 "And Iron, and Migdalel, _____, and Bethanath" (Joshua 19:38)
48 Place of religious training (abbr.)
50 Type of connector
51 King of Assyria (2 Kings 15:19)
52 Peter would deny Christ before the cock crowed this many times (Mark 14:72)
54 "Salute _____ approved in Christ" (Romans 16:10)

58 "I saw the tents of _____ in affliction" (Habakkuk 3:7)
62 "The days of Methuselah were _____ hundred sixty and nine years" (Genesis 5:27)
63 Zophar was one (Job 2:11)
66 Eshcol's brother (Genesis 14:13)
67 Duke that came of Esau (Genesis 36:40)
68 Arad's brother (1 Chronicles 8:15)
69 "My beloved is gone down into his garden, to the _____ of spices" (Song of Solomon 6:2)
70 "Commanding to abstain from _____" (1 Timothy 4:3)
71 Gad's son (Genesis 46:16)

DOWN

1 Joseph mourned for Jacob at his threshingfloor (Genesis 50:10)
2 "Helkath, and _____, and Beten" (Joshua 19:25)
3 Word of agreement or approval
4 "Gave himself a _____ for all" (1 Timothy 2:6)
5 Bela's son (Numbers 26:40)
6 Aaron died in this mountain (Numbers 33:38)
7 "They. . .were forbidden of the Holy Ghost to preach the word in _____" (Acts 16:16)
8 "Every man should _____ rule" (Esther 1:22)
9 Torrents, like with rain
10 "I will send the _____ ahead of you" (Exodus 23:28 NIV)
11 Daniel had a vision by this river (Daniel 8:2)
12 "Of Harim, _____; of Meraioth" (Nehemiah 12:15)
14 Give honor to
18 Abdiel's son (1 Chronicles 5:15)
22 "Now when every _____ turn was come" (Esther 2:12) (poss.)
24 Hodiah's brother (1 Chronicles 4:19)
25 "Whom thou _____ in the valley of Elah" (1 Samuel 21:9)

by N. Teri Grottke

27 Zibeon's son (1 Chronicles 1:40)
28 Bathsheba's first husband
   (2 Samuel 11:3)
29 Joshua's father (Exodus 33:11)
31 "Who gave himself _____ our
   sins" (Galatians 1:4)
32 Rob
35 "To _____ them again unto
   repentance" (Hebrews 6:6)
37 In the _____ and now
39 Live there
40 Type of numeral (abbr.)
41 Hardtack, or a _____ biscuit
46 "Thine enemies have _____ their
   mouth" (Lamentations 2:16)
47 "For _____ are not a terror to
   good works" (Romans 13:3)
49 "They set them up _____ graven
   image" (Judges 18:31) (poss.)
50 "Dwelling was from _____"
   (Genesis 10:30)
53 Slice

54 Canaanite city (Joshua 11:21)
55 Common tree
56 "Engannim, Tappuah, and
   _____" (Joshua 15:34)
57 "Cometh of the _____ of his
   patrimony" (Deuteronomy 18:8)
59 Animal's skin
60 "_____, Hizkijah, Azzur"
   (Nehemiah 10:17)
61 Salathiel's father (Luke 3:27)
64 Area near Babylon (2 Kings 17:24)
65 "Get up, take your _____ and go
   home" (Matthew 9:6 NIV)

ANSWERS

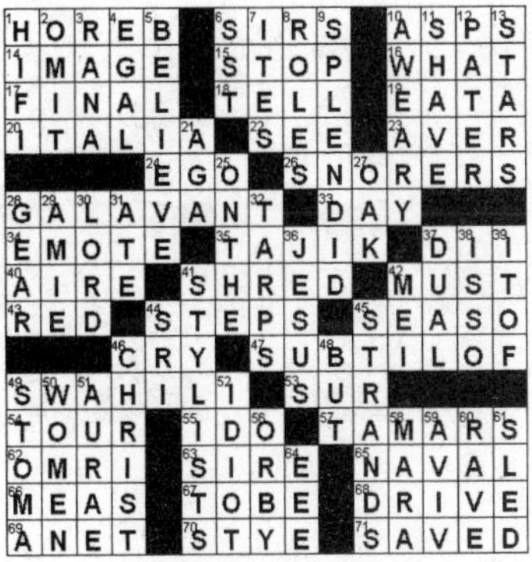

Puzzle 1

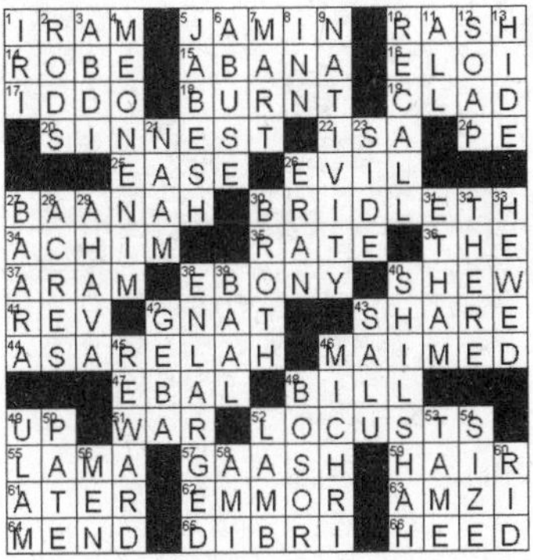

Puzzle 2

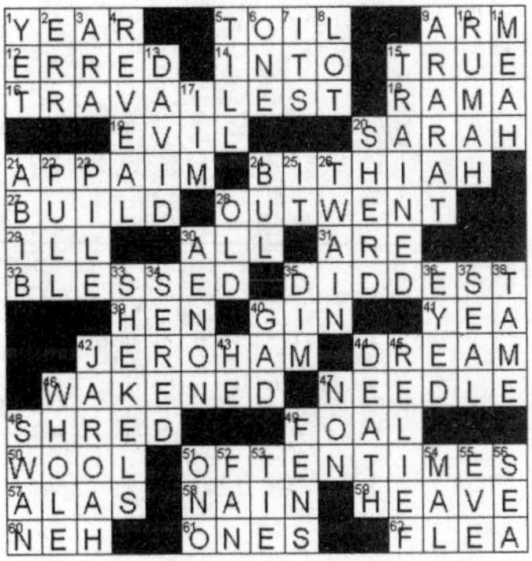

Puzzle 3

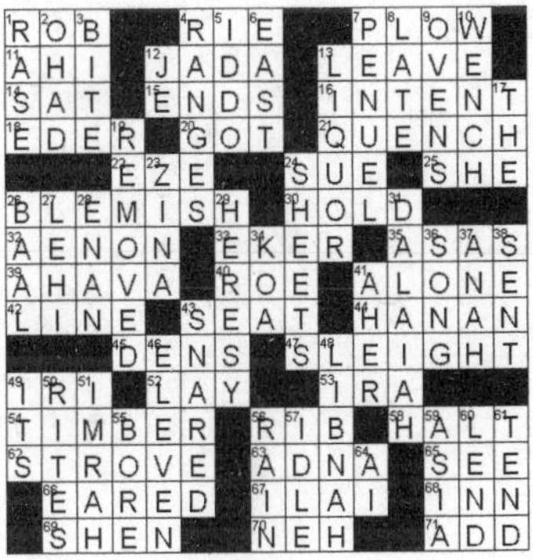

Puzzle 4

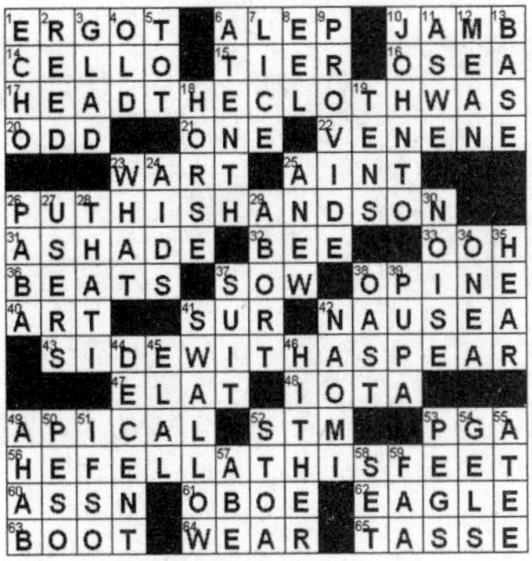

Puzzle 5

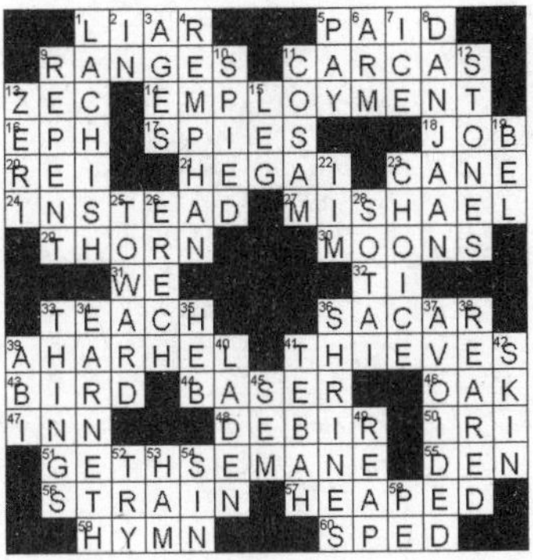

Puzzle 6

Puzzle 7

Puzzle 8

Puzzle 9

Puzzle 10

Puzzle 11

Puzzle 12

PUZZLE 13

PUZZLE 14

PUZZLE 15

PUZZLE 16

PUZZLE 17

PUZZLE 18

Puzzle 19

R	I	E		R	A	M	A		A	R	I	S	E
A	R	M	S		I	R	A	M		H	O	S	E	A
S	O	U	L		N	O	W		M	I	B	H	A	R
E	N	L	A	R	G	E		W	A	R		I	T	S
	S	A	V	E		R	O	H	G	A	H			
		T	E	N		H	I	D		E	D	E	R	
P	A	I		D	O	G		L	A	P		E	W	E
A	D	O		E	V	E		E	L	I		G	E	N
I	N	N		R	E	D		S	A	T		E	S	T
R	A	S	H		R	E	I		H	E	N			
	A	T	R	O	T	H		O	M	E	R			
A	L	L		R	A	N		A	D	M	I	R	E	D
R	E	A	S	O	N		E	R	E		M	A	A	I
T	A	M	E	D		A	R	A	N		S	T	I	R
S	H	A	M	E		S	I	N	S		E	A	T	

Puzzle 19

Puzzle 20

R	E	I		A	S	A				S	H	E	
W	A	Y	S		D	E	W		O	T	H	E	R	S
A	C	E	L	D	A	M	A		A	H	A	S	A	I
R	E	D	E	E	M	E	R		R	E	P	E	N	T
			A	S	I	E	L		F	E	D			
R	E	B	E	L			A	R	T	S				
U	S	E	S	T		R	E	U		H	E	B		
S	A	L	T		S	T	O	L	E		R	U	D	E
H	U	L		A	R	D		G	O	R	E	D		
			R	I	P	E		R	E	I	N	S		
		C	A	B		E	N	S	U	E				
J	A	H	A	Z	A		A	M	R	A	P	H	E	L
A	D	A	M	A	H		B	I	G	T	H	A	N	A
H	A	N	A	N	I		A	T	E		U	L	A	M
R	T	H		L	E	D		T	E	N				

Puzzle 20

Puzzle 21

S	E	W	S		T	A	R	S		S	K	I	P	
A	S	I	A		I	S	I	T		U	N	T	O	
L	A	S	C	I	V	I	O	U	S	N	E	S	S	
T	U	T		W	O	N	T		A	S	E	A	T	
		A	I	L			E	W	E					
D	I	S	S	I	M	U	L	A	T	I	O	N		
M	I	R	T	H		A	N	O	N		S	R	O	
A	D	I	M		G	O	I	N		B	A	A	L	
R	N	A		P	A	R	T		R	I	A	T	A	
C	O	N	C	U	P	I	S	C	E	N	C	E		
		A	R	E			I	C	E					
A	M	O	R	E		I	O	T	A		T	H	E	
S	U	P	E	R	S	C	R	I	P	T	I	O	N	
A	N	E	T		R	O	S	E		E	R	G	O	
P	I	N	S		I	N	K	S		L	E	S	S	

Puzzle 21

Puzzle 22

J	O	B	S		D	R	A	M	S		B	O	N	E
E	L	O	I		R	O	M	A	N		O	M	E	R
R	I	N	G		A	B	A	N	A		A	R	B	A
A	V	E	N		G	E	N	E	R	A	T	I	O	N
H	E	S	E	D			A	H	E	R				
			D	E	N	S			D	E	A	L	E	R
A	V	A		B	E	E	S			S	E	L	A	
R	A	M	A	T	H	A	I	M	Z	O	P	H	I	M
A	L	A	S			R	A	I	N		I	S	A	
H	E	M	A	T	H		N	A	A	M				
			H	A	T	H			N	I	N	T	H	
R	E	F	R	E	S	H	E	T	H		D	U	R	A
E	Z	R	I		H	E	Z	R	O		I	R	A	D
A	R	A	B		U	R	I	E	L		A	S	P	S
D	A	Y	S		M	E	R	E	D			N	E	S	T

Puzzle 22

Puzzle 23

	P	A	T	E		O	M	E	R		H	A	B
H	A	M	O	R		M	O	Z	A		M	A	R	A
A	R	O	E	R		E	R	A	N		A	M	O	K
M	E	S	S	E	N	G	E	R	S		C	A	S	E
			T	O	A	H		O	P	E	N	E	D	
P	I	L	E	H	A		A	M	A	D				
A	M	O	N		H	E	T	H		N	O	D	A	B
W	R	A	T	H		A	H	A		S	N	A	R	E
S	I	N	A	I		S	E	B	A		I	R	A	D
		N	E	S	T		D	E	A	T	H	S		
S	I	N	G	L	E		C	A	N	A				
A	M	A	L		E	M	U	L	A	T	I	O	N	S
C	A	K	E		M	A	R	T		E	Z	B	A	I
A	G	E	D		E	L	S	E		T	R	A	I	N
R	E	D		D	E	E	R		H	I	L	L		

Puzzle 23

Puzzle 24

K	O	R	A	H		A	S	P		S	A	L	T
I	V	O	R	Y		C	H	U	B		A	N	E	R
N	E	S	T	S		H	A	R	A		R	I	P	E
E	R	E		S	T	A	V	E	S		O	S	E	E
			O	A	R	S			O	W	N	E	R	S
Z	A	L	A	P	H		H	E	N	A				
E	N	A	M		A	S	A	S		N	E	B	A	I
R	A	I	M	E	N	T		L	E	T	T	E	R	S
I	N	D	I	A		A	S	I	A		A	R	A	H
			S	O	R	T		T	E	M	A	N	I	
S	O	C	K	E	T		O	M	E	R				
I	R	O	N		H	A	N	A	N	I		I	S	A
A	G	U	E		E	D	E	N		T	A	B	O	R
H	A	R	E		R	A	S	E		E	S	R	O	M
A	N	T	S		M	T	H		S	K	I	N	S	

Puzzle 24

PUZZLE 25

PUZZLE 26

PUZZLE 27

PUZZLE 28

PUZZLE 29

PUZZLE 30

PUZZLE 31

PUZZLE 32

PUZZLE 33

PUZZLE 34

PUZZLE 35

PUZZLE 36

PUZZLE 37

```
MARA  BAJA  CROC
OBIT  ARAM  AARON
ALPO  SANE  EDEMA
BEELZEBUB  SIMON
     LOS  SARAI
REC OTT SAR  SSE
EROS EAT PEANUT
ZAPHNATHPAANEAH
ISRAEL ETC DAVE
PEA HER AIR DER
   MERES OUT
ABRAM  JERUBBAAL
TRAGI EVAS ARCO
MARIA CELL RILL
EACH  TREY  SAUL
```

PUZZLE 38

```
OVEN  SHOT  HALAH
MALE  TARE  ANISE
ALMS  EDEN  MAKER
RESTRAINT  OMERS
     ODD  URI
SURETY HAS MOWN
WREST HOSEN LIE
AGATE ASP ARISE
REI NAVES MOVED
EDAR SEA HEWERS
     OBA  WET
ANGLE  JERAHMEEL
JAALA ELUL EZRA
AMBER WONT ARAD
HEARD SIGH LINE
```

PUZZLE 39

```
CARE  ECC  ASHES
AMOS  DOOM STOLE
GOATS ART  AARON
EZR PIT HA MIND
    FENS  DIP
CHERAN CUMI AMO
LOVER COSAM LEV
OSEE MANEH RULE
DEN EASED RISEN
SAT PREY CEPHAS
    AHA SOME
AGAG HO ELI DIM
NOBAH WON TRADE
INDIA LAST IRON
MEANS  REI  DALE
```

PUZZLE 40

```
DERBE SOAP  LACE
ELIAS ISHI  IRON
BOOTH TEIL  FORT
TITHE HEAL  EDAR
    EAR  HASTILY
DEADNESS  REI
EZR SEEM AMASA
ARAH TELEM EBER
RAMAH RATE DAM
    RED HEARTILY
HERDMAN  TIE
OVEN NUTS SMART
SIZE CROW SENEH
ELIS ESLI ANANI
ASAS SEAM HINDS
```

PUZZLE 41

```
ART  SET  ADORE
BOAS NOAH CORAL
AURA ELSE ITEMS
BYTHEWAYSIDE
ENSILER LBS CIA
BIS SAE AROD
USS STONYGROUND
RANEE FOE OLDIE
AMONGTHORNS EAR
LOUD WIT ATA
SAT SIS AGEDYOU
ONGOODGROUND
ALONE ABLE OBED
DOLCE TOED RATE
ODDER HER  NOR
```

PUZZLE 42

```
JEHU AWARE  LAD
ALAS THROW MICE
NINE TEMPERANCE
NUN CEASE ELEAD
ADAMANT AMENDS
   TENT USES
JOHA IRAD PUA
ANOTHERS SYCHEM
HEN ABIA HALI
   STEP HOUR
ABATED RUBBISH
HADAR AMANA SEA
BANISHMENT FENS
ANAN IMAGE REST
NAH DINED OSEE
```

PUZZLE 43

PUZZLE 44

PUZZLE 45

PUZZLE 46

PUZZLE 47

PUZZLE 48

PUZZLE 49

DAMAGED · OCT · FHA
ERUDITE · LOOKOUT
REMOVAL · IMPINGE
BELIEVEONTHE
PAPERS · VETS
ANIS · WAR · HADA
LYE · DEAL · STORES
LORDJESUSCHRIST
INCISE · ASHE · SIR
DEED · RTE · HERO
OBOE · SCONES
ANDTHOUSHALT
PEASANT · OVATELY
EXTERNE · BESAVED
STE · AYR · OSPREYS

PUZZLE 50

BEES · ABHOR · NOSE
ESLI · BAANA · EVIL
DESOLATION · BENO
KENATH · SHARAI
BEE · POETS
ELIDAD · DUMB · PAW
AENON · BORE · ARBA
SAVE · LIVED · MEAT
EVER · ANER · CEASE
DEN · APES · WANDER
TIRIA · PEN
MAIMED · HASRAH
AMON · OFTENTIMES
IMNA · TRIBE · PALE
DISH · HOPED · ELIM

PUZZLE 51

JEUZ · ASHAN · EBAL
OZNI · THOSE · LAMA
NETOPHATHI · IRAD
MORSEL · GUARDS
ANT · PHEBE
STALLS · TAIL · NER
HEMAM · THIN · ANAH
ENAM · THING · HERE
MOLE · EARS · RESTS
ARE · LAND · HARSHA
KNOCK · SAP
FLIETH · OTHERS
RATE · ENTREATETH
ODED · ROOTS · ABIA
MESS · SEEST · MARS

PUZZLE 52

ZAZA · DEEPS · TOW
WEN · ADLAI · ELIS
DARA · NAILS · LIVE
IRON · GRATE · AVEN
DERIDE · SIR · BEST
URI · ABI
URGE · TOO · ABBA
ESAU · AWAY · AHA
HEIR · GATES · PALM
ITS · DOTH · ULAI
HENA · EST · OREB
EYE · HAB
DARE · ASH · DANNAH
IRAD · CEASE · EASE
MENS · HADAR · THAN

PUZZLE 53

AGORA · IRE · MEAL
ALINED · FIR · OLLA
GILEAD · FOR · REOS
REB · CLAY · OLIVES
ANOUTER · PROA
SARI · CHI · THINE
IVE · OTT · GUR
SEA · EPHRAIM · ONA
OLD · HOE · ACE
PIECE · RBI · NEBO
APAN · DIALECT
ARARAT · COMM · TEE
DORM · OFA · BASHAN
ALIE · NAP · ORIENT
HEAL · ERE · BALLS

PUZZLE 54

ZIZ · FAT · AMASA
USES · ABEL · PADAN
PLAT · SINA · ELIKA
HELI · HATTIL · NEH
REI · HELL
HAS · ROW · LESHEM
AFTERNOON · STOLE
GOOD · SOBER · ASAS
ARROW · LABOURETH
REMMON · OAR · AHA
RARE · RIB
GOT · SHIPHI · AHAB
ABIAH · CHUN · CANE
PALTI · HANG · KINE
SLEEP · ITS · RAN

PUZZLE 55

```
TOWER  SPIN   MELT
ADAMI  ALSO   ELAH
MERED  LOATHSOME
EDER   DEW    AHIAN
       ADAM  TEMA
GALLIM  BENO   SEM
ABODE   DEKAR  HAI
HATS   TAKEN  GIRT
ASA    CORAL  HOMER
MEN    LGTH   DIVIDE
       TOSS  LOSE
ABIHU  GUR    RAMA
HERODIANS     ANGER
ALAS   THAT   COUNT
BADE   SAWS   TREES
```

PUZZLE 56

```
FOOT   SWORD  BRIM
AMMI   HABOR  EASE
MENE   ELIMELECHS
ERI    FALL   SARAIS
       POETS  ASIA
HOSAH  SHESHAN
OUTER  SAITH  BIT
FREE   MICAH  NOSE
FAN    HELAH  TEMAN
ITHAMAR       JABIN
       AMOS   SARON
PASTOR HOPE   ATE
INHERITETH    OBED
POOR   AHLAI  FLAG
ENDS   LYDIA  TYRE
```

PUZZLE 57

```
ASA    LAMAS  SPREE
WOT    AROMA  TROLL
FORWHATISSEENIS
UNEARTH       ANY
LIES   OTTO   RAW
       MANURE RAMA
TEMPORARY     JONAS
ONELAMB  STOMATA
ISLET  BUTWHATIS
TUBA   LESSON
SEA    MADE   MALI
       NEW   REWIPES
UNSEEN  SETERNAL
ROOST  RIDER  ERE
ORASA  AROSE  AND
```

PUZZLE 58

```
LEAP   ILAI   SEM
AHIO   MAST   SHINE
WINEPRESS     WEEDS
       TAIL   LEAVES
LOST   FEARED
JAM    HARVEST
ONE    STAIRS ELI
NERI   MAR    RAGE
ASSS   PILEHA HEN
       BLASTED MAD
HAROEH        MAIL
LEBANA        LEAH
ARISE  ABISHALOM
MEDES  DEEP   BABE
PSA    DENY   SPAN
```

PUZZLE 59

```
WISDOM  ROSH  MAW
ATTIRE  ABIA  IRA
THEE   LAMENT DOR
CART   THEY   SPIED
HIN    USE    OARS
       WARMED WON
JEREMIAS      HORITE
AXE    ABI   OUR  TIP
WOMENS  PURSUETH
       ARA   DUTIES
IMLA   ERR    CAB
SAINT  SPUE   ZOBA
PSA    ONIONS IRAM
ASH    OURS   LEBANA
HAS    KNEE   IDALAH
```

PUZZLE 60

```
HIDE   HENA   GATAM
AVEN   ODED   AHIRA
LAND   GIRD   LAMBS
THYSELF       ZAREAH
       LAY    SELA
HARIPH  THE   HIGH
ABANA   PHEBE TOO
MANNA   ARA   ALTAR
ASK    LEPER  TEATS
NEST   DEW    DEVISE
       ANER   HOR
PARDON        AUSTERE
ADAMI  ANUB   ABIB
SAMOS  HUNT   MEDE
SHARE  ANTS   EDER
```

Puzzle 61

Puzzle 62

Puzzle 63

Puzzle 64

Puzzle 65

Puzzle 66

PUZZLE 67

```
HAM.BEG.ARK...
OBED.ANAH.SEE.
ULAI.ASIA.HANG
RENDERING.ISAAC
..BAGS..MONTH.
ADINO..NATHAN.
DEMAND.YOU.ACRE
DELAYED.ESHBAAL
IRAM.AUL.KELITA
.ASLEEP..SENEH
USETH...THEE...
RAPHU.STANDARDS
THIN.HERS.HARE
.ATE.ESAU.AMON
.HEM..THE..APT
```

PUZZLE 68

```
BAY.HARUM.ERR.
AGE.ANANI.PLEA
DULL.BARNS.LIEN
.ELELOHEISRAEL.
..SIR....OIL..
MOUSE..BAKEN..
ABLE.NAOMIS.EST
LIAR.URIAS.ELAH
ELI.STALLS.SOLE
.FISHS...WHITE.
.BIT....WET...
.BETHMARCABOTH.
HALL.ODOUR.NOAH
ONLY.SNARE.EZE
SKY.TARES.SON
```

PUZZLE 69

```
ASA.SPIN.SNACKS
NAN.AURA.CABANA
DIN.SPUR.EDISON
3DAYSAND3NIGHTS
...EYE..OER....
DAMP..SIR..ITIS
ISA.THOR.SORROW
ANDTHESE3AREONE
NEARER.NOTE.VIE
ARMY..TEN..HEAT
...USA..HOE....
3MEASURESOFMEAL
MILLER.LAST.ABA
ERMINE.ALEE.SLY
NESTOR.MEAN.YES
```

PUZZLE 70

```
EPH.FEWER.EST.
EZRA.ITHAI.ELAH
NAAMATHITE.LIME
DRY.STEP.SIHOR
..GIER.BECAUSE
GILEAD.GAREB..
ABIB.SLAIN.AHA
BROAD.EAR.TAMED
AIN.RHESA.TOLA
..GOODS.SHENIR
PRIESTS.FOUR..
LAMBS.BOWS.ASA
ANNA.AMALEKITES
IGAL.MARKS.RANK
NEH.OWEST.ADD
```

PUZZLE 71

```
RIDE.BEARD..GAP
AMOZ.ENSUE.ARBA
INTREATIES.VAIL
NAH.DURA.OLIVES
.PITY...LATELY.
PACIFY..REACH..
UNITY.HASTE.RAN
ANT.GUILE.USE
HAY.MINNI.BASER
.WITTY..BICHRI.
ASSENT..PORT...
PHALTI.BLOT.AHI
HURL.IRATHITES.
ENOS.ERECH.SALU
KIN..SIDES.ADDI
```

PUZZLE 72

```
LOP.LAWS..ONO
BANI.IZHAR.OBED
OVEN.NAOMI.WARD
YES.LUZ.SOWN..
RITES..OTHER..
POT.TEN.ITEMS
LEHI.HIP.ACHSAH
ADO.NAPHISH.TIE
SARAIS.ARK.WILD
TRUST.SIA.FIT
.STRAW..TITUS.
REBA.COR.THE..
LAMA.DREAD.AIAH
AWAY.AMANA.SODI
DEN..STAY.ANY
```

PUZZLE 73

G	R	I	S	T		C	A	R	T		A	S	T	O
N	I	N	T	H		O	L	E	O		L	O	A	F
A	C	T	O	R		N	I	A	S		G	U	L	F
W	H	O	S	O	E	V	E	R	S	H	A	L	L	
		S	A	Y	O	N		E	Y	E				
P	A	W		T	E	L		S	S	E		C	A	R
A	S	E	A		O	U	C	H		N	U	R	S	E
C	A	L	L	O	N	T	H	E	N	A	M	E	O	F
A	N	T	I	C		E	E	E	E		P	A	N	E
S	Y	S		T	I	S		P	A	T		M	A	R
			G	A	S		E	I	T	E	L			
	T	H	E	L	O	R	D	S	H	A	L	L	B	E
I	R	O	N		B	U	S	H		S	A	V	E	D
R	O	L	E		A	B	E	L		E	M	O	T	E
A	D	D	S		R	E	L	Y		R	A	V	E	N

PUZZLE 73

PUZZLE 74

	B	I	T		N	A	H			M	A	R	A	H
N	E	R	I		A	R	A		O	M	E	G	A	
I	R	O	N		H	A	N	D	S	T	A	V	E	S
G	E	N			A	H	A	R	H	E	L			
H	A	S	H	E	M		N	O	E			H	I	P
			E	D		T	I	P			A	S	A	
	D	A	R	D	A		P	O	R	C	I	U	S	
S	H	E	D	E	U	R		I	N	H	E	R	I	T
P	A	L	S	I	E	S		N	E	E	D	Y		
I	R	A			H	A	G		S	A				
N	A	Y			H	I	S		S	A	R	A	P	H
		E	L	I	S	H	A	H			H	A	I	
E	P	H	R	A	T	H	I	T	E		S	I	R	S
A	H	I	A	M		M	A	R		A	R	T	S	
T	I	M	N	A		A	D	D		W	A	S		

PUZZLE 74

PUZZLE 75

PUZZLE 76

PUZZLE 77

PUZZLE 78

PUZZLE 79

PUZZLE 80

PUZZLE 81

PUZZLE 82

PUZZLE 83

PUZZLE 84

PUZZLE 85

PUZZLE 86

ACROSS

1 "_____ them in pieces, as for the pot" (Micah 3:3)
5 "The words of _____, the son of Jakeh" (Proverbs 30:1)
9 "Of _____ the family of Arelites" (Numbers 26:17)
10 What Miriam was, once
12 The Lord God "_____ upon the high places of the earth" (Amos 4:13 NKJV)
13 Tuft of corn silk
15 Hebrew month
16 Once Barbra's costar
18 Good king of Judah
19 "And _____ lifted up his eyes, and beheld all the plain" (Genesis 13:10)
20 "Out of the half tribe of Manasseh; _____ with her suburbs" (1 Chronicles 6:70)
21 "But Moses _____ from the face of Pharaoh" (Exodus 2:15)
22 Prepare to pray
24 Where Phenice was (Acts 27:12)
25 Mosaic _____
26 Digit
27 Make smooth
31 Make payment for
35 Relax
36 Camino _____
38 "The _____ cannot leave his father" (Genesis 44:22)
39 "A bishop then must be. . ._____ to teach" (1 Timothy 3:2)
40 "The Lord himself shall give you a _____" (Isaiah 7:14)
41 Real or recorded
42 "Neither repented of their. . ._____" (Revelation 9:21)
44 _____ image
46 Eagle's nest
47 "A rough valley, which is neither _____ nor sown" (Deuteronomy 21:4)
48 Before noon, briefly
49 Author Harper and family

DOWN

1 Bring into being
2 "_____, O LORD when I cry" (Psalm 27:7)
3 "Thy counsels of _____ are faithfulness and truth" (Isaiah 25:1)
4 "The name of the first is _____. . . where there is gold" (Genesis 2:11)
5 What Abram built at Shechem
6 Equipment
7 FedEx competitor
8 Garage event, really
9 Caleb's son (1 Chronicles 2:18)
11 Video game button
12 "Should a man full of _____ be justified" (Job 11:2)
14 "Ye _____ men with burdens grievous" (Luke 11:46)
17 NY player
20 "_____! for that day is great" (Jeremiah 30:7)
21 "_____ not thyself because of evil men" (Proverbs 24:19)
23 Or _____ (part of a threat)
24 "One of the seraphims. . .having a live _____ in his hand" (Isaiah 6:6)
27 Turf fuel
28 Binea's son (1 Chronicles 8:37)
29 "I _____ all thy precepts" (Psalm 119:128)
30 "I cannot dig; to _____ I am ashamed" (Luke 16:3)
32 Biblical mount
33 "Ye shall be _____ the Priests of the LORD" (Isaiah 61:6)
34 "The land of Nod, on the east of _____"(Genesis 4:16)
36 "The glory of the LORD is _____ upon thee" (Isaiah 60:1)
37 _____ Gabriel
40 "Grievous words _____ up anger" (Proverbs 15:1)
41 "The spirit _____ him and he fell" (Mark 9:20)
43 To and _____
45 Feminine name

by Evelyn M. Boyington

A JOYFUL SCRIPTURAL REPETITION

This is the day the LORD has made;
let us rejoice and be glad in it.
PSALM 118:24 NIV

ACROSS

1 Parts of minutes (abbr.)
5 "Then _____ you, father, send Lazarus" (Luke 16:27 NIV) (2 words)
9 List parts
14 Molecular constituent
15 "Did _____ serve with thee for Rachel?" (Genesis 29:25) (2 words)
16 Word commonly found in the Psalms
17 _____ time (not ever) (2 words)
18 Kind of tradition
19 Old saw
20 Beginning of **QUOTE** (Philippians 4:4 NIV)
22 Flow's partner
24 Word with wife or way
25 Ft. Worth school (abbr.)
26 "As _____ the east is from the west" (Psalm 103:12) (2 words)
28 **QUOTE**, part 2 (4 words)
35 Rocky hill
36 Gaddi's father (Numbers 13:11)
37 Old copier, briefly
38 "No man taketh it from me, but _____ it down of myself" (John 10:18) (2 words)
40 "M*A*S*H" persona
43 Corn or oat
44 Savants
46 Seth's sire
48 Sib
49 **QUOTE**, part 3 (5 words)
53 Steals a glimpse
54 Elizabeth II's title, for short
55 Exclamation of success
58 Carpet surface
59 End of **QUOTE**
63 "And all men _____ in their hearts of John" (Luke 3:15)
65 German song

67 "Thou art all fair, my love; there is no _____ in thee" (Song of Solomon 4:7)
68 "The labour of the _____ shall fail" (Habakkuk 3:17)
69 Fancy pitcher
70 Nicholas, for one
71 More reasonable
72 Kind of fountain
73 "With sore boils from the _____ of his foot" (Job 2:7)

DOWN

1 Moselle feeder
2 Sermon ending
3 And or but, briefly
4 "And Jacob said to Rebekah. . .I am a _____ man" (Genesis 27:11)
5 Immunization material
6 Make numb
7 Zeta follower
8 "Is there no balm in _____" (Jeremiah 8:22)
9 "There _____ in Gilead" (Old spiritual hymn) (3 words)
10 Hall of Famer Williams
11 "The children of _____" (Ezra 2:7)
12 "_____ from the east came" (Matthew 2:1 NIV)
13 "The love of God is _____ abroad in our hearts" (Romans 5:5)
21 Finishes a cake
23 Swimsuit top
26 Robinson's Man and Detective Joe
27 "The man of God said, Where fell it?. . .and the iron did _____" (2 Kings 6:6)
28 "_____; be not afraid" (John 6:20) (3 words)
29 "Against such there is _____" (Galatians 5:23) (2 words)

by David K. Shortess

30 _____-comedy
31 Sweet ending?
32 Shapeless pond dweller (var.)
33 Beginning of A.D. (2 words)
34 Athenian legislator
39 Bark
41 Despot Amin
42 Bishop's seat
45 Slim
47 Ma Kettle portrayer, to her friends
50 "Hurt not the earth, neither the _____" (Revelation 7:3)
51 "A word fitly spoken is like _____ of gold" (Proverbs 25:11)
52 Specters
55 Old Testament minor prophet
56 Island dance
57 A _____ apple (2 words)
59 "A bruised _____ shall he not break" (Isaiah 42:3)
60 _____ facto
61 "Then flew one of the seraphims. . .

a live _____ in his hand" (Isaiah 6:6)
62 To be, in Paris
64 Actress Arden
66 _____ Jima

3

ACROSS

1 Carnival employees
6 Botch
10 Village in the lowlands of Judah (Joshua 15:34)
11 Jacob's twin
13 Toy for most ages
14 Impart
15 Part of polite request
18 "He _____ his countenance steadfastly" (2 Kings 8:11)
20 Gain
22 Peleg's father (Genesis 10:25)
24 Benjamin's son (Genesis 46:21)
25 Transmit
26 _____ bene
27 View
28 "_____ slayeth the silly one" (Job 5:2)
29 Nuisance
31 "Light is _____ for the righteous" (Psalm 97:11)
33 Jonah was in the _____ belly (Jonah 2:1)
35 David's captain (1 Chronicles 11:42)
38 Haman's son (Esther 9:7)
40 "In the _____ he built castles and towers" (2 Chronicles 27:4)
41 "I will make my covenant between me and _____" (Genesis 17:2)
42 "Over Edom will I cast out my _____" (Psalm 60:8)
43 Word to dog
44 B & B, for one
46 Spin
47 Strange
48 City where multitudes of Gog are to be buried (Ezekiel 39:16)
52 Old Testament prophet (abbr.)
53 Meshullam's father (Nehemiah 3:6)
55 Ethiopian province (abbr.)
56 "In _____ was there a voice heard" (Matthew 2:18)
57 Elkanah's wife (1 Samuel 1)
58 "I am the rose of _____" (Song of Solomon 2:1)

DOWN

1 Archers
2 "He hath the _____ of David" (Revelation 3:7)
3 Seth's son (Genesis 5:6)
4 Comedienne Martha
5 "And thy rod, wherewith thou _____ the river" (Exodus 17:5)
6 "The Cretians are. . .evil beasts, slow _____" (Titus 1:12)
7 "As he saith also in _____ I will call them" (Romans 9:25)
8 "By faith he sojourned in the _____ of promise" (Hebrews 11:9)
9 Shem's son (1 Chronicles 1:17)
12 Gusty
16 "Having _____ in his flesh the enmity" (Ephesians 2:15)
17 Also
19 "In _____ beginning God" (Genesis 1:1)
20 Cyst
21 "Boasters, _____ of evil things" (Romans 1:30)
23 Italian painter of late 1400s
25 "When thou _____ him out" (Deuteronomy 15:13)
30 Calculated guess (abbr.)
32 "The LORD is a man of _____" (Exodus 15:3)
33 "And sounded, and found it twenty _____" (Acts 27:28)
34 Rate
36 Jonathan's brother (1 Samuel 14:49)
37 Joseph's wife (Genesis 41:45)
39 Elkanah's son (1 Chronicles 6:25)
40 "Send unto Babylon _____, that shall fan her" (Jeremiah 51:2)
45 Land where Cain dwelt (Genesis 4:16)
48 Wading bird (arch.)
49 "Were forbidden of the Holy Ghost to preach the word in _____" (Acts 16:6)
50 Father of Saul's concubine (2 Samuel 3:7)
51 City formerly known as Hamath

by Sarah Lagerquist Simmons

53 Big ___
54 Laughing sound

HEROES OF THE FAITH

ACROSS

1 Prostitute who hid spies (Joshua 2)
5 Animal David killed (1 Samuel 17:35–37)
8 "_____ ye therefore, and teach all nations" (Matthew 28:19)
11 Greek letter
13 He penned many Psalms
15 D.C. quadrant
16 Raw mineral
17 Horse's command (var.)
18 He wrestled with God (Genesis 32:24)
21 "Incline thine ear unto _____" (Psalm 102:2)
22 Baking pit
24 Sooner state (abbr.)
25 Mighty man of David (1 Kings 1:8)
27 Reed instrument
29 His face shone after meeting God (Exodus 34:29)
30 His weapon was a jawbone (Judges 15:16)
32 "And it came to pass _____ midnight" (Ruth 3:8)
33 "These are unclean for you: the weasel, the _____" (Leviticus 11:29 NIV)
34 "Here comes. . .a chariot with a _____ of horses" (Isaiah 21:9 NIV)
36 "There was not a man left in _____ or Beth-el" (Joshua 8:17)
37 Blood factor
38 Death notice (abbr.)
39 "Whose shoes I _____ not worthy to bear" (Matthew 3:11)
40 "_____ anger was kindled against Balaam" (Numbers 24:10)
43 "Let _____ build up the wall of Jerusalem" (Nehemiah 2:17)
46 Evil women
49 "They bring thee a _____ heifer without spot" (Numbers 19:2)
51 "_____ all that is in thine heart" (1 Samuel 14:7)
52 NE Canadian province (abbr.)
53 "The LORD _____ with favor on Abel" (Genesis 4:4 NIV)
54 Popular
55 "Shall play on the hole of the _____" (Isaiah 11:8)
57 Printer's measure
59 Governmental county subdivision (abbr.)
60 Encore (Fr.)
62 Great _____, biblically speaking
63 "The portion of their _____" (Psalm 11:6)
65 Discretion
66 Reference info (abbr.)
67 "Give me children, or _____ I die" (Genesis 30:1)
70 "_____ off the gold rings" (Exodus 32:2 NASB)
72 Oriental tea (var.)
73 He was buried near Hebron (Genesis 25:7–10)
74 Midwest state (abbr.)

DOWN

2 "Abimelech took an _____ in his hand" (Judges 9:48)
3 Daddy (Aramaic)
4 Exist
5 Short retort
6 Year of our Lord (abbr.)
7 Sin is like a filthy _____ (Isaiah 64:6)
8 He asked God for a sign (Judges 6:36–38)
9 Curious
10 Noah's son (Genesis 9:18)
12 "King Rehoboam _____ counsel with the old men" (2 Chronicles 10:6)
14 Vigor
15 Issachar's son (Genesis 46:13)
18 "He executed the _____ of the LORD" (Deuteronomy 33:21)
19 "For which of you. . .counteth the _____" (Luke 14:28)

by Marijane G. Troyer

20 "On the two stones the way a
_____ cutter engraves a seal"
(Exodus 28:11 NIV)
23 Lot's son (Genesis 19:36–37)
25 "Take me. . .a _____ of three
years old" (Genesis 15:9)
26 His name means "laughter"
28 "Of the oaks of Bashan have they
made thine _____" (Ezekiel 27:6)
30 Prophet who challenged Saul
31 "Cakes. . .and wafers unleavened
anointed with _____"
(Exodus 29:2)
35 Apiece (abbr.)
41 Baby goat (Isaiah 11:6)
42 She favored Jacob (var.)
44 Narrow opening
45 Esau and Nimrod
46 Brother of Benjamin
47 Atomic number 30 (abbr.)
48 Small portion (John 13:26)
49 First name in country music

50 Royal decree
51 German article
56 Dad, in other words
58 Greek letter
61 What Jacob made Esau (NIV)
64 By means of
65 Hot or cold beverage
68 Musical scale note
69 Quieting sound
71 American tree sloth

5

ACROSS

1 Shammai's brother (1 Chronicles 2:28)
5 Feminine nickname
9 Lawyers' livelihood
14 Addition column
15 Solomon's grandson (Matthew 1:7)
16 Naomi's daughter-in-law
17 "Talmai, the children of _____" (Joshua 15:14)
18 Window part
19 Lift up
20 Good (colloq.)
21 City beside Adam (Joshua 3:16)
23 Perfect score, to some
24 "And _____, which were dukes" (Joshua 13:21)
25 Obtain
26 Luxury car, for short
29 "Whose _____ was the sea" (Nahum 3:8)
32 Exclamation
35 Gad's son (Genesis 46:16)
37 Ripen
38 Duke of Edom (Genesis 36:43)
39 Feminine name
40 House of _____, which reported contentions (1 Corinthians 1:11)
42 "And _____ shall offer gifts" (Psalm 72:10)
43 Sugary finishes?
44 Dine
45 Ezra's son (1 Chronicles 4:17)
46 Resting place
47 Also known as Dorcas (Acts 9:36)
50 Gershwin
51 Owns
52 Spats
53 Pet
56 _____ Hill, in Athens
57 Be pushy
60 Not these
61 Marshes
62 San _____, CA
63 Jahdai's son (1 Chronicles 2:47)
64 In the past
65 "The curse upon Mount _____" (Deuteronomy 11:29)
66 Ashur's wife (1 Chronicles 4:5)
67 Busy ones
68 Musical sign

DOWN

1 "Now _____ was over all the host of Israel" (2 Samuel 20:23)
2 "And there was one _____, a prophetess" (Luke 2:36)
3 _____ Sea
4 Question
5 Sweet melon
6 Eliab's son (Numbers 16:1)
7 Mosaic member?
8 Stop
9 Brassy one?
10 Jether's son (1 Chronicles 7:38)
11 Barbecue bar
12 Comfort
13 "Samuel took a stone and set it between Mizpeh and _____" (1 Samuel 7:12)
21 Jeduthun's son (1 Chronicles 25:3)
22 Concur
26 Esau's brother
27 Jesus ____ from the tomb
28 "Whether he have _____ a son" (Exodus 21:31)
30 Raphu's son (Numbers 13:9)
31 Earlier than the present time
32 Gad's son (Genesis 46:16)
33 "Placed them in Halah and in _____" (2 Kings 17:6)
34 "Look from the top of _____" (Song of Solomon 4:8)
36 _____ *Boot* (honored German film)
38 "A rose _____ rose" (2 words)
40 Discontinue
41 Minor prophet (abbr.)
45 _____ of life
47 "Spreadeth abroad her wings, _____ them" (Deuteronomy 32:11)
48 Daze
49 Belmont beauties
51 Gomer's husband
53 First Christian martyr (abbr., var.)
54 Biblical pronoun

by Tonya Vilhauer

55 Turn over
56 "_____; God hath numbered thy kingdom, and finished it" (Daniel 5:26)
57 Dressing gown
58 "Nevertheless _____ heart was perfect" (1 Kings 15:14)
59 Liquefy
61 Watch pocket
62 Major prophet (abbr.)

ACROSS

1 "If thou canst _____, all things are possible" (Mark 9:23)
7 "He took the seven loaves, and _____ thanks" (Mark 8:6)
8 Despondent
10 Donned
12 Low dam
14 "Members should have the same _____ one for another" (1 Corinthians 12:25)
15 Greek letter
17 "His raiment [was] white as _____" (Matthew 28:3)
19 Number of sons of Sarah
20 "_____ the son of Meshullam" (1 Chronicles 9:7)
22 Father of Hophni and Phinehas
23 Part of the Bible (abbr.)
24 "The _____ is past, the summer is ended" (Jeremiah 8:20)
26 Conjunction (Fr.)
27 Minister (abbr.)
28 Age
29 Judah's firstborn (Genesis 38:6)
31 Heal
34 Preposition (Sp.)
35 Aegean or Adriatic
37 Parable of the _____ (also known as Sower)
38 Affirmative
39 "She became a pillar of _____" (Genesis 19:26)
41 Where Cain dwelt (Genesis 4:16)
42 "Rulers of fifties, and rulers of _____" (Exodus 18:21)
43 "I will _____ bread from heaven for you" (Exodus 16:4)
45 Pad décor?
46 Understands
48 Ready cash
49 "_____ the word with joy" (Luke 8:13)

DOWN

1 "And all _____ him witness" (Luke 4:22)
2 "The serpent beguiled _____" (2 Corinthians 11:3)
3 Article (Fr.)
4 Redactor (abbr.)
5 "_____, and pay unto the LORD your God" (Psalm 76:11)
6 Farm denizens
7 Tipper _____
9 "Doth he not leave the ninety and _____, and goeth" (Matthew 18:12)
10 "The LORD is my shepherd, I shall not _____" (Psalm 23:1)
11 "Work out your own _____ with fear and trembling" (Philippians 2:12)
13 Rhett, to Clark
14 "Whosoever shall _____ that Jesus is the Son of God" (1 John 4:15)
15 Pitch
16 Little (suffix)
18 "Do not bear false _____" (Luke 18:20)
20 What Jesus does
21 Consumers
24 "Every woman shall borrow of _____ neighbor" (Exodus 3:22)
25 Kind of hold
30 "Wilt thou _____ it up in three days" (John 2:20)
32 "The _____ of man is Lord" (Matthew 12:8)
33 _____ gold
34 "Thou shalt _____ me thrice" (Matthew 26:34)
36 Exclamation of regret
38 Cry out
40 Row
42 Mosaic piece
44 Born (Fr.)
45 Fifty-four, to Livy
47 Where Furman U. is (abbr.)
48 Note on musical scale

by Evelyn M. Boyington

CELESTIAL SIGNS OF THE END TIMES

[In] those days shall the sun be darkened,
and the moon shall not give her light,
and the stars shall fall from heaven.
MATTHEW 24:29

ACROSS

1 "And God _____ every thing that he had made" (Genesis 1:31)
4 Jonah follower
9 "The word is _____ thee, even in thy mouth" (Romans 10:8)
13 Asian nursemaid
15 Greek market
16 Referring to (2 words)
17 "As the _____ among thorns" (Song of Solomon 2:2)
18 Cold cream maker
19 Ivan or Peter
20 "God _____ his work which he had made" (Genesis 2:2)
22 "Go and walk through the land, and _____ it" (Joshua 18:8)
24 **CELESTIAL SIGN** (Joel 2:31) (3 words)
27 "Am I _____, or a whale" (Job 7:12) (2 words)
28 University of Oregon locale
31 Little (suffix)
34 Upbeat
36 "I _____ to those whose sin does not lead to death" (1 John 5:16 NIV)
37 **CELESTIAL SIGN** (Amos 8:9) (5 words)
41 Middle Eastern chieftain (var.)
42 Shop with ready-to-serve foods
43 They give TLC
44 Noted lean and fat noneaters
46 Iris locale
48 **CELESTIAL SIGN** (Revelation 8:10) (3 words)
54 Mascara applier
56 Set of steps over a fence
57 Cross or neuron
58 Legume
61 Dutch cheese
62 "_____ are for kids"
63 Swelling from excess fluids
64 San _____, city in northern Italy
65 Unit of time (abbr.)
66 Four-door model, usually
67 "Water _____ round about the altar" (1 Kings 18:35)

DOWN

1 "And Melchizedek king of _____ brought forth" (Genesis 14:18)
2 Kind of organic acid
3 Ralph _____ Emerson
4 "As the men started on their way to _____ out the land" (Joshua 18:8 NIV)
5 "Because _____ to my Father" (John 16:10) (2 words)
6 Tenant-owned apartment, for short
7 Arabic unit of dry measure
8 Bother
9 Four-fifths of the atmosphere
10 "It's cold out here. . . . Why don't you go _____ a while?" (2 words)
11 Kind of bag
12 "And he said, Behold, I am _____, Lord" (Acts 9:10)
14 Serengeti laugher
21 Game player
23 Royal attendants
25 "And they _____ no candle, neither light of the sun" (Revelation 22:5)
26 Source of poi
29 It's a gas
30 European sea eagles
31 "To maintain good works for necessary _____" (Titus 3:14)
32 "A little leaven leaveneth the whole _____" (Galatians 5:9)

by David K. Shortess

33 Peppy
35 Not away from (abbr.)
38 Transmission
39 Neither positive nor negative (abbr.)
40 Thomas _____ Edison
45 Apple and soy
47 "_____ the Fall," Miller play
49 Hebrew letter (var.)
50 "And came and _____ them into the pot of pottage" (2 Kings 4:39)
51 Duck known for its down
52 Alpaca's cousin
53 Detroit dud
54 Medics (abbr.)
55 Time long ago (poet.)
59 Grandma (Ger.)
60 Sure's rival

ACROSS

1 Barbara _____ Geddes
4 Not right
6 Medicinal plant
11 "Thee have I _____ righteous" (Genesis 7:1)
13 Continent
15 Omega, for short
17 Scourge
19 "King David did _____ unto the LORD" (2 Samuel 8:11)
21 Louis XV, to Louis Pasteur
22 Cut down
23 Language of early Bibles
24 Samuel's firstborn son (1 Chronicles 6:28)
27 Resurrection Sunday
28 "Fulfilling the _____ of the flesh" (Ephesians 2:3)
29 Haunt to some
31 Two lengths of a pool
32 Droll
35 City in Simeon's inheritance (Joshua 19:8)
38 Span
41 "He that _____ his life for my sake" (Matthew 10:39)
43 "Their conscience _____ with a hot iron" (1 Timothy 4:2)
44 German article
45 "Whose wife shall _____ be of them" (Mark 12:23)
46 Stories
47 _____ is more
49 Mizraim's son (Genesis 10:13)
51 "They opened their mouth wide against me, and said _____" (Psalm 35:21)
53 Absorbed with, as a topic
54 Youth
55 Give a nickname
56 "Of the tribe of _____ were sealed twelve thousand" (Revelation 7:6)
57 City of Zebulon (Joshua 19:15)
59 To and _____
60 Tebah's mother (Genesis 22:24)
61 Bean curd
62 Query

63 "My speech shall distill as the _____" (Deuteronomy 32:2)
64 Fib

DOWN

2 "Was spoken by _____ the prophet" (Matthew 4:14)
3 Limb
4 "Hear, O Israel: The LORD our God is _____ LORD" (Deuteronomy 6:4)
5 Dim
6 Abet's assistant
7 Pins
8 "In a portion of the lawgiver, was he _____" (Deuteronomy 33:21)
9 All
10 When crocuses may come (abbr.)
12 "So I went, and hid it by _____ as the LORD commanded" (Jeremiah 13:5)
14 _____ system
16 Lion's _____
18 "Thy law do I _____" (Psalm 119:163)
20 Tiger, for one
22 "Yielding fruit after _____ kind" (Genesis 1:11)
25 Missionary with Paul
26 "The land of Zebulon, and the land of _____" (Matthew 4:15)
28 Cote _____ (Gold Coast)
30 "Lend him sufficient for his _____" (Deuteronomy 15:8)
32 Stubborn
33 "The angel of God spoke unto me in a _____" (Genesis 31:11)
34 Sun _____
36 "Being _____ from the commonwealth of Israel, and strangers" (Ephesians 2:12)
37 Godzilla, and others
39 "And he was afraid, and said, How _____ is this place" (Genesis 28:17)
40 Talmai king of _____ (2 Samuel 3:3)
42 Bavai's father (Nehemiah 3:18)

by Sarah Lagerquist Simmons

44 "What then? Art thou _____"
    (John 1:21)
48 Delilah lived in this valley
    (Judges 16:4)
50 Elon's daughter (Genesis 36:2)
52 "Give a dog _____" (2 words)
58 Why's cohort

ACROSS

1 Abraham's hometown
3 Ground bud
7 "There shall come a _____ out of Jacob" (Numbers 24:17)
11 Solidified lava (abbr.)
13 Death investigator
15 "If I _____ the locusts to devour the land" (2 Chronicles 7:13)
17 Concerning
18 God (Lat.)
19 Given to Eve
20 School organization (abbr.)
21 Musical abbreviation (abbr.)
22 "O, _____. . .thou that killest the prophets" (Matthew 23:37)
25 Aquatic mammal
27 "Stand in the _____ before me" (Ezekiel 22:30)
28 "His hands are as gold _____ set with the beryl" (Song of Solomon 5:14)
32 Tear's partner
33 "Israel is a scattered _____" (Jeremiah 50:17)
35 "Render therefore to all their _____" (Romans 13:7)
36 "My moisture is turned into the _____ of summer" (Psalm 32:4)
37 Tribal people settling in Joppa (pl.)
39 Gershwin
40 Magician who opposed Moses (2 Timothy 3:8)
44 Shuthelah's son's family member (Numbers 26:36)
48 Place of Napoleon's exile
49 "Then Joseph commanded to fill their _____ with corn" (Genesis 42:25)
50 Garden flower
51 "And if ye shall say, What shall _____ the seventh year?" (Leviticus 25:20) (2 words)
53 "Be thou diligent to know the _____ of thy flocks" (Proverbs 27:23)
54 Soldier's award (abbr.)
55 "A wicked man is _____" (Proverbs 13:5)

57 _____ Elyon, meaning "God Most High"
59 Celebrity-filled magazine
60 H.S. requirement, usually
61 "When saw we thee an hungred, or _____" (Matthew 25:44)
64 "Whose shoe's latchet I am not worthy to _____" (John 1:27)
68 Electrical unit (abbr.)
69 Donkey (Sp.)
70 Corner

DOWN

1 _____-Berkeley (abbr.)
2 "Just as he was speaking, the _____ crowed" (Luke 22:60 NIV)
3 Not yet in stock (abbr.)
4 "_____ whose wings thou art come to trust" (Ruth 2:12)
5 Unsavory look
6 "For we _____ nothing into this world" (1 Timothy 6:7)
7 "He shall cause the house to be _____ within round about" (Leviticus 14:41)
8 "They _____ not, neither do they spin" (Matthew 6:28)
9 Fossil resin
10 Old German money (abbr.)
11 "Go to the _____, thou sluggard" (Proverbs 6:6)
12 Ohio college town
14 Atomic number 104 (abbr.)
16 News service (abbr.)
21 Political columnist Maureen
22 New name for Gideon (Judges 6:32)
23 College fraternity (abbr.)
24 One of a nomadic tribe that sold Joseph
26 Path for Confucian followers
29 "Down to the grove of _____ trees" (Song of Solomon 6:11 NIV)
30 Equine command
31 Military draft organization (abbr.)
33 "Thy _____ shall be iron and brass" (Deuteronomy 33:25)
34 "_____ of clean and unclean animals" (Genesis 7:8 NIV)

by Marijane G. Troyer

38 Powerful D.C. lobby
40 _____ for Jesus (messianic group)
41 Descendant of Jonathan
   (1 Chronicles 8:36)
42 British military honor (abbr.)
43 Valley of _____
   (1 Chronicles 18:12 NIV)
44 Barely survives (2 words)
45 Golden years' account (abbr.)
46 Is a faithful steward
47 Compass direction
52 Travel packages
53 Facial expression
56 General organization (abbr.)
58 Pituitary hormone (abbr.)
60 River to the Adriatic
61 "Seeing I _____ a great people"
   (Joshua 17:14)
62 Grant Wood's state (abbr.)
63 Via
65 Movie type (abbr.)

66 Seventh-century British language
   (abbr.)
67 _____ Cid

ACROSS

1 Babylonian god (Isaiah 46:1)
5 Old Testament book
9 Poke
12 By oneself
14 Secure
15 Canine command
16 Underground members?
17 "Shalt remain by the stone _____" (1 Samuel 20:19)
18 Israelite leader (Nehemiah 10:26)
19 Omega, for short
20 "The caravans of _____ look for water" (Job 6:19 NIV)
22 Accuse
23 Military branch
24 Compared to
26 Island near Paul's shipwreck (Acts 27:7)
28 Stopover during Hebrews' wandering (Deuteronomy 10:6)
31 "And Moses _____ all the words" (Exodus 24:4)
32 "Then shall the _____ be ashamed" (Micah 3:7)
33 Debtor's declaration (abbr.)
35 "They made upon the _____ of the robe pomegranates" (Exodus 39:24)
36 "Where the birds make their _____" (Psalm 104:17)
37 Micaiah's father (2 Chronicles 18:7)
38 "_____, though I walk through the valley" (Psalm 23:4)
39 One of the cliffs near Philistine outpost (1 Samuel 14:4)
40 Ner's son (1 Samuel 14:50)
41 "Thou. . .art come unto a people which thou _____" (Ruth 2:11)
43 Electrical unit
44 "According to all that her mother in law _____ her" (Ruth 3:6)
45 Double this for deficiency disease
46 "Jair died, and was buried in _____" (Judges 10:5)
49 Powder room (Sp.)
50 Kind of bear
53 Mideast gulf
54 Podiatric problem
56 Famous
58 Extremely
59 Jesse's father (Ruth 4:22)
60 Trap
61 In the style of (suffix)
62 Mistress
63 Instrument (suffix)

DOWN

1 "And his _____ shall be called Wonderful" (Isaiah 9:6)
2 North Carolina college
3 Fearless
4 Single
5 Adversary
6 "Jonathan; Peleth, and _____" (1 Chronicles 2:33)
7 "Wheat and _____ were not smitten" (Exodus 9:32)
8 "_____ power is given unto me" (Matthew 28:18)
9 Simon's father (John 1:42)
10 "_____, and Shema, and Moladah" (Joshua 15:26)
11 Nota _____
13 Property
15 "Is not _____ as Carchemish?" (Isaiah 10:9)
21 Adam's rib?
22 Hurdles
23 New Jersey _____ (pro team)
24 "Hast broken the _____ of the ungodly" (Psalm 3:7)
25 "Restore all that was _____" (2 Kings 8:6)
26 Brook
27 Citizenship Paul claimed
28 "The sin which doth so easily _____" (Hebrews 12:1)
29 Lotan's sister (Genesis 36:22)
30 Became a recluse, with "up"
31 How come
32 Feel in one's bones
34 Former Mideast initials
36 Lack
37 Name meaning "Hebrew"
39 What the ugly duckling became

by Tonya Vilhauer

40 "_____ rod that budded"
   (Hebrews 9:4)
42 "For a present horns of ivory and
   _____" (Ezekiel 27:15)
43 Swampy area
45 Toss about
46 Den
47 Summer coolers
48 Only
49 "It _____ worms, and stank"
   (Exodus 16:20)
50 The sun, for example
51 David, after Goliath
52 First home
54 N.T. book (abbr.)
55 O.T. minor prophet (var.)
57 Canadian province (abbr.)

ACROSS

1 Hebrew
3 Prince of Wales, for one
5 Where Noah's ark landed
10 Men
12 "And the winepress was trodden
. . .even unto the horse _____"
(Revelation 14:20)
14 Meadows
17 Shemida's son (1 Chronicles 7:19)
20 "Fruit of the righteous is a _____
of life" (Proverbs 11:30)
21 Greek letter
23 "Tell ye it in _____, that Moab is
spoiled" (Jeremiah 48:20)
24 Else
25 "_____ the woman saw that the
tree was good" (Genesis 3:6)
26 Poetic contraction
27 Proboscis
29 _____ on parle francais
30 First
32 _____-ed column
33 "Put a _____ on it"
34 "Should be no _____ in the body"
(1 Corinthians 12:25)
37 Coach Parseghian
38 "Breathed _____ his nostrils"
(Genesis 2:7)
40 Huge
42 Judah's daughter-in-law
(Genesis 38:6)
44 "She had made an _____ in a
grove" (2 Chronicles 15:16)
47 "The tongue of the wise useth
knowledge _____" (Proverbs 15:2)
49 "He _____ Pharaoh's heart"
(Exodus 7:13)
51 Facts
52 What "would smell as sweet"
(2 words)
53 Writer Wiesel, and others
56 Man, for one
58 Medieval serf
59 Simeon's son (Genesis 46:10)
60 Cry's partner
61 Cook's measure (abbr.)
62 Old Testament book (abbr.)
63 Coffee, to some

DOWN

2 Does not improve
3 Jephthah fled to this land
(Judges 11:3)
4 Jacques, to Jeanne
5 Any
6 Man who came with Zerubbabel
(Ezra 2:2)
7 Korah's son (Exodus 6:24)
8 Educated, in a way
9 Carrier to Tokyo (abbr.)
11 "For the _____ of this service. . .
supplieth the want of the saints"
(2 Corinthians 9:12)
13 Amalek fought with Israel here
(Exodus 17:8)
15 Peoples (prefix)
16 Dionysius the _____ (Acts 17:34)
18 "I bow my _____ unto the
Father of our Lord Jesus Christ"
(Ephesians 3:14)
19 King of Gezer (Joshua 10:33)
22 "Just a _____"
28 King Azariah built and restored
this city to Judah (2 Kings 14:22)
31 "I have been much _____ from
coming to you" (Romans 15:22)
35 Corp.'s relative
36 Minor prophet
39 O.T. book (abbr.)
41 _____ the Jairite (2 Samuel
20:26)
43 Site of Mars' Hill
44 City of Zebulon (Joshua 19:15)
45 Composer Yoko
46 Bandleader Brown
48 Force of nature?
50 "Nothing runs like a _____"
54 Advocate (Suffix)
55 Start of fall (abbr.)
57 "_____ took of the fruit thereof"
(Genesis 3:6)

by Sarah Lagerquist Simmons

EGYPT'S PLAGUES

"Let my people go. . .or this time I will send
the full force of my plagues against you."

EXODUS 9:13–14 NIV

ACROSS

1 Kilauea product
5 Greek mountain
9 "Now the Valley of Siddim was full _____ pits" (Genesis 14:10 NIV) (2 words)
14 Elliptical
15 Dudley Do-Right's girlfriend
16 "I speak as a _____ am more" (2 Corinthians 11:23) (2 words)
17 Three **PLAGUES** (Exodus 9:9, 8:21, 8:2) (3 words)
20 Have
21 Pre-Aztec Mexican tribe
22 Winglike structures
23 "Is any thing _____ hard for the LORD" (Genesis 18:14)
24 "Who will _____ to every man according to" (Romans 2:6)
26 Another **PLAGUE** (Exodus 7:17) (3 words)
32 Dancer Castle of old
33 Bells ringing
34 "For this is the _____ and the prophets" (Matthew 7:12)
37 "Then Paul stood in the midst of _____ hill" (Acts 17:22)
38 One hundredth of one liter (abbr.) (2 words)
39 Island east of Java
40 That has (suffix)
41 Nemesis
42 "And, lo, a great multitude, which no man _____ number" (Revelation 7:9)
43 Another **PLAGUE** (Exodus 12:29) (3 words)
45 Conversation (var.)
48 Born, in Bordeaux
49 1952 Winter Olympics site
50 "And did _____ showbread" (Mark 2:26) (2 words)

54 "Your lightning _____ up the world" (Psalm 77:18 NIV)
57 Three more **PLAGUES** (Exodus 10:13, 9:22, 8:17) (3 words)
60 Related on mother's side
61 Close to, in a game
62 "I watch, and _____ a sparrow alone upon the house top" (Psalm 102:7) (2 words)
63 "And gave the _____, and caused them to understand the reading" (Nehemiah 8:8)
64 Sicilian volcano
65 "_____ harm yourself! We are all here!" (Acts 16:28 NIV)

DOWN

1 Gray wolf
2 "We have four men which have _____ on them" (Acts 21:23) (2 words)
3 "Shall _____ words have an end" (Job 16:3)
4 "They are _____ gone aside" (Psalm 14:3)
5 "They went through the flood _____" (Psalm 66:6) (2 words)
6 "Go and _____ that thou hast" (Matthew 19:21)
7 Narrow opening
8 Away from the wind
9 "And the publican, standing afar _____" (Luke 18:13)
10 "Looking _____ hasting unto the coming of the day of God" (2 Peter 3:12) (2 words)
11 "To prostitution, _____ wine and new" (Hosea 4:11 NIV) (2 words)
12 Pond organisms
13 Stair part
18 Candy or toy

by David K. Shortess

19 "And the heavens shall be rolled together as a _____" (Isaiah 34:4)
23 Addition column
25 Greek dawn goddess
26 Hoarfrost
27 Persia, today
28 Like grass (Fr.)
29 "The watchman _____ the gate for him" (John 10:3 NIV)
30 "John Brown's Body" poet
31 On the _____
34 Praise
35 "If I give _____ possess to the poor" (1 Corinthians 13:3 NIV) (2 words)
36 "For ____ is the gate" (Matthew 7:13)
38 K-Mart competitor
39 "A _____ of him shall not be broken" (John 19:36)
41 Personal profile, for short
42 Angler's basket
43 Disparages
44 "And they put _____ purple robe" (John 19:2) (3 words)
45 Distributes, with *out*
46 "This _____ of them" (Mark 14:69) (2 words)
47 Alaska Highway, once
51 "_____ forgive our debtors" (Matthew 6:12) (2 words)
52 "And God saw _____ it was good" (Genesis 1:10)
53 Small mountain lake
54 VIP transporter
55 "_____ do all things through Christ" (Philippians 4:13) (2 words)
56 "We should not _____ the Lord" (1 Corinthians 10:9 NIV)
58 "Ye shall not _____ me" (Luke 13:35)
59 Boy

ACROSS

1 Influence
5 Put in a safe place
8 Shammai's brother (1 Chronicles 2:32)
12 Shakespearean traitor
13 Exist
14 General Bradley, to friends
15 "The _____ of my heart are enlarged" (Psalm 25:17)
17 Antitoxins
18 "_____ them about thy neck" (Proverbs 6:21)
19 "He _____ the doors of heaven" (Psalm 78:23)
21 "If thy _____ eye offend thee" (Matthew 5:29)
24 Hit with, as a fine
25 Crude metals
26 "Thy truth _____ unto the clouds" (Psalm 108:4)
30 Cooking utensil
31 "Draw you before the judgment _____" (James 2:6)
32 _____ Lanka
33 "Ye have us for an _____" (Philippians 3:17)
35 Has _____ (former great)
36 "They compassed me about like _____" (Psalm 118:12)
37 "Be ye not unequally _____ together with unbelievers" (2 Corinthians 6:14)
38 Reputation
41 Encountered
42 "Isaac blessed Jacob and _____" (Hebrews 11:20)
43 "Let _____ grow instead of wheat" (Job 31:40)
48 African despot
49 "Give _____, O my people, to my law" (Psalm 78:1)
50 Blood or finish
51 Combine
52 Salon request
53 First home

DOWN

1 Pose
2 Philistine activity
3 Time past
4 "Even the _____ shall faint and be weary" (Isaiah 40:30)
5 Burr's longtime costar
6 Wrath
7 Barren
8 "Israel loved _____ more than all his children" (Genesis 37:3)
9 "Let all the people say, _____" (Psalm 106:48)
10 Challenge
11 Canaanite king (Numbers 21:1)
16 Memory measure, to IBM
20 Cold weather boots
21 Lasso
22 "He hath. . .cut the bars of _____ in sunder" (Psalm 107:16)
23 Understands
24 "Thou art worthy to take the book and to open the _____" (Revelation 5:9)
26 Sought forgiveness
27 Where Isaac named a well (Genesis 26:20)
28 _____ of Life
29 Sight or quarters
31 Small merganser
34 "That ye may _____ in hope" (Romans 15:13)
35 "Every _____ shall be filled with wine" (Jeremiah 13:12)
37 Affirmative
38 Paper quantity
39 Short story by Saki
40 "I will fasten him as a _____ in a sure place" (Isaiah 22:23)
41 Fen
44 Secretariat's supper
45 Cover
46 Compass point
47 Elected official (abbr.)

by Evelyn M. Boyington

14

ACROSS

1 All (comb. form)
4 Elements
9 Legal eagles (abbr.)
12 "Adam was first formed, then
_____" (1 Timothy 2:13)
13 Now (Sp.)
14 Eastern state university (abbr.)
15 Humble
16 Hailed
17 Jacob's son
18 "There was not a man to _____
the ground" (Genesis 2:5)
20 "The Lord shall hiss. . .for the
_____ that is in the land of
Assyria" (Isaiah 7:18)
21 Solomon, for one
22 Tinted
24 Librarian's mantra (pl.)
25 Oath
27 Greek letter
28 "Cornelius, a centurion of the band
called the _____ band" (Acts
10:1)
29 Also known as Cephas
31 "Concerning the fiery _____"
(1 Peter 4:12)
34 "All the world should be _____"
(Luke 2:1)
36 "The words of Job are _____"
(Job 31:40)
38 Millinery
39 Tiny
41 Head over heels
42 "By grace ye _____ saved"
(Ephesians 2:5)
43 "I commend unto you _____ our
sister" (Romans 16:1)
45 Eur. lang.
46 "They _____ in the dry places
like a river" (Psalm 105:41)
47 Hilton, for one
48 Person or thing (suffix)
49 First _____
50 Arlene, Roald, and others
51 Sixties' organization (abbr.)

DOWN

1 Fur
2 Stay away from
3 Afresh
4 Handle clumsily
5 Ahaziah's father (1 Kings 22:49)
6 Fido's friend
7 "The _____ yielding fruit"
(Genesis 1:12)
8 Blue
9 Jacob's offspring
10 Pulls along
11 _____ qua non
19 High priests, tribally
21 Radiant
23 Paid attention to, with on
24 Time _____
26 Combat
27 "He brought me up also out of an
horrible _____" (Psalm 40:2)
29 _____ the Arbite (2 Samuel
23:35)
30 Prolong
32 Sayings
33 Myth
34 "Son of Abraham, which was the
son of _____" (Luke 3:34)
35 "Day nor night _____ sleep"
(Ecclesiastes 8:16)
37 "To quench all the fiery _____"
(Ephesians 6:16)
39 Cowboy's command
40 Watch maker
43 Degree of difficulty? (abbr.)
44 Chicago rails

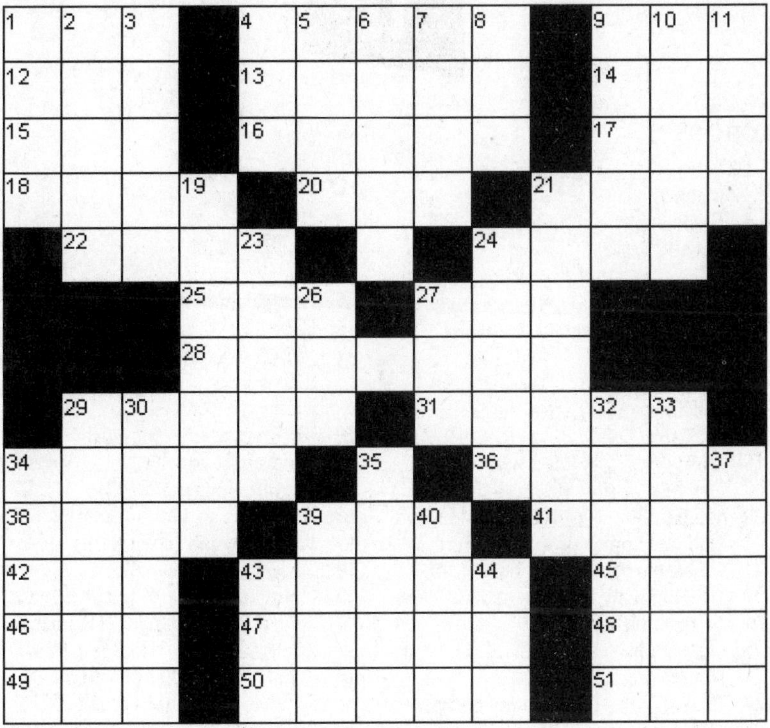

by Tonya Vilhauer

ACROSS

1 Yad _____, Jerusalem Holocaust memorial
4 Bane
9 Awhile back
11 "The _____ of the ox shall be quit" (Exodus 21:28)
13 "Salute _____ my kinsman" (Romans 16:11)
16 Solomon built this fortification (1 Kings 11:27)
17 Deli sub
18 "And _____ walked with God: and he was not" (Genesis 5:24)
20 Widow of _____ (Luke 7:11)
21 Old Testament prophet (abbr.)
22 "Treacherous _____ have dealt treacherously" (Isaiah 24:16)
24 Superlative suffix
26 "Eat, and _____ forever" (Genesis 3:22)
27 "Take, _____: this is my body" (Mark 14:22)
29 People destroyed by Esau's descendants (Deuteronomy 2:12, 22)
30 Samuel's mentor
33 "An _____ for every man" (Exodus 16:16)
35 Pad
36 "From the _____ of thy wood" (Deuteronomy 29:11)
37 Swaddle
38 "I will give unto thee the _____ of the kingdom" (Matthew 16:19)
39 Haggi's brother (Genesis 46:16)
41 Loot
42 O. T. book
45 "They _____ knowledge" (Proverbs 1:29)
48 Susi's son (Numbers 13:11)
49 Change or pail
50 Eleazar was _____ son (Exodus 6:25)
52 The _____ Spoonful, 70s group
55 Sturdy canine, for short
56 _____ paper
57 N. T. book (abbr.)
58 "The _____ that is called Patmos" (Revelation 1:9)
59 _____ Row

DOWN

2 Caress
3 Chief
4 Pride
5 New Testament book (abbr.)
6 Pigs
7 "Then shall there _____ and deliverance arise" (Esther 4:14)
8 Press
10 "There was not among the children of Israel a _____ person than he" (1 Samuel 9:2)
12 Belonging to Hophni's father
13 King of Judah (abbr.)
14 "_____ I saw Elba"
15 "I am _____ both to the Greeks and to the Barbarians" (Romans 1:14)
17 "He that _____ him out a sepulcher on high" (Isaiah 22:16)
19 "If now I _____ found favour in thy sight" (Genesis 18:3)
23 May be more
25 Chief priest (Ezra 8:24)
28 "Look now _____ heaven" (Genesis 15:5)
31 Short poem or song (arch.)
32 "That which groweth of _____ own accord" (Leviticus 25:5)
34 "_____ is broken in pieces; her idols are humiliated" (Jeremiah 50:2 NKJV)
37 "The _____ of heaven were opened" (Genesis 7:11)
40 Poacher's targets?
43 City of Judah (Joshua 15:32)
44 Hurry
45 Exclamation, to Henri
46 "He set my feet on ___" (Psalm 40:2 NIV) (2 words)
47 _____ Gate, in Jerusalem
51 Dauphin's dad (Fr.)
53 LVI divided by VIII
54 Third party (abbr.)

by Sarah Lagerquist Simmons

PAUL'S FIRST MISSIONARY JOURNEY

"Set apart for me Barnabas and Saul. . . ."
So. . .they placed their hands on them and sent them off.
ACTS 13:2–3 NIV

ACROSS

1 Blue Grotto locale
6 Clinton's Attorney General
10 One-time Iranian head
14 Fatty acid
15 Teen follower?
16 Lacquered metalware
17 **CITY** visited by Paul (Acts 13:13)
18 Mrs. Nick Charles
19 MP's target
20 "For _____ a little while" (Psalm 37:10)
21 Corporal or Sergeant (abbr.)
23 Another **CITY** (Acts 13:51)
25 City in southern Turkey
27 "The _____ cannot leave his father" (Genesis 44:22)
28 Another **CITY** (Acts 13:6)
31 "And _____ of heaven shall fall" (Mark 13:25) (2 words)
36 Elevator man
37 Head, in France
39 Subject
40 D-Day craft
41 Another **CITY** (Acts 13:5)
43 "He is of _____; ask him" (John 9:23)
44 "And _____ they sufficed them not" (Judges 21:14) (2 words)
46 Alack's cohort
47 Elvis Presley's middle name
48 Deli meat
50 Another **CITY** (Acts 14:6)
52 Stimpy's pal
53 "What thou seest, write in _____" (Revelation 1:11) (2 words)
55 Another **CITY** (Acts 13:14)
59 "Be not wise in thine _____ eyes" (Proverbs 3:7)
60 "Ye shall not _____ of it" (Genesis 3:3)

63 "Which things the angels desire to _____ into" (1 Peter 1:12)
64 Learn, with of
66 Another **CITY** (Acts 14:6)
68 "That they may be one, even _____ are one" (John 17:22) (2 words)
69 "They have not known the Father _____" (John 16:3 NIV) (2 words)
70 Columnist Goodman
71 Benign cysts
72 "He went into the synagogue. . . and stood up for to _____" (Luke 4:16)
73 Cambodian currency (pl.)

DOWN

1 "This is the _____ of the letter that they sent unto him" (Ezra 4:11)
2 On the sheltered side
3 Bright-eyed and bushy-tailed
4 Semi, to some
5 "_____ all things through Christ which strengtheneth me" (Philippians 4:13) (3 words)
6 Talked a lot (2 words)
7 Kind of trip
8 Salathiel's father (Luke 3:27)
9 "As if a man had enquired at the _____ of God" (2 Samuel 16:23)
10 "To _____ minister in the name of the LORD" (Deuteronomy 18:5) (2 words)
11 "Consider _____ love thy precepts" (Psalm 119:159) (2 words)
12 Baseball's Moises or Felipe
13 At the _____
22 "Let him first _____ stone at her" (John 8:7) (2 words)
24 Drying ovens
25 Words of delight

by David K. Shortess

26 Another **CITY** (Acts 14:25)
28 Coral reef builder
29 "For the king had ___ a navy" (1 Kings 10:22) (2 words)
30 PA univ., familiarly, and frontier fort
32 Blood (prefix)
33 "He went up into a mountain _____ to pray" (Matthew 14:23)
34 _____ mortis
35 La Scala interlude
38 Craggy faced cowboy actor Jack
41 "Be not wroth very _____ LORD" (Isaiah 64:9) (2 words)
42 "Exalt him that _____, and abase him that is high" (Ezekiel 21:26) (2 words)
45 "If someone _____ you on one cheek" (Luke 6:29 NIV)
47 "Or if he _____ a fish, will he give" (Matthew 7:10)

49 "Which hope we have as an _____ of the soul" (Hebrews 6:19)
51 Far off
54 Made numb
55 "Are _____ unto themselves" (Romans 2:14) (2 words)
56 Win by a _____
57 "Out of the _____ of Bethlehem" (John 7:42)
58 "Then said I, _____ am I; send me" (Isaiah 6:8)
60 Perry's creator
61 "Where is _____ thy brother" (Gen. 4:9)
62 "I will not destroy it for _____ sake" (Genesis 18:32)
65 "Seeing I _____ stranger" (Ruth 2:10) (2 words)
67 Hophni's father (1 Samuel 4:4)

17

ACROSS

1 Iron (abbr.)
3 Father of human race
7 Outdoor theater or restaurant
12 Hannah's priest
14 Insistent
16 Midwestern state (abbr.)
17 "Bind this _____ of scarlet thread in the window" (Joshua 2:18)
19 "She let them down by a _____ through the window" (Joshua 2:15)
20 Presage
22 Jacob's devious uncle
24 Make bigger (abbr.)
25 Stiff
26 "The _____ death has no power over them" (Revelation 20:6 NIV)
28 Cell for biomedical research
30 Substitute for pitcher at bat (abbr.)
31 Presidential command when Congress is not in session (abbr.)
32 Sodium (abbr.)
33 Memo abbr.
35 Is there
37 "Became mighty _____. . .of old" (Genesis 6:4)
38 _____ Lewis (initials)
39 "She hath none _____ comfort her" (Lamentations 1:2)
40 Row
42 Prepare for publication
43 College degree (abbr.)
44 "When thou seest the _____. . . shouldest be driven to worship" (Deuteronomy 4:19)
45 One Stooge
46 _____ carte
47 Arm bone
49 "As a _____ is full of birds" (Jeremiah 5:27)
51 Financial officer (abbr.)
53 Composer Anderson
55 Author of Pentateuch
56 Plants new lawn
57 Hawaiian food

58 "_____ me, and deliver me from the hand of strange children" (Psalm 144:11)
59 Antiviral drug for autoimmune infections (abbr.)
61 "Vashti. . .hath not done wrong to the king _____" (Esther 1:16)
63 Teachers' org.
65 Positive
67 "___ tu, Brute"
68 "Falleth to the Chaldeans that _____ you" (Jeremiah 21:9)
71 Salt (Fr.)
72 "And _____ ox also shall they divide" (Exodus 21:35) (2 words)
73 "God made them _____ and female" (Mark 10:6)
74 Highest degree in ministry (abbr.)

DOWN

1 "Cain was very wroth, and his countenance _____" (Genesis 4:5)
2 "There appeared. . .Moses and _____ talking with him" (Matthew 17:3)
4 Lawyer for the state (abbr.)
5 Marketing piece
6 Ancient kingdom north of Greece
7 "Rescue. . .my _____ from the lions" (Psalm 35:17)
8 Circular (abbr.)
9 "_____ maketh no matter to me" (Galatians 2:6)
10 Where New Delhi is capital
11 "Have I _____ of mad men" (1 Samuel 21:15)
13 "My children are with me _____" (Luke 11:7) (2 words)
15 Day of the week (abbr.)
18 "Let _____ esteem other better than themselves" (Philippians 2:3)
20 Caskets
21 Eye
23 "Let _____ joyful voice come therein" (Job 3:7)
25 Amount of moisture in the air (abbr.)

by Marijane G. Troyer

27 "For a camel to go through a
   _____ eye" (Luke 18:25)
29 Widow who lost two sons in
   Moab
34 "And when _____ failed in the
   land of Egypt" (Genesis 47:15)
36 Way (Chinese)
37 "They will look at their _____
   crops" (Jeremiah 12:13 MSG)
38 "God _____ the light Day, and
   the darkness. . .Night"
   (Genesis 1:5)
39 Pronoun (Fr.)
41 Pull back in disgust
43 Government department (abbr.)
44 Precious, bloodred stone
   (Exodus 28:17)
48 "These women had. . .cared for his
   _____" (Mark 15:41 NIV)
50 "Raiment was white _____ the
   light" (Matthew 17:2)
51 Singer _____ Lopez

52 "_____ me from the hand of the
   mighty" (Job 6:23)
54 Bone
55 "And the ark rested in the seventh
   _____" (Genesis 8:4)
57 "My tongue is like the pen of a
   skillful _____" (Psalm 45:1 NLT)
60 Trapper's treasure
62 Irish Breakfast, for one
64 _____ Khan
66 "His eyes shall be _____ with
   wine" (Genesis 49:12)
68 "The genealogy is not to _____
   reckoned" (1 Chronicles 5:1)
69 Plains state (abbr.)
70 _____ Shaddai, name for God

ACROSS

1 Next
6 Baseball stat.
8 Soft drink
12 Tell
13 "Ye have _____ with untempered mortar" (Ezekiel 13:14)
15 Poison
16 Noticed
17 Perjure
18 Joab's "armourbearer" (1 Chronicles 11:39)
21 Aid for indigent
23 Gap
24 "Where thou _____, will I die" (Ruth 1:17)
26 Groovy
27 Blockade
29 Brazil, for one
30 Angelic accoutrement
31 "Open thou my _____" (Psalm 51:15)
34 Benefit
36 "Whose wife shall _____ be" (Mark 12:23)
37 "As. . .sharpens _____" (Proverbs 27:17 NKJV)
38 Korean, for example
39 Bat
41 Living in (suffix)
42 _____ de mer
43 "Stop right there" (2 words)
46 Bon _____, Comet competitor
47 _____ Valley near Los Angeles
50 Scratch
53 Of the chest cavity
55 Remit
56 Liquid measure equaling about six pints (Exodus 29:40)
57 Hebrew month
58 Hew
59 Place in Judah where Saul numbered his forces (1 Samuel 15:4)

DOWN

2 Citizen
3 Number of commandments
4 Esau's father-in-law (Genesis 26:34)
5 Town of Benjamin north of Jerusalem (Joshua 18:25)
6 "The head of Samaria is _____ son" (Isaiah 7:9)
7 Fancy
8 "Father. . .remove this _____ from me" (Luke 22:42)
9 Kimono sash
10 Onionlike vegetables
11 Put together
14 Theatrical gesture
15 Filthy
17 "The world _____ and fadeth away" (Isaiah 24:4)
19 Nun's son (Deuteronomy 32:44)
20 Man who came with Zerubbabel (Ezra 2:2)
22 In awe of
25 Joseph's grandchild (Numbers 1:10)
28 _____ Heights, in Middle East
32 One of twelve disciples
33 "The Lord _____ a mark upon Cain" (Genesis 4:15)
35 Where Ibid. is found (abbr.)
40 Earful?
42 Jesus' earthly mother
44 Den dweller
45 Sarah's son
48 Coin
49 Here, en Paris
50 "He _____ on the ground and made clay" (John 9:6)
51 Walking stick
52 Chedorlaomer was king of _____ (Genesis 14:1)
54 Adam and Eve _____ from God (Genesis 3:8)

by Sarah Lagerquist Simmons

ACROSS

1 Time period
5 Inactive
9 Bosc and Anjou
14 "Of _____, the family of the Oznites" (Numbers 26:16)
15 Cruel
16 Seaweed, for example
17 Save
18 "Till thou hast _____ the very last mite" (Luke 12:59)
19 Morsel
20 Sin
21 "Merchants received the linen _____ at a price" (1 Kings 10:28)
22 Singed
23 Harbor
24 "With a strong ____" (Jeremiah 21:5)
25 "_____ they shall flee away" (Nahum 2:8)
28 Ammihud's son (1 Chronicles 9:4)
31 Type of tie
34 Korah's father (Exodus 6:21)
36 "For every one that _____ shall be cut off" (Zechariah 5:3)
39 "And _____ lived after he begat Peleg" (Genesis 11:17)
40 Pots' partners
42 Lave
43 "I am Alpha and Omega, the first and the _____" (Revelation 1:11)
44 "And _____ did that which was right" (1 Kings 15:11)
45 _____ Colonies, in Iowa
46 "Neither shall ye touch it, lest ye _____" (Genesis 3:3)
47 "With the _____ and deacons" (Philippians 1:1)
50 Strike
51 "Purim after the name of _____" (Esther 9:26)
52 Appeal
53 "Stingeth like an _____" (Proverbs 23:32)
56 "The gods of Hamath, and of _____" (2 Kings 18:34)
58 "Man will _____ thee at the law" (Matthew 5:40)
61 Abram's wife (Genesis 11:29)
62 "Shebam, and Nebo, and _____" (Numbers 32:3)
63 Holler
64 Location
65 Despicable
66 "The province of ____" (Daniel 8:2)
67 "They _____ fig leaves together" (Genesis 3:7)
68 "Gold, and silver, ivory, and _____, and peacocks" (1 Kings 10:22)
69 "Sell that ye have, and give _____" (Luke 12:33)

DOWN

1 "The _____ of my transgressions" (Lamentations 1:14)
2 Son of the ruler of Mizpah (Nehemiah 3:19)
3 "_____ with her suburbs" (1 Chronicles 6:70)
4 Tombstone initials
5 "I may _____ unto you some spiritual gift" (Romans 1:11)
6 "Seven years of _____ began to come" (Genesis 41:54)
7 "I have _____ still and been quiet" (Job 3:13)
8 Omega, briefly
9 "The _____ reeds by the brooks" (Isaiah 19:7)
10 Bathsheba's father (2 Samuel 11:3)
11 End of *teen*
12 "They which run in a _____ run all" (1 Corinthians 9:24)
13 Ranking, as in tennis
21 "Be clean, and change _____ garments" (Genesis 35:2)
22 International org. started in 1865 (abbr.)
25 Submit
26 Naarai's father (1 Chronicles 11:37)
27 "_____ are the generations of Noah" (Genesis 6:9)
29 "The children of _____" (Ezra 2:50)

by Tonya Vilhauer

30 "That which groweth of _____ own accord" (Leviticus 25:5)

31 "And from _____ and from Berothai" (2 Samuel 8:8)

32 Shemaiah's first son (1 Chronicles 26:7)

33 "Barley harvest and of _____ harvest" (Ruth 2:23)

35 "Thou _____ cursed above all cattle" (Genesis 3:14) (sing.)

37 "I know both how to be _____" (Philippians 4:12)

38 Old Testament book (abbr.)

40 Team of two

41 "They laded their _____ with the corn" (Genesis 42:26)

47 "We are _____ with him by baptism" (Romans 6:4)

48 "Instructing those that _____ themselves" (2 Timothy 2:25)

49 Geometric surfaces

51 "Grace be unto you, and _____, from him" (Revelation 1:4)

53 "Poison of _____ is under their lips" (Romans 3:13)

54 Roy's "pard"

55 "Let us _____ near with a true heart" (Hebrews 10:22)

56 "And he said, _____, Father" (Mark 14:36)

57 "I _____ where I sowed not" (Matthew 25:26)

58 "That no man might buy or _____" (Revelation 13:17)

59 Jehush and Eliphelet's brother (1 Chronicles 8:39)

60 "Under oaks and poplars and _____" (Hosea 4:13)

63 "_____, let God be true" (Romans 3:4)

BETHLEHEM'S VISITORS

And thou Bethlehem. . .out of thee shall come a Governor,
that shall rule my people Israel.

MATTHEW 2:6

ACROSS

1 Brig occupant
5 "Who passing through the valley of _____ make it a well" (Psalm 84:6)
9 "If he arrives _____ will come with him to see you" (Hebrews 13:23 NIV) (2 words)
14 Puerto _____
15 Maj. Hoople's favorite expression
16 "But the _____ are the children of the wicked one" (Matthew 13:38)
17 U.S. island occupied by Japan during WWII
18 Goulash
19 Bathsheba's first husband (2 Samuel 11:3)
20 **VISITORS** (Luke 2:15) (2 words)
23 "Yet we did _____ him stricken" (Isaiah 53:4)
24 Mr. Charles
25 O.T. book (abbr.)
28 Scale notes
29 Deteriorate
32 "Praise thy _____ Zion" (Psalm 147:12) (2 words)
33 City from which David took "exceeding much brass" (2 Samuel 8:8)
34 Corolla component
35 More **VISITORS** (Luke 2:4–7) (3 words)
40 "You are worried and _____ about many things" (Luke 10:41 NIV)
41 "The Philistines gathered _____ Dammim" (2 Samuel 23:9 NIV) (2 words)
42 Mend, as a sock
43 Open, as a flag
45 Weasel
48 Golfer Ernie
49 Menlo Park monogram
50 Electrical unit
52 More **VISITORS** (Matthew 2:1–11) (3 words)
55 Stockpile
58 Mariner who discovered Cape of Good Hope
59 Bye-bye
60 "Whom shall _____" (Psalm 27:1) (2 words)
61 Sea eagle
62 Land west of Nod (Genesis 4:16)
63 In accord (2 words)
64 "But in _____ and in truth" (1 John 3:18)
65 "And Jacob _____ his clothes" (Genesis 37:34)

DOWN

1 Top drawer
2 "Compassed about _____ great a cloud of witnesses" (Hebrews 12:1) (2 words)
3 Musical groups
4 Despicable person
5 "Behold now _____, which I made with thee" (Job 40:15)
6 "I had rebuilt the wall and not _____ was left in it" (Nehemiah 6:1 NIV) (2 words)
7 Not "plastic"
8 Stick like glue
9 "_____ to show thyself approved unto God" (2 Timothy 2:15)
10 "Wherein shall go no galley with _____" (Isaiah 33:21)
11 "Give light to my eyes, _____ will sleep in death" (Psalm 13:3 NIV) (2 words)
12 Education assn.
13 Like -*like*

by David K. Shortess

21 What Jesus did at Lazarus's tomb (2 words)
22 "They _____ the ship aground" (Acts 27:41)
25 "But he answered her _____ word" (Matthew 15:23) (2 words)
26 "The twelfth month, which is the month _____" (Esther 3:13)
27 "Sacrifice, _____, acceptable unto God" (Romans 12:1)
30 British rule in India
31 Quiverful
32 Rubies, for example
33 Has _____, kin of also ran
34 "In _____ and hymns and spiritual songs" (Colossians 3:16)
35 Revelation preceder
36 Iridescent gem
37 Belonging to Lithuania and Estonia, once (abbr.)
38 Former cabinet secretary Udall, to his friends

39 "His hand is still _____" (Isaiah 10:4 NIV)
43 Egypt and Syria, once (abbr.)
44 Required
45 Created again
46 "The ten horns which thou sawest _____ kings" (Revelation 17:12) (2 words)
47 Apartment dweller, often
49 "And God said, Let _____ be light" (Genesis 1:3)
51 Andrew's brother
52 Comparison word
53 Ireland, formerly
54 "And your moon will _____ no more" (Isaiah 60:20 NIV)
55 Mole's milieu? (abbr.)
56 Exchange student organization (abbr.)
57 Company bigwig (abbr.)

21

ACROSS

1 Feminine name
4 "They lavish gold. . .and _____ a goldsmith" (Isaiah 46:6)
8 Word in carol title
11 Meat cut
13 Where Adam met Eve
14 "How long _____ ye slack to go" (Joshua 18:3)
15 New Testament prophetess
16 "These six _____ of barley gave he me" (Ruth 3:17)
18 Appear
19 Sign of infection
20 "Thou shalt not _____ the Lord thy God" (Matthew 4:7)
24 "Let the _____ bring forth the living creatures" (Genesis 1:24)
28 Mr. Rogers
30 Bible language (abbr.)
32 Poetic contraction
33 Donkey
34 Chooses
36 Gold (Fr.)
37 Greek letter
38 "To proclaim the acceptable _____ of the LORD" (Isaiah 61:2)
39 Dutch city
40 What Matthew collected
43 "Learn his ways and get a _____ to thy soul" (Proverbs 22:25)
45 "Go to the _____, thou sluggard" (Proverbs 6:6)
47 Minor prophet
50 Feeds
55 Only
56 "And _____ did that which was right" (1 Kings 15:11)
57 "My mercy will I _____ for him for evermore" (Psalm 89:28)
58 Child or ladder
59 Weekday (abbr.)
60 Whirlpool
61 Spicy

DOWN

1 Exclamation
2 "There is _____ like me in all the earth" (Exodus 9:14)
3 Number of rams sacrificed upon Ezra's arrival in Jerusalem (Ezra 8:35)
4 Haw's partner
5 Chemical suffix
6 "They shall _____ the whirlwind" (Hosea 8:7)
7 Follow
8 Upset
9 Raw metal
10 Cable sports network (abbr.)
12 Cite
17 NATO member (abbr.)
21 "A _____ of God came unto me" (Judges 13:6)
22 "_____ one for another" (James 5:16)
23 Subdues
25 "The LORD _____ the soul of his servants" (Psalm 34:22)
26 Walked
27 "He said, _____ am I, my son" (Genesis 22:7)
28 Extremely attentive
29 Greek mountain
31 "What _____ ye by these stones" (Joshua 4:6)
35 Mrs., in Madrid
41 Consume
42 Devilish disguise?
44 Offering options
46 "An ass _____, and a colt with her" (Matthew 21:2)
48 Popular cookie
49 Fall time (abbr.)
50 "They _____ it, and so they marveled" (Psalm 48:5)
51 Employ
52 "When ye fast be not. . .of a _____ countenance" (Matthew 6:16)
53 Masculine name
54 Caleb, for one

by Evelyn M. Boyington

MIRACLES OF JESUS

*Jesus said to them, "I have shown you
many great miracles from the Father."*
JOHN 10:32 NIV

ACROSS

1 Separate
6 Miss or Mrs.
9 Last word in the Bible
   (Revelation 22:21)
13 Abraham's first wife (Gen. 17:15)
14 "But thou shalt give _____ now"
   (1 Samuel 2:16) (2 words)
16 Jacob's third son (Exodus 1:2)
17 "We are true men; we _____
   spies" (Genesis 42:31) (2 words)
18 _____ Valley, CA
19 Chemical suffix (pl.)
20 **MIRACLE** (John 12:1) (2 words)
23 Organic compound
24 Shows or does (suffix)
25 He may save a lot
29 "For my yoke is _____"
   (Matthew 11:30)
31 Police charity (abbr.)
34 Bus or potent preceder
35 Psyche parts
36 Put one foot in front of the other
37 **MIRACLE** (Matthew 14:15–21)
   (3 words)
40 S-shaped moldings
41 Attention-getting word
42 "_____ of a Thousand Days"
43 Prof's lab helpers
44 Italian noble house
46 Took a turn in the lineup
48 Popular sandwich, briefly
49 Vessels (abbr.)
51 **MIRACLE** (Matthew 8:16)
   (3 words)
57 "They will _____ on wings like
   eagles" (Isaiah 40:31 NIV)
58 "Blessed are the _____ in spirit"
   (Matthew 5:3)
59 Get used to
61 Go bad, as fruit
62 Fairytale monster

63 "And, behold, Joseph was _____
   the pit" (Genesis 37:29) (2 words)
64 Flying fish-eaters
65 "Calling on the _____ of the
   Lord" (Acts 22:16)
66 Long lock

DOWN

1 "Like _____ father pitieth his
   children" (Psalm 103:13) (2 words)
2 Catherine _____, last wife of
   Henry VIII
3 Kind of code
4 "Yet they _____ have not spoken
   to them" (Jeremiah 23:21) (2
   words)
5 "But what things were gain. . .
   _____ counted loss"
   (Philippians 3:7) (2 words)
6 Mess up
7 **MIRACLE** (Mark 4:37–39)
   (3 words)
8 "A trap _____ him by the heel"
   (Job 18:9 NIV)
9 "Be on guard! Be _____! You do
   not know when" (Mark 13:33 NIV)
10 Beanery item
11 First lady, and others
12 Serbian city
15 NYC museum
21 Direction from Tucson to Santa Fe
   (abbr.)
22 How or where
25 "And who will _____ us"
   (Isaiah 6:8) (2 words)
26 "I am Alpha and _____"
   (Revelation 1:8)
27 South American range
28 "The Lord is the strength of my
   _____" (Psalm 27:1)
30 Tennis great
31 Sow

by. David K. Shortess

32 *C'est une* _____ *idee*
33 "And all these things shall be _____ unto you" (Luke 12:31)
35 "Will ___ the flesh of bulls" (Psalm 50:13) (2 words)
36 Test taken by HS sophs (abbr.)
38 "Or to which of my creditors did _____ you" (Isaiah 50:1 NIV) (2 words)
39 Old European game with three players and forty cards
45 "Who enter Dagon's temple at Ashdod _____ the threshold" (1 Samuel 5:5 NIV) (2 words)
47 Agree to
48 "Nor gather into _____" (Matthew 6:26)
50 Number of Noah's sons
51 "What, could ye not watch with me one _____" (Matthew 26:40)

52 "And all who _____ their living from the sea" (Revelation 18:17 NIV)
53 "Whom are you pursuing? A dead _____ flea" (1 Samuel 24:14 NIV) (2 words)
54 "So neither _____ my brethren, nor my servants" (Nehemiah 4:23) (2 words)
55 Like a kitten
56 Actor Kristofferson
57 Part of the names of many Quebec towns (abbr.)
60 Printers' measures

ACROSS

1 Hawaii (pl.)
6 Ishmael's son (Genesis 25:14)
11 Attorney
12 Bury
14 Top _____
16 King of Assyria (Isaiah 20:1)
18 "Ye know neither the _____ nor the hour" (Matthew 25:13)
19 Dine
21 Book of the Pentateuch (abbr.)
22 Ax
24 "To day shalt thou be with me in _____" (Luke 23:43)
27 Lot's aunt
29 Nod, to Fido
30 A distance
31 Cut
33 "God created he _____" (Genesis 1:27)
35 Reed
36 Ahiam's father (1 Chronicles 11:35)
38 "Which come to you in _____ clothing" (Matthew 7:15)
41 Naomi's new name (Ruth 1:20)
42 "Jabal; he was the father of such as dwell in _____" (Genesis 4:20)
43 American _____ (college course, briefly)
45 Pointy end
46 Wild
47 Hananiah's son (1 Chronicles 3:21)
49 "I _____ no pleasant bread" (Daniel 10:3)
50 Shobal's son (Genesis 36:23)
51 Whom Abram wed
52 Mail

DOWN

2 "Judge between the _____ and the revenger" (Numbers 35:24)
3 Criminal, for one
4 "Thy _____ and thy she goats" (Genesis 31:38)
5 Vermont product
6 Spouse (abbr.)
7 Tear
8 "There are. . .voices in the world, and none of them is without _____" (1 Corinthians 14:10)
9 Stir
10 Curious
13 Join
15 Survivor of Jericho (Joshua 6:17)
17 King of the Amalekites (1 Samuel 15:8)
20 Foot, to some
23 "He that _____ his father and chaseth away his mother" (Proverbs 19:26)
25 Uncooked
26 Capital city of the Northern Kingdom of Israel
28 Stringed instruments
32 Existed
33 Noah's son
34 Lost
35 "Their _____ exercised to discern both good and evil" (Hebrews 5:14)
37 Benjamin's son (1 Chronicles 8:2)
39 Cook leftovers
40 _____ marker, highway sign
43 "When he came unto _____, the Philistines shouted" (Judges 15:14)
44 Pats
47 Old Testament book (abbr.)
48 "God is _____ judge" (Psalm 75:7)

by Sarah Lagerquist Simmons

ACROSS

1 Government org. in which most have vested interest
4 "Regem, and Jotham, and _____" (1 Chronicles 2:47)
10 Bonkers
14 Thing to pass
15 Resist
16 "Er and _____ died in the land of Canaan" (Numbers 26:19)
17 Jether's son (1 Chronicles 7:38)
18 "The children of Sisera, the children of _____" (Ezra 2:53)
19 Common fear
20 Valley or ravine in Middle East
22 "Mispereth, Bigvai, _____" (Nehemiah 7:7)
24 Old Testament book (abbr.)
25 Scandinavian carrier (abbr.)
28 "Whose soever sins ye _____, they are remitted unto them" (John 20:23)
30 Chuza's wife (Luke 8:3)
33 "_____, come forth" (John 11:43)
37 David was a king of _____ (see 1 Chronicles 22:8)
38 "And I was as a _____ man that openeth not his mouth" (Psalm 38:13)
40 "The sons of Reuel; _____, and Zerah" (Genesis 36:13)
41 "There was one _____, a prophetess" (Luke 2:36)
43 Ruth's love
45 Palti's father (Numbers 13:9)
46 "How long shall this man be a _____ unto us" (Exodus 10:7)
48 "Who shall _____ him up" (Numbers 24:9)
50 Aside from
51 Jehu's father (1 Kings 16:1)
53 "Machnadebai, _____, Sharai" (Ezra 10:40)
55 "And Zimri begot _____" (1 Chronicles 8:36)
57 Time past
58 Book of creation (abbr.)
61 Actress Ward
63 Church areas

68 Comply
70 "And the coast turneth to _____" (Joshua 19:29)
73 "Thou shouldest make thy _____ as high as the eagle" (Jeremiah 49:16)
74 Troubled breath
75 "Johanan, and Dalaiah, and _____" (1 Chronicles 3:24)
76 European dictator
77 Kitchen shapes
78 "He made narrowed _____ round about" (1 Kings 6:6)
79 More than pat

DOWN

1 British playwright
2 "Through faith also _____ herself received strength" (Hebrews 11:11)
3 "And they came to the threshingfloor of _____" (Genesis 50:10)
4 Received
5 New Testament book (abbr.)
6 Unit of measure equivalent to 9 inches
7 "An _____ of barley seed" (Leviticus 27:16)
8 Jonathan's father (Ezra 10:15)
9 "The king was merry with wine, he commanded _____" (Esther 1:10)
10 "And tempted _____ in the desert" (Psalm 106:14)
11 Israelite leader (Nehemiah 10:26)
12 _____ du Nord, in Paris
13 Egyptian symbol of life
21 Amoz's prophet son (abbr.)
23 "From the hill _____" (Psalm 42:6)
26 Also
27 Give the cold shoulder
29 "They departed from _____" (Numbers 33:27)
30 "The son of _____, which was the son of Joseph" (Luke 3:24)
31 "The threshingfloor of _____ the Jebusite" (2 Chronicles 3:1)

by Tonya Vilhauer

32 Minor prophet
34 "Nohah the fourth, and _____ the fifth" (1 Chronicles 8:2)
35 "Of the sons also of Bigvai; _____" (Ezra 8:14)
36 Have nothing to do with
37 Purify
39 "To the moles and to the _____" (Isaiah 2:20)
42 Aminadab's father (Matthew 1:4)
44 "The Nethinims: the children of _____" (Nehemiah 7:46)
47 Cainan's father (Genesis 5:9)
49 Tease
52 "Amram, and _____, Hebron, and Uzziel" (Numbers 3:19)
54 Offspring
56 By oneself
58 "If an ox _____ a man or a woman" (Exodus 21:28)
59 "The curse upon mount _____" (Deuteronomy 11:29)

60 Dickens' "Little" woman
62 "Nevertheless _____ heart was perfect" (1 Kings 15:14)
64 "The _____ are a people not strong" (Proverbs 30:25)
65 "The keepers of the walls took away my _____" (Song of Solomon 5:7)
66 *Como* _____? (Sp. greeting)
67 F-_____ (photography term)
69 Affirmative
71 "Go to the _____, thou sluggard" (Proverbs 6:6)
72 Not hers

ACROSS

1 "The _____ is my Shepherd" (Psalm 32:1)
5 "My grace is _____" (2 Corinthians 12:9)
12 River on Polish border
13 Avoid
14 Year of our Lord (abbr.)
15 French coal-mining region
18 NHL team (abbr.)
19 "The LORD wrought a great _____ that day" (2 Samuel 23:10)
20 Letter abbr.
21 Place (O.E.)
23 Jackie's second
25 "The righteous shall flourish like the palm _____" (Psalm 92:12)
27 Midwest state (abbr.)
28 "Saul, and the archers _____ him" (1 Samuel 31:3)
29 "Joseph's _____ brethren went down to buy corn" (Genesis 42:3)
31 German article
32 Gospel author
34 Prophet who rebuked David
36 Protected product symbol
37 "The words of king _____" (Proverbs 31:1)
41 _____ generis
43 "He will laugh at the _____ of the innocent" (Job 9:23)
46 "Give me children, _____ else I die" (Genesis 30:1)
47 "Who is lord over _____" (Psalm 12:4)
48 Sunny state (abbr.)
49 "Pulse to eat, and water to _____" (Daniel 1:12)
52 Cabinet secretary's domain (abbr.)
53 Where children learn Bible lessons (abbr.)
54 Med. provider
55 Peter or Bridget
56 Coach Parseghian
57 Civil War general
58 Book after Nahum (abbr.)
61 Direction (abbr.)
63 Eye part
65 Nonprescription med. (abbr.)
67 Eastern university (abbr.)
68 "No galley with _____ will ride them" (Isaiah 33:21 NIV)
70 "As a thread of _____ is broken" (Judges 16:9)
71 Eras
73 "Be lord over thy _____" (Genesis 27:29)
74 "Jesus. . .withdrew to _____ places and prayed" (Luke 5:16 NIV)

DOWN

1 "And makes himself rich with _____" (Habakkuk 2:6 NASB)
2 "The _____ number. . .is to be redeemed" (Numbers 3:48)
3 Concerning
4 Ancient Celtic priest
5 "May he. . .be. . .a _____ of your old age" (Ruth 4:15 NASB)
6 "Where is the _____ of the oppressor?" (Isaiah 51:13)
7 Town celebration (abbr.)
8 _____ League
9 "For. . .barley was in the _____" (Exodus 9:31)
10 Home of Fargo (abbr.)
11 Taunts
16 Artery
17 First name of "Exodus" hero
19 King Xerxes' queen
20 "Go to thy fathers in _____" (Genesis 15:15)
22 Down for the count (abbr.)
24 "The _____ of the LORD. . .will perform this" (Isaiah 9:7)
26 Address abbr., for some
29 Weekday (abbr.)
30 Compass direction
32 "Even so, come, Lord _____" (Revelation 22:20)
33 Southwest state (abbr.)
35 Russian ruler
38 "Show Me" state (abbr.)
39 David had him killed
40 "And God said, _____ there be light" (Genesis 1:3)
42 Naval ship's abbr.

by Marijane G. Troyer

43 Absalom killed to avenge her
   (2 Samuel 13:14, 28)
44 Part of a personality
45 Tree of _____ (Genesis 2:9)
48 Savior
50 "Thou shalt have _____ portion"
   (Ezra 4:16)
51 "Mine heart shall be _____ unto
   you" (1 Chronicles 12:17)
57 Place of the seal (abbr., Lat.)
59 Adam's son
60 "Perhaps he is deep in thought, or
   _____" (1 Kings 18:27 NIV)
61 "Will a man _____ God?"
   (Malachi 3:8)
62 "They used. . ._____ for mortar"
   (Genesis 11:3 NIV)
64 You (Ger.)
65 Says who?
66 "I _____ do all things"
   (Philippians 4:13)
69 Indian coin (abbr.)

70 Home of NFL Titans (abbr.)
72 "We bring good things to life"
   company (abbr.)

ACROSS

1 "Look out!"
6 "According as thou _____ me" (Genesis 27:19)
11 "As. . .sharpens _____" (Proverbs 27:17 NIV)
12 Comply
14 Issachar's son (Genesis 46:13)
15 Number of holes on some golf courses
16 Those with a discount (abbr.)
19 Benign cyst
20 Sandra _____ O'Connor
21 Good (colloq.)
23 _____ of America (Minnesota attraction)
25 Now's partner
26 "For we wrestle not _____ flesh" (Ephesians 6:12)
30 Chastises
33 "Every creditor that _____ought unto his neighbour" (Deuteronomy 15:2)
34 Javan's son (Genesis 10:4)
35 Legal exam, familiarly
36 Can
37 Get ready
40 Hagar, and others (var.)
44 "And the _____ in their mount Seir" (Genesis 14:6)
45 "The moving of my lips should _____ your grief" (Job 16:5)
46 So be it
47 Shuthelah's son (Numbers 26:36)
48 Cerise, for one
49 However (var.)
51 Question
54 _____ Khan
55 Jezebel's god
56 Flesh and _____
58 Part of the action
59 Minor prophet
60 Shrines
61 "He _____ him down cedars" (Isaiah 44:14)

DOWN

2 Irony
3 How pretty maids sit, with "all in" (2 words)
4 Job
5 Ahira's father (Numbers 1:15)
6 Shackle
7 Solomon's grandson (Matthew 1:7)
8 Refuse
9 "It is better. . .to enter into the kingdom of God with one _____" (Mark 9:47)
10 Dreary
13 _____-Barnea
17 Anger
18 Maligned
21 Where John was baptizing (John 1:28)
22 Range
24 Top
25 Owns
27 Jeroboam's father (1 Kings 11:26)
28 Gaze intently
29 "Porters keeping the ward at the _____" (Nehemiah 12:25)
30 Part of the northern border of Judah's land (Joshua 15:6)
31 "Moses and _____ talking with him" (Matthew 17:3)
32 Bands
37 Twin son of Judah and Tamar (Genesis 38:29)
38 Paul was a citizen of _____
39 Peg
41 "Stand in _____ and sin not" (Psalm 4:4)
42 "His king shall be higher than _____" (Numbers 24:7)
43 Governing body
49 Iowa town off U.S. 30
50 Hirsute one has plenty
52 A few
53 Understand
55 Louisville Slugger, for one
57 Direction from Minneapolis to Chicago

by Sarah Lagerquist Simmons

## 27

MIRACLES IN DANIEL

*"[God] rescues and he saves; he performs signs
and wonders in the heavens and on the earth."*

DANIEL 6:27 NIV

ACROSS

1 "There is no ___ discerning and
wise as you" (Genesis 41:39 NIV) (2
words)
6 Hearty's cohort
10 "For, lo, the winter is _____"
(Song of Solomon 2:11)
14 Summer TV fare, often
15 Indigo plant
16 He was red all over (Genesis
25:25)
17 Where God intervened to save
Daniel's friends (Daniel 3:20–28)
(3 words)
20 "But Jonathan was very _____ of
David" (1 Samuel 19:1 NIV)
21 "And he will make her wilderness
like _____" (Isaiah 51:3)
22 "Even Assyria has joined them
____ strength to the descendants
of Lot" (Psalm 83:8 NIV) (2 words)
25 "Thou hast not _____ unto men,
but unto God" (Acts 5:4)
26 Haw's opposite
29 In the distance
30 Accumulate
32 "Without _____ of brightness?"
(Amos 5:20 NIV) (2 words)
33 "_____ a girl"
34 Oaf
35 "And in an hour that he is not
_____ of" (Matthew 24:50)
36 Where God intervened to save
Daniel (Daniel 6:16) (3 words)
40 Took a turn (2 words)
42 "Whither have ye made a _____
to day" (1 Samuel 27:10)
43 "And _____ soul sin" (Leviticus
5:1) (2 words)
46 "_____ I trying to please men?"
(Galatians 1:10 NIV) (2 words)
47 "Be self-controlled and _____"
(1 Peter 5:8 NIV)

49 "And _____ hour he is not aware"
(Luke 12:46) (2 words)
50 "Nor standeth in the _____ of
sinners" (Psalm 1:1)
51 Made it home?
52 Go back
54 Bath powder
55 "The _____ came to Jesus by
night" (John 3:2)
56 What God wrote on the wall
(Daniel 5:25 NIV) (3 words)
63 Where Esfahan is
64 "Go and _____ potter's earthen
bottle" (Jeremiah 19:1) (2 words)
65 "Such knowledge _____
wonderful for me" (Psalm 139:6)
(2 words)
66 Prohibitionists
67 Land of Seir (Genesis 32:3)
68 Depends on

DOWN

1 Table scrap
2 Ezra follower (abbr.)
3 "And how long will it be _____
they believe me" (Numbers 14:11)
4 "That the Son of man must
_____ many things" (Mark 8:31)
5 Leek relative
6 "It is _____ for thee to kick
against the pricks" (Acts 26:14)
7 "And see if there be _____
wicked way in me" (Psalm 139:24)
8 "The _____ more than meat"
(Luke 12:23) (2 words)
9 Slips away from
10 Quaker William
11 Jehoshaphat's father (1 Kings
15:24)
12 Biological pouch
13 Calendar abbreviation
18 "I will bring to an _____ the
groaning she caused" (Isaiah
21:2 NIV) (2 words)

by David K. Shortess

19 "By the way of the _____ sea" (Numbers 14:25)
22 _____ chi
23 "This do ye, as _____ as ye drink it" (1 Corinthians 11:25)
24 "And I will raise him up at the _____" (John 6:40) (2 words)
25 "I have _____ to no purpose" (Isaiah 49:4 NIV)
26 Monument rock
27 Give _____ to
28 Pink, at times
31 Pronoun (Fr.)
32 "But my heart standeth in _____ of thy word" (Psalm 119:161)
34 Game, _____, match
35 "Can _____ one cubit unto his stature" (Matthew 6:27)
37 Father of Canaan (Gen. 9:18)
38 "_____ standeth in the way of sinners" (Psalm 1:1)
39 Official under Darius (Daniel 6:1 NIV)
40 "Consider the lilies of the field, _____ they grow" (Matthew 6:28)

41 Jether's son (1 Chronicles 7:38)
44 "Be not _____ from me" (Psalm 38:21)
45 Sluggard's teacher? (Proverbs 6:6)
47 Maintain
48 "Dogs came and _____ his sores" (Luke 16:21)
49 Opposed to
51 "And he _____ down among the ashes" (Job 2:8)
53 Certain correspondence
54 Perfect scores, to some
55 Close forcefully
56 Naval officer (abbr.)
57 "They do alway _____ in their heart" (Hebrews 3:10)
58 "I tell you, _____: but, except ye repent" (Luke 13:3)
59 Ike's command (abbr.)
60 R.R. depot
61 It may be charged?
62 Phone book listings (abbr.)

ACROSS

1 "The cloud the garment. . .thick darkness a _____ for it" (Job 38:9)
11 Chaste
12 Press
14 Remedy
15 "Give _____, O my people, to my law" (Psalm 78:1)
18 "On the hole of the _____" (Isaiah 11:8)
19 Undergraduate degree (abbr.)
20 "If any man will _____ thee" (Matthew 5:40)
22 Robert E., and others
24 Smooth transition
25 Touchy
26 "By the threshingfloor of _____" (1 Chronicles 21:15)
28 "And Joseph said. . .God will surely _____ you" (Genesis 50:24)
29 "_____ of the brooks of Gaash" (2 Samuel 23:30)
30 "The _____ also dwelt in Seir" (Deuteronomy 2:12)
31 Jacob's new name
34 Pontius _____
37 Prophets
40 Sum
41 Proportion
42 Cut costs, with "down"
44 "Didst thou not _____ me" (Genesis 12:18)
45 "He planteth an _____, and the rain doth nourish it" (Isaiah 44:14)
46 Owns
47 Hot _____
49 He did not side with Adonijah (1 Kings 1:8)
50 "The fourth river is _____" (Genesis 2:14)
52 New York Mets' great Tommy
53 Jacob's wife
54 "A man. . .seeketh and _____ with all wisdom" (Proverbs 18:1)

DOWN

2 Germane
3 "In the plain of _____" (Daniel 3:1)
4 Sheath
5 Jumped
6 Halo
7 Diving bird
8 _____ fide
9 Hill builder
10 "And he erected there an altar, and called it _____" (Genesis 33:20)
13 "A sacrifice to God for a _____ savour" (Ephesians 5:2)
16 Aircraft (Prefix, var.)
17 "A voice of the LORD that _____ recompence to his enemies" (Isaiah 66:6)
20 Kinsman saluted by Paul (Romans 16:21)
21 _____ and the Thummim (Exodus 28:30)
23 Not glad
25 Title for Winston Churchill
27 "Adam gave _____ to all cattle" (Genesis 2:20)
28 Become ill
32 "Fill the waters in the _____" (Genesis 1:22)
33 Exist
35 Abraham's nephew
36 Tall one?
38 Yad _____, Jerusalem Holocaust memorial
39 Proclaim
42 "Rock, _____, scissors"
43 Adored, with "on"
46 Gigantic
48 Cope with
50 Consume
51 "_____ shall be called Woman" (Genesis 2:23)

by Sarah Lagerquist Simmons

ACROSS

1 Rebound
6 "The inhabitants of _____ gather themselves to flee" (Isaiah 10:31)
11 Gypsy
14 "Johanan, and Dalaiah, and _____" (1 Chronicles 3:24)
15 "And _____ thereon a great heap of stones" (Joshua 8:29)
16 Master (Sp.)
17 Musical sounds
18 "The children of _____" (Ezra 2:50)
19 Part of HRH
20 "He _____ Abram" (Genesis 12:16)
22 Statue
24 "The appointed barley and the _____" (Isaiah 28:25)
25 "And _____, and Ramah, and Hazor" (Joshua 19:36)
26 "Out of _____ came down governors" (Judges 5:14)
30 Grandmother of Esau
32 Correspond
33 Shimei's father (1 Kings 2:8)
34 _____ Minor
38 Debris
39 Sheresh's son (1 Chronicles 7:16)
40 Remainder
41 "_____ was a great man among the Anakims" (Joshua 14:15)
42 Chemical suffix (pl.)
43 "The children of _____, the children of Darkon" (Nehemiah 7:58)
44 King who was once a shepherd
46 Cruised
47 "And from thence unto _____" (Acts 21:1)
50 Addition total
51 "Henoch, and _____, and Eldaah" (1 Chronicles 1:33)
52 "In _____ were twelve fountains of water" (Numbers 33:9)
54 Shirt maker
58 Church Paul wrote (abbr.)
59 Atone
61 "By the river of _____" (Daniel 8:2)
62 "And Adam called his wife's name _____" (Genesis 3:20)
63 Retaliate
64 Go into the sunset?
65 Saw _____
66 Part of TLC
67 Mound

DOWN

1 Actress Blanchett
2 Soon (arch.)
3 Go on and on
4 Unique person
5 Agonies
6 Grind
7 Comfort
8 Tie up
9 Prophet son of Amoz (abbr.)
10 "Children of _____, the children of Harsha" (Ezra 2:52)
11 Shema's son (1 Chronicles 2:44)
12 "I am Alpha and _____" (Revelation 22:13)
13 Plain of _____, where Abram entered Canaan (Genesis 12:6)
21 Atmosphere
23 "_____ the Netophathite" (2 Samuel 23:28)
25 Ancient Syria, biblically
26 "Call me not Naomi, call me _____" (Ruth 1:20)
27 Jakeh's son (Proverbs 30:1)
28 Baby's bed
29 Ruler of the half part of Keilah (Nehemiah 3:18)
30 Nadab's son who died without children (1 Chronicles 2:30)
31 Coach Parseghian, and others
33 "Jahziel, and _____, and Jezer" (1 Chronicles 7:13)
35 Barrier
36 Sea key
37 "And they came to the threshingfloor of _____" (Genesis 50:10)
42 Actress Gabor
43 Congestion
45 Where the ark came to rest
46 July, for example

by Tonya Vilhauer

47 American Motors model
48 Over
49 Spent
50 Blockade
52 "The land is as the garden of
_____" (Joel 2:3)
53 Loan
54 Issue
55 Jai _____
56 Execute perfectly (colloq.)
57 Cultivate
60 First lady

## 30

ACROSS

1 "Come not _____ your wives" (Exodus 19:15)
3 Sulk
6 "There was a _____ round about the throne" (Revelation 4:3)
11 "Also he sent forth a _____ from him" (Genesis 8:8)
13 Master or sir (Hindi)
14 "Follow _____" (Matthew 4:19 NIV)
15 Irish island
16 Printer's measure
17 "I pray thee, _____ and eat of my venison" (Genesis 27:19)
18 "And Lamech took unto him _____ wives" (Genesis 4:19)
19 _____ de mer
20 Noah's son
22 Rapid marching style (abbr.)
23 "_____ kindness unto my master Abraham" (Genesis 24:12)
26 Lake above Ohio
28 Prophet who anointed Saul
31 "Who will make me a _____" (Job 24:25)
33 Where fall foliage is beautiful in U.S. (abbr.)
35 "Behold, thou art _____, my love" (Song of Solomon 4:1)
36 "The LORD _____ me to the house of my master's brethren" (Genesis 24:27)
37 _____ Shaddai
38 Where there was no room
39 Mark aimed at in curling
40 Bills all paid (abbr.)
41 Do alone
42 "She gave _____ of the tree" (Genesis 3:12)
43 Conjunction (Fr.)
44 Talk aimlessly
46 By virtue of office (Lat., Abbr.)
47 Society of Jesus (abbr.)
49 Regional telephone co. (abbr.)
52 Dear _____
53 Local law (abbr.)
54 Crazy ones (colloq.)
57 Acreage
59 Alas (Ger.)
61 Hidden valuables
62 Numeral (Sp.)
63 American revolutionary Allen
65 "Roaring lions _____ their prey" (Psalm 22:13 NIV)
67 Asian country (abbr.)
68 "But the dove found _____ rest" (Genesis 8:9)
69 Continent (abbr.)
71 Also
72 Broadcast
74 Travel abbr.
75 Noah's son
76 "_____ evil and cultivate good" (1 Peter 3:11 MSG)
77 Quieting sound

DOWN

1 First man and his designees (Genesis 2:20) (2 words)
2 Complete body of Jewish law
3 "They that handle the _____ of the writer" (Judges 5:14)
4 "Neither shall ye _____ enchantment" (Leviticus 19:26)
5 Hats
6 "_____ up and walk" (Acts 3:6)
7 Belonging to king of Gerar (Genesis 20)
8 Southwestern state (abbr.)
9 "It is _____ that I give her to thee" (Genesis 29:19)
10 "Make thee an ark of gopher _____" (Genesis 6:14)
12 Low areas (arch.)
21 Hydrochloric acid (abbr.)
22 Day (Sp.)
24 Flying females in WWII (abbr.)
25 "A calm disposition _____ intemperate rage" (Ecclesiastes 10:4 MSG)
27 "And I will _____ you out of their bondage" (Exodus 6:6)
29 Spouse
30 "And _____ the lamp of God went out" (1 Samuel 3:3)
32 "I. . .do bring a _____ of waters" (Genesis 6:17)

by Marijane G. Troyer

34 Compass direction (abbr.)
36 Lake, in Lyon (Fr.)
37 Forget me nots?
41 Wide river valley
45 Where Joshua sent his men after Jericho (Joshua 7:2)
47 "Get away!"
48 He was seduced by Potiphar's wife
50 Sky description, perhaps
51 NE state (abbr.)
55 When close game is played, maybe (abbr.)
56 Fissile rock
58 Romans' wraps
60 Book division (abbr.)
63 Beige shade
64 Ham's father
66 In a _____ (going nowhere)
69 Garden State (abbr.)
70 Two-year college degree (abbr.)
73 Popular

## 31

A GODLY LIGHT

The people walking in darkness have seen a great light;
on those living in the land of the shadow of death a light has dawned.

ISAIAH 9:2 NIV

ACROSS

1 Sign gas
5 Certain packages (abbr.)
9 Penne, for one
14 Fairytale bad guy
15 Pledge
16 Spicy stews
17 Significant periods
18 _____ cava
19 Card or mat
20 "And God said, _____"
   (Genesis 1:3) (4 words)
23 Jeanne d'Arc, e.g.
24 Northwest Pennsylvania county
25 Mini _____
26 "That _____ after the dust of the
   earth" (Amos 2:7)
27 "For _____ price is far above
   rubies" (Proverbs 31:10)
28 "Silence the _____ and the
   avenger" (Psalm 8:2 NIV)
31 "I _____ and stricken in age"
   (Joshua 23:2) (2 words)
34 Bilhah's first son
   (Genesis 30:4–6)
35 Like a breezeway
36 With 52 Across: "When _____
   spoke again to the people, he
   _____" (John 8:12 NIV) (5 words)
40 He saw a plumb line
41 Barley beard
42 Radon and argon
43 Reagan, familiarly
44 So long
45 Beach acquisitions
47 Asian holiday
48 "And the famine was _____ in
   the land" (Genesis 43:1)
49 Number cruncher (abbr.)
52 See 36 Across (4 words)
57 _____ ear

58 "And _____ not unto thine own
   understanding" (Proverbs 3:5)
59 "Whither have ye made a _____
   today" (1 Samuel 27:10)
60 Military goof
61 "And there was one _____, a
   prophetess" (Luke 2:36)
62 Aussie pal
63 Rich cake
64 Duds
65 Scraped by, with "out"

DOWN

1 Christmas carols
2 Crested wader
3 Hold forth
4 "Then I said, I shall die in my
   _____" (Job 29:18)
5 Grotto
6 "He beheld the city, and wept
   _____" (Luke 19:41) (2 words)
7 Gift recipient
8 Mop a deck
9 "And Jacob took him rods of green
   _____" (Genesis 30:37)
10 Exhausted (2 words)
11 Dross
12 Dash accessory (abbr.)
13 "And upon _____ day Herod. . .
   made an oration" (Acts 12:21)
   (2 words)
21 "Lift up your _____, O ye gates"
   (Psalm 24:7)
22 "I, _____, am the LORD" (Isaiah
   43:11) (2 words)
26 Besides
27 Owned
28 One size _____ all
29 "Whether is greater, he that sitteth
   at meat, _____ that serveth"
   (Luke 22:27) (2 words)
30 Espies

by David K. Shortess

31 "Some cakes and _____ of honey"
   (1 Kings 14:3 NIV) (2 words)
32 Office note
33 "So thou, _____ of man"
   (Ezekiel 33:7) (2 words)
34 "He will silence her noisy _____"
   (Jeremiah 51:55 NIV)
35 Medical test for men (abbr.)
37 "Many will _____ me in that day"
   (Matthew 7:22) (2 words)
38 "Standeth in _____ of thy word"
   (Psalm. 119:161)
39 Former VP Spiro
44 "If ye _____ men, let one of
   your brethren be bound" (Genesis
   42:19) (2 words)
45 "Haman was come. . ._____
   Mordecai on the gallows"
   (Esther 6:4) (2 words)
46 Game sites
47 Grand _____ auto
48 Office aide, briefly

49 Kick the bucket
50 Home _____
51 "These things shall be _____
   unto you" (Matthew 6:33)
52 Itemize
53 "I will _____ wise cast out"
   (John 6:37) (2 words)
54 Snarl (arch.)
55 Not bubbly
56 "Because they have not known the
   Father _____" (John 16:3 NIV)
   (2 words)

## 32

ACROSS

1 "Eloi, Eloi, _____ sabachthani?" (Mark 15:34)
5 Obligation
9 Playwright Henrik
14 "And _____ lived after he begat Peleg" (Genesis 11:17)
15 Always
16 Take care of (2 words)
17 Hebrew month
18 "Their fathers shall they _____ away with them" (Leviticus 26:39)
19 Actor Ed
20 Pathetic
22 Characteristics
24 "For the wine press is full, the _____ overflow" (Joel 3:13 NKJV)
25 Diamonds (colloq.)
26 "Remembering mine affliction and my _____" (Lamentations 3:19)
29 Good (colloq.)
31 "And _____ went out before the men of Shechem" (Judges 9:39)
35 Apart
36 James's brother (Jude 1:1)
37 "The son of _____, which was the son of Nagge" (Luke 3:25)
38 "Man will _____ thee at the law" (Matthew 5:40)
39 Masters
40 _____ of man (Jesus)
41 Rescue
43 Columnist Landers, and others
44 Gem
46 Hushim's father (1 Chronicles 7:12)
47 "I _____ down under his shadow with great delight" (Song of Solomon 2:3)
48 Handbags
49 Agency (abbr.)
51 *Arsenic and Old* _____
52 Admission
55 Mortified
59 "Fine linen, and coral, and _____" (Ezekiel 27:16)
60 Paddles
62 "Calcol, and _____: five of them" (1 Chronicles 2:6)
63 Separate
64 Coax
65 "The tower of _____" (Genesis 35:21)
66 "Some _____ fell by the way side" (Matthew 13:4)
67 "Not _____ unto men, but unto God" (Acts 5:4)
68 Lease

DOWN

1 Take the plunge
2 Kish's father (2 Chronicles 29:12)
3 Protein source
4 Attained, with "at"
5 "Turn away the _____ from the faith" (Acts 13:8)
6 "_____ have compassed me about" (Psalm 40:12)
7 Son of (Heb.)
8 Fixed weight allowance
9 Abraham's son
10 "The Chaldeans that _____ you" (Jeremiah 21:9)
11 Forwarded
12 Hot times in Tours (Fr.)
13 Scandinavian country (abbr.)
21 Transportation fee
23 Doesn't walk
26 Word in spirituals
27 "Imnah, and _____, and Ishuai" (1 Chronicles 7:30)
28 Colander
29 Like some toast
30 Does arithmetic
32 "Met with us at _____" (Acts 20:14)
33 By oneself
34 Boundaries
36 Simon's father (John 1:42)
39 Doesn't expire
42 Built
44 Certain
45 "And the _____ of grapes" (Amos 9:13)
48 Got a C, at least
50 Prophets
51 Immense

by Tonya Vilhauer

52 Shammah's father (2 Samuel 23:11)
53 "A _____, and a stone lay upon it" (John 11:38)
54 "Vexed his righteous _____" (2 Peter 2:8)
56 "And there _____ him a booth" (Jonah 4:5)
57 "Shuthelah: of _____, the family" (Numbers 26:36)
58 Arrow
59 "They laded their _____ with the corn" (Genesis 42:26)
61 First name of "Exodus" hero

ACROSS

1 Man whose sons were David's heroes (2 Samuel 23:32)
7 Most evil
12 _____-ho
13 "We which are _____ and remain unto the coming" (1 Thessalonians 4:15)
14 "Deliver thee from the snare of the _____" (Psalm 91:3)
15 Some at San Quentin
17 Old Testament book (abbr.)
18 In three ways (comb. form)
19 He rode Traveler
20 Greek letter
22 Hophni and Phinehas were _____ sons (1 Samuel 4:16–17)
24 Era
26 "Beguiled you in the matter of _____" (Numbers 25:18)
27 Levite during David's time who was a seer (2 Chronicles 29:30)
29 There are (Sp.)
30 "Israel did eat _____ forty years" (Exodus 16:35)
31 "Of the tribe of Benjamin, an _____. . .a Pharisee" (Philippians 3:5)
33 Reclined
34 "Neither be ye _____as were some of them" (1 Corinthians 10:7)
35 Transformation
38 Judged
42 Amana, for one
43 Computer memory unit
45 Put away
46 Sighing exclamation
47 Attention
48 Deer, biblically
49 Blow
50 Pispah's brother (1 Chronicles 7:38)
52 "That which groweth of _____ own accord" (Leviticus 25:5)
55 Busy one
56 "Let me escape _____. . .and my soul shall live" (Genesis 19:20)
58 "His eyes are like the _____ of the morning" (Job 41:18)
60 Early
61 Deal
62 "Thou shalt break the _____ thereof" (Ezekiel 23:34)
63 Disciple whom Paul greets (Romans 16:14)

DOWN

2 Ahisamach's son (Exodus 31:6)
3 Baste
4 Cease
5 "The LORD shall reign forever and _____" (Exodus 15:18)
6 Baruch's father (Jeremiah 32:12)
7 Dale
8 First name of 70s tennis star
9 Magazine known for its photography
10 Mother of all living (Genesis 3:20)
11 Snake
14 Not real
16 "The sun _____ upon the water" (2 Kings 3:22)
17 "Unto the tower of _____ they sanctified it" (Nehemiah 3:1)
21 Mehujael's father (Genesis 4:18)
23 "Give me also _____ of water" (Joshua 15:19)
25 "I have given order to the churches of _____" (1 Corinthians 16:1)
26 "Every one that _____ among them that are numbered" (Exodus 30:14)
28 "Way of the slothful man is as a _____ of thorns" (Proverbs 15:19)
30 Prince of Persia and Media under Ahasuerus (Esther 1:14)
32 Sorrow
33 What Edom means
35 "He disappointeth the devices of the _____" (Job 5:12)
36 Assyrian area where Israelites were taken by Sargon (2 Kings 17:6)
37 Maaseiah's father (Nehemiah 3:23)
39 Ruth, originally
40 "And be it indeed that I have _____" (Job 19:4)
41 Hate

by Sarah Lagerquist Simmons

43 Chef James, and others
44 Testeth
50 Hushim's father (1 Chronicles 7:12)
51 "_____ in the audience of the people" (Exodus 24:7)
53 Hiram was king of _____ (2 Samuel 5:11)
54 Oracle
57 _____ *Robe*, Lloyd C. Douglas novel
59 Old Testament book (abbr.)

ACROSS

1 He ruled over almost a billion people for more than 25 years
3 Low-ranked naval officer (abbr.)
6 "And I saw as the colour of _____ as the appearance of fire" (Ezekiel 1:27)
9 Scandinavian carrier (abbr.)
11 "And ere the lamp of God went out in the _____ of the Lord" (1 Samuel 3:3)
14 He wears a mask at home
16 Southern state (abbr.)
17 Expert
19 _____ Cid
21 Feminine name
22 "Nevertheless David took the _____ of Zion" (1 Chronicles 11:5)
24 Large truck, to some
26 House or ground
28 On the summit
30 Copied
32 In the manner of
33 Parent, to some
34 Not too good or bad (abbr.)
35 "Some bread and some _____ stew" (Genesis 25:34 NIV)
38 "And there accompanied him into Asia Sopater of _____" (Acts 20:4)
40 For example (L.)
42 "You alone are to be _____" (Psalm 76:7 NIV)
44 Where children learn about God (abbr.)
45 "Slew a lion in a pit in a _____ day" (1 Chronicles 11:22)
47 "None is so fierce that _____ stir him up" (Job 41:10)
50 Musical singing note
51 "_____ what?"
52 Sandwich (abbr.)
54 "And a _____ of three years old" (Genesis 15:9)
55 "Their calls will _____ through the windows" (Zephaniah 2:14 NIV)
57 Ridge
59 "The _____ shall eat and be satisfied" (Psalm 22:26)
61 Slippery ones
63 Continent (abbr.)
64 New England state (abbr.)
65 2,000 pounds
66 "And _____ the seventh day God ended his work" (Genesis 2:2)
68 Spy who brought back good report
70 Um's cousin
71 Wandering one
73 False sense, to Christians (abbr.)
74 "As the trees of lign _____" (Numbers 24:6)
75 Hebrew letter
76 "And one more thing" (abbr.)

DOWN

1 Led Hebrews to Promised Land
2 Big Ten school (abbr.)
3 See
4 "Each man _____ a sword to his side" (Exodus 32:27 NIV)
5 "I _____ the LORD" (Leviticus 22:3)
6 "_____, master! for it was borrowed" (2 Kings 6:5)
7 "Or in things too high for _____" (Psalm 131:1)
8 "For ye tithe mint and _____ and all manner of herbs" (Luke 11:42)
10 One of the twelve spies (Numbers 13:12)
12 Engineering major (abbr.)
13 Part of Costa del Sol (Sp.)
15 Emerald Isle (abbr.)
17 "But ye shall destroy their _____" (Exodus 34:13)
18 Company VIP (abbr.)
20 "Seven days shall there be no _____ found in your houses" (Exodus 12:19)
22 "She shall be _____ Woman" (Genesis 2:23)
23 Do to a shrew
25 Brit. politician, maybe
27 Wild animal's dwelling
29 Princess's nemesis, in tale
31 Rebel against

by Marijane G. Troyer

36 Location of NH and VT
37 Dosage, maybe
39 Vashti's successor
41 "And thou shalt dwell in the land of _____" (Genesis 45:10)
43 Women's historical organization (abbr.)
45 "_____ took of the fruit" (Genesis 3:6)
46 "Behold, I will put a fleece of _____" (Judges 6:37)
48 Egyptian sun god
49 Village 7 miles from Jerusalem
52 College degree (abbr.)
53 Grad student, at times (abbr.)
56 Lowest Anglo-Saxon freeman
58 19th-century evangelist
60 Asa and Ahab
62 "And he begat _____ and daughters" (Genesis 5:4)
63 Got rid of
65 Ceylon, for example

67 "But the dove found _____ rest for the sole of her foot" (Genesis 8:9)
68 Affirmative (Ger.)
69 Almost (abbr.)
72 Salem's state (abbr.)

## 35

ACROSS

1 "_____; Thy kingdom is divided" (Daniel 5:28)
6 "Let me do it" (2 words)
10 Cracked open
14 "Duke Timnah, duke _____" (1 Chronicles 1:51)
15 Spray weapon
16 Character on TV's "Hawaii 5-0"
17 Wear away
18 "Between blood and blood, between _____" (Deuteronomy 17:8)
19 "Belly is as wine which hath no _____" (Job 32:19)
20 "Not by the door into the _____" (John 10:1)
22 "Between Nineveh and _____" (Genesis 10:12)
23 Son of Zorobabel (Luke 3:27)
24 "Showed thee, O _____, what is good" (Micah 6:8)
25 Hymn (abbr.)
28 "_____ no man any thing" (Romans 13:8)
29 "Causeth contentions to cease, and _____ between the mighty" (Proverbs 18:18)
33 Paddles
35 "Unto him was Carshena, Shethar, _____" (Esther 1:14)
36 Helez's son (1 Chronicles 2:39)
40 "Thou art _____ in the balances" (Daniel 5:27)
41 "Said unto her, _____ cumi" (Mark 5:41)
42 "Glean _____ of corn" (Ruth 2:2)
43 "Herds that fed in Sharon was _____" (1 Chronicles 27:29)
44 New Testament book (abbr.)
47 _____ income
48 Old Testament book (abbr.)
49 "The sin which doth so easily _____" (Hebrews 12:1)
51 Remit
54 _____ nest
58 Iridescent stone
60 Glimpse
61 "Johanan, and Dalaiah, and _____" (1 Chronicles 3:24)
62 Mud
63 Fabled creature
64 Actor Jack, and others
65 "That _____ after the dust of the earth" (Amos 2:7)
66 "And unto Enoch was born _____" (Genesis 4:18)
67 Clean

DOWN

1 "And whatsoever goeth upon his _____" (Leviticus 11:27)
2 "Whom thou slewest in the valley of _____" (1 Samuel 21:9)
3 Ascend
4 "Fall into the mouth of the_____" (Nahum 3:12)
5 "Ebal, _____, and Onam" (Genesis 36:23)
6 Foist upon
7 _____ lily
8 Did well, as on an exam
9 Teachers' org.
10 Benefit
11 She slew Sisera
12 "There was one _____, a prophetess" (Luke 2:36)
13 Kind of IRA
21 Not many
22 "Pharez, Hezron, and _____" (1 Chronicles 4:1)
24 "And there _____ him a booth" (Jonah 4:5)
25 "As certain also of your own _____" (Acts 17:28)
26 Eber's father (Genesis 11:14)
27 Gad's son (Genesis 46:16)
29 "Delivered me out of the _____ of the lion" (1 Samuel 17:37)
30 _____ Frome, Wharton novel
31 Yonder
32 "For thou _____ cast me into the deep" (Jonah 2:3)
34 "For thus _____ the LORD of hosts" (Haggai 2:6)
37 Dried grain stalks
38 Ahaziah's father (1 Kings 22:49)

by Tonya Vilhauer

39 "Bethel on the west, and _____
   on the east" (Genesis 12:8)
44 "Ye have _____ treasure
   together" (James 5:3)
45 Cornerstone abbr.
46 "I have yet to speak on God's
   _____" (Job 36:2)
49 "Shilshah, and Ithran, and _____"
   (1 Chronicles 7:37)
50 Choir member
51 "_____ and Circumstance"
52 Capital of Western Samoa
53 "Merchants received the linen
   _____ at a price"
   (1 Kings 10:28)
54 Anxiety
55 "And it is a _____ thing"
   (Daniel 2:11)
56 Expires
57 Platter
59 Allow
60 Greek letter

## 36

THREE MONETARY LESSONS

*The three theme answers are possible titles for
the three lessons cited, all dealing with coins.*

ACROSS

1 "An _____ pleasing to the Lord" (Leviticus 1:9 NIV)
6 Transcript data (abbr.)
9 "Crying, _____, Father" (Galatians 4:6)
13 Largest Philippine island
14 "Eat not of it _____, nor sodden" (Exodus 12:9)
15 Chunk of earth
16 **LESSON 1:** When a sinner repents (Luke 15:8–10 NIV) (4 words)
19 Daily Planet reporter
20 "He _____ and worshipped him" (Mark 5:6)
21 "Men condemned to die in the _____" (1 Corinthians 4:9 NIV)
22 "How long will it be _____ they believe me" (Numbers 14:11)
23 Valley of _____ Hinnom (Joshua 18:16 NIV)
24 "Walking after their _____ lusts" (Jude 16)
25 Links gadget
26 Sure competitor?
27 _____ Mahal
30 Get soaked?
33 Obtain
34 Woody's son
35 **LESSON 2:** On the paying of taxes (Matthew 17:27 NIV) (5 words)
38 "From the lions' _____" (Song of Solomon 4:8)
39 "You may know the hope to which he _____ called you" (Ephesians 1:18 NIV)
40 Philistines' god (Judges 16:23)
41 112° 30' from N
42 "Their conscience seared with a _____ iron" (1 Timothy 4:2)

43 "_____ it is written" (Matthew 4:6)
44 "And the _____ of Carmel shall wither" (Amos 1:2)
45 Push hard
46 Mineral spring
49 "And _____ Aaron of his garments" (Numbers 20:26)
52 "A wise _____ maketh a glad father" (Proverbs 10:1)
53 _____ Street
54 **LESSON 3:** True sacrifice (Mark 12:41–44) (3 words)
57 "They _____ perverse and crooked generation" (Deuteronomy 32:5) (2 words)
58 "_____ no man any thing" (Romans 13:8)
59 Esso competitor
60 Signs of spring
61 "For our _____ is come" (Lamentations 4:18)
62 "She maketh fine _____" (Proverbs 31:24)

DOWN

1 "Cast alive into _____ of fire" (Revelation 19:20) (2 words)
2 "I will make thee _____ over many things" (Matthew 25:21)
3 Earth's natural UV blocking layer
4 "It is _____ holy unto the LORD" (Exodus 30:10)
5 "Go to the _____" (Proverbs 6:6)
6 "For in this we _____" (2 Corinthians 5:2)
7 "The _____ as of a woman in travail" (Jeremiah 22:23)
8 Rye bristle
9 Sign of fall
10 "And he made a vail of _____" (Exodus 36:35)
11 Former capital of West Germany

by David K. Shortess

12 "Then he shall _____ fifth part" (Leviticus 27:13) (2 words)
17 Manitoba tribe
18 Forest youngster
23 _____ there, done that
24 "And again he denied with an _____" (Matthew 26:72)
25 "Give us _____ day our daily bread" (Matthew 6:11)
26 All _____ are off
27 Math branch
28 "Sweeter _____ than honey" (Psalm 19:10)
29 Zebedee's son (Matthew 10:2)
30 Said (arch.)
31 Hits a hole-in-one
32 Musical sound
33 Pest
34 "So is good news from _____ country" (Proverbs 25:25) (2 words)
36 Where "pancake" is understood (abbr.)

37 Esau's land
42 Arizona tribe
43 "Who _____ the coals into flame" (Isaiah 54:16 NIV)
44 Natives of northern New Mexico
45 "Nevertheless the men _____ hard" (Jonah 1:13)
46 "And _____ the right hand of God" (Mark 16:19) (2 words)
47 _____ work (such as sewing)
48 "Happy Days" actor Williams
49 Pierce
50 "No _____ Street"
51 "A _____ shaken with the wind" (Matthew 11:7)
52 "That which was _____ in his heart" (Matthew 13:19)
53 "La Boheme" role
55 "A loving _____, a graceful deer" (Proverbs 5:19 NIV)
56 Last O.T. book

ACROSS

1 Formerly Persia
5 "Woe to _____ that is filthy and polluted" (Zephaniah 3:1)
8 Axis
12 Spire
13 Where Sargon took some captive Israelites (2 Kings 17:6)
15 "Hold the _____" (deli order)
16 Coin
17 City in Naphtali (Joshua 19:33)
18 David's grandfather
19 City between Zoreah and Zanoah (Joshua 15:33–34)
21 "Grafted contrary to _____ into a good olive tree" (Romans 11:24)
23 Quaint
24 Presidential initials
25 Court's partner
28 Actress Sandra
29 Dell models, e.g.
32 Taut
33 "Ye shall speak into the _____" (1 Corinthians 14:9)
34 Apartment, in England
35 "As a bowing wall. . .as a _____ fence" (Psalm 62:3)
37 Geometric surface
38 Addition column
39 Wail
40 Depends, with "on"
41 By
42 Greek letter
43 Slang
44 Pronoun (Fr.)
45 Slob
46 Realm
49 Having feet (pl.)
53 Twelve months
54 "That's all, _____"
56 Newspaper sect.
58 Rim
59 Perspire
60 Broccoli _____
61 "With your _____ after you" (Genesis 9:9)
62 Old Testament book (abbr.)
63 Wall Street abbr.

DOWN

1 Govt. regulatory agency
2 "Deliver thyself as a _____ from the hand of the hunter" (Proverbs 6:5)
3 New Testament prophetess
4 NJ pro team
5 Bedad's son (Genesis 36:35)
6 Shimei's father (1 Kings 4:18)
7 "A _____ caught in a thicket by his horns" (Genesis 22:13)
8 Struck, biblically
9 Fragrance by Dana
10 One who stares
11 Type
13 What Paul touched to heal the sick (Acts 19:12)
14 Block
20 Mount, to some
22 Summer drink
25 Rock
26 Also known as Cephas
27 Hill builders
28 Burrow
29 City near Dallas
30 Biblical verb
31 Jeanne d'Arc (abbr.)
33 At all
34 Tire
35 Lid
36 Ezbon's brother (1 Chronicles 7:7)
37 "They came to _____ in Pamphylia" (Acts 13:13)
40 "Thou takest up that thou _____ not down" (Luke 19:21, var.)
42 _____ favor (Sp.)
44 Stuck
45 Remaliah's son (2 Kings 15:25)
46 "Your _____ shall be opened" (Genesis 3:5)
47 Darius the _____ (Daniel 11:1)
48 Leaf
49 _____ bargain
50 Unable to decide
51 Popular Internet site
52 Brothers and sisters, for short
55 Have
57 Summer shirt

by Sarah Lagerquist Simmons

JESUS AND THE SEA

Note that of the long theme answers, only 17 Across is a direct quote from scripture. The other two, 41 and 65 Across, are not.

ACROSS

1 Georgetown jocks
6 One of two countries that claims Everest
11 "Which of you shall have. . .an ox fallen into a _____" (Luke 14:5)
14 Not hidden
15 "And if a man shall _____ pit. . . and not cover it" (Exodus 21:33) (2 words)
16 Jazz, for one
17 "And in the fourth watch of the night Jesus went unto them, _____" (Matthew 14:25) (4 words)
20 "It shall be _____ with him" (Isaiah 3:11)
21 "Praise the _____" (Psalm 115:18)
22 "He _____ his meat and eats his fill" (Isaiah 44:16 NIV)
23 David, to many
24 Forks in the road
25 Leaf attachment point
28 "_____ art thou" (Genesis 27:32)
30 "Neither could any man _____ him" (Mark 5:4)
34 Hemoglobin deficiency
37 "And his word is not _____" (1 John 1:10) (2 words)
40 Shea spectator
41 What happened when a great storm arose on the sea (Mark 4:39) (4 words)
44 NATO member (abbr.)
45 Edible plant of the genus Brassica
46 "But if thou _____ go down, go thou with. . .thy servant" (Judges 7:10) (2 words)
47 CIA operative
49 "Get up! Pick up your _____ and walk" (John 5:8 NIV)
51 "_____ John" (missive type)
52 "Barnabas they called _____" (Acts 14:12 NIV)

55 French 101 verb
58 "A young _____ and told Moses" (Numbers 11:27 NIV) (2 words)
61 _____ vera
62 "They that _____ in tears shall reap in joy" (Psalm 126:5)
65 What Peter, James, and John found in their nets (Luke 5:4–7) (5 words)
68 Vote cast
69 "In the first month, that is, the month _____" (Esther 3:7)
70 Clear the board
71 Poem of praise
72 Alamogordo's county
73 "Art thou a _____" (Acts 22:27)

DOWN

1 "Consider _____ love thy precepts" (Psalm 119:159) (2 words)
2 Track shape
3 Give a holler
4 "Take up the _____ of the covenant" (Joshua 3:6)
5 Steps on a fence
6 "He causeth the grass _____ for the cattle" (Psalm 104:14) (2 words)
7 Trendy digital accessory
8 _____-oni, Rachel's son
9 "She crieth. . .at the _____ of the city" (Proverbs 8:3)
10 California/Nevada border lake
11 "And it came to _____" (Genesis 6:1)
12 "Through thy precepts _____ understanding" (Psalm 119:104) (2 words)
13 Herbal and green
18 Than
19 _____ of Eden, Steinbeck opus
23 Blood (prefix)
24 Habit

by David K. Shortess

25 Follower of Micah

26 "As the Lord hath called every _____ let him walk" (1 Corinthians 7:17) (2 words)

27 Transferable picture

29 "And shall _____ multitude of sins" (James 5:20) (2 words)

31 "And the tongue is _____, a world of iniquity" (James 3:6) (2 words)

32 Devilfish

33 "There is a woman that hath a familiar spirit at _____" (1 Samuel 28:7)

35 Type

36 "Seeing I _____ stranger" (Ruth 2:10) (2 words)

38 Most TV channels (abbr.)

39 Understand

42 "Under oaks and poplars and _____" (Hosea 4:13)

43 Trudge through

48 Old Testament scribe

50 "They should _____ man of him" (Mark 8:30) (2 words)

53 "Ye shall _____ manner of fat" (Leviticus 7:23) (2 words)

54 Not qualified

56 "It was _____ painful for me" (Psalm 73:16)

57 Direct toward

58 Minnesota clinic

59 "Ish-bosheth, who lay on _____ at noon" (2 Samuel 4:5) (2 words)

60 "These are a smoke in my _____" (Isaiah 65:5)

61 Like a wing

62 Burma neighbor, once

63 Greek mountain

64 "_____ I was a child" (1 Corinthians 13:11)

66 "_____ not vain repetitions" (Matthew 6:7)

67 "From going to and _____ in the earth" (Job 1:7)

ACROSS

1 Mountain range considered boundary between Europe and Asia
5 Riches' predecessors
9 Jeroboam's father (2 Kings 15:18)
14 Expensive perfume, such as Mary used
15 Chelub's son (1 Chronicles 27:26)
16 "Adam, Sheth, _____" (1 Chronicles 1:1)
17 Everglades critter, for short
18 Resemble
19 "To the battle at _____" (Numbers 21:33)
20 Was first
21 "Children of base men: they were _____ than the earth" (Job 30:8)
22 We should be not just hearers but _____ of the Word
23 "Of Eri, the family of the _____" (Numbers 26:16)
25 "And Simeon that was called _____" (Acts 13:1)
26 Hill builders
28 Bani's son (Ezra 10:34)
31 "_____ the Carmelite" (1 Chronicles 11:37)
34 Linger
37 "Even the city of _____ the father of Anak" (Joshua 15:13)
38 Ahithophel's son (2 Samuel 23:34)
39 "And over the fowl of the _____" (Genesis 1:26)
40 Sharar's son (2 Samuel 23:33)
41 Saw, for one
42 "_____ and Caiaphas being the high priests" (Luke 3:2)
44 Maui is one
45 "_____ builders did hew them" (1 Kings 5:18)
47 Hoover, for example
49 Hirsute
52 Cleansed
57 "Child shall play on the hole of the _____" (Isaiah 11:8)
60 "And Serug lived thirty years, and begat _____" (Genesis 11:22)
62 Complete

63 Ezra's son (1 Chronicles 4:17)
65 "Maaz, and Jamin, and _____" (1 Chronicles 2:27)
67 "As he saith also in _____" (Romans 9:25)
68 Single
69 Cush's son (Genesis 10:7)
70 Construe
71 More sunburned
72 "And _____ gave names to all cattle" (Genesis 2:20)
73 Finishes

DOWN

1 Sam, for one
2 More precious
3 "Shuni, and Ezbon, Eri, and _____" (Genesis 46:16)
4 Third world countries, mostly (abbr.)
5 Withstand
6 "Eleasah his son, _____ his son" (1 Chronicles 8:37)
7 Jade, for example
8 Hosah's son (1 Chronicles 26:10)
9 "And _____ not that any should testify of man" (John 2:25)
10 Witch of _____
11 Drill
12 "Phanuel, of the tribe of _____" (Luke 2:36)
13 "_____ is the day which the LORD hath made" (Psalm 118:24)
21 Ire
24 "And Rekem, and Irpeel, and _____" (Joshua 18:27)
27 "And the _____, and the pelican, and the gier eagle" (Leviticus 11:18)
28 Author Leon
29 "The curse upon Mount _____" (Deuteronomy 11:29)
30 Whom Jesus healed, with "the"
31 "And Ephron dwelt among the children of _____" (Genesis 23:10)
32 "_____, lama sabachthani?" (Mark 15:34)

by Tonya Vilhauer

33 "Which is Hebron, and _____"
   (Joshua 15:54)
35 "On the east side of _____"
   (Numbers 34:11)
36 "And unto Enoch was born
   _____" (Genesis 4:18)
37 Aram's brother (1 Chronicles 7:34)
42 Continent
43 Adage
46 Mien
48 Gullet
50 Zorobabel's son (Luke 3:27)
51 "Be ye not unequally _____
   together" (2 Corinthians 6:14)
53 Lake _____ Drive, in Chicago
54 "Their _____, and their hats"
   (Daniel 3:21)
55 "Shuthelah his son, and Ezer, and
   _____" (1 Chronicles 7:21)
56 Actions
57 Partly open
58 Parlor (Sp.)

59 Till
61 Singer McEntire
64 "Thou believest that there is
   _____ God" (James 2:19)
66 "And a _____ of three years old"
   (Genesis 15:9)

ACROSS

1 King of Judah for 41 years
4 Split rattan
8 "The king of Israel is come out to seek a _____" (1 Samuel 26:20)
12 New Testament book (abbr.)
13 Kind of code
14 Base
15 Be a gymnast
17 "A time to cast away _____, and a time to gather" (Ecclesiastes 3:5)
19 Cuddle, in earlier days
20 Judge of Israel
21 Overweight
24 Gad's son (Genesis 46:16)
27 Pest
29 Close
31 _____ Sea
32 I _____ (name of God)
33 "We were driven up and down in _____" (Acts 27:27)
34 D.C. quadrant
35 "I will _____ you out of their bondage" (Exodus 6:6)
37 Abbey, for one
38 "Many of them. . .used curious _____" (Acts 19:19)
40 Tempest
42 "They make _____ to shed innocent blood" (Isaiah 59:7)
44 "Samuel said unto the _____, Bring the portion" (1 Samuel 9:23)
46 Situate
49 "I will _____ again unto you" (Acts 18:21)
51 More intense
52 "The words of _____, who was among the herdmen of Tekoa" (Amos 1:1)
53 Tie
55 Samuel's mentor
56 "Drink the _____ blood of the grape" (Deuteronomy 32:14)
57 "There is no _____ to them that fear him" (Psalm 34:9)
58 80 or 66 (abbr.)

DOWN

1 "Praise him for his mighty _____" (Psalm 150:2)
2 Pea _____
3 Just about
4 "Is not _____ as Carchemish" (Isaiah 10:9)
5 Is
6 Iowa's neighbor (abbr.)
7 "Take thine _____, eat, drink, and be merry" (Luke 12:19)
8 Whole wheat, for one
9 "As with the _____, so with the borrower" (Isaiah 24:2)
10 "Set seven _____ lambs of the flock by themselves" (Genesis 21:28)
11 Much of magazines
16 "They were baptized, _____ men and women" (Acts 8:12)
18 Abraham's father (Luke 3:34)
22 Disentangle
23 "_____ lived seventy years and begat Abram" (Genesis 11:26)
25 In case
26 March time
27 _____ Hill, in Athens
28 Leave out
30 Verdi opera
33 "Put on the full _____ of God" (Ephesians 6:11 NIV)
36 Luke, for one
38 Tamarisk tree
39 Grim one?
41 "An old lion; who shall _____ him up" (Genesis 49:9)
43 "She. . .had _____ all that she had" (Mark 5:26)
45 "They _____ that he had spoken the parable against them" (Mark 12:12)
47 Ancient European
48 Great Lake
49 Strike
50 Flightless bird
51 Lair
54 Kind of hospital (abbr.)

by Evelyn M. Boyington

ACROSS

1 Grandmother of Jesse
5 Jether's son (1 Chronicles 7:38)
8 Mordecai's nemesis
13 Region
14 "_____, TEKEL, UPHARSIN"
(Daniel 5:25)
16 God's love for man (Gr.)
17 "Who will make me a _____"
(Job 24:25)
18 Ellipsoidal
19 Yarns
20 Relaxes, with "up"
22 "_____ lived ninety years"
(Genesis 5:9)
24 Ease
25 Descendants of a Manassite clan
of Gilead (Numbers 26:32)
28 "He may _____ mercy upon you"
(Jeremiah 42:12)
29 Odious
34 "_____ did that which was right
in the eyes of the LORD"
(1 Kings 15:11)
37 Enan's son (Numbers 1:15)
38 Issue
41 "Hast thou entered into the
_____ of the sea?" (Job 38:16)
43 Squeak
44 As well
45 "I do _____ my bow in the cloud"
(Genesis 9:13)
46 Asp
49 "They did _____ it with an omer"
(Exodus 16:18)
51 "As a bride _____ herself with
her jewels" (Isaiah 61:10)
53 Guitarist's aid, briefly
56 Grant's _____, in NYC
59 Craft
60 Senior
62 John's time on Patmos, for example
64 "Observe the month of _____"
(Deuteronomy 16:1)
66 Lazy
67 Prince of Persia and Media under
Ahasuerus (Esther 1:14)
68 Alike
69 Rivals
70 All
71 "The soldiers _____ him away"
(Mark 15:16)
72 Chemical suffixes

DOWN

1 Abnormal breathing sound
2 Bathsheba's husband
3 Antagonize
4 Beth-gader's father
(1 Chronicles 2:51)
5 Master (Sp.)
6 Worship
7 Elioenai's son (1 Chronicles 3:24)
8 Derby, for one
9 Sarai's handmaid (Galatians 4:24)
10 Gender
11 Mimics
12 "As an eagle stirreth up her
_____" (Deuteronomy 32:11)
15 Uzziah rebuilt this city
(2 Chronicles 26:1–2)
21 _____ Na Na, "oldies" group
23 "Joseph gathered corn as the sand
of the _____" (Genesis 41:49)
26 "The fire shall _____ be burning"
(Leviticus 6:13)
27 What the Magi followed
30 Naaman's brother (Genesis 46:21)
31 "Whatsoever hath _____ and
scales in the waters" (Leviticus
11:9)
32 "The Pharisees began to _____
him vehemently" (Luke 11:53)
33 "That which shall befall you in the
_____ days" (Genesis 49:1)
34 Belonging to NCAA's eastern
conference (abbr.)
35 Holding a grudge
36 Mamre's brother (Genesis 14:13)
39 Competent
40 Got by
41 Once
42 Bard
47 "City of the priests"
(1 Samuel 22:19)
48 "Came unto them to _____ in
five days" (Acts 20:6)
50 "I am _____ door" (John 10:9)

by Sarah Lagerquist Simmons

52 Abigail's husband (1 Samuel 25:3)
53 Make room for? (2 words)
54 Noisy scene
55 Beg
56 "The inhabitants of the land of
_____ brought water to him"
(Isaiah 21:14)
57 Farm team?
58 "The _____ places thereof and
the marishes" (Ezekiel 47:11)
61 "Breathed into his nostrils the
breath of _____" (Genesis 2:7)
63 Dec. in NYC
65 Put to _____

## 42

CELEBRATION!

"The kingdom of heaven is like a king who prepared a wedding banquet for his son."
MATTHEW 22:2 NIV

ACROSS

1 "Do not stand up for _____ cause" (Ecclesiastes 8:3 NIV) (2 words)
5 Official records
9 Memorable shrine
14 "With what measure ye _____, it shall be measured to you" (Mark 4:24)
15 "A threefold _____ is not quickly broken" (Ecclesiastes 4:12)
16 "And it came to pass in the month _____" (Nehemiah 2:1)
17 "That in the _____ to come" (Ephesians 2:7)
18 Altitude (abbr.)
19 Slip by
20 Start of **QUOTE** (Song of Solomon 2:4 NIV) (4 words)
23 "_____ by Starlight," pop hit of the 40s
24 Olds model
25 IRA kin
28 **QUOTE**, part 2 (3 words)
32 Wee sizes (abbr.)
35 "And they will _____ out of his kingdom" (Matthew 13:41 NIV)
36 Leah's first son (Genesis 29:32)
37 **QUOTE**, part 3 (1 word)
39 To _____
41 "Drunk my wine with my milk: _____ friends" (Song of Solomon 5:1) (2 words)
42 "The priest is to offer _____ sin offering" (Numbers 6:11 NIV) (3 words)
45 Shem's father (Genesis 6:10)
48 Tennis shot
49 **QUOTE**, part 4 (3 words)
52 _____ Cruces, NM
53 Soap staple, once

54 "What _____ is that to you" (Luke 6:32 NIV)
58 End of **QUOTE** (4 words)
61 Over's partner
64 County or party
65 "Be as I am; for I _____ ye are" (Galatians 4:12) (2 words)
66 "From the _____ of thy wood" (Deuteronomy 29:11)
67 "And it had great _____ teeth" (Daniel 7:7)
68 "And pitched his _____ there" (Genesis 26:25)
69 "In darkness have _____ great light" (Isaiah 9:2) (2 words)
70 Aerie
71 "For my yoke is _____" (Matthew 11:30)

DOWN

1 Asian nannies
2 "When thou shalt _____ children" (Deuteronomy 4:25)
3 "While they _____ stood near them under a tree" (Genesis 18:8 NIV) (2 words)
4 Use reverse osmosis
5 Old movie film material
6 Soda pop flavor
7 "Star _____"
8 Verb modifier
9 Windflower
10 "Man shall not _____ by bread alone" (Matthew 4:4)
11 Abijam's successor (1 Kings 15:8)
12 "I am not _____, most noble Festus" (Acts 26:25)
13 "Was not arrayed like _____ of these" (Matthew 6:29)
21 "The Lord is _____ to anger" (Nahum 1:3)

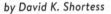

by David K. Shortess

22 "Let us draw _____ with a true heart" (Hebrews 10:22)
25 Japheth's son (Genesis 10:2)
26 "David, _____ thine own house" (2 Chronicles 10:16) (2 words)
27 "As yet shall he remain _____ that day" (Isaiah 10:32) (2 words)
29 "_____ thee two tables of stone" (Exodus 34:1)
30 Minneapolis suburb
31 What, in Juarez
32 Sandbar
33 "Our fathers did eat _____ in the desert" (John 6:31)
34 Iditarod vehicles
38 _____-dee-dah
40 Large amount
43 "And I'll give you ten shekels of _____ year" (Judges 17:10 NIV) (2 words)

44 "Carried away unto these dumb idols, even _____ were led" (1 Corinthians 12:2) (2 words)
46 _____ of days
47 Not his
50 "Alexander's Ragtime Band" composer
51 Integrate
55 "She replied, _____ special favor" (Judges 1:15 NIV) (3 words)
56 "The Great" and "The Terrible"
57 Irritable
58 "They are all hot as an _____" (Hosea 7:7)
59 "I sink in deep _____" (Psalm 69:2)
60 Adam's grandson (Luke 3:38)
61 Relatives of oohs
62 Bonnet occupant?
63 "_____ no man any thing, but to love one another" (Romans 13:8)

43

ACROSS

1 "Whatsoever creepeth upon the earth, after their _____" (Genesis 8:19)
6 Throng
10 Daddy (Aramaic)
14 Sarah's son
15 Not ending
16 Seethe
17 Abishag the _____, a young virgin (1 Kings 1:3)
19 Suggestion
20 "And put _____ into the garden of Eden" (Genesis 2:15)
21 Understand
22 "Like a serpent; _____ poison is under their lips" (Psalm 140:3)
24 Line formed at the joint of two pieces of material
25 "They which are in _____ be turned away from me" (2 Timothy 1:15)
26 Grant Wood, for example
29 "The _____ of a wound cleanseth away evil" (Proverbs 20:30)
33 Brief
34 Squash, for one
35 White or bald-faced
36 "And straightway they forsook their _____" (Mark 1:18)
37 "But I _____ you. . .to go and bear fruit" (John 15:16 NIV)
38 Wheel
39 "And there was war between _____ and Baasha" (1 Kings 15:16)
40 Man of the _____
41 "Were with him from _____ of Judah" (2 Samuel 6:2)
42 Shallum's father (Nehemiah 3:12)
44 "Take of them of the captivity, even of _____" (Zechariah 6:10)
45 Turf
46 "And _____ it with the king's ring" (Esther 8:8)
47 Neoteric
50 "They _____ to and fro" (Psalm 107:27)
51 "Moses went. . .and _____ him up into the mount" (Exodus 24:18)
54 Judah's son (Genesis 38:4)
55 "The robber _____ up their substance" (Job 5:5)
58 Farm measure
59 "Trode them down with _____ over against Gibeah" (Judges 20:43)
60 Magi, for example
61 Bow
62 Colored, as Easter eggs
63 "Thou shalt rise up before the _____ head" (Leviticus 19:32)

DOWN

1 Saul's father (1 Samuel 9:3)
2 Zoheth's father (1 Chronicles 4:20)
3 "Son of Amos, which was the son of _____" (Luke 3:25)
4 Jacob's son
5 "Then thou _____ me with dreams" (Job 7:14)
6 Lotan's son (Genesis 36:22)
7 Roman poet
8 Group
9 "For where your _____ is, there" (Matthew 6:21)
10 Gideoni's son (Numbers 10:24)
11 Augur
12 Coffin
13 "They shall say in all the highways, _____" (Amos 5:16)
18 "And did all eat the same spiritual _____" (1 Corinthians 10:3)
23 Withered away
24 "Saying, _____, ye are brethren" (Acts 7:26)
25 "Departed from Dophkah, and encamped in _____" (Numbers 33:13)
26 "The children of _____" (Ezra 2:50)
27 Zorobabel's son (Luke 3:27)
28 Aggregate
29 "Made him a _____, and sat under it" (Jonah 4:5)

by Tonya Vilhauer

30 "Shuthelah his son, and Ezer, and _____" (1 Chronicles 7:21)
31 "House of Millo, which goeth down to _____" (2 Kings 12:20)
32 "Mattathias, which was the son of _____" (Luke 3:26)
34 "They were all filled with the Holy _____" (Acts 2:4)
37 "He that is to be _____ shall wash" (Leviticus 14:8)
38 Corridor
40 Former spouse of Sonny
41 "Ziph, and Telem, and _____" (Joshua 15:24)
43 Unlocked
44 Canine command
46 Nadab's son who died without children (1 Chronicles 2:30)
47 Orpah's land
48 Formerly
49 Mend
50 Destroy (Brit.)

51 Shimei's father (1 Kings 2:8)
52 "The children of _____ of Hezekiah" (Ezra 2:16)
53 "Thy rod and thy staff _____ comfort me" (Psalm 23:4)
56 "Turn again, my daughters, go your _____" (Ruth 1:12)
57 "That he _____ loveth God love his brother" (1 John 4:21)

ACROSS

1 Stool or stone
5 New grass
8 Chest, maybe
12 Stew
13 First woman
14 Retired, in a way
15 God
16 Stomach
17 Affection
18 Ms. Horne, and others
20 Torn apart
21 "God trieth the hearts and _____" (Psalm 7:9)
23 Japheth's son (Genesis 10:2)
24 City of Asher (Judges 1:31)
26 "He that _____ a matter separateth very friends" (Proverbs 17:9)
30 Buddhist sect
31 "I am _____ door" (John 10:9)
32 O.T. book (abbr.)
34 Actor Lugosi
35 Owns
36 Smooth
38 Build
39 Fee
40 Hot _____
41 Bela's son (1 Chronicles 7:7)
43 "_____, lama sabachthani?" (Mark 15:34)
44 Being
45 _____ sequitur
46 Meek
47 Pronoun, to King James
48 Relative
49 Zerubbabel's son (1 Chronicles 3:20)

9 Over's partner
10 Temperature
11 Utopia
19 Nip
20 Toga
22 "Destroy all the children of _____" (Numbers 24:17)
23 "And the ___ of hell shall not prevail" (Matthew 16:18)
25 "And Isaac came from the way of the well _____" (Genesis 24:62)
26 Set free
27 One who is subject to law
28 "Make _____ a crown of gold" (Exodus 25:24)
29 Joktan's son (Genesis 10:29)
30 Haman's spouse (Esther 5:10)
33 Grow
34 Consumed with troubles
37 Town on the boundary between Zebulun and Asher (Joshua 19:27)
41 "I wrote them with _____ in the book" (Jeremiah 36:18)
42 Where there was no room?

DOWN

1 Go 9 to 5
2 More mature, maybe
3 Solo
4 _____ Lama
5 Noah's son (Luke 3:36)
6 Egg-shaped
7 Mist
8 City near Aenon where John the Baptist baptized (John 3:23)

by Sarah Lagerquist Simmons

## 45

ACROSS

1 "But Noah found _____ in the eyes of the Lord" (Genesis 6:8)
5 Advanced degree (abbr.)
7 IOU, in other words
11 Fabled dwarflike creature
12 "Have I _____ of mad men" (1 Samuel 21:15)
13 Some votes
15 Hawaiian island
16 "And it is a _____ thing that the king requireth" (Daniel 2:11)
17 "For thee have I seen righteous before _____ in this generation" (Genesis 7:1)
18 O.T. time
19 Marching cadence (abbr.)
20 "And there shall come forth a rod out of the _____ of Jesse" (Isaiah 11:1)
21 Thanks (Brit.)
22 Andy Capp's wife
23 "_____, Joy of Man's Desiring"
26 "I will not be afraid what man can _____ unto me" (Psalm 56:11)
28 Proofreader's mark
30 Highway sign of years past
32 "Containing the gold _____ of manna" (Hebrews 9:4 MSG)
34 "Wake up, harp! wake up, _____" (Psalm 57:8 MSG)
35 Egg
37 Spineless one (colloq.)
39 "And Abraham was old, and well stricken in _____" (Genesis 24:1)
41 Ship's initials
42 Time long past
43 Salary _____ (pl.)
44 _____ Canals in U.S. and Canada
46 Volunteer state (abbr.)
47 Blind, in falconry
48 Chesapeake, for one (abbr.)
50 "Yea, hath God said, _____ shall not eat of every tree of the garden" (Genesis 3:1)
51 "_____ teach us to number our days" (Psalm 90:12)
52 Affirmative
55 Ocean shelf made of coral

57 "And the _____ he prepared. . .to set there the ark" (1 Kings 6:19)
60 Pine _____
62 College degree (abbr.)
63 "And fell on their faces in _____ worship" (1 Kings 18:39 MSG)
66 College plant?
68 Article (Ger.)
69 "In all places where I _____ my name" (Exodus 20:24)
71 Baking chamber
73 "And it came to pass _____ the seventh day" (2 Samuel 12:18)
75 "By man shall his blood be _____" (Genesis 9:6)
76 Greek letter
77 Weekday (abbr.)
78 "And I shall be whiter than _____" (Psalm 51:7)
79 Eugene's home? (abbr.)
80 "And thou shalt make a _____ seat of pure gold" (Exodus 25:17)

DOWN

1 "The dust will become _____" (Exodus 8:16 NIV)
2 _____ Tae Woo, South Korean president
3 Entertains
4 Time from Christ's birth (abbr.)
5 *Mal de* _____
6 Holy _____
8 "Neither shall thine _____ pity him" (Deuteronomy 13:8)
9 "He will not suffer thy foot to _____ moved" (Psalm 121:3)
10 What Moses brought down from Mount Sinai (pl.)
11 "For _____ so loved the world" (John 3:16)
12 "I will never blot out his _____" (Revelation 3:5 NIV)
14 Teatime treats
16 "For God had made them _____ with great joy" (Nehemiah 12:43)
17 "So that thou shalt be _____ for the sight of thine eyes" (Deuteronomy 28:34)

by Marijane G. Troyer

24 "But my God shall _____ all your need" (Philippians 4:19)
25 Abraham's homeland
27 Spread
29 "And rejoiced with great _____" (1 Kings 1:40)
30 "_____ your bread there" (Amos 7:12 NIV)
31 D.C. quadrant
33 Continent (abbr.)
36 Adult U.S. citizen, maybe
38 Actress West
40 Where Brownies bake? (abbr.)
45 Midianite priest killed by Gideon (Judges 7:25)
47 Energy or system
49 Library sect.
50 Alpine sound
51 Where Clemson U. is (abbr.)
53 French conjunction
54 Mentioned

56 "But the just shall live by his _____" (Habakkuk 2:4)
58 David's son, who coveted his half sister
59 "From following the _____ great with young" (Psalm 78:71)
61 Home on wheels (abbr.)
64 "Their calls will _____ through the windows" (Zephaniah 2:14 NIV)
65 "For the LORD. . .plentifully rewardeth the proud _____" (Psalm 31:23)
67 "Then _____ eyes shall be opened" (Genesis 3:5)
70 Byway (abbr.)
72 Prodigal son's nadir, in a word
74 _____ show
76 Augusta is its capital (abbr.)

## 46

WHOM WILL YOU SERVE?

Serve the LORD with gladness:
come before his presence with singing.

PSALM 100:2

ACROSS

1 Start of **QUOTE** (Joshua 24:15 NIV)
4 Takes a dip
9 Took on
14 Cabinet wood
15 "Their strength is _____ still" (Isaiah 30:7) (2 words)
16 Range maker
17 "We sailed to the _____ of Crete" (Acts 27:7 NIV)
18 "Like men condemned to die in the _____" (1 Corinthians 4:9 NIV)
19 Country singer Travis
20 **QUOTE**, part 2 (5 words)
23 *Kiss Me, _____*
24 Glide on water or snow
25 Inhabitant of northern Iraq
29 Rave's other half
33 "Let the young _____ arise" (2 Samuel 2:14) (2 words)
35 "_____ is this King of glory" (Psalm 24:8)
38 Call her Mara (Ruth 1:20)
41 "Most _____ Felix" (Acts 24:3)
42 **QUOTE**, part 3 (3 words)
45 "How long shall _____ with you" (Mark 9:19 NIV) (2 words)
46 "So, as much as in me _____ ready to preach" (Romans 1:15) (3 words)
47 Latin case (abbr.)
48 "Beware of the _____ of the Pharisees" (Mark 8:15)
50 Prohibitionists
52 "Woe to them that are at _____ in Zion" (Amos 6:1)
53 Row
56 ¿*Cómo _____ usted?*
60 End of **QUOTE** (3 words)
65 "For who _____ save the LORD" (Psalm 18:31) (2 words)

68 "Such _____ in darkness and in the shadow of death" (Psalm 107:10) (2 words)
69 Pooh's pal
70 "And it shall be to the LORD for _____" (Isaiah 55:13) (2 words)
71 "Out of _____ the issues of life" (Proverbs 4:23) (2 words)
72 What Malchus lost, for a time
73 "_____ are trapped by evil times" (Ecclesiastes 9:12 NIV) (2 words)
74 Nostrils
75 ID number (abbr.)

DOWN

1 Moabite king (Numbers 22:4)
2 "Whoever touches thorns _____ tool of iron" (2 Samuel 23:7 NIV) (2 words)
3 Felony
4 "And I will give him the morning _____" (Revelation 2:28)
5 "And the _____ shall eat them like wool" (Isaiah 51:8)
6 "Lo, _____ four men loose" (Daniel 3:25) (2 words)
7 Biblical currency (pl.)
8 Offended, in a way (var.)
9 "Do thyself no _____: for we are all here" (Acts 16:28)
10 "That _____ how frail I am" (Psalm 39:4) (3 words)
11 Bled, like fabric
12 "World without _____. Amen" (Ephesians 3:21)
13 "Give us this _____ our daily bread" (Matthew 6:11)
21 "_____ the land of the free"
22 "Mine eye also is _____ by reason" (Job 17:7)
26 Not asked for
27 "_____ great stone unto me this day" (1 Samuel 14:33) (2 words)

by Marijane G. Troyer

28 "And Isaac _____ in Gerar" (Genesis 26:6)
30 "Moment, in the twinkling of ____" (1 Corinthians 15:52) (2 words)
31 Minor prophet (abbr.)
32 "This _____ say, is meaningless" (Ecclesiastes 8:14 NIV) (2 words)
34 Nemesis
35 "In that, _____ we were yet sinners" (Romans 5:8)
36 Beeri's son (Hosea 1:1)
37 "Hast thou not poured me _____ milk" (Job 10:10) (2 words)
39 D.C. United is one of its teams (abbr.)
40 "She gave me of the tree, and _____ eat" (Genesis 3:12) (2 words)
43 "I may provoke to emulation. . . and might_____ of them" (Romans 11:14) (2 words)
44 "Neither shall they learn _____ any more" (Micah 4:3)

49 Conjunction
51 Salt, in Bordeaux
54 "Why do. . .the people imagine _____ thing" (Psalm 2:1) (2 words)
55 "Come. . .into a desert place, and _____ while" (Mark 6:31) (2 words)
57 One of Job's afflictions (pl.)
58 "And they passing by Mysia came down to _____" (Acts 16:8)
59 "That women _____ themselves in modest apparel" (1 Timothy 2:9)
61 Perfect place
62 Romanov despot
63 Employ
64 Summers on the Seine
65 Belonging to Midwest state (abbr.)
66 _____-cone
67 Herd of whales

## 47

ACROSS

1 "The _____ looks of man shall be humbled" (Isaiah 2:11)
5 Flock tenders (Luke 2:8)
13 Expert
14 "They look and _____ upon me" (Psalm 22:17)
15 "He cuts me off from the _____" (Isaiah 38:12 NKJV)
16 Crabapple
18 Ahira's father (Numbers 1:15)
19 The valley of _____ (Psalm 84:6)
20 Rules etched in stone (Exodus 34:1) (2 words)
23 "My _____ is no longer central" (Galatians 2:20 MSG)
24 Sluggard's suggested role model (Proverbs 6:6)
25 "_____! Susanna" (song)
26 Maternal bird (Luke 13:34)
28 "They came to meet us. . .on the _____ Way" (Acts 28:15 NLT)
31 "He hath given occasions of speech against _____" (Deuteronomy 22:17)
32 Samarian prophet (2 Chronicles 28:9)
34 Subway's opposite (abbr.)
35 Follows Old Testament (abbr.)
37 Hiel's youngest son (1 Kings 16:34)
38 "And ye shall _____ in plenty" (Joel 2:26)
40 "It will be built again, with _____ and moat" (Daniel 9:25 NASB)
43 Isaac's well (Genesis 26:20)
44 Head (obsolete)
45 Son in Aramaic (Matthew 16:17)
46 Where Abraham lived (Genesis 22:19) (2 words)
49 Comedian Caesar
50 Trifle
51 Maacah to Absalom (2 Samuel 3:3)
53 Causes sibling tears (Matthew 7:5)
55 Divorced his foreign wife (Ezra 10:24)
57 "Will cause the sun to go down at _____" (Amos 8:9)
59 "Nor is his _____ satisfied with riches" (Ecclesiastes 4:8 NKJV)
60 "And Arad, and _____" (1 Chronicles 8:15)
61 Where Samson lived (Judges 15:8)
63 What the stone will do (Habakkuk 2:19)
65 Serious (Titus 2:6)
67 Flying saucer's opposite (abbr.)
68 Og's chief city (Deuteronomy 1:4)
69 "For these _____ I weep" (Lamentations 1:16)

DOWN

1 Israel's sheep (Matthew 15:24)
2 "The faith which _____" (Galatians 1:23) (3 words)
3 Frond-producing plant
4 "I will cut off every _____ of Baal" (Zephaniah 1:4 NKJV)
5 "A rod out of the _____ of Jesse" (Isaiah 11:1)
6 Musical priest (Nehemiah 12:36)
7 Ephraim's grandson (Numbers 26:35–36)
8 Earring style (Song of Solomon 1:10 MSG)
9 Luz renamed (Genesis 35:6–7)
10 Reddish-brown and spotted
11 "Gamaliel, a _____ of the law" (Acts 5:34)
12 What God will do to sacred stones (Exodus 34:13 NIV)
17 West Indian fish
21 "How long are you going to _____ over Saul?" (1 Samuel 16:1 MSG)
22 North Star state (abbr.)
26 Married a prostitute on God's command (Hosea 1:2)
27 Southern desert region (Genesis 13:1 AMP notes)
29 Enjoyments (Titus 3:3)
30 "Broke into an _____ of praise" (Luke 2:38 MSG)
33 Tribal leader (Genesis 36:15)
36 "She came to prove him with _____ questions" (1 Kings 10:1)
39 Tree (Isaiah 44:14)

by Mary Ann Sherman

40 Greek philosopher
41 "Though I be _____ the flesh" (Colossians 2:5) (2 words)
42 Where Joram smote the Edomites (2 Kings 8:21)
44 "He is a _____ man" (Habakkuk 2:5)
47 Country code for Cervantes' land
48 "Linen _____ upon their heads" (Ezekiel 44:18) (sing.)
52 Used to cultivate the hills (Isaiah 7:25 NIV)
53 "With what measure ye _____" (Mark 4:24)
54 "Lest he _____ my soul like a lion" (Psalm 7:2)
56 "And the _____ did swim" (2 Kings 6:6)
58 "Then answered _____. . .but I was an herdman, and a gatherer of sycomore fruit" (Amos 7:14)
60 A Gadite (1 Chronicles 5:15)

62 Southwest Asian country (abbr.)
64 Contemporary version of AD (abbr.)
66 Blood type that can be positive or negative

48

ACROSS

1 "Goeth out to Remmon-methoar to _____" (Joshua 19:13)
5 Minor prophet
10 "For this _____ is mount Sinai" (Galatians 4:25)
14 "And the sons of _____" (1 Chronicles 7:39)
15 Range maker
16 Contemptible
17 Uproar
18 "Magpiash, Meshullam, _____" (Nehemiah 10:20)
19 Belonging to Hophni's father
20 Devil
22 Slangy denial
23 Confirm
24 "Came unto the valley of _____" (Deuteronomy 1:24)
26 "Of the sons of _____, Jonathan" (2 Samuel 23:32)
27 Captain _____, Peter Pan's nemesis
29 Reveal
30 Abram's nephew
33 Noxious
35 Brazil, for one
38 Farm females
39 Slug
40 Shaphat's father (Numbers 13:5)
41 Benign cyst
42 "Leave off contention, before it be _____ with" (Proverbs 17:14)
44 Lade
45 "And straightway they forsook their _____" (Mark 1:18)
46 Spume
48 Jehoiada's father (Nehemiah 3:6)
52 "Seven times more than it was wont to be _____" (Daniel 3:19)
56 "Then sent I for Eliezer, for _____" (Ezra 8:16)
57 Haw's partner
59 Whittle
60 "A colt _____, whereon yet never man sat" (Luke 19:30)
61 "Hodiah the sister of _____" (1 Chronicles 4:19)

63 Range
64 "Unto the custody of _____" (Esther 2:3)
65 Fictional Miss Doolittle
66 Tabernacle, once
67 Cast off
68 "And _____ counsellors against them" (Ezra 4:5)
69 Biblical verb

DOWN

1 "Even as a _____ cherisheth her children" (1 Thessalonians 2:7)
2 "What the scripture saith of _____" (Romans 11:2)
3 "Was in Asher and in _____" (1 Kings 4:16)
4 "Again Esther spake unto _____" (Esther 4:10)
5 Nope
6 So be it
7 "Wall of Jerusalem, and _____" (1 Kings 9:15)
8 Apartment
9 Disfigure
10 "Securely as men _____ from war" (Micah 2:8)
11 "And Goshen, and Holon, and _____" (Joshua 15:51)
12 Animated
13 "And _____ between Nineveh and Calah" (Genesis 10:12)
21 "High _____"
23 Peel
25 "The LORD _____ the prisoners" (Psalm 146:7)
26 "And Meshobab, and _____" (1 Chronicles 4:34)
28 Types
29 "Smote Job with sore _____" (Job 2:7)
30 Actor Ayres
31 "_____ no man any thing" (Romans 13:8)
32 "Heaven be likened unto _____ virgins" (Matthew 25:1)
34 Blue
35 "Dwelt in the land of _____" (Genesis 4:16)

by Tonya Vilhauer

36 Bezaleel's father (Exodus 38:22)
37 Gratuity
42 Corn _____
43 Fees
45 "And _____ not that any should testify of man" (John 2:25)
47 "Elkanah, the son of _____" (1 Chronicles 6:35)
48 Trails
49 "King's house, with Argob and _____" (2 Kings 15:25)
50 "The days of the _____ are fulfilled" (Ezekiel 5:2)
51 "Chelub the brother of Shuah begat _____" (1 Chronicles 4:11)
53 "Melech, and _____, and Ahaz" (1 Chronicles 8:35)
54 "That one _____ happeneth to them all" (Ecclesiastes 2:14)
55 "He. . .became obedient unto _____" (Philippians 2:8)

57 Border town in Asher (Joshua 19:25)
58 Confusing layout
61 Old Testament book (abbr.)
62 Irate

## 49

ACROSS

2 A town of Benjamin, north of Jerusalem (Joshua 18:25)
7 "According to all the _____ of it" (Numbers 9:3)
13 "The morning _____" (Genesis 19:15)
14 Abraham's old name
15 "Unto him was Carshena, Shethar, _____" (Esther 1:14)
17 Alms
19 "Barley and the _____" (Isaiah 28:25)
20 "Brought _____ unto the man" (Genesis 2:22)
21 "LORD God _____ not caused it to rain" (Genesis 2:5)
22 Duty
23 "Whither thou _____" (Deuteronomy 3:21)
25 Descendants of one of Gad's sons (Numbers 26:16)
27 Not far
28 Lamprey
30 Den
31 Spars
32 Type of satellite (abbr.)
33 "Then shall the people of the Lord go down to the _____" (Judges 5:11)
35 Ulam's brother (1 Chronicles 7:16)
40 Society for women descended from 1776 fighters (abbr.)
43 Sheshan's children (1 Chronicles 2:31)
47 Alternative spelling for Abraham's wife
48 Opposite of WNW
49 "_____ that is above the liver" (Exodus 29:13)
50 Tingles
52 "Should be no _____ in the body" (1 Corinthians 12:25)
54 Begone
55 King of Hamath (2 Samuel 8:9)
56 Before Colossians (abbr.)
57 Dactyl
59 "Not a _____" (1 Timothy 3:3)
61 Factor

63 "_____ are the generations" (Genesis 2:4)
64 "They _____ fields" (Micah 2:2)
65 "The _____ of the LORD" (Exodus 12:41)
66 "_____ white with milk" (Genesis 49:12)

DOWN

1 Piercing
2 Pharaoh
3 Pispah's brother (1 Chronicles 7:38)
4 "They say to their _____" (Lamentations 2:12)
5 "I have eaten _____ like bread" (Psalm 102:9)
6 "And every wise _____ man" (Exodus 36:8)
7 Belonging to Joseph's mother
8 One of David's sons (1 Chronicles 3:6)
9 Swapping
10 "Master shall bore his _____" (Exodus 21:6)
11 "Wherefore _____ thou thy fellow?" (Exodus 2:13)
12 Agate
16 "Great is _____ of the Ephesians" (Acts 19:28)
18 "Touch not; _____ not; handle not" (Colossians 2:21)
24 "They that _____ at meat with him" (Luke 7:49)
26 Pekoe
29 Mononucleosis virus (abbr.)
31 Longitude and latitude, not prime
34 _____ whale
36 "Esar-haddon king of _____" (Ezra 4:2)
37 One of twelve cities (Joshua 19:15)
38 Gad's son (Genesis 46:16)
39 Capes
40 "Fulfilling the _____ of the flesh" (Ephesians 2:3)
41 "Ye shall be _____ gods" (Genesis 3:5)
42 Honor

by Sarah Lagerquist Simmons

43 Gain
44 Another form of Ai (Genesis 12:8)
45 "Thy soul _____ after" (Deuteronomy 12:15)
46 "____ with her suburbs" (Joshua 21:18)
51 "Whither _____ thou?" (John 16:5)
53 "Which are of the house of _____" (1 Corinthians 1:11)
54 "Over the camels also was _____" (1 Chronicles 27:30)
58 One of five cities (1 Chronicles 4:32)
60 "_____ hath done this thing" (Genesis 21:26)
62 "A lion _____ him by the way" (1 Kings 13:24)

## 50

WOMEN OF THE BIBLE

And many women were there, beholding afar off,
which had followed Jesus from Galilee, ministering unto him.
MATTHEW 27:55

ACROSS

1 "Hitherto have ye _____ nothing in my name" (John 16:24)
6 Singer Fitzgerald
10 Carpet
13 **WOMAN** of Cenchrea, who went to Rome (Romans 16:1)
14 Advertising gas
15 Used car lot stat. (pl.)
17 Drive back
18 Among
19 "As soon as the sun _____, thou shalt rise early" (Judges 9:33) (2 words)
20 **WOMAN** from Egypt, who went to Kadesh (Numbers 20:1)
22 "And he began again to teach by the _____" (Mark 4:1) (2 words)
24 New Deal org.
26 "Caraway is not threshed with a _____" (Isaiah 28:27 NIV)
27 **WOMAN** of Rome, who went to Ephesus by way of Corinth (Acts 18:1–19)
33 "Guard against all kinds of _____" (Luke 12:15 NIV)
34 Soundtracks
35 Hair "ado"
37 "But ye have not so _____ Christ" (Ephesians 4:20)
39 **WOMAN** of Nahor, who went to Canaan (Genesis 24) (var.)
44 New Mexican pueblo
46 Shady spots
47 Greek goddess
51 **WOMAN** of Judah, whose Nazarene cousin came to visit (Luke 1:36–40) (var.)
53 Negatively charged atoms
55 Lyric poem
56 Crucial
58 **WOMAN** of Jerusalem, who went to Babylon (Esther 2:5–7)
63 City on the Oka
64 Singer Horne
66 Ratty residence
68 Fern spore cases
69 South African river
70 "Good night" girl of popular song
71 _____ King Cole
72 Resistance units
73 **WOMAN** of Ur, who went to Canaan via Haran (Genesis 11:31)

DOWN

1 Spring month (abbr.)
2 Ark passenger (Genesis 7:13)
3 French military cap
4 Shem's great-grandson (Genesis 10:22–24)
5 It's full of bologna
6 Tooth protector
7 Moon buggy
8 **WOMAN** of Lystra, whose grandson went to Macedonia (2 Timothy 1:5)
9 Chilean range
10 "Then shall stand up in his estate a _____ of taxes" (Daniel 11:20)
11 _____ down
12 "_____ not one against another" (James 5:9)
16 Rapidity
21 "If there _____ matter too hard for thee" (Deuteronomy 17:8) (2 words)
23 High school subject
25 "In _____ thy ways" (Proverbs 3:6)
27 Buddy
28 "For ye tithe mint and _____ and all" (Luke 11:42)
29 Mrs. Cantor

by David K. Shortess

30 Dear _____
31 "And his brethren were _____"
(Genesis 37:27)
32 "To meet the Lord in the _____"
(1 Thessalonians 4:17)
36 Discontinues
38 "Naphtali is a _____ set free"
(Genesis 49:21 NIV)
40 Kind of tide
41 Runner Sebastian
42 TV screen, often (abbr.)
43 "And lifts the needy from the
_____ heap" (Psalm 113:7 NIV)
45 School zone sign (abbr.)
47 Guitar add-ons
48 "Whose feet they hurt with
fetters: he was laid _____" (Psalm
105:18) (2 words)
49 Pitcher Mariano
50 "Pipe down!" (2 words)
52 Standards of excellence
54 Burst of applause

57 **WOMAN** of Haran, who went to
Canaan (Genesis 31)
59 Not that
60 Israeli dance
61 At any time
62 California rockfish
65 Site of modern conflict, briefly
67 Oahu wreath

ACROSS

1 Rezia's father (1 Chronicles 7:39)
5 "LORD spoke unto Moses and Aaron in mount _____" (Numbers 20:23)
8 Married woman (abbr.)
11 "They _____ to and fro" (Psalm 107:27)
12 "Food for your little ____" (Genesis 47:24)
14 "Bore his ear through with an _____" (Exodus 21:6)
15 Icon
16 Babylonian town from which some Jews returned to Judea with Zerubbabel (Ezra 2:59)
18 Lay
20 "We have borne the image of the _____" (1 Corinthians 15:49)
21 Cut
23 Phares's brother (Matthew 1:3)
24 Micah's son (1 Chronicles 8:35)
25 Viper
26 Yonder
29 Benjamin's son (Genesis 46:21)
30 "Who provideth for the _____ his food?" (Job 38:41)
31 Lod's son (Nehemiah 7:37)
32 Aye
33 Tamar's grandson (Matthew 1:3)
35 Atop
38 Site
39 "The _____ was very fair to look upon" (Genesis 24:16)
42 "He then having received the _____ went immediately out" (John 13:30)
43 "Shama and Jehiel the sons of Hothan the _____" (1 Chronicles 11:44)
46 Krishna
49 Damp
50 Flat
51 Shuthelah's son (Numbers 26:36)
52 Before Habakkuk (abbr.)
53 Drive
54 Assay

DOWN

1 Bezaleel's son (Exodus 31:2)
2 "But God _____ the people about" (Exodus 13:18)
3 "Their horses also are swifter than the _____" (Habakkuk 1:8)
4 Entice
5 Fiery
6 Ace
7 This is to be made at the end of every seven years (Deuteronomy 15:1)
8 Shop
9 Hie
10 Kill
13 "Lest being present I should use _____" (2 Corinthians 13:10)
17 Pispah's brother (1 Chronicles 7:38)
19 Rip
21 Don't go
22 Rabbit
23 Ezer's son (1 Chronicles 1:42)
26 "The _____ stuck fast" (Acts 27:41)
27 Soon
28 _____ wasn't built in a day
34 Twenty years
35 Wear
36 "_____; Thy kingdom is divided" (Daniel 5:28)
37 "In her mouth was an _____ leaf" (Genesis 8:11)
39 "Until the day _____" (2 Peter 1:19)
40 Extent
41 "A garment that is _____ eaten" (Job 13:28)
44 Decade
45 Finish
47 Scar
48 Part

by Sarah Lagerquist Simmons

52

ACROSS

1 "I a _____ of babes" (Romans 2:20)
8 "And Jesus called a little _____ unto him" (Matthew 18:2)
12 Apiece
13 "Have them make a chest of _____ wood" (Exodus 25:10 NIV)
16 Aunt (Sp.)
17 "I went down to the grove of _____ trees" (Song of Solomon 6:11 NIV)
18 Portion of the Bible (abbr.)
19 Zilpah's son by Jacob (Genesis 30:10–11)
20 Pa's partner
21 SMU's state (abbr.)
22 "To know _____ and instruction" (Proverbs 1:2)
24 Grad student, maybe (abbr.)
25 "Wait, I say, _____ the Lord" (Psalm 27:14)
26 Be in poor health
27 Collection of Jewish laws
29 Mend
32 Things to fill in
35 "And one _____ lamb of the first year without blemish" (Leviticus 14:10)
36 Thing to doff
38 "And the Pharisees began to _____ him vehemently" (Luke 11:53)
39 Crimson Tide state (abbr.)
40 The results will _____ the conclusion (2 words)
42 Legume
44 Poetic contraction
45 Abhor
46 _____ de la Cite, en Paris
48 Pox reminder
51 Type of love
52 "He had a firm _____ on the staff of God" (Exodus 4:20 MSG)
53 Break in the action
54 Get on someone's nerves
56 Hospital area (abbr.)
57 One (abbr.)
59 Italian commune in northern Italy

63 Wire measure
65 "And _____ was a keeper of sheep" (Genesis 4:2)
67 Messiah College state (abbr.)
68 "_____ thy way may be known upon earth" (Psalm 67:2)
71 "For God _____ loved the world" (John 3:16)
72 That is (abbr.)
73 Balance due on current debt (abbr.)
74 "My lover is to me a cluster of _____ blossoms" (Song of Solomon 1:14 NIV)
75 Indian rhythmic pattern
76 "He rested on the seventh day from all his _____" (Genesis 2:2)

DOWN

1 "He ran to meet them from the _____ door" (Genesis 18:2)
2 Waters (Fr.)
3 "The _____ of violence is in their hands" (Isaiah 59:6)
4 Part of a book (abbr.)
5 "The person who _____ any of it will be held responsible" (Leviticus 7:18 NIV)
6 _____ Cola
7 Con artist's specialty
8 Pepperdine University state (abbr.)
9 Collegiate racquet org. (abbr.)
10 Where Montauk is (abbr.)
11 "Until the day _____, and the day star arise in your hearts" (2 Peter 1:19)
14 Time past
15 Part of personality
18 What OPEC controls, briefly
20 "He will set up a _____ beside it" (Ezekiel 39:15 NIV)
22 Come out on top
23 "I can _____ all things through Christ which strengtheneth me" (Philippians 4:13)
24 "A nation whose _____ thou shalt not understand" (Deuteronomy 28:49)
25 Exclamation

by Marijane G. Troyer

26 Place
27 Pitch
28 Simile word
29 Young woman entering society, briefly
30 Reverence
31 Belonging to French composer Gabriel
33 Christian of Gentile descent (Philemon 24)
34 "And she made him _____ upon her knees" (Judges 16:9)
36 Iowa college
37 Book section (abbr.)
41 California oak
43 Soiled
45 Israeli dance
47 Fabricate
48 Hercule Poirot, for one
49 "Every _____ in his misbegotten brood" (1 Samuel 25:22 MSG)
50 _____ dente

52 Main body of the United Nations (abbr.)
54 "She bare also. . .Sheva the father of Machbenah, and the father of _____" (1 Chronicles 2:49)
55 Feminine name
58 I _____ (name of God)
59 "But Mordecai found out about the _____ and told Queen Esther" (Esther 2:22 NIV)
60 Colorado ski town
61 "Let their way be _____ and slippery" (Psalm 35:6)
62 "He _____ to meet them from the tent door" (Genesis 18:2)
64 "The LORD _____ my shepherd" (Psalm 23:1)
66 "Both _____ and high, rich and poor" (Psalm 49:2)
67 Average
69 "_____ taught me also" (Proverbs 4:4)
70 Vanderbilt U. state (abbr.)

## 53

LOOK BEYOND THE PRESENT!

For now we see through a glass, darkly;
but then face to face.

1 CORINTHIANS 13:12

ACROSS

1 "She is _____ of life"
   (Proverbs 3:18) (2 words)
6 "Ye have not gone up into the
   _____" (Ezekiel 13:5)
10 Legally impede
15 "Along the _____ man said to
   him" (Luke 9:57 NIV) (2 words)
16 Mine opening
17 Start of **VERSE** (Psalm 126:5 NIV)
18 Ladder parts
19 South American cow catcher
20 Plantain lily
21 Music makers
23 "But the name of the wicked shall
   _____" (Proverbs 10:7)
24 Anesthetic
25 **VERSE**, part 2 (4 words)
28 _____ Four (musical
   phenomenon)
29 Game piece
30 "Will a man _____ God"
   (Malachi 3:8)
33 Object of casting lots
37 Ancient arsonist
40 City on Lake Michigan
42 Brick ones
44 **VERSE**, part 3
46 "Come unto me, all ye that. . .are
   heavy _____" (Matthew 11:28)
47 Church John was to write
   (Revelation 3:1)
49 Take the bark off
51 "And thou puttest thy _____ in a
   rock" (Numbers 24:21)
52 Main Street pillar
53 _____ *volente* (God willing)
55 _____ chi
57 **VERSE**, part 4 (3 words)
64 Where the humerus meets the
   ulna
67 "Crib" predecessor (colloq.)

68 Part of R.L.S.
69 Lariat
70 "And thou shalt rule _____ him"
   (Genesis 4:7)
72 City Paul and Silas entered by
   night (Acts 17:10)
73 End of **VERSE** (2 words)
74 "Where thou dwellest, even where
   Satan's _____ is" (Revelation
   2:13)
75 "_____ as the east is from the
   west" (Psalm 103:12) (2 words)
76 Roebuck's partner
77 Gaelic
78 Takes five

DOWN

1 Contained in FedEx logo (look
   closely!)
2 "Put forth thine hand. . .and
   _____ all that he hath" (Job 1:11)
3 "His sister's son, that he _____
   meet him" (Genesis 29:13) (2
   words)
4 "The sharp sword with two
   _____" (Revelation 2:12)
5 "The land of Nod, on the _____
   Eden" (Genesis 4:16) (2 words)
6 Yak
7 "You _____ yourself in vain"
   (Jeremiah 4:30 NIV)
8 "They are steered. . .wherever
   the _____ wants to go"
   (James 3:4 NIV)
9 Pronounced
10 Diaphanous
11 Photos
12 Nonsense, in Nottingham
13 Bony beginning
14 Partridge's tree
22 What ugly duckling became
26 Powerful union (abbr.)

by David K. Shortess

27 "For ye shall speak into the
_____" (1 Corinthians 14:9)
30 Get a lift
31 Arithmetic column
32 "He hath _____ his bow"
(Lamentations 3:12)
33 _____ of Sharon
34 Noted office
35 Found along the road
36 "But the _____ is not yet"
(Matthew 24:6)
38 Tear
39 Corrida cheer
41 "An open door, and no man
_____ shut it" (Revelation 3:8)
43 Laterally
45 Latvian native
48 Dead or Salt
50 Garland's costar in Oz
54 Vie
56 Line on a weather map
57 Helicopter lifter

58 "Yet he did not _____ through
unbelief" (Romans 4:20 NIV)
59 Thoughts
60 More than portly
61 Squishy toy balls
62 "How _____ Thou Art"
63 "Which. . .and sealeth up the
_____" (Job 9:7)
64 Statue located in Piccadilly Circus
65 "Narrow is the way, which leadeth
unto _____" (Matthew 7:14)
66 _____ California
71 66 or 30, e.g.

ACROSS

1 Kimono sash
4 Lab _____
6 Ike's initials
9 Stumble
11 Deer, biblically
13 "The governor under _____ the king" (2 Corinthians 11:32)
16 Shamer's son (1 Chronicles 7:34)
18 "Thou shalt _____ covet" (Exodus 20:17)
19 "The vision of _____ the Elkoshite" (Nahum 1:1)
21 "Ye tithe mint and _____ and all manner of herbs" (Luke 11:42)
22 Slay
24 Cave
25 "And will _____ the caul of their heart" (Hosea 13:8)
26 She with the tender eyes (Genesis 29:17)
28 Bard
29 Name of God
30 Salary
31 Pine for
34 Cleanse
37 Radio host Limbaugh
38 "In the month _____, which is the second month" (1 Kings 6:1)
40 Pastures
42 Lubricant
43 Salu's son (Numbers 25:14)
45 He thought Hannah was drunk
46 Saudi Peninsula
48 Ronald Reagan, for one
50 Late afternoon activity, for some
52 Wood
53 Bring in
54 "Eber, Peleg, _____" (1 Chronicles 1:25)
55 "The son of _____, which was the son of Noe" (Luke 3:36)

DOWN

2 Scarab
3 NYC subway (abbr.)
5 Morning (abbr.)
6 Play-_____
7 Bachelor of arts, for example
8 Grade
10 "They _____ in the dry places like a river" (Psalm 105:41)
11 CD-_____
12 Storage building
14 Agitate
15 Gloomy
16 Operate
17 "Thou shalt not approach to his wife: she is thine _____" (Leviticus 18:14)
20 "Who had taken _____ for his daughter" (Esther 2:15)
23 "Cause it to be heard unto _____" (Isaiah 10:30)
25 "Thy servant dwell in the _____ city" (1 Samuel 27:5)
27 Possesses
28 "Delivered me out of the _____ of the lion" (1 Samuel 17:37)
31 Naturalist John
32 "He shall deliver the _____ of the innocent" (Job 22:30)
33 _____ sum, Chinese specialty
35 "Let them _____ the bones of it therein" (Ezekiel 24:5)
36 Angelic glow
37 Path
38 "Jachan, and _____, and Heber, seven" (1 Chronicles 5:13)
39 Backward
41 Dear _____ (pl.)
43 Energy
44 Gershwin brother
47 Evil
49 "They laded their _____ with the corn" (Genesis 42:26) (sing.)
51 Gym class (abbr.)

by Tonya Vilhauer

ACROSS

1 Children
5 "Moab shall howl over _____"
(Isaiah 15:2)
9 "Set thy face against _____"
(Ezekiel 38:2)
12 "A bedstead of _____"
(Deuteronomy 3:11)
13 A city of Simeon (1 Chronicles 4:29)
14 Abijam's son (1 Kings 15:8)
15 "In _____ was there a voice heard" (Matthew 2:18)
16 Atoned
18 Caleb's son (1 Chronicles 4:15)
20 Granted
21 Inside
23 "Beyond the tower of _____" (Genesis 35:21)
24 "Neither _____ up the people" (Acts 24:12)
26 "_____ shall be called Woman" (Genesis 2:23)
28 Spanish word for master
29 Abbreviation for last Old Testament book
31 King of Assyria (2 Kings 15:19)
32 "Then began _____ to call" (Genesis 4:26)
33 Descendants of Salma (1 Chronicles 2:54)
35 As
37 Look for
38 Seem to be
41 "LORD God _____ not caused it to rain" (Genesis 2:5)
42 "The _____ cease" (Ecclesiastes 12:3)
45 "_____ thou hast not hated blood" (Ezekiel 35:6)
48 Bani's son (Ezra 10:34)
49 "Who can stand before the children of _____" (Deuteronomy 9:2)
50 "_____, lama sabachthani?" (Mark 15:34)
51 "Mine _____ mourneth" (Psalm 88:9)
52 Abjure
53 Tinted

DOWN

1 "_____ of Moab is laid waste" (Isaiah 15:1)
2 Ikkesh's son (1 Chronicles 11:28)
3 Rule
4 "_____ of death" (2 Samuel 22:6)
5 Abner's father (1 Samuel 14:50)
6 Old Testament prophet (abbr.)
7 Hadad's father (Genesis 36:35)
8 The end
9 Monopoly is one
10 "As he saith also in _____" (Romans 9:25)
11 Sodi's son (Numbers 13:10)
17 Sin
19 "Judgment of _____" (Numbers 27:21)
21 Duke of Edom (Genesis 36:43)
22 Dub
23 "Joshua passed unto _____" (Joshua 10:34)
25 "He shall be called a _____" (Matthew 2:23)
26 Apace
27 Bran
30 Saul's father (1 Samuel 9:3)
34 Ribbed
35 Before eleven
36 "_____ being yet a little child" (1 Kings 11:17)
38 "The burning _____" (Leviticus 26:16)
39 Victim
40 Load
43 "Living creatures _____ and returned" (Ezekiel 1:14)
44 Heavens
46 Part of the foot
47 "Jacob _____ them under the oak" (Genesis 35:4)

by Sarah Lagerquist Simmons

56

ACROSS

1 Moses' sister
6 "And the two sons of _____, Hophni and Phinehas" (1 Samuel 1:3)
8 "The. . .faith. . .which dwelt first in thy grandmother _____" (2 Timothy 1:5)
12 Utah city
13 Ailing
14 Plains state (abbr.)
16 Genetic letters
17 "They will eat their food. . .and _____ their tiny portions of water" (Ezekiel 12:19 NLT)
18 Bend, as in the road (var.)
19 Snake or scarf
21 Borrowed money payable upon request (abbr.)
22 Education (abbr.) _____
23 Cold storage
25 Dash
27 "The rich _____ in low place" (Ecclesiastes 10:6)
29 Where it's _____
30 Bitter (Fr.)
32 Cap
33 Villain
35 Undetonated weapon (abbr.)
36 Article (Ger.)
39 Things to connect
41 Apiece (abbr.)
43 "I have _____ to eat that ye know not of" (John 4:32)
46 David's daughter (2 Samuel 13:1)
48 "With the scab, and with the _____" (Deuteronomy 28:27)
50 Esau (Genesis 25:30)
52 Tokyo, once
53 Ahasuerus's wife (Esther 8:1)
55 "Eat it as a thing offered unto an _____" (1 Corinthians 8:7)
56 Oxidizes
58 Southern state (abbr.)
60 David's wife (2 Samuel 3:3)
65 "Pick up your _____, and walk" (Mark 2:9 NLT)
67 Lazarus' sister
69 Boys' group (abbr.)
70 He died of diseased feet (2 Chronicles 16:12–13)
71 "He went _____ into a mountain apart to pray" (Matthew 14:23)
72 John (Gael.)
73 "A _____ was under the first pair of branches" (Exodus 37:21 NASB)
74 Secret competitor?
76 "There shall be a time of trouble, such as _____ was" (Daniel 12:1)
77 Beverage
78 "Rejoice, O _____ man, in thy youth" (Ecclesiastes 11:9)
79 Alms box
80 "Woe _____ me now" (Jeremiah 4:31)

DOWN

1 Joshua succeeded him (Numbers 27:18–23)
2 Relating to part of the eye
3 Elected official (abbr.)
4 Within (prefix)
5 Coastal city (Acts 20:15)
6 "Even _____. . .is going to have a child in her old age" (Luke 1:36 NIV)
7 Innate
9 Produced when needed (abbr.)
10 Asian country
11 She brought spices to Jesus' tomb (Mark 16:1)
15 "Then said I, What come these to _____" (Zechariah 1:21)
18 Time period
20 Down or from (prefix)
24 Long dash
26 Legal in some states on red (abbr.)
28 Trading center rebuilt by Solomon (1 Kings 9:17–18)
31 "I saw the _____ pushing westward" (Daniel 8:4)
34 Deceased beforehand (abbr.)
37 "_____ thou hast forgotten the law of thy God" (Hosea 4:6)
38 "There is but a _____ between me and death" (1 Samuel 20:3)
40 Very (Fr.)
42 Professional

by Marijane G. Troyer

44 "If any man shall _____ unto these things" (Revelation 22:18)
45 "Shall there arise _____ much contempt" (Esther 1:18)
47 _____ *nauseum*
48 Belonging, say, to a pet
49 Nationally elected body (abbr.)
51 Metric measure (abbr.)
54 "_____ on your armor and be shattered" (Isaiah 8:9 ESV)
57 "Who can be against _____" (Romans 8:31)
58 Musical note
59 Type of fuel
60 Babylonian town (Ezra 8:15)
61 Deadly poisons (arch.)
62 Adjoins
63 _____ of Patmos
64 Rachel's father
65 First to discover the Resurrection (Matthew 28)
66 Fragrance by Dana

67 Rope-making grass
68 Row
75 "For they shall be _____ ornament of grace" (Proverbs 1:9)
76 Does not pertain (abbr.)

JESUS, THE I AM

*Again the high priest asked him. . .Art thou the Christ,
the Son of the Blessed? And Jesus said, I am. . . .*

MARK 14:61–62

ACROSS

1 Word frequently used in Matthew 1:2–16
6 "And the _____ lying in a manger" (Luke 2:16)
10 Wear's cohort
14 "Of Christ, who is the _____ of God" (2 Corinthians 4:4)
15 It goes with milk
16 "To speak evil _____ man" (Titus 3:2) (2 words)
17 "Encourage the _____, help the weak" (1 Thessalonians 5:14 NIV)
18 Eras
19 "And were as swift as the _____ upon the mountains" (1 Chronicles 12:8)
20 British gun
21 Univ. employee
22 "A wholesome tongue is _____ of life" (Proverbs 15:4) (2 words)
23 "Then said Jesus unto them. . .I am the _____" (John 10:7, 11) (2 words)
26 Existed
29 Wrong (prefix)
30 One who excels
31 "In earth, _____ in heaven" (Matthew 6:10) (3 words)
33 Course for immigrants (abbr.)
34 "Then Herod called the _____ secretly" (Matthew 2:7 NIV)
38 "Then spake Jesus again unto them, saying, I am the _____" (John 8:12) (4 words)
41 "Citizen _____"
42 Gov't. med. research agency
43 Void
44 "_____ the land of the free"
45 Catchall abbreviation
46 Half a donkey bray

47 "Jesus said unto her, I am the _____" (John 11:25)
53 Incensed
54 Actor Guinness
55 Parched
59 "That _____ after the dust of the earth" (Amos 2:7)
60 Unique individual
61 Theatrical device
62 Italian noble family
63 "Thy god, _____, liveth" (Amos 8:14) (2 words)
64 "All ye that labour and are heavy _____" (Matthew 11:28)
65 "Ye know that summer is _____" (Mark 13:28)
66 Fabled creature
67 Country call

DOWN

1 "Behold, we put _____ in the horses' mouths" (James 3:3)
2 Give off
3 "The lazy man does not roast his _____" (Proverbs 12:27 NIV)
4 "Senior moment" cause
5 Newsman Baxter, from 70s TV hit
6 Companies' directors
7 Ancient Greek city
8 Corned _____ (breakfast favorite) (2 words)
9 Greek goddess of dawn
10 Value
11 Said or thought?
12 Disparaging look
13 Washed, as a deck
21 Murderer, at times
22 Mimic
24 "Command you, do not _____ a word" (Jeremiah 26:2 NIV)
25 Unusual
26 Traffic light instruction

by David K. Shortess

27 "Unto the seven churches which are in _____" (Revelation 1:11)
28 "For the Jews require a _____" (1 Corinthians 1:22)
32 "Blessed are _____ meek" (Matthew 5:5)
33 Biblical suffix
34 Calendar abbreviation
35 _____ angel
36 Delight
37 "Every _____ word that men shall speak" (Matthew 12:36)
39 "An offering made by _____ sin offering" (Numbers 15:25 NIV) (3 words)
40 Baylor University locale
44 Mine output
45 Ageless (arch.)
47 Mature
48 Expunge
49 _____ Maria, CA
50 Say

51 "Like unto _____ glass" (Revelation 21:18)
52 Kind of tone
56 Sit in the saddle
57 "The _____ seemed good to me" (Deuteronomy 1:23 NIV)
58 Fender flaw
60 "That is so cool"
61 Priest's robe

ACROSS

1 Jerk
4 "As he saith also in _____"
(Romans 9:25)
8 Battle
11 Joseph's son (Numbers 13:7)
13 Facial hair
15 Level
16 Tattletale
17 Canaanite king (Numbers 21:1)
18 Shred
19 Borders
21 Naaman was a _____ (2 Kings 5:1)
23 "The children of Keros, the children of _____" (Nehemiah 7:47)
24 "From _____ eastward" (Joshua 19:12)
25 Argument
29 "Where thou _____, will I die" (Ruth 1:17)
30 "Ye _____ men with burdens" (Luke 11:46)
31 Before Zephaniah (abbr.)
33 They came from here to live in Samaria (2 Kings 17:24)
34 "Which is neither _____ nor sown" (Deuteronomy 21:4)
35 Elah's brother (1 Chronicles 4:15)
36 "The people _____ together" (Acts 21:30)
37 Shimei's son (1 Chronicles 23:10)
38 Kinds
40 Replies
43 "The _____ wind blew" (Acts 27:13)
44 "Hena, and _____" (2 Kings 18:34)
45 Merari's son (1 Chronicles 24:27)
46 "The wall of _____" (2 Chronicles 26:6)
49 Yarn
51 "Mine _____ also is dim" (Job 17:7)
54 "He called the name of the well _____" (Genesis 26:20)
55 "The family of the _____" (Numbers 3:27)

58 Become weary
59 "At _____ appointed" (Nehemiah 13:31)
60 "Fowl _____ may fly" (Genesis 1:20)
61 Assist
62 "And Dishon, and _____" (1 Chronicles 1:38)

DOWN

1 Humor
2 Sarai's handmaid (Galatians 4:24)
3 "The _____ received him" (John 4:45)
4 Submitted
5 Ocean
6 "Master shall bore his _____" (Exodus 21:6)
7 "How long will it be _____ they believe me" (Numbers 14:11)
8 "All manner of _____" (Nehemiah 13:16)
9 "_____ heart was perfect" (1 Kings 15:14)
10 Cherry
12 "Cleanse the _____" (Matthew 10:8)
14 This was done to the bullock (1 Kings 18:26)
15 Saruch's father (Luke 3:35)
20 Bail
22 Hole
24 The third month (Esther 8:9)
25 Mend
26 Notion
27 After the twenty-ninth
28 "The _____ was without form" (Genesis 1:2)
29 Zerah's son (1 Chronicles 2:6)
30 Phalti's father (1 Samuel 25:44)
32 Mass transport
34 "Ethan the _____" (1 Kings 4:31)
38 Sane
39 "Thou art _____ sister" (Genesis 24:60)
41 Blinked
42 "The serpent beguiled _____" (2 Corinthians 11:3)
43 He prayed with Paul (Acts 16:25)

by Sarah Lagerquist Simmons

46 Ebony
47 "Preach the word in _____"
   (Acts 16:6)
48 Zophah's son (1 Chronicles 7:36)
49 "The troops of _____ looked"
   (Job 6:19)
50 Hushim's father (1 Chronicles 7:12)
52 Affirmative oral vote
53 Old Testament book about a Jewish queen (abbr.)
56 "By the cliff of _____"
   (2 Chronicles 20:16)
57 "That which groweth of _____ own accord" (Leviticus 25:5)

## 59

DIVINE ILLUMINATION

Then spake Jesus. . .I am the light of the world:
he that followeth me. . .shall have the light of life.

JOHN 8:12

ACROSS

1 Sail support
5 "And he shall pluck away his
 _____ with his feathers"
 (Leviticus 1:16)
9 Pentateuch, at times
14 "But the tongue can no man
 _____" (James 3:8)
15 Burr's "Perry Mason" costar
16 Relating to the flock?
17 "But such _____ common to
 man" (1 Corinthians 10:13) (2
 words)
18 With, in Paris
19 "Then began _____ call upon the
 name of the Lord" (Genesis 4:26)
 (2 words)
20 Start of **QUOTE** (1 John 1:5)
 (5 words)
23 Cain's land (Genesis 4:16)
24 "Ye shall not _____ of it"
 (Genesis 3:3)
25 Aswan, for one
28 "They compassed me about like
 _____" (Psalm 118:12)
31 In the distance
36 "Renew our days _____ old"
 (Lamentations 5:21) (2 words)
38 Circle segments
40 "Let us get up _____ to the
 vineyards" (Song of Solomon 7:12)
41 Honda model
43 Tattletale
44 "Am I in God's _____"
 (Genesis 30:2)
45 City in Egypt or Illinois
46 Thick slice
48 Satisfy fully
49 Weak blooded
51 "She also lieth in wait as for a
 _____" (Proverbs 23:28)
53 *Mal de* _____

54 Collar
56 Diving sea bird
58 **QUOTE**, part 2 (4 words)
67 End of **QUOTE** (2 words)
68 "The wringing of the _____
 bringeth forth blood"
 (Proverbs 30:33)
69 Aunt Bee's charge
70 Familiar greeting
71 "To maintain good works for
 necessary _____" (Titus 3:14)
72 Traveled
73 "But there went up _____ from
 the earth" (Genesis 2:6) (2 words)
74 Hot _____
75 Loch _____ monster

DOWN

1 "My lover is like a gazelle or a
 young _____" (Song of Solomon
 2:9 NIV)
2 El _____, Texas
3 "God has ascended _____ shouts
 of joy" (Psalm 47:5 NIV)
4 Tree exudate
5 "And _____ shall be a spoil"
 (Jeremiah 50:10)
6 Sitarist Shankar
7 Designer Cassini
8 _____ Melba, *en Paris*
9 Love apples
10 "Our skin was black like an
 _____ " (Lamentations 5:10)
11 Fruit coating
12 Against
13 "But _____ whom it falls will be
 crushed" (Matthew 21:44 NIV)
 (2 words)
21 _____ sister
22 _____-Sachs disease
25 Bangladesh capital
26 Flu type

by David K. Shortess

27 Theater offering
29 Makes a mistake
30 Can be flaky
32 King Cole, and namesakes
33 "And, behold, it was a _____"
(Genesis 41:7)
34 Bring joy to
35 U-Haul rival
37 "His heart is as _____ as a stone"
(Job 41:24)
39 "There fell a great _____ from
heaven" (Revelation 8:10)
42 Pay phone feature (2 words)
47 "Thou _____ record of thyself"
(John 8:13)
50 "Saying, Who then _____ be
saved" (Matthew 19:25)
52 Expression of disgust (var.)
55 More than expected
57 Acquainted
58 "Tee hee"
59 Piece in the paper

60 West African country
61 "Not plagued by human _____"
(Psalm 73:5 NIV)
62 Quantity of medicine
63 "There was _____ of glass like
unto crystal" (Revelation 4:6) (2
words)
64 Pointless weapon
65 "Though your _____ be as
scarlet" (Isaiah 1:18)
66 "The lowly he _____ on high"
(Job 5:11 NIV)

ACROSS

1 Word in a threat
5 "I will take _____ to my ways" (Psalm 39:1)
9 Blue
12 "_____ Irae"
13 Tear down
14 Digit
15 "Jesus. . .overthrew. . .the _____ of them that sold doves" (Matthew 21:12)
17 Thing (Lat.)
18 Number of Sarah's sons
19 Consumed
21 "Ye have _____ the people of the Lord" (Numbers 16:41)
23 Simulate
27 *Norma* _____, Oscar winner
28 "His soul shall dwell at _____" (Psalm 25:13)
29 By dying on the cross, Jesus _____ us
31 Nonmetric measure (abbr.)
33 Needle part
34 "The child was _____ from that very hour" (Matthew 17:18)
35 Exist
36 Letter abbreviation
37 Act like a peacock
38 "All the people said, _____, and praised the LORD" (1 Chronicles 16:36)
39 King (Fr.)
40 What Thomas did
42 Kingdoms
45 *Mme* (Eng.)
46 Son of (Arabic)
47 Weekday (abbr.)
49 He came with Zerubbabel to Jerusalem (Nehemiah 7:7)
53 Droop
54 Eliphaz's son (1 Chronicles 1:36)
56 "There is _____ of you that is sorry for me" (1 Samuel 22:8)
57 Compass point (abbr.)
58 Word heard in fast-food restaurant
59 Jacob, to Esau

DOWN

1 Sullivan and Wynn
2 Fabrication
3 Salt _____, biblical body
4 "Let the king give her royal _____ unto another" (Esther 1:19)
5 Part of a day (abbr.)
6 "The _____ of the wise seeketh knowledge" (Proverbs 18:15)
7 O.T. book
8 "Whatsoever mine eyes _____ I kept not from them" (Ecclesiastes 2:10)
9 Evening wear, formerly
10 Top quality
11 Board game item
16 Jeanne d'Arc, *par exemple* (abbr.)
20 "Let him seek peace, and _____ it" (1 Peter 3:11)
22 Male friend (Brit.)
23 Heard in the hen house
24 Beams
25 Compass point (abbr.)
26 Threw down the gauntlet
30 "The cruel _____ of asps" (Deuteronomy 32:33)
31 Release
32 "The thoughts of the diligent _____ only to plenteousness" (Proverbs 21:5)
34 "Though they be red like _____" (Isaiah 1:18)
35 Quantity (abbr.)
37 Seasoned elected one
38 "At home in the body, we are _____ from the Lord" (2 Corinthians 5:6)
39 Amana, for one
41 Planter
42 "It shall _____ up wholly like a flood" (Amos 9:5)
43 Israeli diplomat of note
44 "The _____ came to Jesus by night" (John 3:2)
48 Strain
50 "_____ fair is thy love, my sister" (Song of Solomon 4:10)
51 One only (comb. form)

by Evelyn M. Boyington

52 "They have wandered as blind
_____ in the streets"
(Lamentations 4:14)
55 _____ Rev. (abbr.)

ACROSS

1 Acts
6 "_____ crieth at the gates" (Proverbs 8:3)
9 Follows Luke (abbr.)
12 The Ashterathite (1 Chronicles 11:44)
13 Lane
14 Dark wood
16 "Yet I _____ not" (Psalm 119:110)
17 Beholden
18 Bane
19 Nethinim whose descendants returned to Jerusalem after Babylonian exile (Nehemiah 7:47)
20 Prowl
22 "Take away all thy _____" (Isaiah 1:25)
23 Colored
24 Own
27 Meshullam's father (Ezra 10:29)
30 Ham's brother (Luke 3:36)
31 Jether's son (1 Chronicles 7:38)
33 Gad's children built this city (Numbers 32:34)
35 Descendants of Kohath (Numbers 3:27)
38 Day before today
39 Vashni's brother (1 Chronicles 6:28)
40 Enhakkore (Judges 15:19)
41 Sick
42 "In _____ sight I shall find grace" (Ruth 2:2)
43 "The Highest gave _____ voice" (Psalm 18:13)
44 "_____ is confounded" (Jeremiah 50:2)
45 City in western half of the tribe of Manasseh (1 Chronicles 6:70)
46 Call
48 Costly
51 "Where _____ seat is" (Revelation 2:13)
54 "Am I in _____ stead" (Genesis 30:2)
55 Club
58 "They shall _____ him" (Deuteronomy 22:19)
59 "It is God that _____ me" (2 Samuel 22:48)
60 One twelfth of a year
61 King of Sodom (Genesis 14:2)
62 Serug's father (Genesis 11:20)
63 "The _____ of the staves" (1 Kings 8:8)
64 "Great _____ the company" (Psalm 68:11)
65 "My gray _____" (Genesis 42:38)

DOWN

1 Fees
2 Chelub's son (1 Chronicles 27:26)
3 Jether's father (1 Chronicles 4:17)
4 Perish
5 Glumly
6 "By thy _____ shalt thou live" (Genesis 27:40)
7 "Doth the _____ fly by thy wisdom" (Job 39:26)
8 "None _____ pitied thee" (Ezekiel 16:5)
9 After Obadiah (abbr.)
10 Hadid's brother (Ezra 2:33)
11 Ode
14 Bad
15 Jaaziah's son (1 Chronicles 24:26)
21 Amram's brother (Ezra 10:34)
22 "The inhabitants of the land of _____ brought water to him" (Isaiah 21:14)
23 "When a man _____ in a tent" (Numbers 19:14)
24 Emerald
25 State
26 Fat
27 Arch
28 Ziphion's brother (Genesis 46:16)
29 Beaks
30 Little
32 Zilpah's son (Genesis 35:26)
34 Was not with Adonijah (1 Kings 1:8)
35 Maasiai's father (1 Chronicles 9:12)
36 Crop
37 One of David's sons (1 Chronicles 3:6)

by Sarah Lagerquist Simmons

44 Ignoble
46 Barbs
47 Move slowly
48 Pigeons
49 Mahli's brother (1 Chronicles 23:23)
50 This man's children were among the Nethinim returning from captivity (Ezra 2:50)
51 Ditto
52 Became king in Jerusalem at 22 (2 Kings 21:19)
53 Keep watch over
54 City of Benjamin (Joshua 18:24)
55 Suah's brother (1 Chronicles 7:36)
56 The children of _____ were among the porters (Ezra 2:42)
57 So

ACROSS

1 But where is the _____ for a burnt offering?" (Genesis 22:7)
5 Ceramic fragment, biblically speaking
11 "Thou mayest _____ them for the calling of the assembly" (Numbers 10:2)
12 "From the firstborn of Pharaoh that _____ on his throne" (Exodus 12:29)
13 Russian space station
14 One for your thoughts (abbr.)
15 State official (abbr.)
16 Mature
18 First state (abbr.)
19 British pilots' organization (abbr.)
21 The Commandments, for example
22 Round wooden nail
23 Perky
25 Twosome
26 High navy officer (abbr.)
27 Fastener
30 Carry a load
32 "Shall rule with a _____ of iron" (Revelation 19:15)
33 High standards
36 "Let them shout for joy, and be _____" (Psalm 35:27)
38 Hosp. area
39 Weekday
40 "But his delight _____ in the law of the LORD" (Psalm 1:2)
41 Cable channel (abbr.)
42 "Then they _____ unto the LORD in their trouble" (Psalm 107:19)
44 Born (Fr.)
45 "They were filled with. . . amazement _____ that which had happened" (Acts 3:10)
46 "Wherefore think _____ evil in your hearts?" (Matthew 9:4)
47 Australian marsupial
49 Comforted
53 Witty
54 "_____ I Love You" (Beatles' hit)
55 Sticky substance
57 Great Lake
59 "That in the _____ to come he might show. . .his grace" (Ephesians 2:7)
63 Interjection

65 One of the ten spies (Numbers 13:17)
67 "Let them _____ shout for joy" (Psalm 5:11)
69 Adriatic feeder
70 Certain collegians (abbr.)
72 "He also wrote letters to _____ on the LORD God of Israel" (2 Chronicles 32:17)
73 Addict
75 Indefinitely long periods
76 Small letters (abbr.)
77 "_____ they did eat, and were filled" (Nehemiah 9:25)
78 English singing poet

DOWN

1 "Not greedy of filthy _____" (1 Timothy 3:3)
2 *The Thin Man* pet
3 "But as for _____, I will come into the house" (Psalm 5:7)
4 "And he sent forth a _____" (Genesis 8:7)
6 Hatefully
7 Took to court
8 Printer's measure
9 "And they have caused him to _____ upon the king's mule" (1 Kings 1:44)
10 "Thou hast drunken the _____ of the cup of trembling" (Isaiah 51:17)
12 "Turn Moab into a drunken ____, drunk on the wine of my wrath" (Jeremiah 48:26 MSG)
16 "Mayberry _____," spin-off TV series
17 Arafat's origin (abbr.)
20 "But Jonathan was very _____ of David" (1 Samuel 19:1 NIV)
22 "Then Saul, (who also is called _____), filled with the Holy Ghost" (Acts 13:9)
24 Cannot pertain to (abbr.)
26 "And took thence old cast clouts and old rotten _____" (Jeremiah 38:11)
27 "And failing of eyes, and _____ of mind" (Deuteronomy 28:65)
28 City near Dresden
29 Passover feasts

by Marijane G. Troyer

31 "Then one of them, which was a
_____" (Matthew 22:35)
32 "He is the _____, his work is
perfect" (Deuteronomy 32:4)
34 "For in the day that thou eatest
thereof thou shalt surely _____"
(Genesis 2:17)
35 Ten-step organization (abbr.)
37 "And understood that Saul was
come in very _____" (1 Samuel
26:4)
40 "That which groweth of
_____ own accord of thy harvest"
(Leviticus 25:5)
43 Ready (arch.)
45 "My soul shall be satisfied _____
with marrow and fatness" (Psalm
63:5)
48 "With anthems of praise to God
using _____ by David"
(2 Chronicles 29:30 MSG)
50 "For thou hast made him a little
lower than the _____" (Psalm
8:5)

51 Ogden's state (abbr.)
52 "Eat not of it _____, nor sodden
at all with water" (Exodus 12:9)
54 "Every several gate was of one
_____" (Revelation 21:21)
56 "And it is a _____ thing that the
king requireth" (Daniel 2:11)
58 One who checks out details (abbr.)
60 Burst of energy (abbr.)
61 D.C. quadrant
62 "O _____, why hast thou made
us to err from thy ways" (Isaiah
63:17)
64 Court
66 Resinous substance
68 "Take some of its blood and
_____ it on Aaron's right earlobe"
(Exodus 29:20 MSG)
69 According to
71 Davy Crockett's home state (abbr.)
74 Organization begun by Gen. and
Mrs. Booth (abbr.)

ACROSS

1 Chew
5 Canyon
10 "That _____," 60s TV series
14 Unique
15 Medal
16 Solomon's grandson (Matthew 1:7)
17 Tenth part of an ephah (Exodus 16:36)
18 "Moza begat _____" (1 Chronicles 8:37)
19 Zerahiah's father (1 Chronicles 6:6)
20 Hit with, as a snowball
21 Rage
22 Swimmer's lengths
23 High priest in Shiloh
25 Obtain
27 Minor prophet (abbr.)
28 Firearm
30 Plead
32 Hearing
33 Cures
35 Search
36 Gait
37 "In all _____ there is profit" (Proverbs 14:23)
39 "Leave their wealth to _____" (Psalm 49:10)
41 Ziphion's father (Genesis 46:16)
42 Bezaleel's father (Exodus 38:22)
43 Compete
44 And so forth (abbr.)
46 Learning handicap (abbr.)
47 Group
48 Stumble
49 Jether's son (1 Chronicles 7:38)
50 "That lieth before _____ by the way of the wilderness" (2 Samuel 2:24)
52 "Who had taken _____ for his daughter" (Esther 2:15)
54 "Adonijah, Bigvai, _____" (Nehemiah 10:16)
55 Turn up one's nose at
57 Deface
58 Theatrical device
59 Stuffed animal maker
60 "And there was war between _____ and Baasha" (1 Kings 15:16)
61 Adam lived _____ hundred and thirty years (Genesis 5:5)
62 Scandinavian carrier (abbr.)
63 Cooped-up one?
64 License plate

DOWN

1 Fumble around
2 To wit
3 Gad's son (Genesis 46:16)
4 "If thou _____ pure and upright" (Job 8:6)
5 "The men of Ramah and _____" (Nehemiah 7:30)
6 In debt
7 Grasslands
8 Welcome
9 "The tower of _____" (Genesis 35:21)
10 Ancient region of western Europe
11 Judge of Israel (Judges 12:8)
12 Saul's concubine (2 Samuel 3:7)
13 "Cause it to be heard unto _____" (Isaiah 10:30)
24 Harmful
26 Suede, for example
28 Chow
29 Evidence of creation
30 "Then thou shalt _____ thyself" (2 Samuel 5:24)
31 Joy
32 "Lebbaeus, whose surname was _____" (Matthew 10:3)
34 Going from one to another
37 Cargo
38 "Departed from Hazeroth, and pitched in _____" (Numbers 33:18)
39 Invaded
40 Pace
41 Practical jokes
45 Candy _____
51 "The gods of Sepharvaim, _____, and Ivah" (2 Kings 18:34)
53 State of being comfortable

by Tonya Vilhauer

54 "Stayed in _____ for a season"
   (Acts 19:22)
56 Aves.
58 "Go to the _____, thou sluggard"
   (Proverbs 6:6)

ACROSS

1 Crippled
6 Separated
10 Midianite King slain by the Israelites (Numbers 31:8)
11 Stop
13 One of Berah's sons (1 Chronicles 8:15)
14 Old Testament prophet (abbr.)
15 Before
18 Set
21 Timothy's mother (2 Timothy 1:5)
22 "Save the _____ sort" (2 Kings 24:14)
24 "Be _____ of the Spirit" (Galatians 5:18)
25 Kohath's son (Numbers 3:19)
27 Tint
28 "_____ with her suburbs" (1 Chronicles 6:73)
29 Bang
30 "Become an astonishment, a _____, and a byword" (Deuteronomy 28:37)
33 Hedge
35 "In _____ was there a voice heard" (Matthew 2:18)
36 "He is a _____ of them" (Hebrews 11:6)
39 Chill
40 Zeruiah's son (2 Samuel 2:18)
42 "The children of _____" (Ezra 2:57)
43 "Would they not give _____" (Nehemiah 9:30)
44 Party
45 Mother _____
46 Patmos was one (Revelation 1:9)
47 _____ of Galilee
49 "Barley and the _____" (Isaiah 28:25)
50 Fall
51 Way
52 Roman province in Asia Minor (Acts 27:5)

DOWN

2 The Jairite (2 Samuel 20:26)
3 Cure
4 The Philistines brought the ark from _____ to Ashdod (1 Samuel 5:1)
5 Move quickly
6 Barak's father (Judges 4:6)
7 Parson
8 Jephunneh's brother (1 Chronicles 7:38)
9 "Make them like a _____" (Psalm 83:13)
12 "Moses _____ all the words" (Exodus 24:4)
16 Regret
17 Final
19 After Galatians (abbr.)
20 Ahaz's son (1 Chronicles 8:36)
23 Chief
26 Hug
28 Assyrian king brought inhabitants from here to live in Samaria (2 Kings 17:24)
29 "Called these days Purim after the name of _____" (Esther 9:26)
30 "He was the _____" (Genesis 14:18)
31 A Jewish term of contempt (Matthew 5:22)
32 "Fill an _____ of it" (Exodus 16:32)
33 Loft
34 Beverages
37 One of Benjamin's sons (Genesis 46:21)
38 Vare
40 Elkanah's brother (Exodus 6:24)
41 "The _____ of the feet" (Joshua 3:13)
46 Caleb's son (1 Chronicles 4:15)
48 Bow

by Sarah Lagerquist Simmons

BIBLICAL BIRDS

The spellings of some birds' names differ with some printings of the KJV. The older (Authorized) version is used here.

ACROSS

1 "And the _____, because he cheweth the cud" (Leviticus 11:6)
5 Gov't. industrial safety group
9 Editor's mark
14 Enthusiastic
15 _____ dunk
16 Minneapolis suburb
17 **BIRD** (Psalm 55:6)
18 Crow calls
19 Choir boy?
20 Three **BIRDS** (Leviticus 11:13–19)
23 Poetic preposition
24 Type
25 Airport abbr.
26 St. crosser
27 Nick and Nora's dog
29 Noah's son (Genesis 5:32)
32 Hindu mystic
35 Tennis great
36 Little bit
37 Three more **BIRDS** (Leviticus 11:13–19)
40 "It goes through _____ places seeking rest" (Matthew 12:43 NIV)
41 Utah natives
42 Beldam
43 Buttons or Adair
44 "Ye have made it _____ of thieves" (Matthew 21:13) (2 words)
45 Part of many Quebec city names (abbr.)
46 Runner
47 "And I _____ smooth man" (Genesis 27:11) (2 words)
48 **BIRD** (Luke 13:34)
51 Three more **BIRDS** (Leviticus 11:13–19)
57 "Men condemned to die in the _____" (1 Corinthians 4:9 NIV)
58 "Whither have ye made a _____ to day" (1 Samuel 27:10)
59 Persia, today
60 Hog breed
61 "He rolled _____ stone in front" (Matthew 27:60 NIV) (2 words)
62 "The _____ that is in thy brother's eye" (Luke 6:41)
63 **BIRD** (Psalm 104:17)
64 Asherah, for one
65 Adam's grandson (Luke 3:38)

DOWN

1 Biblical verb
2 "And fulfill _____ made to the Lord" (2 Samuel 15:7 NIV) (3 words)
3 David, to Saul
4 First home
5 Sponge's mouth
6 "Let not thine hands be _____" (Zephaniah 3:16)
7 **BIRD** (Job 39:26)
8 "I _____ troubled that I cannot speak" (Psalm 77:4) (2 words)
9 Et _____
10 "He is _____ brother, a faithful minister" (Colossians 4:7 NIV) (2 words)
11 "And the king took off his _____" (Esther 8:2)
12 Organic compound
13 Biblical weed
21 Honda model
22 Living _____ (what Jesus promised)
26 "God has ascended _____ shouts of joy" (Psalm 47:5 NIV)
27 Pale, as a face
28 "_____ the right one for me" (Judges 14:3 NIV)
29 Tramp

by David K. Shortess

30 "Whose breaking cometh suddenly _____ instant" (Isaiah 30:13) (2 words)
31 "Be gathered, every one with her _____" (Isaiah 34:15)
32 Nautical support
33 Existed
34 "Every open container without _____ fastened on it" (Numbers 19:15 NIV) (2 words)
35 Poker prose
36 Memo heading (2 words)
38 Part of multimedia
39 Of eight
44 Have _____ for (2 words)
45 Kind of pot
46 Madrid mister
47 To no _____
48 Part of HOMES
49 Muse believed to inspire poets
50 Endangered Hawaiian birds
51 Units of ionizing radiation

52 Experiencing ennui, with "in" (2 words)
53 _____ Beach, Florida
54 It's a _____ (showbiz talk)
55 Gray wolf
56 "I have sinned this _____" (Exodus 9:27)

66

ACROSS

1 Lax
7 Sow
11 Town in the territory of Ephraim (1 Chronicles 7:28)
12 Ado
14 "_____ have emptied them out" (Nahum 2:2)
16 "At the river of _____" (Ezra 8:21)
17 Coffee holder
18 David and Samuel dwelt here (1 Samuel 19:18)
20 City in the extreme south of Judah (Joshua 15:29)
21 Cad
23 Forswear
24 "Put it on a blue _____" (Exodus 28:37)
25 Senior
27 "They _____ them" (Joshua 7:5)
29 Head
32 Cut
33 "Distributing to the _____ of saints" (Romans 12:13)
34 "I know that thou _____ God" (Genesis 22:12)
36 Town of Canaanites later belonging to Judah (Genesis 38:5)
40 "That the iniquity of _____ house" (1 Samuel 3:14)
41 You
43 Hill
44 Do not lose
46 "These nations shalt thou find no _____" (Deuteronomy 28:65)
48 Angry
49 Ilk
51 Judas' son (Matthew 1:3)
53 After Joshua (abbr.)
54 Urge
55 Precise
56 Before Job (abbr.)
57 "Fill the _____ sacks" (Genesis 44:1)

DOWN

1 Prophet who anointed David as king

2 "The number of them that _____" (Judges 7:6)
3 Craft
4 Abel's murderer
5 Mold
6 "Assaulted the house of _____" (Acts 17:5)
7 Beri's brother (1 Chronicles 7:36)
8 Before Philippians (abbr.)
9 "Was spoken by _____ the prophet" (Matthew 4:14)
10 "He disappointeth the _____" (Job 5:12)
11 Pharaoh _____, king of Egypt (2 Kings 23:29 NKJV)
13 Broken
15 "The wheat and the _____ were not smitten" (Exodus 9:32)
19 "My state shall _____ declare" (Colossians 4:7)
22 "The _____ are cleansed" (Matthew 11:5)
24 Legalist
26 Clan
28 "Ephron dwelt among the children of _____" (Genesis 23:10)
30 Exam
31 Mordecai was _____ cousin (Esther 2:7)
33 Jesus raised the widow's son to life at this city's gate (Luke 7:11)
34 Rare
35 A mighty man of valor from the tribe of Benjamin (2 Chronicles 17:17)
37 Abraham's son (1 Chronicles 1:32)
38 Abraham was _____ father
39 Cot
42 "Perform unto the Lord thine _____" (Matthew 5:33)
45 "Cruel venom of _____" (Deuteronomy 32:33)
47 A city of Simeon (1 Chronicles 4:29)
50 Away
52 "Shall the _____ boast itself" (Isaiah 10:15)

by Sarah Lagerquist Simmons

ACROSS

1 "His kingdom was _____ into darkness" (Revelation 16:10 NIV)

7 "Caused it not to rain upon _____ city" (Amos 4:7)

13 Paul imprisoned there (Acts 28:16)

14 "So the men sat down, in _____ about five thousand" (John 6:10)

15 Shimei's father (1 Kings 4:18 NIV)

16 "Wild beasts of the _____" (Isaiah 13:22)

18 Jesus spoke this language

20 "All of God's _____ children" (Hebrews 12:23 CEV)

21 "In those days Israel had _____ king" (Judges 17:6 NLT)

22 In addition

23 Hebrew year's sixth month

24 "_____, we wept" (Psalm 137:1 NKJV)

26 New Zealand bird

27 City where Paul stayed seven days (Acts 21:3–4)

29 "The damsel _____ not dead" (Mark 5:39)

31 How Peter reached Jesus' tomb (Luke 24:12)

32 King of Bashan (Numbers 21:33)

34 "The Jesus whom Paul _____" (Acts 19:13 NKJV)

38 People from here were brought to Samaria (Ezra 4:9–10) (var.)

41 Roman numeral two

42 Harvest (Jeremiah 12:13)

43 "_____ into clay, and tread morter" (Nahum 3:14)

45 "_____ have compassion, making a difference" (Jude 22)

46 "At him they _____ stones" (Mark 12:4)

48 "I will leave _____ men of them" (Ezekiel 12:16) (2 words)

50 Long, fluffy scarf

51 Sermonizing spots

54 "Every _____ from his place" (Zephaniah 2:11)

55 Jane Austen title

57 Reading, 'Riting, and 'Rithmetic: the three _____

58 Early plainsman (Genesis 13:12)

59 About

60 "I am at the point to _____" (Genesis 25:32)

61 "He that loveth _____ shall be a poor man" (Proverbs 21:17)

64 Olympic gymnast _____ Korbut

67 "Who also hath made us _____ ministers" (2 Corinthians 3:6)

69 Satan's minion (Matthew 9:33 NKJV)

70 "He will show you a large upper _____" (Mark 14:15)

71 A _____-do-well (contraction)

72 Wild prairie rose is state flower (abbr.)

73 Extended His mercy to whom? (Ezra 9:9)

74 "Whether they be young ones, or _____" (Deuteronomy 22:6)

75 "None can _____ his hand" (Daniel 4:35)

76 "_____, that great city Babylon" (Revelation 18:10)

DOWN

1 Precedes destruction (Proverbs 16:18 NKJV) (3 words)

2 A worthless person

3 Diacritical mark above vowel

4 Close to

5 "Great unto the _____ of the earth" (Micah 5:4)

6 "Buried in a dry and _____ grave" (Jeremiah 17:13 NLT)

7 Damascus river (2 Kings 5:12)

8 Roman ruler, Paul's contemporary (Acts 25:21 NASB, note)

9 "_____ pro nobis" (Latin) (trans.: "Pray for us")

10 "Apostles, prophets, teachers, miracle workers, _____" (1 Corinthians 12:28 MSG)

11 Shaphat's son (1 Kings 19:19)

12 Masked mammal (var.)

17 Yankeedom (abbr.)

19 "On their way to _____ out the land" (Joshua 18:8 NIV)

25 "_____ they believe me" (Numbers 14:11)

by Mary Ann Sherman

28 Biblical pleasure-seekers (Acts 17:18)
29 "Out of whose womb came the _____?" (Job 38:29)
30 Tibetan sheep
33 "I clothed Lebanon with _____" (Ezekiel 31:15 NIV)
35 Iranian currency (pl.)
36 What Jonathan gave his lad (1 Samuel 20:40)
37 Government watchdog (abbr.)
39 Town in Judah (Joshua 15:26)
40 "Have mercy on _____" (Matthew 15:22)
43 "Uphold me by your _____ spirit" (Psalm 51:12 NKJV)
44 "_____ no man any thing" (Romans 13:8)
47 Without issue (Latin) (abbr.)
49 "As far as Appii _____" (Acts 28:15)
52 Part of the foot

53 Telescopic surveying method for elevation
56 "Even over them that had not sinned after. . ._____ transgression" (Romans 5:14) (possessive)
61 Guilty or not guilty
62 "Shut up the words, and _____ the book" (Daniel 12:4)
63 Lowest-ranking naval officer (abbr.)
65 Measure of oil (Leviticus 14:10)
66 "I am against thee, O _____" (Ezekiel 38:3)
68 Wager

JESUS, MY ROCK

ACROSS

1 Kind of exam
4 Flight to the fjords (abbr.)
7 "And the _____ God said, It is not good that the man should be alone" (Genesis 2:18)
12 Cape Town's country (abbr.)
13 High jinks
15 Balmoral Castle's river
16 "God shall send forth his _____ and his truth" (Psalm 57:3)
18 "Thus saith the LORD, I have _____ these waters" (2 Kings 2:21)
21 Its capital is Pierre (abbr.)
22 Town in northeastern Pennsylvania
24 "That he should still _____ for ever" (Psalm 49:9)
25 Meadow
26 Mode of transportation (abbr.)
27 Make lace
29 Compete
30 "The mouth of the righteous man _____ wisdom" (Psalm 37:30 NIV)
34 State for newlyweds (abbr.)
35 Tree or street
36 Indian currency (abbr.)
38 Hawaiian bird
39 Title Paul gave to other Christians (abbr.)
40 "Why did we _____ leave Egypt" (Numbers 11:20 NIV)
42 "To offer unto the LORD the _____ sacrifice, and his vow" (1 Samuel 1:21)
44 Own (Scot.)
46 "And thou shalt _____ up the tabernacle according to the fashion" (Exodus 26:30)
48 "Thou trustest in the staff of this broken _____" (Isaiah 36:6)
49 _____ mode
50 Calling or greeting
51 Classic car
52 Model Cheryl
53 "And saveth such _____ be of a contrite spirit" (Psalm 34:18)

55 "But if the LORD make a _____ thing" (Numbers 16:30)
58 Certain parchment scroll (var.)
60 Emergency crew (abbr.)
61 "And ten asses _____ with the good things of Egypt" (Genesis 45:23)
64 "And _____ of Rehoboth by the river reigned in his stead" (Genesis 36:37)
66 Cornhusker state (abbr.)
67 Jacob _____ Israel (abbr.)
68 Pharaoh name
70 Sal of songdom was one
72 "Locks with the _____ of the night" (Song of Solomon 5:2 NASB)
74 "The same came for a witness, _____ bear witness of the Light" (John 1:7)
76 What Santa says
77 Name of God
78 "Let us build us a city and a _____" (Genesis 11:4)

DOWN

1 Bone
2 "Behold behind him a _____ caught in a thicket" (Genesis 22:13)
3 "You got fat, became obese, a tub of _____" (Deuteronomy 32:15 MSG)
4 Pig's home
5 City in Canaan
6 "It is only a _____ from the burn" (Leviticus 13:28 NIV)
8 Paean
9 "For my flesh is _____ food" (John 6:55 NIV)
10 "The LORD is my rock, and my fortress, and my _____" (2 Samuel 22:2)
11 "For I know that my _____ liveth" (Job 19:25)
14 Billy Graham's home state (abbr.)
17 Rebekah's son

by Marijane G. Troyer

18 "And God called the firmament _____" (Genesis 1:8)
19 "Some _____ beast hath devoured him" (Genesis 37:20)
20 "Tabernacle shall be sanctified by my _____" (Exodus 29:43)
22 "He who hurries his footsteps _____" (Proverbs 19:2 NASB)
23 European country (abbr.)
26 Property (abbr.)
28 Hebrew letter
31 "Then Joshua _____ his clothes and fell facedown" (Joshua 7:6 NIV)
32 "And the servant _____ Isaac all things that he had done" (Genesis 24:66)
33 Trite
37 Dried up
41 "_____ abode at Corinth" (2 Timothy 4:20)
43 Time period (var.)
45 *Othello* role

47 Twelfth month of the Jewish year
49 Irish nobleman
51 "Which shall be cities of _____" (Numbers 35:14)
54 "Praise be to my Rock! Exalted be God my _____" (Psalm 18:46 NIV)
56 Certain railway, familiarly
57 Famed pianist Landowska
59 Spanish cheer
62 "And the _____ beast shall be his" (Exodus 21:34)
63 _____ Valley, California
64 "Moses _____ to judge the people" (Exodus 18:13)
65 Golfer Ernie
69 "Pull me out of _____ net" (Psalm 31:4)
71 Selma's state (abbr.)
73 One who heals (abbr.)
75 First part of the Bible (abbr.)

A PROVERBIAL FACELIFT

LORD, lift thou up the light of thy countenance upon us.
Thou hast put gladness in my heart.
PSALM 4:6–7

ACROSS

1 "In _____ was there a voice heard" (Matthew 2:18)
5 Lupino, and others
9 Group of jurors
14 "Ahira the son of _____" (Numbers 1:15)
15 ICBM hangar
16 "That I _____ not my power in the gospel" (1 Corinthians 9:18)
17 Big Island city
18 "And she shall bring forth _____" (Matthew 1:21) (2 words)
19 Oscar de la _____
20 Start of **QUOTE** (Proverbs 15:13) (3 words)
23 Sew
24 Class of dog
25 _____-relief
28 _____ for Humanity
32 "If I wash thee not, thou hast no _____ with me" (John 13:8)
33 Commercials
36 Zhivago's love
37 "The _____ of the mountains is his pasture" (Job 39:8)
38 **QUOTE**, part 2 (3 words)
42 "They of _____ salute you" (Hebrews 13:24)
43 Brain wave records (abbr.)
44 Amount owed
45 "But only one _____ the prize" (1 Corinthians 9:24 NIV)
46 Motown
49 Sugary finish?
50 Big _____, California
51 Grain for grinding
55 End of **QUOTE**
59 Expunge
63 Thunderclap
64 Tribe
65 Violinist's aid
66 Scarlett's home
67 Architect Saarinen
68 Wince
69 "There is no _____ in thee" (Song of Solomon 4:7)
70 End of road?

DOWN

1 Substance abuse treatment, briefly
2 Soul, according to psychologist Jung
3 Gender members
4 "As _____ wind brings rain" (Proverbs 25:23 NIV) (2 words)
5 "_____ unto thee, Arise" (Mark 2:11) (2 words)
6 Gossip (colloq.)
7 Medicinal plant
8 Beethoven's "Moonlight _____"
9 Political group
10 "Honest" one
11 Joshua's father (Joshua 1:1)
12 Winter time in PA
13 Meadow
21 Property for sale
22 "But the name of the wicked shall _____" (Proverbs 10:7)
25 National park west of Calgary
26 "Will you _____ the case for God" (Job 13:8 NIV)
27 Stone marker
29 Scrooge's syllable
30 "And _____ also the Jairite was a chief ruler about David" (2 Samuel 20:26)
31 Musically silent
32 Average
33 Juan's buddy
34 "Times and _____ we do not need" (1 Thessalonians 5:1 NIV)
35 Stingray
37 Call it quits

by David K. Shortess

39 Golfer Ernie
40 Not his
41 Part of psyche
46 Pair
47 Bursts forth
48 Copies
50 "Yet through the _____ of water
   it will bud" (Job 14:9)
52 Water strip
53 Frighten
54 "And we told him according to the
   _____ of these words"
   (Genesis 43:7)
56 Tide type
57 Poi source
58 Red Sea port
59 Sounds of hesitation
60 Permanent CD
61 Righteous king of Judah
   (1 Kings 15:11)
62 _____ Walter Scott

## 70

ACROSS

1 "Get thee up into this mountain
    _____" (Deuteronomy 32:49)
7 "_____, why do ye these things?"
    (Acts 14:15)
11 "Three days _____ I fell sick"
    (1 Samuel 30:13)
12 "I will _____ off from the top"
    (Ezekiel 17:22)
14 "The _____ owl also shall rest
    there" (Isaiah 34:14)
16 Ancestral head of one of the
    subdivisions of porters of the
    temple (Ezra 2:42)
18 Type of tree
19 Head vermin
21 Hangout
22 Big cat
24 Duke of Edom (Genesis 36:43)
25 "Make a mercy _____ of pure
    gold" (Exodus 25:17)
26 Flag
28 Back
30 Even
31 "What am I _____" (Job 16:6)
32 "The wicked is _____"
    (Psalm 9:16)
35 Skill
36 "Bread to the _____" (Isaiah
    55:10)
38 Method
42 "_____, against my sanctuary"
    (Ezekiel 25:3)
43 Mask
45 "My heart standeth in _____"
    (Psalm 119:161)
46 "A third part shall be at the gate of
    _____" (2 Kings 11:6)
47 Moses was _____ brother
49 Zephaniah's son (Zechariah 6:14)
50 Damp
52 "Riotous _____ of flesh"
    (Proverbs 23:20)
54 Joyce Kilmer wrote about one
55 Gape
56 On this day Abraham saw the far-
    off place (Genesis 22:4)
57 "Like a _____ of scarlet"
    (Song of Solomon 4:3)

DOWN

2 Head of one of the families of the
    Nethinims who returned from the
    exile with Zerubbabel (Ezra 2:53)
3 Eon
4 A kind of deer or hart
5 "Hearts _____ to follow"
    (Judges 9:3)
6 Eshton's father (1 Chronicles 4:11)
7 Plan
8 Ikkesh's son (1 Chronicles 11:28)
9 "Tree that will not _____"
    (Isaiah 40:20)
10 "Whose trust shall be a _____
    web" (Job 8:14)
13 "My heart _____" (Isaiah 21:4)
14 "The _____ of thy foot"
    (Deuteronomy 28:35)
15 Eve's son
17 Pick on
20 Vehicle
23 "As vinegar upon _____, so is he"
    (Proverbs 25:20)
25 "The chief _____ in the
    synagogue" (Matthew 23:6)
27 "Pelican, and the _____ eagle"
    (Deuteronomy 14:17)
29 "It was _____ good" (Genesis
    1:31)
32 "Abundance of the _____, and of
    treasures" (Deuteronomy 33:19)
33 Follows Micah
34 City on the border of Ephraim
    (Joshua 16:2)
35 Daughter of the priest of On
    (Genesis 41:45)
37 Mr.
39 Melech's brother (1 Chronicles
    9:41)
40 "Following the _____ great with
    young" (Psalm 78:71)
41 "When _____ began to multiply"
    (Genesis 6:1)
43 Despised
44 "Thou _____ well" (Genesis 4:7)
47 "Of the tribe of _____ were
    sealed twelve thousand"
    (Revelation 7:6)
48 Ace

by Sarah Lagerquist Simmons

51 Uzziel's brother (1 Chronicles 7:7)
53 Rather

ACROSS

1 "Paul, an apostle of Jesus Christ and _____ our brother" (2 Corinthians 1:1)
7 Japanese coin
9 Held up arms of Moses (Exodus 17:12)
12 Biblical region (Genesis 35:21)
13 "And it is a _____ thing that the king requireth" (Daniel 2:11)
15 "In the twentieth year of Jeroboam king of Israel reigned _____ over Judah" (1 Kings 15:9)
16 Mid-twentieth-century failed car
18 "Tracks of a wild donkey in _____" (Jeremiah 2:24 MSG)
19 "If a maiden _____ out to draw water" (Genesis 24:43 NIV)
20 "For they were _____ strong for me" (Psalm 18:17)
21 Type of response system (abbr.)
23 "For they shall _____ an ornament of grace unto thy head" (Proverbs 1:9)
24 Aurora or dawn
25 Yes for Juan
26 "They'll cover every square _____ of ground" (Exodus 10:5 MSG)
29 "Which are blackish by reason of the _____" (Job 6:16)
30 "The name of it [is] called _____; because the LORD did there confound the language of all the earth" (Genesis 11:9)
32 Short laugh
33 Archie Bunker's wife
35 Accepted standard
36 "When you _____ at them with drawn bow" (Psalm 21:12 NIV)
37 Not
38 Persian coin
40 Sunshine state (abbr.)
41 South American country
43 "_____ shall I keep thy law continually" (Psalm 119:44)
44 Meadow
46 "Jacob took him rods. . .of the _____ and chesnut tree" (Genesis 30:37)
47 Bronze Chinese coin
49 Actress Amanda _____
50 "They fled before the men of _____" (Joshua 7:4)

52 "For _____ have I seen righteous before me in this generation" (Genesis 7:1)
54 "And, _____, I am with you always" (Matthew 28:20)
56 "Again, _____ made seven of his sons to pass before Samuel" (1 Samuel 16:10)
58 Rejects
60 A Catholic woman who dedicates her life to Christ
62 Fuegan Indian
63 Rodent
65 "Go to the _____, thou sluggard; consider her ways" (Proverbs 6:6)
66 "So the officials took Jeremiah and lowered him into an empty cistern in the prison _____" (Jeremiah 38:6 NLT)
68 "It is vain for you to rise up early, to sit up _____" (Psalm 127:2)
70 Sounds an owl makes
71 Opposite of oohs
72 "They're already at Hazazon Tamar, the _____ of En Gedi" (2 Chronicles 20:2 MSG)

DOWN

1 "The flesh was still between their _____" (Numbers 11:33)
2 A leader of the tribe of Manasseh (1 Chronicles 27:21)
3 Stone worker
4 Raw mineral
5 Sixty minutes makes one (abbr.)
6 "She shops around for the best _____ and cottons" (Proverbs 31:13 MSG)
7 Prepare flax
8 "Then Abraham. . .picked out a _____ plump calf" (Genesis 18:7 MSG)
9 "_____ came to the banquet with Esther" (Esther 7:1)
10 "_____ hospitality one to another" (1 Peter 4:9)
11 Tablets discovered in Syria (2 words)
14 Eurasian country (abbr.)
17 Horseleach (Proverbs 30:15 NIV)
22 Fish eggs
23 Worn to protect baby's clothes
25 Clothes worn by Indian women

by Marijane G. Troyer

(pl.)

26 State of Chicago (abbr.)
27 Greek letter
28 Hebrew name for God, translated "Lord" (Preface NIV)
29 "_____ waxeth old because of all mine enemies" (Psalm 6:7)
30 "And shut and _____ the gates" (Nehemiah 7:3 MSG)
31 President's command (abbr.)
33 Printer's measure
34 Rural Midwestern state bordering Ohio (abbr.)
35 "_____, a servant of Jesus Christ, called to be an apostle" (Romans 1:1)
36 Words to praise God (Revelation 19:1) (pl.)
38 One who heals (abbr.)
39 Firm (abbr.)
41 "Can you make a _____ of him like a bird?" (Job 41:5 NIV)
42 Aboveground trains (abbr.)
45 Collar
46 Samuel's mother (1 Samuel 1:20)

48 "That which groweth of _____ own accord" (Leviticus 25:5)
49 "Found this man a real _____" (Acts 24:5 NASB)
51 Girl's name
53 "Then Joseph _____ husband, being a just man" (Matthew 1:19)
55 "For _____ you is born this day. . . a Saviour" (Luke 2:11)
56 "Oh, the _____ of those who trust in him" (Psalm 34:8 NLT)
57 "Through faith also _____. . . conceived strength to conceive seed" (Hebrews 11:11)
59 "When he _____ how good is his resting place" (Genesis 49:15 NIV)
61 Colorful card game
64 "For then I would fly away, and be _____ rest" (Psalm 55:6)
67 Person who bats in place of the pitcher (abbr.)
68 New Orleans state (abbr.)
69 Seventh note of a musical scale

## 72

ACROSS

1 "Be clean, and change _____ garments" (Genesis 35:2)
5 "_____, let God be true" (Romans 3:4)
8 "Dwelled between Kadesh and _____" (Genesis 20:1)
12 "Woe to them that are at _____ in Zion" (Amos 6:1)
13 Antique
14 Employ
15 "The righteous shall flourish like the palm _____" (Psalm 92:12)
16 "Carried the people of it captive to _____" (2 Kings 16:9)
17 Rim
18 "Then I will give you rain in _____ season" (Leviticus 26:4)
20 "And Rekem, and _____, and Taralah" (Joshua 18:27)
22 "He that findeth his life shall _____ it" (Matthew 10:39)
24 "Waters bring forth. . .the. . . creature that _____ life" (Genesis 1:20)
25 _____ money
26 Sleeping dogs do this
28 Belonging to slugger Sammy
32 Gem shape
34 "They passed through the Red sea as by _____ land" (Hebrews 11:29)
35 "And Abimelech took an _____ in his hand" (Judges 9:48)
36 "Put on the new man, which is _____ in knowledge" (Colossians 3:10)
38 "I will make thee _____ over many things" (Matthew 25:21)
40 Esther's king
42 "He lieth under the _____ trees" (Job 40:21)
45 "_____ not the poor" (Proverbs 22:22)
46 "Straightway the spirit _____ him" (Mark 9:20)
47 Fire starter?
49 Jezebel's "better" half
53 Sadoc's father (Matthew 1:15)
54 "And Adam called his wife's name _____" (Genesis 3:20)
55 Letter
56 Cincinnati team
57 Pop
58 Perfect place

DOWN

1 "_____ they shall flee away" (Nahum 2:8)
2 Row
3 Employ
4 "The _____ and flags shall wither" (Isaiah 19:6)
5 "The _____ of my transgressions" (Lamentations 1:14)
6 "Samuel arose and went to _____" (1 Samuel 3:6)
7 "We were driven up and down in _____" (Acts 27:27)
8 "Ebal, _____, and Onam" (Genesis 36:23)
9 Conceal
10 "Pharisees began to _____ him vehemently" (Luke 11:53)
11 "They _____ to and fro" (Psalm 107:27)
19 Bani's son (Ezra 10:34)
21 Football positions (abbr.)
22 Not taped
23 Judah's son with Shuah (Genesis 38:4)
24 "The firstlings of our _____" (Nehemiah 10:36)
25 _____ favor, amigo.
27 Thought
29 Zimri's father (Numbers 25:14)
30 "Come against her with _____" (Jeremiah 46:22)
31 Sunday speech (abbr.)
33 "They be blind _____ of the blind" (Matthew 15:14)
37 "_____ hast thou forsaken me" (Psalm 22:1)
38 Antique auto
39 Suave
41 Pleaded
42 "When they saw the _____, they rejoiced" (Matthew 2:10)

by Tonya Vilhauer

43 Confusion
44 Nickname of baseball standout Alex
47 "Thou in thy mercy hast _____ forth the people" (Exodus 15:13)
48 Eggs
50 "Bezer, and _____, and Shamma" (1 Chronicles 7:37)
51 "I _____ no pleasant bread" (Daniel 10:3)
52 David _____-Gurion

## 73

ACROSS

1 Sihon and Israel fought here (Deuteronomy 2:32)
6 Isaac's grandfather (Genesis 11:26)
11 Equal
12 "Beyond the tower of _____" (Genesis 35:21)
14 A bunch of this was dipped in blood (Exodus 12:22)
16 Amateur
18 Peleg's son (Genesis 11:18)
20 King of Moab (2 Kings 3:4)
21 "Under oaks and poplars and _____" (Hosea 4:13)
23 "_____ hath done this thing" (Genesis 21:26)
25 Amos's father (Luke 3:25)
26 "According to the _____ of grace" (Romans 11:5)
28 "Purge away our _____" (Psalm 79:9)
29 Spoiled
31 Leah's son (Genesis 29:33)
34 Below
38 Aware of
39 Samson was buried between _____ and Zorah (Judges 16:30–31)
42 "That which groweth of _____ own accord" (Leviticus 25:5)
43 "As he saith also in _____" (Romans 9:25)
44 "I _____ not" (Luke 17:9)
46 "Swift as the _____ upon the mountains" (1 Chronicles 12:8)
48 City on the coast of Syria (Acts 13:4)
50 Ready
51 Old Testament prophet
52 Sales is one type
53 Frock

7 Another name for Esau (Genesis 25:30)
8 "The _____ brought him bread" (1 Kings 17:6)
9 "Parmashta, and _____, and Aridai" (Esther 9:9)
10 Trey
13 "Row of cedar _____" (1 Kings 6:36)
15 Scream
17 One of the cities of Hadarezer (1 Chronicles 18:8)
19 Fired a gun
22 Turn
23 "Of whom it is _____ that he liveth" (Hebrews 7:8)
24 Each
27 Besides
30 Almond
31 "I spread my _____ over thee" (Ezekiel 16:8)
32 "From thence it was parted, and became _____ four heads" (Genesis 2:10)
33 Aaron died and was buried here (Deuteronomy 10:6)
35 "Partakers of the divine _____" (2 Peter 1:4)
36 Tabitha (Acts 9:36)
37 "_____, lama sabachthani?" (Mark 15:34)
40 Look
41 Baanah's son (1 Chronicles 11:30)
45 Combat
47 After five
49 Follows 2 Chronicles (abbr.)

DOWN

2 Feign
3 "The Sovereign LORD _____ sworn" (Amos 6:8 NIV)
4 Old Testament prophet
5 Before Haggai (abbr.)
6 After nine

by Sarah Lagerquist Simmons

## 74

SLICES OF THE BREAD OF LIFE—
THE SCRIPTURES

Search the scriptures; for in them. . .
ye have eternal life.

JOHN 5:39

ACROSS

1 Kind of door
5 "And I will _____ sign among them" (Isaiah 66:19) (2 words)
9 **Small slice**
13 "The LORD shall _____ over you" (Judges 8:23)
14 **Small slice**
15 "The wife of _____ the Hittite" (2 Samuel 11:3)
17 Elevator man
18 One under Columbus
19 St. _____, Paris suburb
20 **Large slice** (3 words)
23 "Just a _____"
24 _____ polloi
25 Snug place
28 Kind of code
31 **Medium slice**
36 Hessian house
38 What a wheel rotates on
40 Spunk
41 Fungal spore sacs
42 **Whole loaf**
44 "Thou shalt not _____" (Exodus 20:13)
45 Coach Amos Alonzo _____
47 "I may _____ all my bones" (Psalm 22:17)
48 Thailand, once
49 **Small slice**
51 "And parted them to all men, as every man had _____" (Acts 2:45)
53 Title or occupation (suffix)
54 Refusals
56 Bill's partner
58 **Large slice** (3 words)
67 Seeps
68 Choir member
69 Fencing need

70 Limbless bodies (var.)
71 "Let the sea _____, and the fulness thereof" (Psalm 98:7)
72 Essence
73 Bridge response
74 Makes a lap
75 **Small slice**

DOWN

1 Pony gait
2 **Small slice**
3 "Who changed the truth of God into _____" (Romans 1:25) (2 words)
4 Mexican moola (pl.)
5 Beach crustacean (2 words)
6 Give off
7 Atmosphere
8 "A woven tunic, a turban and _____" (Exodus 28:4 NIV) (2 words)
9 Reform or Conservative
10 Utah city
11 "_____ Kleine Nachtmusik"
12 "He had _____ in the grave four days already" (John 11:17)
16 FDR follower
21 Meadow
22 Big _____ (circus tent)
25 Moon appearance
26 Kilns
27 Old European coin
29 Way out
30 Harry's vice president
32 Affirmations from space
33 VII x IX=_____
34 La Scala locale
35 Alabama civil rights town
37 Sound of regret
39 Fashion magazine
43 Registered voters

by David K. Shortess

46 **Medium slice**
50 Tiff
52 Accident fatality, often (abbr.)
55 "When the morning _____ sang together" (Job 38:7)
57 "I am Alpha and _____" (Revelation 21:6)
58 Small child
59 Hula-_____
60 **Small slice**
61 "The Untouchables" role
62 "_____, lama sabachthani" (Mark 15:34)
63 Immediately, in a hospital
64 Heroic tale
65 "I shall die in my _____" (Job 29:18)
66 Asian holidays

A TIME OF REVELATION

ACROSS

1 "And which had not worshipped the _____" (Revelation 20:4)
6 "They bring thee a red _____ without spot" (Numbers 19:2)
11 Baseball player who only bats (abbr.)
13 Boredom
14 Large amount
15 Mediocre grade
16 African antelope
18 Army volunteer (abbr.)
19 La _____ tar pits
20 American Indian
22 Church in Revelation
25 "_____ no more so exceeding proudly" (1 Samuel 2:3)
27 Amazon tributary
28 One who rents
29 "Abram passed through the land unto the place of _____, unto the plain of Moreh" (Genesis 12:6)
30 Person in early 20s (abbr.)
32 Biblical language (abbr.)
34 Place of the seal (Lat.)
37 "And behold a great red _____" Revelation 12:3)
39 Sinai wanderer (abbr.)
41 "I will give unto thee the _____ of the kingdom of heaven" (Matthew 16:19)
44 President's command (abbr.)
45 Mid-Atlantic state (abbr.)
47 "Shall tribulation, or distress, or persecution. . .or _____, or sword" (Romans 8:35)
49 Early Christian pulpit or lectern
51 "The _____ of Jesus Christ, which God gave unto him, to shew unto his servants" (Revelation 1:1)
54 "One to his _____, another to his merchandise" (Matthew 22:5)
55 "And the LORD _____ me of thee" (1 Samuel 24:12)
56 Home of the von Trapp family (abbr.)

57 _____ Peng, Chinese prime minister
58 "_____ waxeth old because of all mine enemies" (Psalm 6:7)
59 Jet (abbr.)
60 "For the _____ is touching the whole multitude thereof" (Ezekiel 7:13)
63 American _____, coll. course
66 Cooling system (abbr.)
68 Church to whom Paul wrote (abbr.)
69 Major network (abbr.)
71 Revelation was written to _____ (2 words)

DOWN

1 "That I may dwell in the house of the LORD. . .to behold the _____ of the LORD" (Psalm 27:4)
2 Printer's short measure
3 "For he shall give his _____ charge over thee" (Psalm 91:11)
4 "And unto the great sea toward the going down of the _____" (Joshua 1:4)
5 Germanic god
7 Einsteinium (abbr.)
8 Nailed (colloq.)
9 "Of whom the whole _____ in heaven and earth is named" (Ephesians 3:15)
10 Mr. Sullivan
11 North Sea feeder
12 "In the beginning God created the _____ and the earth" (Genesis 1:1)
15 "Better a dry _____ with peace and quiet than a house full of feasting" (Proverbs 17:1 NIV)
17 "And rejoiceth as a strong man to run a _____" (Psalm 19:5)
21 Instructor's helper (abbr.)
22 "And Israel sent messengers unto _____" (Numbers 21:21)
23 "A voice is heard in _____" (Matthew 2:18 NIV)

by Marijane Troyer

24 "When he had opened the fourth _____" (Revelation 6:7)
26 "So Saul took the _____ over Israel" (1 Samuel 14:47)
31 "An _____ pleasing to the Lord" (Leviticus 2:9 NIV)
33 "Wherefore I abhor myself, and _____ in dust and ashes" (Job 42:6)
35 Amateur play
36 "In thee, O LORD, do I put _____ trust" (Psalm 31:1)
37 "And they bring unto him one that was _____" (Mark 7:32)
38 Precursor to modern language (abbr.)
40 EU country (abbr.)
42 "One for Moses, and one for _____" (Matthew 17:4)
43 "And I, even I, will chastise you seven times for your _____" (Leviticus 26:28)
46 Book of laws (abbr.)
48 "Facts of Life" actress Charlotte
50 Siblings (abbr.)

51 "For the LORD God had not caused it to _____ upon the earth" (Genesis 2:5)
52 "And the _____ of the temple was rent in twain from the top to the bottom" (Mark 15:38)
53 "He sendeth _____ his word" (Psalm 147:18)
57 "_____, I am with you always" (Matthew 28:20)
59 Elm, for one (abbr.)
60 "And when one came to the wine _____ to draw fifty measures" (Haggai 2:16 NASB)
61 Connected wiring (abbr.)
62 Eisenhower's nickname
63 Gehrig of baseball
64 Not normal (abbr.)
65 "I will saddle me with an _____" (2 Samuel 19:26)
67 Without name (Lat.)
68 Abram, originally (abbr.)
69 Trials occur here (abbr.)
70 Exist

ACROSS

2 Mattathias's son (Luke 3:26)
5 Pet
8 "Israel mine _____" (Isaiah 45:4)
10 Asher's son (1 Chronicles 7:30)
12 "No man that _____ entangleth himself" (2 Timothy 2:4)
14 Not false
15 Pass away
16 "Riotous _____ of flesh" (Proverbs 23:20)
18 "A spider's _____" (Job 8:14)
19 Name
20 "The borders of _____ on the west" (Joshua 11:2)
22 Abdiel's son (1 Chronicles 5:15)
24 "_____, I am warm" (Isaiah 44:16)
27 Reuben's son (Joshua 18:17)
29 "Sailed into Syria, and _____ at Tyre" (Acts 21:3)
31 "Upon all the _____ of Bashan" (Isaiah 2:13)
32 "The children of _____" (Nehemiah 7:23)
33 Pispah's brother (1 Chronicles 7:38)
34 One of Simeon's descendants (1 Chronicles 4:36)
37 Slip
38 Guy
40 Shobal's son (1 Chronicles 1:40)
43 "He left nothing _____" (Joshua 11:15)
46 Belonging to Isaac's son
47 "Give a distinction in the _____" (1 Corinthians 14:7)
48 "_____ art thou wroth?" (Genesis 4:6)
49 Jonathan's son (Ezra 8:6)

DOWN

1 Morning moisture
2 Place where the Israelites murmured for want of water (Deuteronomy 32:51)
3 "As it were a half _____ of land" (1 Samuel 14:14)
4 "_____ the sacrifices of the dead" (Psalm 106:28)
5 Dry mud
6 Variant of Hosea (Romans 9:25)
7 Watch over
9 Load
11 More
13 "Brought _____ unto the man" (Genesis 2:22)
17 Eliphaz's son (Genesis 36:12)
19 "The iron, the _____, and the lead" (Numbers 31:22)
21 Free
23 "The Sovereign LORD _____ sworn" (Amos 6:8 NIV)
25 Pildash's brother (Genesis 22:22)
26 Town in the southern part of Judah (Joshua 11:21)
27 "There came other _____" (John 6:23)
28 Blade
30 "With the point of a _____" (Jeremiah 17:1)
32 Exclude
34 Hanani's son (1 Kings 16:1)
35 Get up
36 "He put forth his _____" (Genesis 3:22)
39 Bird's home
41 Gash
42 Wage
43 Utilize
44 "The priests that were in _____" (2 Samuel 22:11)
45 "Rain in _____ season" (Leviticus 26:4)

by Sarah Lagerquist Simmons

## 77

HOW GREAT A LOVE!

*Greater love hath no man than this,
that a man lay down his life for his friends.*

JOHN 15:13

ACROSS

1 Goose or thistle
7 "Out of the _____ of Jesse"
   (Isaiah 11:1)
11 Company agent (abbr.)
14 "An ephod, a robe, _____ tunic"
   (Exodus 28:4 NIV) (2 words)
15 _____ dweller
16 _____ *Town*, Wilder play
17 Start of **VERSE** (from 1 John 3:1)
18 Locale
19 Exist
20 **VERSE**, part 2 (3 words)
23 Pacific _____
26 Inhabitant of (suffix)
27 Incline
28 What came out of Lazarus' tomb
30 What Alice's cookie said (2 words)
34 "A certain man. . .went into
   _____ country" (Mark 12:1) (2
   words)
35 A root of evil
37 Scorches
39 **VERSE**, part 3 (3 words)
44 "Which I have _____ will
   declare" (Job 15:17) (2 words)
45 "Do not be _____ together with
   unbelievers" (2 Corinthians 6:14
   NIV)
47 Soft drink, to a New Yorker
51 Groups of three
53 "For the sake of _____ will not
   destroy it" (Genesis 18:32 NIV)
   (2 words)
54 What Jesus did on Easter
56 H.S. student's hurdle (abbr.)
58 "_____, thy sins be forgiven
   thee" (Mark 2:5)
59 **VERSE**, part 4 (2 words)
64 Esquire (abbr., var.)
65 Tenth of a homer (Ezekiel 45:14)
66 End of **VERSE** (2 words)

70 Louis XV, *par exemple*
71 Hairy one
72 "The stones of the _____ carcase
   trodden under feet" (Isaiah 14:19)
   (3 words)
73 Is
74 Actress Susan and family
75 Unfired bricks of the Southwest

DOWN

1 Thing to hail
2 "Stand in _____, and sin not"
   (Psalm 4:4)
3 Formal Japanese drama
4 "We have four men which have
   _____ on them" (Acts 21:23)
   (2 words)
5 City on the Jumna
6 "I took the little book out of
   the angel's hand, _____ it up"
   (Revelation 10:10) (2 words)
7 Swindler's game
8 O'Hara estate
9 Tied
10 Wherewithal
11 "Listen to the _____ the lions"
   (Zechariah 11:3 NIV) (2 words)
12 Jupiter's moon
13 "If I _____ not Jerusalem above
   my chief joy" (Psalm 137:6)
21 "Thou art a _____ come from
   God" (John 3:2)
22 Shimei's dad (1 Kings 4:18 NIV)
23 N.T. book
24 Baal, for one
25 Not stereo
29 Gun a motor
31 "_____ said unto you, Dread not"
   (Deuteronomy 1:29) (2 words)
32 Member of the mob
33 Notable period
36 Affirmative

by David K. Shortess

38 Pig's place
40 Lunar New Year, in Vietnam
41 "My heart was _____ within me" (Psalm 39:3)
42 Scrimps, with "out"
43 Nevada city
46 "He will silence her noisy _____" (Jeremiah 51:55 NIV)
47 African desert
48 Tertullus, for one (Acts 24:1)
49 Feminine nickname
50 _____ Wednesday
52 _____ tree (make firewood or lumber) (3 words)
55 Slipped away
57 Lukewarm
60 At _____
61 "Or who can _____ the bottles of heaven" (Job 38:37)
62 Therefore
63 "What profit shall this birthright _____ me" (Genesis 25:32)

(2 words)
67 Catch a crook
68 "_____ not vain repetitions" (Matthew 6:7)
69 Airline to Oslo (abbr.)

## 78

ACROSS

1 The Nethinims dwelt here (Nehemiah 3:26)
6 A lawyer (Titus 3:13)
11 Eleventh month of the Jewish year (Zechariah 1:7)
13 "Lot lifted up his _____" (Genesis 13:10)
15 "He _____ on my hand" (2 Kings 5:18)
17 A range of mountains (Song of Solomon 2:17)
19 Unwell
20 Opined
22 Sack
23 Song, "_____ and Circumstance"
25 "As a _____ is shaken" (1 Kings 14:15)
26 In time
27 Ishuah's brother (Genesis 46:17)
29 "_____, Jesus Christ maketh thee whole" (Acts 9:34)
32 "Appointed barley and the _____" (Isaiah 28:25)
34 Rip
35 Grave
38 "A third part shall be at the gate of _____" (2 Kings 11:6)
40 "And I will punish _____ in Babylon" (Jeremiah 51:44)
41 Be gone
44 Not less
46 "Solomon made a _____ of ships" (1 Kings 9:26)
47 "She is not afraid of the _____" (Proverbs 31:21)
49 Tear down
51 Herod's brother (Luke 3:1)
53 Add
54 "The _____ of your faith" (1 Peter 1:7)
57 "A people great and _____" (Deuteronomy 9:2)
58 "For God took _____" (Genesis 5:24)
59 "God is _____ judge" (Psalm 75:7)
60 "Master shall bore his _____" (Exodus 21:6)
61 Continent
62 Old Testament book about a Jewish queen (abbr.)
63 "We will go with _____ young" (Exodus 10:9)

DOWN

2 Hymns
3 Rooster's mate
4 Gaal's father (Judges 9:26)
5 After
6 John and James were _____ sons (Matthew 4:21)
7 "Saul _____ David from that day and forward" (1 Samuel 18:9)
8 Gain
9 "The house of _____" (1 Chronicles 4:21)
10 Skid
12 "So be it done unto _____" (Matthew 8:13)
14 Coax
16 "_____, lama sabachthani?" (Mark 15:34)
18 "_____ to hear" (Deuteronomy 29:4)
21 "It shall be for _____" (Genesis 1:29)
24 "_____ purge away thy dross" (Isaiah 1:25)
28 "They departed from _____" (Numbers 33:45)
30 Esli's son (Luke 3:25)
31 Mistake
33 "Adam, Sheth, _____" (1 Chronicles 1:1)
36 Old Testament prophet (abbr.)
37 After Exodus (abbr.)
39 "Of _____" (Numbers 26:44)
42 Come together
43 Phuvah's brother (Genesis 46:13)
45 Hasty
46 "_____ of checker work" (1 Kings 7:17)
48 "Vex you with their _____" (Numbers 25:18)
50 Abraham purchased a sepulcher from the children of _____ (Acts 7:16)

by Sarah Lagerquist Simmons

51 Prayer
52 "Cast him into the _____ of ground" (2 Kings 9:26)
55 Possessive pronoun
56 Rohgah's brother (1 Chronicles 7:34)

## 79

ACROSS

1 Alaskan city
4 "My heart _____ for Moab like a harp" (Isaiah 16:11 NIV)
9 "Which we have heard. . .and our fathers have told _____" (Psalm 78:3)
11 High priest, to Samuel
12 Two _____ in one month equals a blue one
13 Tell Legend site
14 "And I will make thy seed to multiply as the stars of _____" (Genesis 26:4)
16 Hawaiian dish
17 Hair _____
18 Sea arm of the Mediterranean between Greece and Turkey
20 "That I should not _____ down to the pit" (Psalm 30:3)
21 Chief federal law officer (abbr.)
22 "But God _____ it for good" (Genesis 50:20)
24 "_____ panteth my soul after thee" (Psalm 42:1)
25 Greek letter
26 "I will both lay me down _____ peace, and sleep" (Psalm 4:8)
27 Jewish homeland
31 Minor prophet (abbr.)
33 Love (Lat.)
34 "And out of the midst thereof as the colour of _____" (Ezekiel 1:4)
35 Loud noise
37 Popular greeting
38 "_____ the good shepherd" (John 10:11) (2 words)
39 Engineer (abbr.)
40 Nevada city
41 "_____ LORD is my strength and my shield" (Psalm 28:7)
43 More infused with rosy hues
47 Certain votes
48 Cool drink
49 Common navy man (abbr.)
50 "Four days _____ I was fasting until this hour" (Acts 10:30 NKJV)
52 Fads

54 Door part
55 "The hand of God has turned the _____" (Psalm 118:15 MSG)
58 Afterward
59 International organization for peace (abbr.)
60 "And he made the waters to stand as _____ heap" (Psalm 78:13)
61 Mallards' flight
62 Giant
65 Organization aiding in disasters (abbr.)
66 "Be quiet"
68 Alert
70 "More to be desired are they than gold, yea, than much _____ gold" (Psalm 19:10)
71 "David took _____ of gold that were on the servants" (2 Samuel 8:7)
72 "Likewise, ye _____, be in subjection to your own husbands" (1 Peter 3:1)

DOWN

1 He rebuilt the temple walls
2 Heard at bullfight
3 Not accounted for in war (abbr.)
4 "How _____ shall the wicked. . . triumph" (Psalm 94:3)
5 Money ledger belonging to (abbr.)
6 Midwestern state (abbr.)
7 Cable sports channel
8 Triangular-shaped musical instrument (Daniel 3:5–10 NASB)
9 Bathsheba's husband
10 "The time of the _____ of birds is come" (Song of Solomon 2:12)
12 "When my brother Esau _____ you and asks, To whom do you belong" (Genesis 32:17 NIV)
13 "I will lift _____ my hands in thy name" (Psalm 63:4)
15 "Vanity of _____, saith the Preacher" (Ecclesiastes 1:2)
19 City in Judah (Joshua 15:34)
23 "And I will put _____ between thee and the woman" (Genesis 3:15)

by Marijane Troyer

25 Promised land (var.)
28 "Consider well her _____, view her citadels" (Psalm 48:13 NIV)
29 "The Philistines took the ark of God, and brought it from _____ unto Ashdod" (1 Samuel 5:1)
30 Onion relative
32 Presidential nickname
36 "Because there is _____ light in them" (Isaiah 8:20)
40 Freight transportation (abbr.) (pl.)
42 "Christ is the _____ of the church" (Ephesians 5:23)
44 Baking potatoes (var.)
45 Greek goddess
46 Unruly crowd
47 Sacred places
51 City of refuge (Deuteronomy 4:43)
53 "He shall surely _____ her to be his wife" (Exodus 22:16)

54 "And he took the fire in his hand, and a _____; and they went. . . together" (Genesis 22:6)
56 "They'll cover every square _____ of ground" (Exodus 10:5 MSG)
57 Word in a threat
59 Mormon state (abbr.)
63 Poetic contraction
64 "Behold, I make all things _____" (Revelation 21:5)
67 Parliament chamber (abbr.)
69 Nation's revenue (abbr.)

80

ACROSS

1 "Salvation thereof as a _____ that burneth" (Isaiah 62:1)
4 Flow
8 Esau dwelt in this mount (Genesis 36:8)
10 To
12 "_____ thou hast not hated blood" (Ezekiel 35:6)
14 Aaron was one (Exodus 4:14)
16 Manahath's brother (Genesis 36:23)
18 A lawyer (Titus 3:13)
19 "Jael went out to meet _____" (Judges 4:18)
20 "Be _____ upon her knees" (Isaiah 66:12)
22 "Took the little book out of the angel's hand, and _____ it up" (Revelation 10:10)
24 Yep
26 Eyot
29 "My lips should _____ your grief" (Job 16:5)
32 "Cast him _____ this pit" (Genesis 37:22)
34 "Like the _____ of a calf's foot" (Ezekiel 1:7)
35 "Rushed with one accord into the _____" (Acts 19:29)
37 Before Song of Solomon (abbr.) (var.)
39 "He that _____ me before men" (Luke 12:9)
42 After Micah (abbr.)
43 Old Testament prophet (abbr.)
44 Ill
47 King of Hamath (1 Chronicles 18:9)
48 Defy
50 Guni's grandson (1 Chronicles 5:15)
51 Corrode
53 Bustle
54 Aaron and _____ held up Moses' hands (Exodus 17:12)
55 Shammah's father (2 Samuel 23:11)
56 After Galatians (abbr.)

DOWN

1 Claim
2 Island whose inhabitants are associated with Tyre (Ezekiel 27:8)
3 Set down
4 "God, the _____ of heaven and earth" (Genesis 14:22)
5 "Good works for necessary _____" (Titus 3:14)
6 Mature
7 "All the Chaldeans, Pekod, and _____" (Ezekiel 23:23)
9 "For the _____ sake" (Matthew 24:22)
11 Poor
13 Mob
15 Before Jeremiah (abbr.)
17 "With thy _____ treasure" (Psalm 17:14)
21 "I am the _____ in my father's house" (Judges 6:15)
22 "What _____ thee" (Psalm 114:5)
23 "_____ marked her mouth" (1 Samuel 1:12)
25 "_____ no man any thing" (Romans 13:8)
27 "He will be _____" (Jeremiah 20:10)
28 "_____ have said" (Acts 17:28)
30 "The LORD _____ him" (Genesis 38:7)
31 Per
33 "I am _____ root" (Revelation 22:16)
36 Ahitub's son (1 Samuel 14:3)
37 Ample
38 Make happen
40 Before Daniel (abbr.)
41 Zeruah's son (1 Kings 11:26)
45 One of the cities of Hadarezer (1 Chronicles 18:8)
46 "Syria shall go into captivity unto _____" (Amos 1:5)
47 Net
48 "They _____ the ship aground" (Acts 27:41)
49 One of three cities built by Elpaal's sons (1 Chronicles 8:12)
52 Before eleven

by Sarah Lagerquist Simmons

ACROSS

1 "_____, though I walk through the valley" (Psalm 23:4)
4 "Thy _____ shall return upon thine own head" (Obadiah 1:15)
10 Holler
14 Row
15 "Arisai, and _____, and Vajezatha" (Esther 9:9)
16 "_____, lama sabachthani?" (Mark 15:34)
17 Try out
18 Hana Mandlikova's game
19 Rescue
20 Bring up
22 "Let them praise his name in the _____" (Psalm 149:3)
24 "As a _____ doth gather her brood" (Luke 13:34)
25 Corp.'s cousin
28 North Carolina Tar _____
30 Actress Shirley, and others
33 "Thou _____ up mighty rivers" (Psalm 74:15)
37 Harsh
38 "Thou art my _____ and my deliverer" (Psalm 40:17)
40 "Tekoa had two wives, Helah and _____" (1 Chronicles 4:5)
41 Scraped by, with "out"
43 Distort
45 Onesimus, for one
46 "And from _____, and from Berothai" (2 Samuel 8:8)
48 Banner, for one
50 Level
51 "And Jiphtah, and _____, and Nezib" (Joshua 15:43)
53 "For as ye have _____ your members" (Romans 6:19)
55 "That at the name of Jesus every ____ should bow" (Philippians 2:10)
57 "Wheat and _____ were not smitten" (Exodus 9:32)
58 "_____ they shall flee away" (Nahum 2:8)
61 Soil
63 Dense

68 Like a track
70 Grind
73 "By the river of _____" (Daniel 8:2)
74 _____ avis
75 "Shall move out of their _____ like worms" (Micah 7:17)
76 "There is a sound of abundance of _____" (1 Kings 18:41)
77 "I _____ that thou art a gracious God" (Jonah 4:2)
78 Cure
79 "Thy land shall be divided by _____" (Amos 7:17)

DOWN

1 "Be clean, and change _____ garments" (Genesis 35:2)
2 "Woe to them that are at _____ in Zion" (Amos 6:1)
3 _____ code
4 Rodent
5 Poetic contraction
6 "He caused an east _____ to blow in the heaven" (Psalm 78:26)
7 "Captains of thousands; _____ the chief" (2 Chronicles 17:14)
8 "And had _____ down manna upon them to eat" (Psalm 78:24)
9 "I could not _____ the form thereof" (Job 4:16)
10 Positive response
11 "Whom thou slewest in the valley of _____" (1 Samuel 21:9)
12 "They shall prosper that _____ thee" (Psalm 122:6)
13 "Though ye have _____ among the pots" (Psalm 68:13)
21 _____ Grande
23 "What the scripture saith of _____" (Romans 11:2)
26 _____ degree
27 Masticate
29 "Ye are _____ unto the day of redemption" (Ephesians 4:30)
30 Makes cookies, say
31 "If he hath wronged thee, or _____ thee" (Philemon 1:18)

by Tonya Vilhauer

32 "Surely thou wilt _____ the wicked" (Psalm 139:19)
34 "And he _____ them from the judgment seat" (Acts 18:16)
35 Rescued
36 Next
37 "And _____, which were dukes" (Joshua 13:21)
39 Victim
42 Marred by mildew
44 Couple
47 "The night is far spent, the day is at _____" (Romans 13:12)
49 "And _____, and the mighty men" (1 Kings 1:8)
52 Stature
54 Allow
56 Mistake
58 Duke of _____
59 Apparel maker _____ Picone
60 "Straightway the spirit _____ him" (Mark 9:20)

62 "They gave them in full _____ to the king" (1 Samuel 18:27)
64 Pitch
65 "_____ the Ahohite" (1 Chronicles 11:29)
66 "They have gone in the way of _____" (Jude 11)
67 "Hear this word, ye _____ of Bashan" (Amos 4:1)
69 Mosaic _____
71 Pekoe, for one
72 Agency (abbr.)

82

ACROSS

1 Not back
5 Mesha's son (1 Chronicles 2:42)
8 Banes
10 "_____ lieth at the door" (Genesis 4:7)
12 A town of Judah (Nehemiah 11:29)
14 Aria
17 "It is _____ for a camel" (Luke 18:25)
18 Before Proverbs (abbr.)
20 City of David (2 Samuel 5:7)
22 "Sorrows of _____ compassed me" (2 Samuel 22:6)
23 King before David
24 Jamin's brother (1 Chronicles 2:27)
26 Free
28 Raamah's son (Genesis 10:7)
30 "Under oaks and poplars and _____" (Hosea 4:13)
31 It's rude to do this
32 One of the cities of Zebulon (Joshua 19:15)
34 "By his _____ a light doth shine" (Job 41:18)
36 Japheth's son (Genesis 10:2)
38 Vow
39 Pile
41 Mary's father-in-law (Luke 3:23)
42 "He planteth an _____" (Isaiah 44:14)
43 Belonging to Abigail's husband (1 Samuel 25:14)
45 Ham's brother (Luke 3:36)
46 Make fun of
48 Manahath's brother (1 Chronicles 1:40)
49 Stir
50 "He that is dead is _____ from sin" (Romans 6:7)
51 Elizabeth Barrett Browning was one

DOWN

2 Beholden
3 Nary
4 Sarah's father-in-law (Genesis 11:31)
5 Town in the mountain district of Judah (Joshua 15:54)
6 Hostel
7 David's great-grandfather (1 Chronicles 2:12–15)
9 This man was killed by a woman (Judges 5:26)
10 "LORD _____ a sweet savor" (Genesis 8:21)
11 Colt
13 5,280 feet
15 City in the extreme south of Judah (Joshua 15:29)
16 "He _____ roast and is satisfied" (Isaiah 44:16)
18 "Cry from the _____" (Jeremiah 22:20)
19 Take to civil court
21 An Ammonite (1 Samuel 11:1)
23 Fifth in line of the ancient kings of Edom (Genesis 36:36–37)
25 Mattithiah's brother (1 Chronicles 25:3)
27 Shem's son (Genesis 10:22)
29 King of Syria (1 Kings 20:1)
31 "Thou shalt be broken by the _____" (Ezekiel 27:34)
32 Abraham's son
33 Pit
34 Belonging to Ham, Shem, and Japheth's father
35 City in Benjamin (Isaiah 10:31)
37 A town captured by the Philistines in the reign of Ahaz (2 Chronicles 28:18)
40 Purple or red fruit
43 Adam lived _____ hundred and thirty years (Genesis 5:5)
44 Trip
46 "Deliver thyself as a _____" (Proverbs 6:5)
47 After Genesis (abbr.)

by Sarah Lagerquist Simmons

## 83

ACROSS

1 "When he _____ the lamps" (Exodus 30:7 NASB)
6 Summit of Mt. Pisgah
10 "Saw no _____ come to him" (Acts 28:6)
14 Forbidden
15 Right away (abbr.)
16 Choir member
17 "My sister just _____ here" (Luke 10:40 NLT)
18 Radar target
19 "Even _____ the tongue is a little member" (James 3:5)
20 List of government deceased beneficiaries (abbr.)
21 One who suits to please?
23 "_____ hospitality one to another" (1 Peter 4:9)
25 "Guilded with silver _____" (Jeremiah 10:9 MSG)
26 "Unto the angel of the church in _____ write; these things saieth he" (Revelation 3:1)
28 "A shameful wife _____ his strength" (Proverbs 12:4 NLT)
30 "Arba, a great _____ of the Anakites" (Joshua 14:15 NLT)
31 Doctors' group (abbr.)
32 "Give us our food for _____" (Matthew 6:11 NLT)
35 "Thou hast made heaven. . .the _____, and all things that are therein" (Nehemiah 9:6)
38 Netherlands Antilles Island
40 Highest navy rank (abbr.)
41 "Naphtali is a _____ let loose" (Genesis 49:21 NASB)
42 Something not to drop
43 "_____ the man" Musial
45 "Coated it with _____ and pitch" (Exodus 2:3 NIV)
47 Anesthetic
49 The *New York Times*, and others
51 "The ways of Zion _____ mourn" (Lamentations 1:4)
53 Former Princess of Wales, familiarly
54 "A sword is upon the liars; and they shall _____" (Jeremiah 50:36)
55 "Prophets that make my people _____" (Micah 3:5)
57 Cush's son (1 Chronicles 1:10)
61 San Francisco, for one
65 "Who lay on a bed _____ noon" (2 Samuel 4:5)
67 Bright sign
68 Television diva
69 Major prophet
70 "Have you not put _____ around him and his household" (Job 1:10 NIV) (2 words)
71 So be it
72 Above
73 Man's title
74 D.C. quadrant (abbr.)

DOWN

1 Puts words on a machine (abbr.)
2 Ancient Canaanite city Ugarit, today (2 words)
3 In the same place (abbr.)
4 Dominant themes
5 "Help!"
6 Abigail's first husband
7 Christ's ancestor (Luke 3:25)
8 "After they had posted _____" (Acts 17:9 NLT)
9 "Instructing those that _____ themselves" (2 Timothy 2:25)
10 "The leech _____ two daughters" (Proverbs 30:15 NASB)
11 "Cry _____ at Beth-Aven" (Hosea 5:8)
12 Way to veer (abbr.)
13 Zipporah's husband (Exodus 2:21)
21 Former European dictator
22 "A _____ thing that the king requireth" (Daniel 2:11)
24 Seventh tone of diatonic scale
27 "Whither have ye made a _____ today?" (1 Samuel 27:10)
28 Swedish import
29 Missionary with Silas
30 "They had sung an ____" (Mark 14:26)

by Marijane G. Troyer

32 Grad student, maybe (abbr.)
33 "It is now out of _____" (Hebrews 8:13 NLT)
34 "Went up to _____, and fetched a compass to Karkaa" (Joshua 15:3)
36 Memorization using repetition
37 "And _____ their claws in pieces" (Zechariah 11:16)
39 Jesus _____ and died for me
43 "Be quiet"
44 "I _____ down under his shadow" (Song of Solomon 2:3)
46 Indian currency (abbr.)
48 "With silver, iron, _____, and lead" (Ezekiel 27:12)
49 Pea holder
50 Salt's companion
51 Erase (abbr.)
52 "Whether therefore ye eat, _____ drink" (1 Corinthians 10:31)
54 Put on
56 "Remember. . .against the sons of Edom. . .who said. . ._____ it to its very foundation" (Psalm 137:7 NASB)
58 Amazon cetacean genus
59 "And it was not _____ for us to see" (Ezra 4:14)
60 Candy bar
62 Former California military base
63 "All our righteousnesses are as filthy _____" (Isaiah 64:6)
64 Biblical "you"
66 "And he wrote. . .the words of the covenant, the _____ commandments" (Exodus 34:28)
68 Unit of electrical resistance
69 Dorothy's Auntie _____

## 84

ACROSS

1 "The body by _____ and bands" (Colossians 2:19)
6 Amasai's son (2 Chronicles 29:12)
11 "When he came unto _____" (Judges 15:14)
12 Yes
14 "Should I have _____ still" (Job 3:13)
15 Group of cows
16 Type of tree
19 "I gave ear to your _____" (Job 32:11)
21 Dampen
23 "When ye _____ the harvest" (Leviticus 19:9)
25 "Every plant of the _____" (Genesis 2:5)
26 "If his offering be a _____" (Leviticus 3:12)
27 Jephunneh's son (Numbers 26:65)
29 It's beside Ezion-geber (1 Kings 9:26)
30 "I have in a figure _____ to myself" (1 Corinthians 4:6)
35 "Let him go _____" (Exodus 21:26)
36 Alternative spelling for Abraham's wife
38 "Godliness with _____ is great gain" (1 Timothy 6:6)
42 "I have seen thy _____" (2 Kings 20:5)
44 A city of Lycaonia (Acts 14:6)
46 Mar
47 Bukki's father (Numbers 34:22)
51 Certificate of land ownership
52 Skill
53 Noah's son
55 "_____ blessed Elkanah and his wife" (1 Samuel 2:20)
56 Jeroham's grandfather (1 Chronicles 6:34)
57 Colorado ski resort
59 "Their border was Helkath, and _____" (Joshua 19:25)
60 If not
61 Kohath's son (Numbers 3:19)
62 "There sat a certain man at _____" (Acts 14:8)

DOWN

2 Bad
3 Close
4 Crook
5 "Came to the Desert of _____" (Exodus 19:2 NIV)
6 Heman's father (1 Kings 4:31)
7 Alter
8 "If the firstborn son be _____" (Deuteronomy 21:15)
9 Plus
10 Hunt
13 "Elam, _____, Bani" (Nehemiah 10:14)
17 "Joseph gathered corn as the sand of the _____" (Genesis 41:49)
18 Stop
20 I
21 Log
22 Sup
24 "I will _____ the oath" (Genesis 26:3)
26 "So she _____ in the field" (Ruth 2:17)
28 "So shall thy _____ be filled" (Proverbs 3:10)
29 "They also that _____ in spirit" (Isaiah 29:24)
31 Mesh
32 Eye
33 Before Job (abbr.)
34 Bump into
37 City in Judah where David sent the spoil of his enemies (1 Samuel 30:30)
38 Dray
39 "Time drew _____ that Israel must die" (Genesis 47:29)
40 Maple is one
41 Mean
43 "Give _____ to his commandments" (Exodus 15:26)
45 "_____ boweth down" (Isaiah 46:1)
47 Solomon's servant (Ezra 2:56)
48 "Brought gold from _____" (1 King 10:11)
49 Straighten

by Sarah Lagerquist Simmons

50 Aquila and Priscilla came from
    here (Acts 18:2)
53 Asaph's son (2 Kings 18:18)
54 Snake sound
56 "All _____ counsel of God"
    (Acts 20:27)
58 "_____ there be light"
    (Genesis 1:3)

## 85

ACROSS

1 "As thou _____ to do unto those that love thy name" (Psalm 119:132)
6 Appendage
10 Israeli leader Golda
14 End of many psalms
15 "Kish the son of _____" (2 Chronicles 29:12)
16 River in Italy
17 Make amends
18 Seek
19 "Whosoever shall say to his brother, _____" (Matthew 5:22)
20 Hard to locate merchandise (pl.)
21 Stubborn one
22 Peter, for one (var.)
23 "John also was baptizing in _____" (John 3:23)
25 "And he said, _____; but I will die here" (1 Kings 2:30)
27 "And Hadoram, and _____, and Diklah" (Genesis 10:27)
30 Terminate
31 "The king will _____ him with great riches" (1 Samuel 17:25)
35 "His _____ come to honour" (Job 14:21)
36 Effortless
38 Glamorous accessory
39 "Bezaleel the son of _____" (2 Chronicles 1:5)
40 "Cast all their sins into the _____ of the sea" (Micah 7:19)
42 "Dishon, and _____, and Dishan" (1 Chronicles 1:38)
43 Level (Brit.)
45 "And when he came unto _____" (Judges 15:14)
46 Demean
47 "I commend unto you _____ our sister" (Romans 16:1)
49 Terms of duty
50 Rodent
51 Nun's son (Numbers 13:8)
53 "And the coast reacheth to _____" (Joshua 19:22)
56 "The righteous shall flourish like the palm _____" (Psalm 92:12)
57 Window part
61 Middle East gulf
62 "Shall come forth a vessel for the _____" (Proverbs 25:4)
63 "Stayed in _____ for a season" (Acts 19:22)
64 "Call me not Naomi, call me _____" (Ruth 1:20)
65 "Absalom made _____ captain of the host" (2 Samuel 17:25)
66 Annoying person (colloq.)
67 Shechaniah's father (Nehemiah 6:18)
68 "Abraham gave a _____ part of all" (Hebrews 7:2)
69 Former game show host Monte

DOWN

1 Academy in CO (abbr.)
2 Egyptian king
3 College in North Carolina
4 "The thongs of whose _____ I am not worthy" (John 1:27 NIV)
5 "_____ are the generations of Noah" (Genesis 6:9)
6 "The porters, Akkub, _____" (Nehemiah 11:19)
7 "Consolation also _____ by Christ" (2 Corinthians 1:5)
8 Baal, for one
9 Effigy
10 "Antipas was my faithful _____" (Revelation 2:13)
11 Ages
12 Peruvian tribe
13 Lion's lament
24 "The north side of Bethemek, and _____" (Joshua 19:27)
26 Some
27 "Nor to _____ authority over the man" (1 Timothy 2:12)
28 "The coast of their inheritance was _____" (Joshua 19:41)
29 Dill seed
32 Judge of Israel (Judges 12:8)
33 Something that may be clear
34 Speedy mammals
37 Aram's brother (1 Chronicles 7:34)
41 Pin down

by Tonya Vilhauer

42 "Elkanah his son, and _____ his son" (1 Chronicles 6:23)
44 "From Jotbathah, and encamped at _____" (Numbers 33:34)
46 Dined
48 Give _____ to
49 "And his daughter was _____" (1 Chronicles 7:24)
51 "The threshingfloor of _____ the Jebusite" (2 Chronicles 3:1)
52 "_____ thou a man diligent in his business" (Proverbs 22:29)
53 Iowa town on U.S. 30
54 "On the thirteenth day of the month _____" (Esther 9:17)
55 "That these made war with _____" (Genesis 14:2)
56 Again's partner
58 _____ Minor
59 Place for a flowerpot
60 Corridor
62 Obese

## 86

ACROSS

1 "The plowman shall overtake the
_____" (Amos 9:13)
6 "Beauty is a _____ flower"
(Isaiah 28:1)
11 "There was no _____"
(Judges 18:28)
13 Drop
14 New Testament prophetess
15 Mr. and _____
18 The Netophathite
(1 Chronicles 27:13)
20 To and _____
22 Tree juice
23 Fancy
24 Atmosphere
25 Shade of red
27 After nine
28 Mute
30 "Joseph is without doubt _____
in pieces" (Genesis 37:33)
31 "I shall die in my _____" (Job
29:18)
32 "_____ the sacrifices of the dead"
(Psalm 106:28)
35 Bar
37 Criticize
41 "Sweet _____ unto the God"
(Ezra 6:10)
45 Arodi's brother (Genesis 46:16)
46 Discharge
48 Slap
49 Cure
50 Walker
51 After Amos (abbr.)
52 "Written not with _____"
(2 Corinthians 3:3)
53 Joseph's nephew (Genesis 46:21)
54 Abner's father (1 Samuel 14:50)
55 Prepare for crops
57 "Whether it be fat or _____"
(Numbers 13:20)
60 Variant of Hosea (Romans 9:25)
61 Besides
62 "_____, and sacrificeth unto the
Lord" (Malachi 1:14)
63 Uz's father (Genesis 36:28)

DOWN

2 Put together
3 Let
4 Bathsheba's father (2 Samuel 11:3)
5 Gomer's son (Genesis 10:3)
6 "_____ the wrath of the king"
(Hebrews 11:27)
7 A descendant of David (1
Chronicles 3:21)
8 "I _____ him not" (1 Kings 20:7)
9 The Jairite (2 Samuel 20:26)
10 "Blast with the _____ horn"
(Joshua 6:5)
12 "Sin lieth at the _____"
(Genesis 4:7)
16 Odd
17 "Whose heart stirred them up in
wisdom _____ goats' hair"
(Exodus 35:26)
19 Ripen
20 "His _____ was noised"
(Joshua 6:27)
21 "He took one of his _____"
(Genesis 2:21)
26 Sun
29 Open
33 Turtle
34 Always
35 Ruin
36 "They _____ the deeds of the
wicked" (Jeremiah 5:28)
37 "_____ ye from him" (2 Samuel
11:15)
38 Shuthelah's son (Numbers 26:36)
39 Baby girl color
40 City built by Reuben's children
(Numbers 32:37)
41 "They _____ him" (1 Kings
13:27)
42 On
43 Toga
44 "As the _____ fly upward"
(Job 5:7)
47 "Let thine _____ now be
attentive" (Nehemiah 1:6)
55 "Strong shall be as _____"
(Isaiah 1:31)
56 Allow

by Sarah Lagerquist Simmons

58 Priest who raised Samuel
    (1 Samuel 1:25)
59 Before Esther (abbr.)

ANSWERS

Puzzle 1

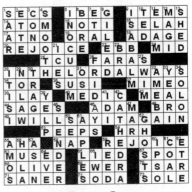

Puzzle 2

Puzzle 3

Puzzle 4

Puzzle 5

Puzzle 6

PUZZLE 7

PUZZLE 8

PUZZLE 9

PUZZLE 10

PUZZLE 11

PUZZLE 12

Puzzle 13

Puzzle 14

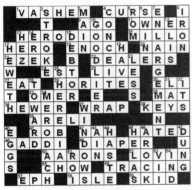

Puzzle 15

Puzzle 16

Puzzle 17

Puzzle 18

Puzzle 19

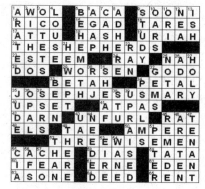

Puzzle 20

Puzzle 21

Puzzle 22

Puzzle 23

Puzzle 24

PUZZLE 25

PUZZLE 26

PUZZLE 27

PUZZLE 28

PUZZLE 29

PUZZLE 30

Puzzle 31

```
N E O N # C O D S # P A S T A
O G R E # A V O W # O L L A S
E R A S # V E N A # P L A C E
L E T T H E R E B E L I G H T
S T E # E R I E # V A N # # #
# # # P A N T # H E R # F O E
A R N O L D # D A N # A I R Y
J E S U S S A I D I A M T H E
A M O S # A W N # G A S E S #
R O N # B Y E # T A N S # # #
# # # T E T # S O R E # C P A
L I G H T O F T H E W O R L D
I N N E R # L E A N # R O A D
S N A F U # A N N A # M A T E
T O R T E # T O G S # E K E D
```

Puzzle 32

```
L A M A # D E B T # I B S E N
E B E R # E V E R # S E E T O
A D A R # P I N E # A S N E R
P I T I F U L # T R A I T S #
# # # V A T S # I C E # # # #
M I S E R Y # B A D # G A A L
A S I D E # J U D E # E S L I
S U E # L O R D S # S O N # #
S A V E # A N N S # S T O N E
A H E R # S A T # P U R S E S
# # # E S T # L A C E # # # #
# A C C E S S # A S H A M E D
A G A T E # O A R S # D A R A
S E V E R # U R G E # E D A R
S E E D S # L I E D # R E N T
```

Puzzle 33

```
# J A S H E N # V I L E S T
# H E A V E # A L I V E #
# F O W L E R # L I F E R S
M A L # T R I # L E E # P H I
E L I S # A G E # P E O R #
A S A P H # H A Y # M A N N A
H E B R E W # L # R E S T E D
# # # I D O L A T E R S # # #
C H A N G E # T # D E E M E D
R A N G E # B I T # S T O R E
A L A S # E A R # H A R T #
F A N # A R A # I T S # B E E
T H I T H E R # E Y E L I D S
Y # A H E A D # T R E A T # T
# # S H E R D S # H E R M E S
```

Puzzle 34

```
M A O # E N S # A # A M B E R
O # S A S # T E M P L E # U #
S U M P I R E # L A # A C E #
E L # M Y R A # C A S T L E #
S E M I # P L A Y # A T O P #
A P E D # A L A # M A # E # #
A V # L E N T I L # B E R E A
# E G # F E A R E D # S S # #
S N O W Y B # D A R E # T I #
H # S O # B L T # R A M # H #
E C H O # S E A M # M E E K #
E E L S # T # O # S A # R I #
T O N # O N # J O S H U A # N
E R # N O M A D # E S P # G #
A L O E S # A # Y O D # P P S
```

Puzzle 35

```
P E R E S # I C A N # A J A R
A L I A H # M A C E # D A N O
W A S T E # P L E A # V E N T
S H E E P F O L D # C A L A H
# # R H E S A # M A N # # # #
P S A # O W E # P A R T E T H
O A R S # A D M A T H A # # #
E L E A S A H # W E I G H E D
T A L I T H A # E A R S # # #
S H I T R A I # H E B # N E T
# # # H A B # B E S E T # # #
P A Y # W # F E A T H E R E D
O P A L # P E E P # A N A N I
M I R E # H A R E # L O R D S
P A N T # I R A D # F R E S H
```

Puzzle 36

```
A R O M A # G P A # A B B A
L U Z O N # R A W # C L O D
A L O S T C O I N F O U N D
K E N T # R A N # A R E N A
E R E # B E N # O W N # # #
# # T E E # B A N # T A J #
B A T H E # G E T # A R L O
A C O I N I N T H E F I S H
D E N S # H A S # D A G O N
E S E # H O T # F O R # # #
# # T O P # R A M # S P A #
S T R I P # S O N # M A I N
T H E W I D O W S M I T E S
A R E A # O W E # A M O C O
B U D S # E N D # L I N E N
```

Puzzle 37:

```
I R A N . . H E R . S T E M
C O N E H A L A H M A Y O
C E N T A D A M I O B E D
. A S H N A H . N A T U R E
. . O D D . . D D E
S P A R K . D E E P C S
T E N S E A I R F L A T
T O T T E R I N G P L A N E
O N E S C R Y L E A N S
P E R P H I A R G O T
. M O I . P I G
E M P I R E P E D A T E S
Y E A R F O L K S O B I T
E D G E S W E A T R A B E
S E E D . N A H N Y S E
```

PUZZLE 37

PUZZLE 38

PUZZLE 39

PUZZLE 40

PUZZLE 41

PUZZLE 42

PUZZLE 43

PUZZLE 44

PUZZLE 45

PUZZLE 46

PUZZLE 47

PUZZLE 48

Puzzle 49

Puzzle 50

Puzzle 51

Puzzle 52

Puzzle 53

Puzzle 54

PUZZLE 55

KIDS · NEBO · GOG
IRON · EZEM · ASA
RAMA · REDEEMED
· IRU · AGREED
INNER · EDAR · I
RAISING · · SHE
AMO · MAL · K · PUL
MEN · ZORITES
· THAN · SEEK
APPEAR · · HAD
GRINDERS · SITH
UEL · ANAK · ELOI
EYE · DENY · DYED

PUZZLE 56

MIRIAM · ELI · LOIS
OREM · ILL · ND · DNA
SIP · EL · I · BOA · DL
ED · FREEZER · BRIO
SIT · AT · AMER · TAM
CAD · UXB · DAS · E
S · DOTS · EA · MEAT
TAMAR · ITCH · EDOM
EDO · ESTHER · IDOL
P · RUSTS · TN
G · S · R · ABIGAIL
MAT · MARTHA · BSA
ASA · UP · IAN · BULB
R · BAN · NEVER · TEA
YOUNG · ARAS · IS · N

PUZZLE 57

BEGAT · BABE · WASH
IMAGE · OREO · OFNO
TIMID · AGES · ROES
STEN · PROF · ATREE
· GOODSHEPHERD
WAS · MIS · ACE
ASITIS · ESL · MAGI
LIGHTOFTHEWORLD
KANE · NIH · CANCEL
· OER · ETC · HEE
RESURRECTION
IRATE · ALEC · ARID
PANT · ONER · ASIDE
ESTE · ODAN · LADEN
NEAR · HARE · BLEAT

PUZZLE 58

WAG · OSEE · WAR
IGAL · BEARD · RASE
TALEBEARER · ARAD
RIP · Y · EDGES
LEPER · SIA
SARID · DISPUTE
DIEST · LADE · HAB
AVA · EARED · IRU
RAN · ZINA · SORTS
ANSWERS · SOUTH
· IVAH · IBRI
JABNEH · TALE · EYE
ESEK · ZEHARITES
TIRE · TIMES · THAT
AID · EZAR · S

PUZZLE 59

SPAR · CROP · TORAH
TAME · HALE · OVINE
ASIS · AVEC · MENTO
GODISLIGHTANDIN
· NOD · EAT
DAM · BEES · YONDER
ASOF · ARCS · EARLY
CIVIC · RAT · STEAD
CAIRO · SLAB · SATE
ANEMIC · PREY · MER
· NAB · AUK
HIMISNODARKNESS
ATALL · NOSE · OPIE
HELLO · USES · WENT
AMIST · SEAT · NESS

PUZZLE 60

ELSE · HEED · SAD
DIES · RAZE · TOE
SEATS · RES · ONE
· ATE · KILLED
PRETEND · RAE
EASE · SAVED · FT
EYE · CURED · ARE
PS · PREEN · AMEN
· ROI · DOUBTED
REALMS · MRS
IBN · SAT · NEHUM
SAG · OMAR · NONE
ENE · NEXT · TWIN

Puzzle 61

```
D E E D S   S H E     J O H
U Z Z I A   W A Y   E B O N Y
E R R E D   O W E   V E N O M
S I A   L U R K   T I N   N
    D Y E D   B E L O N G
B A N I   L   S E M   A R A
A R O E R   A M R A M I T E S
Y E S T E R D A Y   A B I A H
  L E H I   I L L   W H O S E
H I S   B E L   A N E R
    D I A L   D E A R
S A T A N S   G O D S   B A T
A M E R C E   A V E N G E T H
M O N T H   B E R A   R E U
E N D S   W A S   H A I R S
```

PUZZLE 61

Puzzle 62

```
L A M B   R   P O T S H E R D
U S E   S A T   D   U   M I R
C T   G O V   R I P E N   D E
R A F   T E N F O L D   P E G
E   O N   N   D U O   R A   S
  S N A P   S   S   H A U L
R O D   I D E A L S   G L A D
O R   F R I D A Y   I S   W E
C R Y   N E E   A T   Y E
K O A L A   R E A S S U R E D
  W R Y   P S   N   T A R
R   E R I E   A G E S   W   L
A W   I G A L   E V E R   P O
R O T C   R A I L   U S E R
E O N S   L C   S O   B A R D
```

PUZZLE 62

Puzzle 63

```
G N A W   G O R G E   G I R L
R A R E   A W A R D   A B I A
O M E R   B I N E A   U Z Z I
P E L T   A N G E R   L A P S
E L I   R   G E T   L   N A H
  Y   G U N   S   B E G   H
    T R I A L   H E A L S
    H U N T     S T E P
  L A B O U R   O T H E R S
G A D   U R I   V I E   E T C
A D D   S E T   E R R   A R A
G I A H   H E R   A D I N
S N E E R   M A R   A S I D E
  G U N D   A S A   N I N E
    S A S   H E N   T A G
```

PUZZLE 63

Puzzle 64

```
  M A I M E D   A P A R T
W   R E B A   B A R     W
H   A D E R   I S A     R
E R E   I N T E N T   J   O
E U N I C E   P O O R E S T
L E D   I Z E H A R   H U E
      A N E M   M   P O P
P R O V E R B   G U A R D
R A M A   R E W A R D E R
I C E   A S A H E L   A M I
E A R   S O C I A L   H E N
S   I S L E   S E A     K
T   R I E   E R R     S
C O U R S E   L Y C I A
```

PUZZLE 64

Puzzle 65

```
H A R E   O S H A   C A R E T
A V I D   S L A M   E D I N A
D O V E   C A W S   T E N O R
S W A N C U C K O W E A G L E
T I L   I L K     A R R
    A V E   A S T A   H A M
S W A M I   A S H E   I O T A
P E L I C A N H E R O N B A T
A R I D   U T E S   C R O N E
R E D   A D E N   S T E
    S K I   A M A   H E N
R A V E N O W L V U L T U R E
A R E N A   R O A D   I R A N
D U R O C   A B I G   M O T E
S T O R K   P O L E   E N O S
```

PUZZLE 65

Puzzle 66

```
S L A C K   J   S E E D
N A A R A N   A   U P S E T
E M P T I E R S   A H A V A
C U P   N A I O T H   I M
H E E L   D E N Y   L A C E
O L D E R     C H A S E D
    P A T E   H E W   S
    N E C E S S I T Y
F E A R E S T   C H E Z I B
E L I S   T H O U   R I S E
W I N   A   E A S E   M A D
A     S O R T   Z A R A
J D G   P U S H   E X A C T
A   E S T   S   M E N S
```

PUZZLE 66

PUZZLE 67

PUZZLE 68

PUZZLE 69

PUZZLE 70

PUZZLE 71

PUZZLE 72

PUZZLE 73

PUZZLE 74

PUZZLE 75

PUZZLE 76

PUZZLE 77

PUZZLE 78

PUZZLE 79

```
N O M E . L A M E N T S . U S
E L I . M O O N S . R . U R I
H E A V E N . P O I . P I N
E . A E G E A N . G O . A G
M E A N T . N . S O . C H I
I N . I S R A E L . N A H . N
A M A T . A M B E R . B A N G
H I . I A M . E E . R E N O
T H E . P I N K E R . A . M
A Y E S . A D E . O S . A G O
L . A . C R A Z E S . K N O B
T I D E . T H E N . U N . L
A N . L . S O R D . T I T A N
R C . S H . E . O N . F I N E
S H I E L D S . W I V E S . W
```

PUZZLE 80

```
. L A M P . P O U R . S
S E I R . U N T O . S I T H
L E V I T E . S H E P H O
Z E N A S . E . S I S E R A
C . D A N D L E D . O
A T E . Y E S . O N
I S L E P . A S S W A G E
L . I N T O . S O L E . A
E . T H E A T R E . E C C
D E N I E T H . W . N A H
Z E C . S I C K . T O U
R E B E L . A H I . R U S T
A . A D O . H U R . A G E E
N . T . D . N . E P H . N
```

PUZZLE 81

```
Y E A . R E W A R D . Y E L L
O A R . A R I D A I . E L O I
U S E . T E N N I S . S A V E
R E A R . D A N C E . H E N
. I N C . H E E L S
B O O T H S . D R I E D S T
R A W . H E L P . N A A R A H
E K E D . W A R P . S L A V E
B E T A H . Y E A R . E V E N
A S H N A H . Y I E L D E D
. K N E E . R I E
Y E T . D I R T . T H I C K
O V A L . G R A T E . U L A I
R A R A . H O L E S . R A I N
K N E W . T R E A T . L I N E
```

PUZZLE 82

```
F R O N T . Z I P H
B . W O E S . S I N . F
O . E N R I M M O N . O
A I R . E A S I E R . P S A
Z I O N . H E L L . S A U L
M A A Z . R E L E A S E
S H E B A . E L M S
S T A R E . I D A L A H
N E E S I N G S . M A G O G
O A T H . H E A P . H E L I
A S H . N A B A L S . S E M
H . R I D I C U L E . Z
S . O N A M . M I X . O
F R E E D . P O E T
```

PUZZLE 83

```
T R I M S . N E B O . H A R M
T A B O O . A S A P . A L T O
. S I T S . B L I P . S O . S
S S D I . T A I L O R . U S E
H . F O I L . S A R D I S
S A P S . T . H E R O
A M A . T O D A Y . E A R T H
A R U B A . A D M . D O E
B A L L . S T A N S . T A R
. E T H E R . P A P E R S
D O . D I . D O T E
E R R . N I M R O D . P O R T
L . A T . N E O N . O P R A H
. E Z E K I E L . A H E D G E
A M E N . A T O P . M R . S E
```

PUZZLE 84

```
J O I N T S . M A H A T H
S . L E H I . A M E N . Z
E . L A I N . H E R D . A
A S H . R E A S O N S . W E T
R E A P . F I E L D . G O A T
C A L E B . L . E L O T H
H . T R A N S F E R R E D . U
. F R E E . S A R A
A . C O N T E N T M E N T . M
T E A R S . I . D E R B E
H A R M . J O G L I . D E E D
A R T . J A P H E T H . E L I
C . T O A H . V A I L . A
H . H A L I . E L S E . N
I Z E H A R . L Y S T R A
```

Puzzle 85

Grid (across answers): USEST, TAIL, MEIR / SELAH, ABDI, ARNO / ATONE, LOOK, RACA / FINDS, MULE, TSAR / AENON, NAY / UZAL, END, ENRICH / SONS, I, EASY, BOA / URI, DEPTHS, EZAR / RASE, LEHI, ABASE / PHEBE, G, STINTS / RAT, OSHEA / TABOR, TREE, SASH / ADEN, FINER, ASIA / MARA, AMASA, PILL / ARAH, TENTH, HALL

Puzzle 86

Grid (across answers): REAPER, FADING / R, DELIVERER, D / A, DRIP, ANNA, O / MRS, MAHARAI, FRO / SAP, IMAGINE, AIR / RUST, TEN, DUMB / RENT, H, G, NEST / ATE, ROD / REPROVE, SAVOURS / ERI, RELEASE, POP / TAN, TREADER, OBA / INK, O, ARD, P, NER / R, TILL, LEAN, K / E, OSEE, ELSE, S / VOWETH, DISHAN

MORE GREAT BIBLE PUZZLES!

Love word searches? Love the Bible? Here are 365 puzzles to challenge and expand your knowledge of the Good Book every day for a whole year. They feature thousands of words for your searching pleasure, all drawn from the beloved King James Version of scripture.

Paperback / 978-1-63609-279-9